This book makes an important contribution to the literature of creative studies. Drawing on contemporary research in the field with particular insight into the value of recent digitally based practice, Linda Candy introduces a rigorous and illuminating analysis of the often enigmatic nature of the creative process, grounded in lively interviews with practising artists, scientists and technologists, providing a deeper understanding of the ways in which artworks, and indeed any other creative outcomes, evolve in all their complexity.

— **Siân Ede**, *author of* Art & Science

Linda Candy shows us how the powerful paradigm of reflective practice can be used to understand creative thought in such diverse fields as science, engineering, art, design and music. Her interviews with distinguished practitioners provide a privileged glimpse into especially creative minds and her analysis reveals fascinatingly generic aspects of cognition. This book deserves to become a standard text in the field; there is every chance that it will.

— **Bryan Lawson**, *Emeritus Professor: Dip Arch (Dist) (Oxford), MSc (Dist), PhD (Aston), RIBA, Registered Architect*

Linda Candy has created an incredible book on creativity. Her deep reflections on the nature of creativity will be of vital importance to anyone engaging with reflective creative practice. Through the voice of many significant artists and practitioners from a broad range of fields and disciplines, she weaves together a framework with which to understand their reflective practices, but more importantly how we, the readers, can benefit and enhance our own creativity.

— **Craig Vear**, *Professor of Digital Performance (Music), De Montfort University, Leicester, UK*

THE CREATIVE REFLECTIVE PRACTITIONER

The Creative Reflective Practitioner explores research and practice through the eyes of people with a wholehearted commitment to creative work. It reveals what it means to be a reflective creative practitioner, whether working alone, in collaboration with others, with digital technology or doing research, and what we can learn from listening and observing closely. It gives the reader new insights into the fascinating challenge that having a reflective creative mindset can bring.

Creative reflective practice is seen through practitioner ideas and works which have informed the writing at every level, supported by research studies and historical accounts. The practitioners featured in this book represent a broad spectrum of interdisciplinary creative activities producing works in film, music, drama, dance and interactive installations. Their work is innovative, full of new ideas and exciting to experience, offering engagement and challenge for audiences and participants alike. Practitioner interviews give a direct sense of how they see creative practice from the inside. The ways in which these different situations of practice stimulate and facilitate reflection in practice and how we can learn from this are described. Variations of reflective practice are discussed that extend the original concepts proposed by Donald Schön, and a contemporary dimension is added through the role of the digital in creative reflective practice as a tool, mediator, medium and partner.

This book is relevant to people who wish to understand creativity and reflection in practice and how to learn from the practitioners themselves. This includes researchers in any discipline as well as students, arts professionals and practitioners such as artists, curators, designers, musicians, performers, producers and technologists.

Dr Linda Candy lives in the Peak District of England. She was born in County Durham, England and grew up near Richmond, North Yorkshire and Adelaide, South Australia. She is a writer and researcher and is active in promoting awareness about interdisciplinary creative practice in art, technology and science. She has a BA (University of Adelaide), a Masters by Research (De Montfort University) and a PhD in Computer Science (Loughborough University). After working in academic research for many years, she now works freelance and is a co-director of ArtworksrActive (ArA) an independent consultancy in art and technology. She has written over 100 articles and edited several books about the creative process and the role of digital technology in interdisciplinary creative practice.

THE CREATIVE REFLECTIVE PRACTITIONER

Research Through Making
and Practice

Linda Candy

Routledge
Taylor & Francis Group

LONDON AND NEW YORK

First published 2020
by Routledge
2 Park Square, Milton Park, Abingdon, Oxon OX14 4RN

and by Routledge
52 Vanderbilt Avenue, New York, NY 10017

Routledge is an imprint of the Taylor & Francis Group, an informa business

British Library Cataloguing-in-Publication Data
A catalogue record for this book is available from the British Library

Library of Congress Cataloging-in-Publication Data
A catalog record for this book has been requested

ISBN: 978-1-138-63274-5 (hbk)
ISBN: 978-1-138-63276-9 (pbk)
ISBN: 978-1-315-20806-0 (ebk)

Typeset in Bembo
by Apex CoVantage, LLC

Printed in the United Kingdom
by Henry Ling Limited

For Emma, Catriona, Lulu and Eric

CONTENTS

FIGURES

PRACTITIONER PORTRAITS

Andrew Johnston. Photograph reproduced courtesy the University of Technology Sydney

Brigid Costello. Photograph: Brigid Costello

Roger Mills. Photograph: Linda Candy

Esther Rolinson. Photograph: Fraser Kent

Julie Freeman. Photograph: Bret Hartman/TED

Ken Arnold. Photograph: Ken Arnold, reproduced courtesy University of Copenhagen

Anthony Rowe. Photograph: Erik Johan Worsøe Eriksen

Shona Illingworth. Photograph: Mark Sealy

David Clarkson. Photograph David Clarkson

Matthew Connell. Photograph: Ryan Hernandez, reproduced courtesy of the Museum of Applied Arts and Sciences

Anna Ledgard. Photograph: James Runcie

Anthony Marshall. Photograph: Christine Marshall

Sue Hawksley. Photograph: Maria Falconer

Sarah Fdili Alaoui. Photograph: Uwe Homm

George Poonkhin Khut. Photograph: Max Doyle, courtesy of *The Australian Way* magazine

Andrew Bluff. Photograph: Danielle Bluff

Ben Carey. Photograph: Benjamin Carey

ACKNOWLEDGEMENTS

To the practitioners who gave their time and were so open and generous, I am deeply grateful. Listening to their reflections on creative practice and experiencing their remarkable works has been a great privilege. I am profoundly indebted to Sarah Fdili Alaoui, Ken Arnold, Denise Bate, Karen Battersby, Andrew Bluff, Oliver Bown, Benjamin Carey, David Clarkson, Matthew Connell, Brigid Costello, Sue Crellin-McCarthy, Ernest Edmonds, Julie Freeman, Vince Frost, Robert Hall, Sue Hawksley, Shona Illingworth, George Poonkhin Khut, Andrew Johnston, Roger Kneebone, Anna Ledgard, Anthony Marshall, Tom McCarthy, Roger Mills, Esther Rolinson, Anthony Rowe, Stephen Scrivener, Jennifer Seevinck, Thecla Schiphorst, Gregory Shannon.

Thank you especially to my wonderful family and to my dear friends for the many lively and stimulating conversations we have had and are still enjoying together. Over many years I have been extremely fortunate to have known deeply reflective people who have helped me think and write. Amongst them are Graham Bate, Zafer Bilda, Micheline Beaulieu, Maggie Boden, Mike Burrows, Meroë Candy, Tony Crook, Jenny Crook, Nigel Cross, Rob Edmonds, Ian Gwilt, Nicola Ham Edmonds, Tom Hewett, Bryan Lawson, Lian Loke, Roger Malina, Debbie Michaelson, Jonathan Michaelson, Derek Teather, Deborah Turnbull-Tillman, Craig Vear and many others.

Last but not least, I am very grateful to my editor Hannah Shakespeare for her encouragement and support throughout the writing process and to the Routledge team for their helpful advice.

PREFACE

When I first began to explore the world of the creative practitioner, I thought that to be able to understand how it all worked you needed to observe, record and analyse what was going on with a cool objective eye. Naturally, these observations would be informed and framed by theory. I was a practitioner myself at the time, but like so many, I was not aware of how much everyday practice was a significant source for my professional knowledge. My understanding began to change once I became a practitioner researcher and discovered the writings of Donald Schön. The experience of finding value in research through practice was only the beginning of what became an enduring pursuit.

Since those early days, my fascination with creative practice and its practitioners has not diminished. In this book, my interest in how people think and produce works is taken forward into a deeper examination of living creative practice reflectively. My aim is to convey something of the rich and varied ways in which practitioners engage in their creative lives and produce imaginative, stimulating and challenging works. These works take different forms in music, art, movement and performance and come in many combinations of those elements and materials. They have the power to make us think again and again and sometimes to transform our experience of ourselves and how we see the world in which we live. As individuals, when we practice bringing awareness to our present state of thinking and feelings, we learn through that experience. Focusing our attention in a deliberate way enhances our capacity to break out of habitual patterns of thought. In doing so, we are better able to reveal what we have known only tacitly until then. Practising awareness benefits the individual and, indirectly, those with whom we come into contact. It is something that enriches our understanding of ourselves through self-reflection. Through sharing the experience of their creative works with others, practitioners contribute to reflective thinking more broadly.

The creative practitioner takes something that emerges within themselves out into the external world through making artefacts or taking action in order to make things happen. The results of these activities then become part of a shared experience that enables creative practitioners to reflect on what ever preoccupations they have at the time, a pattern of thinking that continues throughout their creative lives. Equally it offers opportunities for others to share the experience of the works. The making in the present moment stimulates awareness and also lends itself to contemplation beyond the present. In this way the search for understanding that underlies so much of creative practice has impact beyond the individual. Creative practice is a path towards revealing and reflecting on what it is to be human. Practice and creative practice seen this way are conscious reflective processes.

The approach I have taken in writing this book is to try to represent how creative practice is seen from the inside. It is a view that is hard to get at from the outside alone, by which I mean by classical studies based on the observations of researchers, theorists and historians. In my conversations with practitioners, I am an empathetic listener who records and responds to what I have learnt. I am also a researcher whose challenge is to present a wider perspective without sacrificing the practitioner's individual voice. I have tried to give space to those voices as my primary sources of inspiration and guidance and, at the same time, to offer some general insights. I want to emphasise the central place and value of the practitioners speaking for themselves and urge readers to give their words the attention they deserve. I hope in this way to offer the reader a window into reflective creative practice that is firmly grounded in practitioner experience.

Linda Candy
September 2019

1

REFLECTION, PRACTICE AND THE CREATIVE PRACTITIONER

In this first chapter, the main themes, the approach and methods are introduced. Creative reflective practice is seen through the perspective of practitioners whose ideas and works have informed the writing at every level. The approach offers a view 'from the inside' of practice itself that is both valuable and distinctive. Practitioner interviews are the primary sources of inspiration and guidance for the insights into creative practice and the role of reflection. These are supported by narratives and diaries, research studies and historical accounts. The challenge has been to present a more general perspective of creative reflective practice at the same time as giving space to the individual practitioner voices.

The book explores reflective practice in different contexts: professional, creative, collaborative, digital and research. Professional practice is differentiated from creative practice in terms of the purpose and manner in which the practice is undertaken. Whilst professional and creative practitioners can be both professional and creative, there are differences to be explored and revealed. As will become clear, it is the context – the situation of practice – that influences the nature of reflection in practice, whether working alone or collaboratively.

Creative practice, creative works

People engage in creative acts by simply doing what is natural to them. Activities like drawing, singing, dancing and thinking, are the essentials of creativity that express who we are as human beings. Creative works on the other hand, in the sense of art, take those activities further. For there to be art, a process that explores, reveals and exhibits creative acts and works is necessary. This is a process that creates experiences that may ultimately lead to a change in how we see ourselves as human beings whether as artists or audiences. Viewed this way, the practitioners who have contributed to this book can be seen as 'artists' whose 'works' pose searching questions and challenge assumptions that reframe existing activities in a potentially transformational way for themselves and for all of us.[1] However, rather than getting tied up in making distinctions between what is creative and what is art, in the discussion throughout this book, creativity is framed within 'creative practice' and art is encompassed within 'creative works'.

Creative practitioners in different fields and disciplines produce 'works' that exhibit 'artistry', a feature that is found in creative practice more generally and is characterised in a variety of ways. The motivational forces, the private goals and public service demands drive, shape and constrain creative activities and how practitioners respond to new and unexpected situations. There are distinct elements within a life of practice in which the creation of works is central, be they sculptures, images, compositions, films, installations, performances, exhibitions or events.

Creating 'things' (in the broadest sense of the word) is the core activity around which many others take place. The creative process also includes reading inspiring books and exploring the potential of new materials and tools, as well as talking with other people who are directly or indirectly involved in the work either in a formal collaboration or in casual encounters. A single focus on the making of artworks can change over time and other kinds of activity take place in parallel. Many practitioners also work in areas that appear, on the face of it, tangential to the creative practice but provide paid employment and space to create. Others work in organisations that afford opportunities to be creative: for example, as project managers or exhibition curators or teachers. Deciding to live on the proceeds of a creative life is not a practical choice for most, however, and there are many different routes to survival without the established career paths available to the professional practitioner. It is the life-long commitment to creative practice that distinguishes the practitioners in this book. That commitment involves pursuing original ideas relentlessly until they reach tangible form as finished works.

Living creative practice usually begins in early years with a natural facility to draw and paint, compose and perform music, dance and sing, and often this leads to encouragement into formal training. The creative practitioners in this book are all characterised by living creatively throughout their lives. Some mentioned being recognised in childhood as having a talent for some kind of artistic pursuit. It raised the question for me when considering how important living a creative life was to them, whether that early talent had raised expectations in themselves and their families that influenced the direction they took later on. Can we recognise an artist by early signs in childhood proficiency? It seems that the quick answer to this is 'not necessarily'. Many children are very skilled at drawing and painting, but that does not necessarily mean they will be outstanding artists in adulthood, and in any case, proficiency in drawing strikingly accurate portraits or beautiful landscapes does not always presage a life-long pursuit.[2] Just 'being good' at doing something creative is for some practitioners never quite enough. For many, there is a constant search for deeper understanding that generates personal challenges.

The essence of the creative process is in the minutiae of creating, when lines are drawn, sounds are composed, movements performed and tentative ideas emerge.

The ideas spring from multiple sources, all of which are widely available to anyone. However, it is being highly alert to the potential of this material and working closely to exploit its properties in a novel way that sets the creative practitioner apart. When trying to understand the creative process as an observer, it soon becomes clear that this is the nub of it all. And yet, it is the hardest part to convey from the practitioner's perspective – beyond the obvious mechanics. Sometimes during the creative process, the thinking becomes reflective: these moments can happen as a result of external factors such as interruptions or more frequently, deliberate pauses imposed by uncertainty of what to do next. Sometimes, conscious reflection is seen as undesirable because the practitioner is striving for a different state of mind when brain and body work in unison, as in the case of improvisation discussed in Chapter 3 on reflective creative practice. To achieve this, practitioners devise ways of setting aside conscious reflection using techniques devised for that purpose such as rules for drawing. In other cases, creative actions can seem to come almost automatically from deep within, perhaps from emotional or aesthetically charged forces. This condition is very familiar to creative practitioners.

Placing a value on the outcomes of creative practice is often assumed to be the business of the viewer, the buyer, the critic or historian: the creator's own perspective is less frequently considered. And yet it is on them we depend for achieving originality and quality. They are the first in line to appraise and evaluate the works, although their voices are somewhat muted when it comes to how they go about doing that.

There are many questions that come to mind in trying to understand creative practice from a practitioner point of view including: What frames of reference do artists use to think about the works they make? What do they say to themselves about whether they like what they see once the making process is done? What kind of things are they looking for? Do they have explicit criteria or standards to judge their works? When appraisal takes place, does it involve asking questions about whether the work has qualities that are pleasing or satisfying or challenging? Over time do they establish criteria for appraising all works or is each work judged by a different set of values? For some practitioners developing a way of judging whether a work is good or not arises from the making process itself. If the intention is to create works that express particular ideas or moods, this will mean using particular criteria that will in themselves determine what the work is like. This assumes that the principal judge is the creator but what happens when there is an explicit intention to involve the viewer or audience? If the aim is to make the audience respond in a particular way, what is the effect of unexpected behaviour?

These are some of the questions that are considered throughout this book in the exploration of reflective practice seen through the eyes of creative practitioners and informed by studies of historical and contemporary practices. My aim is to reveal the diverse ways in which practitioners engage in their creative practices and produce extraordinarily imaginative, stimulating and challenging works of many different forms.

How can we better understand the nature of reflective creative practice through the eyes of the practitioner?

Let us consider different ways of viewing the practitioner's perspective on their practices and works. We can listen to what they say and write about their work in journals and narratives. We can also read accounts carried out by sensitive facilitators: Katharine Kuh and David Sylvester, for example, show us how to tease out the practitioner's perspective through conversations around the works themselves.[3] These are avenues open to anyone who is curious to learn what lies behind the enormously diverse repertoire of creative works that comprise our cultural wealth. Examples of these approaches are described next. This is followed by an introduction to my general approach in writing this book.

***

Intentions, accidents and meaning

> From music people accept pure emotion but from art they expect explanation.

These words by Agnes Martin, the great North American painter, are a challenge to the way that some forms of creative works are presented to the public and what is expected of their experience.[4] I hear what she says every time I enter an exhibition or attend a performance. They remind me to allow myself to look with open eyes and mind so that I can dwell in the experience of the moment instead of rushing to wonder how to interpret it in the manner I learnt through training and teaching. Too often, when we visit exhibitions we are offered audio guides to provide commentary on the works as we move through the show, encouraging us to listen first rather than look at the visual images. By contrast, when we go to a music or dance performance, we embrace the experience directly and feel the sensations of sound and movement and how they evoke emotion within us. Experiencing the art and 'explaining' it, are both important, of course, and once the creators give their work to the world to experience, it becomes open to interpretation by all. Some people focus on the works and their meaning, others want to know more about why and how they came to be.

For an artist of pure abstraction like Agnes Martin, the general desire for 'explanation' is problematic. Her beautifully executed paintings, the ultimate expression in surface simple form and colour, are designed using complicated mathematics as their organising structure and painted by hand – an exacting and immersive method. The absence of representation in her painting leaves little room for a narrative to be constructed about its meaning. This opens the door to explanation by analysis of how the work is made- a film of Martin painting is there to help.[5] But knowing what it is made of and how the material was used does not necessarily offer the viewer a better way of experiencing it, nor does jumping to conclusions about what it 'means'. If, instead, we resist the urge to find an explanation and see the art work as a path to our inner responses, something that can unlock our senses and spirits, we have made a crucial step towards achieving an understanding of the deeper wells of the art experience. In viewing creative work in this way, we can begin to see that our experience does not have to be shaped by symbolic significance, historical and cultural narratives, at least in the first instance. Our immediate 'understanding' can reside principally within our capacity to experience the art directly.

For the writer about creative practice, this first step to understanding by way of experiencing the works does not take you far enough, however. There is a need to find another avenue that reveals the nature of creative practice beyond 'explaining' its outcomes. One approach is to change the main focus from the artefact to the artist in a quest to come closer to the thinking and making process. An alternative to interrogating the artwork is to listen to conversations between artists talking or writing about their works or responding to questions from adroit observers like Katharine Kuh and David Sylvester.

Kuh's approach to understanding the nature of art and art making in her 1960 book *The Artist Voice*, is to give more space to the words of the practitioners than she allows herself. In the short commentary she provides, she highlights some differences in the way critics have interpreted the work of the celebrated modern artists she interviews. She draws attention to a disparity between those interpretations of artistic intention made by commentators and what artists themselves say regarding intention recollected well after the art has been made. For example, there are those who say that Edward Hopper's art is related to loneliness and nostalgia: in response Hopper says: 'If they are, it isn't at all conscious'.[6]

From Kuh's account, we learn that the artists come to their work from inside themselves and when audiences see the results 'from the outside' so to speak, there is no reason to assume that these realities coincide. Few artists articulate their intentions prior to making works but, when time has allowed for observers to make claims about the work, faced with these viewpoints, they sometimes feel obliged to respond by providing an 'intention' of their own. Many artists will say they expect their artworks to speak for themselves and prefer to avoid talking about their intentions. Those who write about their work do so in ways that are important to them but to others can seem tangential to the art itself. Piet Mondrian was deeply interested in theosophy and wrote about that subject.[7] Paul Klee left a more practical legacy by developing a theory of colours that was intended to help other artists. He wrote about using complementary colours to balance each other out, and how integrating the bold tones of yellow and violet together into an artwork was difficult, a source of valuable advice that is now available online.[8]

What is meant by the word 'intention' in relation to creative work can be difficult to pin down and few artists use that word, although they may talk about 'my idea', or 'desire' or indeed 'vision' (this last usually with a self-conscious smile at allowing such a seemingly pompous word to pass their lips). In creative practice, it is perhaps more accurate to think of 'intention' as an initial, often vague or loosely conceived aim, goal or objective that evolves as a result of unplanned changes of direction. Intention may in that way actually reside in the thoughts, perceptions and feelings that emerge unanticipated from the process itself almost as if by accident. Experiencing art as the artist intended is possibly the least likely expectation that most people have. Because our ways of seeing art have been mediated by education and cultural expectations, many people are nervous about their capacity to handle the simple question, 'What did you think of that?' This often leads to a search for understanding based upon the commentaries of experts in the field whose views do not necessarily arise from talking with the artists and trying to understand their intentions. This path to understanding is hampered by a lack of direct access to the voices of past generations and for the most part, we have the artworks alone to provide us with insights into the artist's thinking. Fortunately, in the more recent past, there are notable exceptions: for example, the conversations between artist Francis Bacon and historian David Sylvester are the product of a strong relationship and a singular ability to articulate on both sides.

Sylvester's conversations with Bacon give many insights into the way the artist thinks about intention and his artistic process. We learn not only how artworks emerge from the creative process, but also how the very attempt to draw reveals the unexpected: as he tries to draw a bird, suddenly something else emerges that becomes a different picture, one that he had no intention of doing when he started:

> I was attempting to make a bird alighting on a field . . . but suddenly the lines that I'd drawn suggested something totally different and out of this suggestion arose this picture. I had no intention to do this picture, I never thought of it that way. It was like one continuous accident mounting on top of another.[9]

In Bacon's case (and I don't think this is at all uncommon), a work emerges as if by accident. However, this is not to say that accidental production is an accurate description of the way all artists generate new works. Although Bacon uses the word 'accident' repeatedly, he questions whether it is so and whether it is rather more about selecting what to keep when surprising things happen:

> I don't in fact know very often what the paint will do and it does many things which are very much better than I could make it do. Is that an accident? Perhaps one could say it's not an accident because it becomes a selective process which part of this accident one chooses to preserve. One is attempting, of course to keep the vitality of the accident and yet preserve a continuity.[10]

What is interesting in this statement is that it suggests that Bacon, faced with a so-called 'accident', first decides whether to preserve or reject it. The second thing he reveals is that in making the decision to keep an 'accident', he bases that decision on two related things – we might call them criteria, which are that the work should exhibit vitality without compromising continuity. What he appears to be saying is that achieving vitality in his works is a high-level goal- we might say his artistic intentions are revealed. In this way, Bacon's process of making a work leads to transformations in his initial intentions by way of so-called 'accident'. These accidents act as triggers for creating new works: 'suggestions' he says not 'ambigui- ties' as Sylvester proposes. He muses on why his particular way of painting leads to accidents, a kind of unconscious working: 'So that the artist may be able to open up, or rather unlock the values of feeling and therefore return the onlooker to life more violently'.[11] Here Bacon's thinking about his intentions for emotional effect on the viewer are revealed. Sylvester then asks him about when something 'clicks' and he replies: 'there is a possibility that you get through this accidental thing something much more profound than what you really wanted'.[12] In other words, the accidents that arise whilst working with material (oil paint) and tools (paint brushes) can lead to something much more than your original expectation.

It becomes clear from this exchange that for an artist, setting out with well- defined fixed intentions is not the most rewarding or fruitful way to proceed. Instead, being open to the creation of forms that emerge unexpectedly, combined with an ability to select from those forms and going on to make a work, seems to represent the essence of the creative process as it happened in this case and, to my knowledge, that of many other artists. The practitioner's response to surprise and the unexpected, as a defining characteristic of creative practice, will be explored later in this book.

The practitioner's voice

Practitioners can speak for themselves through personal diaries that record daily acts, events and thoughts. Those like me who are fascinated by the working prac- tices of artists and scientists learn a great deal from the diaries written as part of a Calouste Gulbenkian Foundation programme that was designed to encourage practitioners to give time for open ended exploration of new ideas. The artist diaries are rich in compelling accounts of the vicissitudes of practice and provide a story that 'shadows and illuminates the act of making art'.[13] The commentary, although brief, gives a way into the raw material that is made possible by taking a broad view of the whole rather than the individual case. We learn that art does not happen by chance, nor is it 'self-expression', both ideas that are commonly found in popular perception. The diaries provide evidence of risk taking, insatiable curi- osity and unapologetic pragmatism as well as the entrepreneurial spirit that drives many artists today in the search for survival in a competitive world. The scientists' diaries reveal a world even more competitive but in a very different sense. Whilst the artists are constantly struggling with the problems of how to find the means to make their art, they are ultimately responsible for themselves. For the scientists in these accounts, as well as being original thinkers, they are answerable to others in everything they do.[14]

As the examples described earlier show, gaining insight into the inner life of the creative practitioner can be done in different ways. Interviewers can facilitate the opening up of thoughts that might otherwise remain hidden. Combining com- mentary with first person accounts gives the reader signposts into creative thinking and making that might otherwise be tacit. Diaries that record every day events and ideas provide a sense of immediacy that only such journaling can convey. At the same time, they can be fragmentary and partial in a way that systematic field studies would try to avoid. Taken together, first hand, first person narratives are witness to the everyday thinking and actions of the practitioner. They are the primary sources from which researchers and historians can draw out patterns and events as they attempt to situate their observations in real practitioner experience. They are invaluable inroads into the tacit and private world of the creative practitioner.

My primary sources are interviews and conversations with practitioners working in a wide variety of creative and professional fields. Thirty audio recorded interviews were carried out using a semi-structured method which centred around three broad topics: the history and nature of the practitioner's creative practice and its outcomes, their experience of collaboration and their awareness of reflection in practice. I asked additional questions that followed the drift of the practitioner's narrative and at times, probed further into particular issues that were mentioned. My method was to transcribe each interview myself and put it back to the practitioner so he or she could reflect further and make any changes. Most interviews were conducted face to face with follow up exchanges by email. Two interviews were conducted through questions by email following discussions in person. The result is a very varied set of extensive first-person accounts. I then carried out my own analysis of the complete interview protocols to differentiate features and identify similar ones. The interviews selected for inclusion in the book are of necessity reduced in size but I have tried to retain the essence of the practitioner's perspective. I have made the complete set of interviews available online through my personal website and links are provided in each case.[15] In addition to the interviews, my ideas are grounded in the many encounters I have had with practitioners over thirty years as a researcher. Early studies of bicycle design and collaboration between artists and technologists were foundational.[16] In the exploration of creative reflective practice more generally, I have also referred to research that relies directly on first-hand accounts as well as a variety of historical writings. All these sources have contributed to bringing the material together in the form about to enfold.

Creative reflective practice arises in many contexts, disciplines and domains and is not confined to those traditionally associated with creativity such as artists. Creative work takes many forms whether making artefacts, coming up with novel ideas, facilitating events, mounting exhibitions, or creating dance performances. Through their creations and initiatives, practitioners show us what it means to be both creative and reflective. Some inspire us as role models to emulate or simply admire; others empower us through their actions whilst others facilitate new experiences through events and exhibitions. They are people living creative lives in its fullest sense with all the attendant struggles that are the inevitable consequences of pursuing courses of action that are challenging to accepted norms and not always understood or valued by society at large.

The creative practitioners who appear throughout the book are well known in their respective fields and beyond. They enjoy success in the public realm having exhibited or performed their works in galleries, museums, exhibition spaces and events across the globe. Their works represent contemporary preoccupations and forms, many of which are digitally enabled: drawings, prints, sculpture, films, interactive installations and performances, as well as interdisciplinary connections and collaborative ventures. Some of the works involve audiences being immersed in visually stunning shapes and lights, or hearing culturally diverse music improvised across the internet, or seeing circling colours and sounds generated by heart beat and breath, or digitally visualised small animal data on screen, not to mention stopping in wonder before slices of the brain of Albert Einstein. Behind the works are the people whose creative practices make it possible. It is through the looking, the listening, the feeling, the responding, that we begin to understand the challenges that the creators of these works are grappling with. For the curious reader wishing to know more, links to the images, sounds, videos, events and texts are provided.

An overview of the main themes follows from which readers are invited to choose their own path.

Overview

The following presents an overview of the main themes considered through the prism of reflective practice as proposed by Donald Schön in his book, *The Reflective Practitioner*, first published in 1983. Reflective practice as a concept and practice is explored and extended in five contexts: professional practice, individual creative practice, collaborative practice, practice amplified with digital technology and the role of research. The final chapter sums up what we can learn from practitioners working in different situations of reflective practice.

We begin, in Chapter 2, with the origins and legacy of the concept of reflective practice and revisit Schön's ideas about the role of reflection *in* and *on* action in the artistry of professional knowledge. His challenge to the prevailing Technical Rationality model of knowledge of the time, whereby professional practice is seen as problem solving expertise using scientifically derived facts, is as relevant today as it was when he first proposed it. Those readers who feel very familiar with Schön's concepts are advised to move quickly to the second half of the chapter. Although reflective practice is now a familiar term in many fields and it has become a byword in professional competency frameworks, our understanding of practitioner knowledge is limited, an issue that is considered before moving to the voices of contemporary professional practitioners. These accounts from medicine, social work, law and architecture give us invaluable insights into the role of reflection in the complex and demanding world of providing professional services to the community. From here, the narrative turns towards situations of reflective practice that have different drivers and circumstances to those of the traditional professional world. We start with individual creative practice before going into what happens in the collaboration situation and the way reflection works in both.

How reflective practice takes place in creative situations is explored and reframed in Chapter 3, drawing on the views and experience of practitioners in art, design, music and digital work. Creative reflective practice involves many interwoven activities as practitioners search for understanding through making works of various forms. We look at creative practice through the prism of the practitioner process- the activities. The outcomes – the 'works' – are considered insofar as they are integral to the process, but they are not the main focus of attention. Variations of reflection *in* and *on* action have been identified within the creative process and five categories are described that extend the original concept. Practitioner observations about personal practice and the way they appraise and learn from making works appear as examples throughout the discussion. The characterisation of reflective creative practice is drawn from interviews with practitioners currently working in a range of fields, a selection of which are included at the end of the chapter and as with all the practitioner interviews available in full online.[17]

Creative practitioners learn to be reflective in practice through individual activities honed over many years. But what happens when their creative work involves collaboration with others? How much does collaboration itself influence the way the practitioner creates new ideas and works and reflects on the process and its outcomes? In Chapter 4, a picture of the world of collaborative creation emerges in which different patterns and structures influence how practitioners generate ideas, realise them in tangible forms and reflect before, during and after the activities. By shifting the context of creative practice from solo to shared concerns, we can see how this extends the concept of reflective practice again. Sources include studies of art, science and journalism and interdisciplinary collaboration. Research on organisations working collaboratively, including artistic collectives, news media operations and design companies have also provided valuable examples of real-world collaborative practice. Above all, interviews with artists, designers, curators, entrepreneurs, musicians and technologists who collaborate extensively have been invaluable. Together these sources represent a broad spectrum of co-creation and provide the foundation for the discussion of co-reflection.

Practitioners throughout the world are amplifying their creative processes with digital technology. Chapter 5 explores how this has had a profound effect on the way practitioners think and make creative works, a process that is continually evolving as the technologies advance at a rapid pace. Digitally amplified practice provides practitioners with new ways of generating fresh insights into their processes and the creative works that emerge. It raises questions like: how do creative practitioners view the technologies they use: as tools for making objects, as mediators between thinking and action, as media for making or as partners with whom to interact and perform? Or perhaps, a combination of one or more of these categories? What do these terms tell us about how creative practitioners think about their relationship to the digital in their practice and the influence on reflection in action? Four kinds of amplification are defined in which the digital role is differentiated as tool, mediator, medium and partner. The discussion is illustrated by the ideas and works of established creative practitioners in the field for whom digital technology is integral to the way they work.

Donald Schön believed that reflective practice made the practitioner into a researcher who was then able to construct new theory from unique cases revealing the true nature of practitioner knowledge. Chapter 6 explores practitioner approaches to making, appraising and documenting their creative work in the context of personal and shared research practices. Reflective practice is undergoing a renaissance driven by new forms of research carried out in conjunction with creative practice. What is more, it is the practitioners themselves who are making that knowledge about practice available to a wider community of expertise by undertaking formal research. We explore the way new research practices are generating practice-based evidence in a quest for greater understanding of the nature of practitioner knowledge in creative practice. Examples of the kinds of knowledge from this research are provided drawing on a range of practitioner PhD research projects.

Being a reflective practitioner means cultivating the many ways we can learn through experience. Reflective practice has benefits in increasing self-awareness, a key element of emotional intelligence and, at the same time, in developing a better understanding of others. Chapter 7 asks whether reflective practice can be learnt and what reflective practitioners offers in professional and creative contexts, in collaboration with others, in digitally amplified practice and through research. The student of reflective practice can draw on print literature and online web resources and some useful starting points are provided. General guidance is useful for students and researchers coming to reflective practice for the first time. In the professions, there is copious advice from professional associations and regulatory codes of practices. This advice is valuable for established practitioners undertaking new regimes for self-assessment as part of a programme of continuous professional development.

Try as we might, writers can take the reader only to the doorstep of first-hand experience of creative work in the different situations of practice that practitioner choose to work in. Creative works stand for themselves of course, but what gives rise to them? Why do creative practitioners do what they do? What can we learn about creative reflective practice from the practitioner? This book asks questions that take us beyond the concerns that Schön addressed in his studies of reflective practice amongst professional practitioners. From the creative practitioner's voice, we can discover the kinds of reflection that are so vital to successful practice. By listening to those on the front line of creative practice, it soon becomes evident that having a reflective mindset is at the heart of creativity whether in professional, individual, collaborative, digital or research situations of practice.

Notes

1 Gombrich said in the introduction to his book The Story of Art, 'There really is no such thing as art. There are only artists' (Gombrich, 1950, p. 4).
2 Some of the assumptions commonly held about this subject are explored by Drake and Winner, 2013.
3 Kuh (1962); Sylvester (1975).

4 Agnes Martin was born in Canada in 1912 and later went to the USA hoping to teach where she became a citizen: www.moma.org/artists/3787#works and www.tate.org.uk/whats-on/tate-modern/exhibition/agnes-martin/who-is-agnes-martin
5 An Introduction to Agnes Martin: www.youtube.com/watch?v=65Sd-L03X84
6 Kuh (1962, Da Capo 2000 edition, p. 5).
7 Holtzman and James (1986).
8 https://thechromologist.com/3900-pages-colour-notes-paul-klee-now-online/ accessed 13/05/2019.
9 Sylvester (1975, p. 11).
10 Sylvester (1975, p. 17).
11 Sylvester (1975, p. 17, para 3).
12 Sylvester (1975, p. 17, para 5).
13 Ede, p. 1 in Allen (2001).
14 Ede, p. 8 in Turney (2003).
15 The interviews in full may be accessed at http://lindacandy.com/CRPBOOK
16 Candy and Edmonds (1996); Candy et al. (2018)
17 Selected interviews are included in the book as a shortened version of the original transcriptions. The interviews in full may be accessed at: http://lindacandy.com/CRPBOOK

2

REFLECTIVE PROFESSIONAL PRACTICE

Chapter 2 is about the role of reflection in professional practice. The springboard is Donald Schön's contribution to our understanding of the way professional knowledge operates and evolves through reflective practice. Some key foundational concepts are reviewed followed by a recap of his original characterisations of reflection *in* and *on* action and his challenge to 'technical rationality' with the artistry of reflective practice. The legacy of these ideas on a range of professional fields is discussed. The second half presents examples of practitioner perspectives from the front line of contemporary professional practice. The voices of practitioners in medicine, social work, law and architecture provide glimpses into the intimate world of practice and give us invaluable insights into the role of reflection.

Situating Schön's reflective practice: context and contribution

The Reflective Practitioner, first published in 1983, is the best known of Donald Schön's writings. It is cited widely in fields as various as education, management, health and arts research.[1] Schön's case for a total reassessment of the state of professional knowledge was made on the grounds that the existing competencies were inadequate to deal with the changing situations that professional practitioners faced with, as he put it: 'the complexity, uncertainty, instability, uniqueness, and value conflicts which are increasingly perceived as central to the world of professional practice'.[2] He refers to a time when post-World War II enthusiasm for increased professionalism was at its height, from his time of writing twenty years later, when those high expectations had been replaced by a loss of faith in professional expertise. Over that period, the professions came under attack because they were deemed to be unable to deliver remedies for the complex, systemic problems that had become prevalent in the Western world. It was an era of rapid change when society was questioning the legitimacy of professional autonomy, and professional practitioners did not appear able to respond to the criticisms. As Schön saw it, the crisis was rooted in a misconceived but dominant view of professional knowledge, as: 'instrumental problem solving made rigorous by the application of scientific theory and technique',[3] what he refers to as 'technical rationality'. He argued that the neglect and ignorance of the kind of knowledge that practitioners actually use in their practice contributed to the crisis of confidence in professional effectiveness. He was motivated by a desire to put this right by offering a new epistemology of practice 'implicit in the artistic, intuitive processes which some practitioners do bring to situations of uncertainty, instability, uniqueness and value conflict' that promoted reflection in action as a 'legitimate form of professional knowing'.[4]

Schön's contribution was to propose a new model of professional knowledge based on reflective practice. By 'reflective practice' he meant the integration of thought and action within a specific context. A reflective practitioner according to Schön's characterisation, is someone for whom continuous reflection is an integral part of the way they practice on a daily basis. Reflective practice involves taking actions and making judgements that are informed by the domain knowledge and wisdom of a particular professional field.[5] It is by implication something that is acquired through extensive training and deep experience in continually evolving practice. The importance of these ideas to competence and proficiency is recognised today in their widespread adoption in professional development programmes and educational curricula, of which more later.

Writing as I am, in the second decade of the 21st century, Schön's contributions to our understanding of practitioner knowledge and the value of professional expertise, remain highly pertinent. The role of specialist expertise in informing opinion and guiding behaviour, coupled with persistent doubts about the ability of professional knowledge not only to cure medical and social diseases, but more broadly, to address the major global problems faced today, from climate change to the spread of contagious disease, is the subject of contemporary debate. Much is expected of professional expertise and yet scepticism about what experts have to say has become emblematic of our times. This is reflected in popular culture through print and online media and can have serious repercussions that can affect the personal choices of individuals as well as those of whole nations.[6]

Until the 1990s, it was an Internet and World Wide Web free world for most people, when the very idea of consulting 'Dr Google' before heading off to your general practitioner armed with possible explanations for your medical symptoms, would have seemed unimaginable. Nowadays, medical practitioners, having spent many years acquiring professional knowledge and expertise, can expect to have 'ePatients'[7] presenting them with diagnoses based upon a few hours of their own online investigations. Another example of public participation, is the emergence of 'citizen science' in which non-professional scientists have opportunities for taking part in scientific research without any prior training in the field.[8]

The shift towards people power has had significant implications for how we relate to professional practitioners whose knowledge is hard won and has been so highly prized in the past. Whilst it cannot be claimed that the role of the expert has been completely superseded, nevertheless, there has been a significant shift in contemporary culture in relation to public perception of the relationship between users and providers of professional services. As faith in the power of expert knowledge has diminished, there has been a growth in regard for what the 'non-expert' can contribute to fields that have traditionally been the territory of highly trained professionals. Of course, this is not to say we have a reached the point where anything goes and we are happy to permit amateurs to operate on us – there are still some limits! These are, nevertheless, significant developments that herald a change in expectations with implications for professionals and experts in many fields.

Seen from a broader perspective, the advent of greater public participation in the use of professional services, has inevitably challenged traditional ways of thinking including long standing paternalistic approaches operating within well-established fields such as medicine and law. Those professions with a more recent history such as social work have in some ways led the way in breaking down barriers between service 'users' and professional 'providers' although the costs in terms of effectiveness and retention have yet to be fully assessed.[9] What is clear is that the professions are undergoing considerable changes in ways that were not necessarily anticipated in the 1980s of Schön's time. The notion of a clear distinction between those who deliver services and those who receive them no longer captures the contemporary context accurately. When users are seen to be active and knowledgeable participants in their own care, health, education, this must of necessity transform the way professional practitioners think and act. Moreover, this brings with it challenges to expectations borne of a belief in the omniscience of professional expertise. That there are positive benefits to these developments in the role of the professional practitioner is evident for 'users' but, nevertheless, there remain questions as to whether it also leads to increased stress on 'providers' who are unable to respond appropriately.[10]

The decline of faith in the effectiveness of professional knowledge that motivated Schön's work, has persisted, albeit for different reasons, some of which are associated with ubiquitous Internet availability and the massive change in access to information afforded by it. This change in attitude is an important part of the backdrop to the place of professional 'expert' knowledge in society today and represents a wholly different cultural context for anyone coming across Schön's ideas for the first time, or indeed, revisiting them as I have been doing. The enormous shift over the last forty or so years has seen a deepening of the kind of scepticism that Schön was addressing in his time but with the added dimension of higher expectations of active public participation in decision making that was once the sole province of the professional. What has not changed, however, is that professional people throughout the world are subject to strict training and accreditation requirements within national and international legal frameworks that govern their ability to practice. If anything, we are seeing a tightening up of the regulatory frameworks making them even more stringent than in the 20th century.[11]

Foundations of reflective practice

In order to place Schön's contribution to knowledge in the wider context of the history of ideas, let us first briefly situate his work in relation to its antecedents. Whilst it is generally acknowledged that Schön first made the term 'reflective practice' widely known and proposed a relationship between this and the development of practitioner knowledge, the underlying concepts go back much further. The student, educator, researcher or practitioner coming to Schön's ideas for the first time, and perhaps even those who consider themselves already familiar with his thinking, are encouraged to take a longer look at the foundational philosophical ideas for a deeper perspective on their relevance for learning and practice.[12]

In weighing up the significance of Schön's work from the vantage point of in the early part of the 21st century, his theories continue to be explored and extended further in a diverse range of fields of professional practice[13] as well as in making a link between action research and practitioner knowledge.[14] It is the concept of reflective practice that has travelled furthest and widest and continues to do so even in the face of criticism. The basic concepts of reflective practice focus on practitioner knowledge and extend the traditional frames of reference for systematic research methodologies into counterview approaches.[15] However, the legacy of Schön's ideas is not without its critics and questions have been raised as to the value of his theories for all situations of practice. One consequence of that legacy has been a tendency to focus on making reflective practice one element of a set of competencies that can be acquired during professional training. In going down this road, there is a danger of losing sight of the deeper questions that Schön raised. This is particularly so with regard to his attention to how we conceive and interpret the kind of knowing that arises from, and is used in, real-world practice. His challenge to the dominant authority of the Technical Rationality model of knowledge remains unresolved. This is discussed in the next section in relation to the artistry of reflective practice.

But let us begin at the beginning and assume we are newcomers to the theory behind Schon's concept of reflective practice. We will start with the word 'reflection' and how it became a cornerstone for a new epistemology of knowledge.

How thought becomes reflection

John Dewey, in *How We Think*, begins his exploration of the nature of reflection by asking a fundamental question, 'what is thought?'[16] In his search for a consistent meaning, he distinguishes between the many loose ways we define 'thinking'. There is the thinking based upon some kind of testimony or evidence of which there are two kinds: the first is thinking something but without proffering grounds to support that belief; the second, by contrast, involves a deliberate attempt to find evidential grounds for thinking something – and it is here that reflection comes into play: 'This process is called *reflective* thought; it alone is truly educative in value'[17] (my emphasis).

Dewey goes on to draw out the difference between ordinary types of thinking and reflective thinking in respect of the 'random coursing of things through the mind'. He argues that whilst randomness might be true of most kinds of successive thoughts, this is not characteristic of reflection, which is:

> not simply a sequence of ideas, but a consequence, a consecutive ordering in such a way that each determines the next as its proper outcome while each in turn leans back on its predecessors. The successive portions of the reflective thought grow out of one another and support one another. . . . Each phase is a step from something to something. . . . The stream or flow becomes a train, chain, or thread.[18]

Whilst not necessarily associated with pure rational thinking, in this context, the word reflection is, nevertheless, connected to thinking as a conscious cognitive process. The 'consecutive ordering' Dewey refers to suggests a process of working through chains of events or identifying the subtle threads that connect events and experiences in a way that seems to 'make sense'. Teasing out links that relate ideas or actions of one kind or another also suggests a sense of judging or appraising those relationships and, in that way, can appear to be both a rational and a self-critical process. For Schön, reflection is the fundamental element of strategic think-ing and a word that is always accompanied by another – action. Throughout his writings, the words reflection and action are inextricably combined. These notions of reflection *in* and *on* action are key to understanding reflective practice and its challenge to the prevailing wisdom about the nature of knowledge.

Reflection in and on action

The concepts of reflection *in* action and reflection *on* action are crucial to under-standing of what Schön meant by reflective practice and its relationship to the 'knowing' that resides in action. This kind of knowledge is comprised of criteria, procedures, judgments and previous experiences that are tacit at the time of use. Schön showed that practitioners are capable of bringing tacit understandings to solving problems, and that they produce well-founded insights based on experi-ence. Whilst such knowing may not be clearly articulated, practitioners do think about what they are doing at the time and are usually asking themselves questions during the process of dealing with a problem or unexpected situation that has arisen, questions like: What am I seeing here? What criteria am I using to judge this? What procedures am I using, and does it work?

Schön defined reflection-*in*-action as:

> When someone reflects-in-action, he becomes a researcher in the practice context. He is not dependent on the categories of established theory and technique but constructs a new theory of the unique case. His inquiry is not limited to a deliberation about means which depends on a prior agreement

about ends. He does not keep means and ends separate but defines them interactively as he frames a problematic situation. He does not separate thinking from doing, ratiocinating his way to a decision which he must later convert to action. Because his experimenting is a kind of action, implementation is built into his inquiry. Thus reflection-in-action can proceed, even in situations of uncertainty or uniqueness, because it is not bound by the dichotomies of Technical Rationality.[19]

In this way, reflection-in-action is characterised as an intertwined and reflexive process of thinking about the actions being taken, or about to be taken, in a unique situation. Thinking and acting together form a dialogue through which the practitioner assesses his or her actions and, in doing so, learns how to develop better ways of addressing the problem faced.

Reflection-*on*-action on the other hand, involves reflecting on how practice can change by evaluating a situation after it has happened:

> We reflect on action, thinking back on what we have done in order to discover how our knowing-in-action may have contributed to an unexpected outcome. The reflection takes place after the event and draws on knowledge of previous events and their connection to an unexpected event; it includes working out what has to now be done to address this in the future.[20]

Schön dismisses the belief that thinking interferes with doing and cites examples of how practitioners describe their own intuitive understandings through reflection-in-action. He rejects the claim that by reflecting you might stop the action altogether, that is, paralyse it, and argues that taking this view is to misunderstand the complementary relationship between thought and action:

> If we separate thinking from doing, seeing thought only as a preparation for action and action only as an implementation of thought, then it is easy to believe that when we step into the separate domain of thought we will become lost in an infinite regress of thinking about thinking. But in actual reflection-in-action, as we have seen, doing and thinking are complementary. Doing extends thinking in the tests, moves, and probes of experimental action, and reflection feeds on doing and its results. Each feeds the other, and each sets boundaries for the other. It is the surprising result of action that triggers reflection, and it is the production of a satisfactory move that brings reflection temporarily to a close.[21]

As we see here, Schön is very clear about the reciprocity of thinking and doing and the role of surprise in provoking reflection. Nevertheless, he does acknowledge that there are circumstances when reflecting in the moment of acting might not work. Thinking can interfere with doing where it would be dangerous to stop and think, for example, when quick action is necessary to avoid a collision or in sports performance at the highest level when the differences between competitors are measured in split seconds.

Schön's theories were based on direct observations of reflective practice in action; he considered different kinds of reflection in terms of the time frame in which it takes place – what he calls the 'action present'.[22] He acknowledges that we often think *before* taking an action; nevertheless, there are many examples of actions that do not depend on thinking through matters beforehand and that take place quickly and spontaneously. However, it is when the practitioner is faced by unusual and unexpected situations for which there is no ready-made response that reflection comes into play and marks out the truly effective practitioner. The ability to reflect on what is there and to test out what he or she already knows against the new phenomenon enables the practitioner to arrive at a better understanding of what to do.[23]

The relationship between thinking and action has been the subject of much debate over many years and is discussed further in Chapter 3, *Reflective Creative Practice*.

Challenging the technical rationality model with the artistry of reflective practice

Schön makes a case for reflective practice in opposition to the technical rationality model of knowledge which represents practice as a problem-solving process that can be conducted using scientific theory and techniques. This view of professional knowledge has, he believes, exerted too much influence over academic writing about the professions, and he goes to some length to counter that view.[24] He argues that the malign effect goes beyond scholarship, embedded as it is in: 'the institutional context of professional life . . . and the institutionalised relations of research and practice'.[25] His objection to the technical rationality position, according to which testable facts are the basis of knowledge and professional competence is a technical expertise, is set against the position in which the practitioner constructs the situations of practice. The practitioner is not a problem solver but rather an artist, a maker of things:

> A constructionist view of a profession leads us to see its practitioners as world-makers whose armamentarium gives them frames with which to envisage coherence and tools with which to impose their images on situations of their practice.[26]

In our increasingly complex world, practitioners are often faced with unexpected situations that are hard to resolve using an approach designed for well-defined, familiar problems as distinct from the 'swampy lowland'[27] of the real world of practice. Enter the concept of 'problem setting', which involves selecting what are considered to be the more critical features of the situation, identifying what matters and imposing a framework that enables the practitioner to identify what is wrong and how to change it.

Schön's notion of reflective practice challenges the hold that a reductive scientific method has on our understanding of how new knowledge is acquired and developed in practice. He argues that the practitioner's dilemma hinges on the positivist view of science rather than science itself. Science seen from a positivist perspective is a set of established propositions derived from research and there are limits to the value of these in practice. Instead, he proposes an alternative view of science as a process in which scientists grapple with uncertainties, one that more in tune with the arts of practice. Whilst both views of science exist today, the second has begun to garner more attention, particularly in fields where the limitations of objective measurable criteria and results have been recognised. An emerging counterview to the dominance of scientific materialism differentiates between 'true' science and what is called 'scientism' or 'reductive materialism'.[28]

Scientific method has many dimensions and ways of seeking evidence, from double blind controlled studies to observational protocol data analysis. The subject is too large to cover adequately here but it is important to be aware of the existence of differences when it comes to arguing a case for evidential knowledge. This issue matters a great deal in relation to what we take to constitute reliable knowledge in the context of reflective practice. The rise of the evidence-based practice movement, which favours quantitative over qualitative, and established protocols over intuitive practice, carries on the reductive approach.[29] For Schön, reflective practice was the core of 'professional artistry' and its ability to address problems in an entirely different way to the rigorous application of science relied on case studies of practitioners thinking in practice.

Revealing the artistry of practice through protocols and cases

Schön's theories have firm foundations in philosophical antecedents, but he goes further by basing his theories on cases and protocol studies in the 1983 book. The protocol data comes from observations of cases of very different kinds of professional practice: architectural design, psychotherapy, town planning and management in organizational learning. In each case study, a conversation is observed and recorded between practitioners about a situation that is proving difficult to resolve; the dialogue, the events and media used are described and interpreted in relation to a set of initial questions. Having considered the two cases in architectural design and psychotherapy, he then compares them in terms of what they reveal about the structure of reflection-in-action in practice, before going on to take a similarly close look at the more 'science-based professions'. He then considers the four cases from which some common features and some differences are identified, providing a set of useful pointers for comparison. His overall conclusion is that they reveal an underlying similarity in their practice, and especially in the 'artful inquiry by which they sometimes deal with situations of uncertainty, instability, and uniqueness'.[30]

The similarities of pattern are most evident in the way the problem solving starts with an existing situation but then is transformed by

> a frame experiment made possible by the practitioner's willingness to step into the problematic situation, to impose a frame on it, to follow the implications of the discipline thus established, and yet to remain open to the situation's back-talk.[31]

The similarity described here is one of following a procedure guided by the knowledge of the professional but adopting an exploratory and open-minded responsiveness when faced with unfamiliar conditions. The differences, he notes, are in the common features ('constants') that that various practitioners bring to their reflection-in-action: for example, the media, languages and repertoires; the 'appreciative systems', 'overarching theories' and 'role frames'.[32] These features, which he acknowledges are not unchanging despite the connotation of the word 'constant', are, in effect, the domain specific tools and methods by which practitioners conduct the core business of their field.[33]

Schön describes the artistry of reflection-in-action drawing on case studies of different kinds of professional practitioners. His analysis method could be described as a form of 'protocol analysis'[34] or 'grounded theory[35] whereby records of verbal exchanges between participants are analysed according to 'events' that the researchers identify, label and connect by similarity and difference.[36] By basing his observations on a close examination of dialogue between practitioners, he gives much more than simply a ring of truth to his theory. Moreover, the findings provide Schön with a springboard for embarking on a wider discussion of the critical issues that emerge from this analysis. From the case studies, he draws conclusions that are not numbers in a data set but rather interpretations of narratives about practitioner processes. These 'rich pictures' enable the observer to consider the implications of complicated and subtle approaches to difficult problems. He is not seeking to quantify the characteristics of such situations by focusing on or isolating single issues or variables because to do so would be to endanger his capacity to describe its multidimensional complexity fully. Nevertheless, there are, he acknowledges, limitations to what can be described accurately.[37] The descriptions of practitioner knowledge are inevitably incomplete, limited as they are by the gap between what is known to work – 'the feel' – and what can be expressed in words – 'the external descriptions'. This is the artistry that cannot be fully described, or from the viewpoint of the practitioner, be expressed in words alone.

Influences that endure: legacy and critique

In the years since the publication of *The Reflective Practitioner*, the theory of reflective practice has been embraced in a variety of professional domains from nursing, social work and health care to town planning and education. With the rapidly growing extension of academic research into the fields of art and design, the search for new conceptual frameworks that harmonise with a more practice-based ethos in research has led to a revival of interest in his ideas. In particular, his notions of reflection in and on action are now much more widely known. That is not to say that the concepts are necessarily well understood, nor are they always being appropriated in ways that he would have recognised as true to the original drivers that motivated his thinking. Nevertheless, this resurgence of interest in the basic idea of reflective practice, as a model for understanding knowledge derived from practice-based evidence, has proved durable as its application to many professional development courses in a variety of fields testifies.

Inevitably, with widespread uptake comes criticism about the value of the original theory and its applicability to all domain contexts. Some see a lack of coherence in Schön's theories and it is not unreasonable to view his ideas as being somewhat imprecise when it comes to how they might be used to enhance practice. Misreadings abound about the implications of his theory. It could be argued that many of the efforts to inculcate reflective practice in professional development have been based on a misguided notion of what reflective practice actually is. In the following discussion of some of those initiatives and the criticism engendered, I suggest we can proceed confidently – but with respectful caution.

Reflective practice and its key elements: reflection-*in*-action and reflection-*on*-action, has achieved an established status amongst curriculum planners and researchers looking for an alternative to the technical rationality paradigm. However, questions about its plausibility and relevance to different fields of professional practice have been raised. Some criticism is based upon a view that gives primacy to empirical evidence tailored to specific domain needs and a recognition of the limits imposed by practical considerations such as time and resources. Ixer argues that reflection-in-action as a model for understanding knowledge in practice was based on those professions not subject to challenging problems and tight time constraints.[38] In social work, the demands of the moment are such that exercising judgments is frequently undertaken under extreme pressure, leaving little time for considered reflection. However, it is perhaps a tribute to the success of Schön's reflective practice theory that it has led to the kind critique that is asking for more, a fact not unrelated to the flexibility and adaptability of the ideas.

The implications of critiques such as those of Ixer and others, are relevant to the time dimension of reflective practice. Some have questioned whether or not practitioners can reasonably be expected to reflect in the moment of action when there is heavy demand on both cognitive and emotional states. The pertinence of this issue to time poor intensive work is apparent and also relevant for certain kinds of creative activities. In situations of high stress and heavy cognitive load,[39] such as handling unexpected incidents and emergencies, or indeed creating an intensely absorbing work of art, the thinking and the action are typically felt as a unified experience. As Michael Eraut says, once a practitioner reflects, he or she has cognitively 'left the action'.[40] In that sense, reflection seen as separate from action, could be disruptive to its smooth operation acting as a form of interruption to embedded procedures that normally require no conscious thinking.[41] Anyone who has switched to a right-hand drive car using a manual floor shift for changing gear, having been used to left hand drive (or vice versa) will know how the sudden change to a different hand can affect one's ability to drive confidently. Conscious awareness of this kind can be disruptive to the habitual knowledge that is embedded in the action.

Reductive reflective practice

It is apparent from a reading of commentaries across different disciplines that there is scepticism about making reflective practice a professional competency. For some, technical rationality appears to have reasserted itself by the back door. This is manifested in its dominance of professional accreditation, university research and curricula for professional development where it has given rise to increased 'proce-duralisation'[42] of practice and a reliance on bureaucratic processes and priorities. By reducing professional reflective practice in this way, it could be argued that, as always, technical rationality strikes hard at the subtleties of practice. Practition-ers often find themselves battling against constraints that have been laid down by organisational regulations that do not take account of the prevailing factors that govern good practice.

Della Fish regards the prevalence of technical rationality in professional practice as a case of being 'under siege' in a hostile world where practitioners are being forced to be 'accountable' using professional criteria based solely on measurable competencies.[43] Practitioners are hampered by the difficulties of articulating the tacit aspects of practice that do not lend themselves to simple forms of verbal reporting or checkbox assessments. Some argue that this lack of clarity about the subtle aspects of practice supports the claim that there is too much mystique in practice. This can help justify the paring down of professional scope into those skills – 'competencies' – that are easily identifiable, hence measurable and thereby open to simple forms of appraisal. By focusing on developing those qualities that can be readily evaluated, the expectation is that this is a route to improve practice. Unfortunately, it can also be a view of professional practice which lends itself to administrative and bureaucratic control.

The most negative view of the tests and targets that are set (often by non-professionals) in medicine, education, health and social care is that they hand responsibility to external bodies and in doing so take autonomy away from the professionals and with it, a good measure of their confidence in their own profes-sional judgment. An example from health care is the way that clinical judgments maybe affected by non-clinical decisions based on criteria such as cost: e.g. choice of cheaper anaesthetic drug over a more expensive one that reduces recovery time: the medical practitioner makes a clinical judgment based on what is good for the patient's wellbeing overall whilst the hospital management decides on the narrow basis of direct costs. The practitioner's knowledge is based upon the unique situa-tion of a particular patient's needs and the impact of using a more expensive drug on operating conditions. However, this judgement may be given lower priority than meeting cost targets set by the organisation. Here, professional judgement is subordinate to bureaucratic control.

In order to counter the ongoing dominance of technical rationality over professional practice, Fish believes that practitioners should be encouraged to become more aware of the artistry in their practice. Seeing practice as artistry means expressing its affective, intuitive elements in artistic forms- narrative, autobiography and other art forms. Art and science use different methods but rigour and discipline are features of both. She suggests that practitioners should be able to draw upon the artistry of practice wherever they are faced with unique cases: Professionals – like artists – need to be able to make new meaning out of what is happening within a practical situation rather than applying to it predetermined procedures.[44]

There is increasing recognition that professional practice has a dimension that involves different kinds of knowledge: science and evidence-based approaches have an important role to play but are not the only solution to the difficult 'swampy' problems that many professional practitioners have to address. The tide started to turn in the 1980s, with Schön's first efforts to challenge the technical rationality view of knowledge in practice and the need for a shift away from reductive views of professional expertise. How much has that continued since then? The spread of targets for professional effectiveness expressed in terms of 'measurable' competencies seems to have become unstoppable. If the love affair with technical rationality was thought to be over, it would seem nevertheless that the marriage is still in place and is far from reaching a point of breakdown. Technical rationality is as firmly entrenched as ever despite the voices from the front line urging more nuanced representations of the true nature of professional practice.

The persistence of what some regard as retrogressive views of how professionals practice, combined with a widespread drive to improve performance has given rise to a new industry: the design of guidelines and prescriptions for evaluating professional skills based on a competencies model of practice. These are continuous efforts to inject into professional training the means and measures for assessing how well a trainee is meeting standards of professional competence. Professions with public service remits governed by legal frameworks, have to renew rights practice throughout professional life times and there is an obligation on individuals and companies alike to ensure they meet competency standards. The role of reflection in professional practice plays a vital role in many programmes for assessing professional learning and development.

Reflective practice and professional development

Professional practice is founded upon high levels of specialist training which enables a practitioner to provide expert advice and services to other people. Most professions require forms of further professional development in order to keep up to date and for the purposes of promotion. A professional practitioner's ability to practice is dependent upon acquiring recognition according to professional standards and legal requirements.[45] Traditionally, professional practice is one where practitioners have a high degree of autonomy and operate on a self-regulating basis subject to informal control by peers. However, over recent times the extent of that autonomy has been eroded by the application of stricter statutory regulations and stronger controls over accreditation. Increasingly, professional practice involves conducting work that not only conforms to certain norms but is also subject to social and legal control. Most professions whether regulated by law or operating under charters require members to have liability insurance cover and not having it may result in disciplinary proceedings. Court judgments may also establish precedents for extending liability in terms of the period over which professionals can be held liable. Public service authorities will cover all their employees and some professional associations may hold funds that extend liability cover for employees in private practice. What sets certain professions apart from other forms of advisory and service provision is the existence of statutory regulations that govern the legal responsibilities of the practitioners and their associations. All this means that the professions are answerable for the manner and quality of their practice.

Reflection in practice is increasingly playing a role in programmes for professional learning and development in a drive to maintain and improve professional performance. This has given rise to the design of frameworks and systems for evaluating professional skills and competence. There are ongoing efforts to introduce into professional training the means and measures for assessing how well a practitioner is meeting standards of their particular profession. As will be apparent from the accounts by practitioners in the next section, reflection takes different forms and its existence depends on the particular situations of practice.

Schön's theories about the role of reflective practice in the development of professional expertise are based on observational cases and protocol studies. Observation by itself whilst invaluable does not provide a complete picture of real-world practice. In the following section, we hear from practitioners in medicine, social work, law and architecture in conversation and in writing.

The voices of professional practitioners

In historical and critical accounts of practice, the way practitioners think and work is often obscured in part because most commentary is made by external observers. In academic research, the interpretation of what happens in practice is frequently represented by theoretical models that say something very general *about* practice but not *within* or *through* it. I confess that as a researcher I have presented models of creativity that represent an over simplified, generalised view of the process and its elements.[46] Even in participative research where the people concerned are included in the research design, it is still notoriously difficult to gain access to the true voices of the practitioners and even harder to arrive at a coherent picture about different people operating in variable circumstances. In those research areas where practice plays a major part, the practitioner perspective on how they reflect and act and develop new understandings, is limited and the existing knowledge remains deeply unsatisfactory. There is a need for new approaches to understanding practice-based knowledge and the role of practitioners in this is critical.

Having access to the inner voices of the practitioner at work is particularly hard to acquire in those professions where time and effort are highly pressurised. Nevertheless, where they exist, first person narratives can give us valuable insights into reflective thinking and its relationship to actions from an insider's perspective. Professional practitioners who speak or write their own accounts provide glimpses into the intimate world of practice and reveal much about how they reflect on their problems and solutions. By listening to and reading of experiences in different professional fields, we see that each situation of practice imposes its own constraints as well as demands for continual reflection. The examples that follow represent practitioners speaking and writing about their experiences in medicine, law, social work and architecture:

- The first practitioner is that of a neurologist whose writings about her practice provide insight into that most difficult of worlds: the conundrum of being presented with patients with chronic illnesses for which there is no apparent physical explanation.
- The second is a practitioner in law working as a legal educator responsible for the training of colleagues at a time of significant changes in professional development requirements.
- The third is a social worker whose practice is no less difficult, being responsible for ensuring safety and support in family crises and where other service agencies are involved.
- The fourth is an architect working on complex projects with multiple stakeholders and facing challenges that are both professional and creative.

The medical practitioner

> All my patients are individuals with their own story to tell. . . . Each of them teaches me something important, just as each new patient I meet reminds me that there is always more to learn.[47]

In Suzanne O'Sullivan's account of her medical practice, *It's All in Your Head*,[48] she relates stories of patients presenting with illnesses for which all the standard tests can find no pattern of disease, that is, no physiological cause that can be demonstrated on scans and in blood tests. Her expertise as a neurologist is founded on years of training and experience and the use of powerful technological tools that exist today to assist in diagnosis. And yet there are conditions that require a different approach to the conventions of evidence-based medicine because they do not conform to normal expectations. Some doctors react to patients who manifest physical symptoms for which no disease can be found scientifically with scepticism and disbelief: 'they must be faking it'. On the other hand, other doctors respond by confronting their own assumptions: 'there must be another explanation, possibly psychological, and if I look hard enough I may discover it'. O'Sullivan recounts her personal experiences throughout her career and shows how she learnt to question her prejudices and hasty conclusions through puzzling individual cases that did not respond to conventional medical procedures. She shows how she was sometimes wrong: for example, having dismissed a patient's condition as not physical, having relied too heavily on negative test results, only later to discover that one additional scan revealed a physical cause- a tumour. On other occasions having been convinced of a physiological cause, she discovers through a chance encounter that the patient was indeed 'faking it'.

Refection in medical practice

Throughout O'Sullivan's book, we hear the voice of the reflective practitioner at work, thinking, questioning, observing closely and connecting with and listening to the patients at the same time as negotiating difficult situations in which they do not welcome the news she has to convey. She demonstrates very clearly how a practitioner, in meeting the challenges of the unexpected, is made more highly effective by a capacity for reflection in the 'action present'.[49] Additionally, by offering a longer-term reflection on events, she opens up a wholly different dimension, that of a practitioner who can connect her everyday practice as a doctor in the 21st century with the evolution of medical knowledge from the distant past. Interleaved with the individual stories are accounts of how conditions such as hysteria and neurasthenia, were diagnosed and treated by the star practitioners of the time. She shows how this knowledge went out of fashion or was superseded by other theories in a less 'evidence-based'[50] context than modern medicine would find acceptable and yet was firmly believed at the time. Providing this kind of perspective serves to alert the contemporary reader to the dangers of assuming that what we believe today is totally reliable and unlikely to change – the only certainty is that new knowledge will eventually overturn the old.

O'Sullivan's voice conveys a palpable sense of the complexities of her medical practice and the struggle to address problems that do not slot nicely into familiar disease patterns that are readily treatable. Her portrayal of practice is a powerful and convincing testimony to the value of the reflective practitioner's 'knowing in action' combined with 'theories-in-use'.[51] Her account relies on close intimacy with individual cases that reveal the dilemmas and conflicts faced on a daily basis, at the same time as drawing on an historical perspective that provides a certain kind of rationale for the medical practice. This combination of personal practice knowhow and documented medical knowledge illustrates very nicely the need for more than a purely scientific 'technical' approach to medical practice. At the same time, the place of science in medicine is secured by the vital role of diagnostic tests, such as Functional MRI scans, leading to more accurately targeted treatments. Even here the reflective practitioner proffers a cautionary note:

> we have new ways of thinking about and looking at the brain and the mind. Psychosomatic symptoms are far less likely to be considered symbolic than

they were in the past and less likely to be considered 'all in the mind'. But still it feels to me, and to my patients, that we are as far away from answering any of the mysteries that surround hysteria as we were when Charcot, Freud and Janet were alive.[52]

The role of the reflective practitioner in navigating the difficulties of healing the troubled human condition cannot be under-estimated. An especially moving and instructive account of the life of a brain surgeon, whose professional reputation can veer from hero to villain depending on the outcome of an operation, can be found in Henry Marsh's *Do No Harm*. Unusually, and courageously, he writes about surgical actions and decisions taken that lead to mistakes, on which the more he reflects, the more they rise to the surface, 'like poisonous methane stirred up from a stagnant pond'. The act of writing about these submerged events is crucial here: 'I found that if I did not immediately write them down I would often forget them all over again'.[53] Marsh's honest and insightful reflections offer an invaluable window into the heart wrenching dilemmas faced by professionals working with life threatening conditions. Accounts such as those of O'Sullivan and Marsh, reveal that to be effective in treating complex health problems, practitioners cannot rely solely on measurable, evidence-based treatments, as valuable as these are. Understanding the role of the mind in physical illness is a vital part of a practitioner's therapeutic repertoire, much of which is learnt through case by case experience.

The social work practitioner

> What came across from all the stories is the unpredictable, complex and highly individual nature of social work.[54]

Becoming a social worker not only involves years of university or college degree level study, it also requires continual professional development. The training includes significant requirements for practical work placements often comprising 50 per cent of the curriculum. Social workers are usually required to be licensed before they can operate as a practitioner in the field or in management positions. The licence is based on having validated qualifications as well as practical work experience. Having obtained an initial first licence, each individual is responsible for his or her continued professional development and must provide evidence supporting the application.[55] In recent years, there has been a tightening up of regulations in some countries which may suggest that there are higher expectations of social workers compared with other related professions, such as occupational therapy, counselling, and health care. It may also be a reaction to failures in the system and the resulting increased public and political pressure to act. The social work profession of the UK achieved a critical mark of recognition after years of campaigning when in 2000–2001, laws were passed that protected the title of 'social worker' conditional on having the required qualifications including registration. This was viewed as an indication of the strengthened status of the profession alongside doctors, teachers and nurses and brought with it a hope of more public confidence.

Reflection in social work

Social work from the practitioner perspective is seen first through the eyes of Denise Bate, a senior manager of many years' experience, now retired, reflecting on the constraints and complexities of her field.[56] This is followed by other voices from the inside of social work, including the users of services and the practitioners who provide them.[57]

There are many players involved in social work: families ('clients' or 'service users'), neighbours, police, medical practitioners, health visitors, all of whom have to be dealt with at any given time. Problematic situations, such as a report of child abuse, require rapid decisions about, for instance, who is to carry out interviews with a child, when to inform the police, and when to contact medical assistance. When things go badly wrong and tragedy happens, such as the death of a vulnerable child known to the social services, often the immediate response is to call for action, to lay blame at the door of the social workers for their apparent lack of professional competence. When subsequent enquiries report systemic failures, governments are bound to act and this can mean legislating stiffer regulations. However, these measures may not always take sufficient account of the practical difficulties on the ground, and the chances of solving the problems the legislation is intended to address may be poor. From the perspective of a practitioner like Denise Bate, the lack of human resources is often more critical. As she says:

> If things go wrong it has less to do with the strength or weakness of the regulatory system but more to do with overwork, unfilled posts, expectations, changing policies and procedures, changing the criteria you need to access services. To my mind that's where the difficulties and constraints are around the profession.

It is often the case that a social work manager is monitoring several active situations simultaneously. Workloads are often heavy and continuity of staffing not always available. The manager is responsible for allocating new cases to social workers in the field and this is sometimes on top of already heavy caseloads and at inopportune times. The situation has worsened in countries where cuts in public expenditure have given rise to an increase in vacancies in social work positions:

> A massive frustration is that whatever you learn, whatever good training you have and however you come to know your own value system, the difference techniques, the different theoretical things behind whatever you are trying to do, it hits up against the reality which is that there are not enough staff, there are too many pressures.

Many decisions have to be taken on the fly and quite fast when faced with dire situations and people who are sometimes unable or unwilling to co-operate. The training regimes that aim to bring in reflective practice into social work skills and competency, do not always take account of the pressures on practitioners in the field when it comes to decision-making. Having to make a quick judgment in a highly fraught situation may not lend itself to carefully considered thinking about the various options available. Moreover, for the individual social worker, the process of making judgments and deciding on courses of action is one normally carried out in consultation with other people, for example with supervisors. In rapid response situations of everyday practice, there can be a mismatch between the ideal of considered reflective practice and the actual experience faced by the practitioner, which demands fast thinking. In terms of the educational goals for achieving reflective attributes in practice, the constraints and conditions are different in every professional field of practice.

Given the tight constraints and pressurised conditions, are there any opportunities at all for reflection in social work practice? Because so much time is taken responding to urgent situations, the opportunities for reflection are often limited to the regular supervision process when the individual social worker meets with the manager and reviews active cases. A key part of that process is helping the practitioner on the ground handle the emotional fall out that comes from working with people in highly emotional states. It is often a matter of identifying how much a person can actually take and giving the practitioner support in understanding their own limits. Addressing questions such as: who or what can you trust? How should I deal with threatening client? Whose safety is the critical issue when deciding whether to go in alone?

> It is a dynamic process. Things don't stand still. You can't do something, reflect on it, be critical about it and then – that's it. It's dynamic until you get to the point when you say we've done as much as we possibly can . . . There are times when things are deeply distressing as a result of decisions you have taken – it's deeply personal.

For the social worker, the impact of having responsibility for decisions and actions taken is immediate. Such decisions may have highly significant effects both positive and negative. Once retired however, the social worker employed by a public organisation does not bear personal liability. This does not mean that decisions taken are easily forgotten when they have not worked out as planned.[58]

In a different scenario, social work practitioners were asked to tell their stories in response to questions about what motivated their entry into the field, their career history and examples of critical incidents that seemed to make a difference. They were also asked to reflect on the lessons they learnt that could inform future thinking about the direction of the profession.[59] Many 'service users' expressed a wish for social workers to be well trained and knowledgeable, but it was the practitioners who had most to say about the importance of working on the basis of evidence.

The influence of a 'what works' agenda in social work was acknowledged to be strong by many and whilst they were aware of research relevant to their practice, they believed that actions taken – 'intervention' – should be focused and helpful. Being able to acquire knowledge based on research was often lost in the heat of being on the front line of practice. The 'unique' situation is an everyday reality that involves balancing rights and risks where, for example, the complexity of ensuring that an individual's right to independent living is balanced against risks to personal safety and that of others.

Practitioner interventions are often crisis driven because in a climate of limited resources and personnel, support for maintaining 'normal living' is a lower priority. The notion of social workers as maintainers of stability in previously chaotic lives suggests a trajectory seeking calm and predictability. And yet it is the challenge of finding solutions to complex and intractable problems that practitioners cite as an important reason for being attracted to the job:

> I love what I do. . . . I never cease to marvel at the diverse range of people. . . . I like the unexpected – you may have pre-formed opinions and you get out there and get the unexpected.[60]

What makes a good practitioner in the field is the capacity to continue to ask questions of social work even after years of experience. In the words of one recipient:

> It's the ones who struggle with what they are doing and why they're doing it, whilst they've got lots of experience, they're still questioning what they're doing and why they're doing it, because they're so committed and they're so frustrated by the process and the way that departments and systems work- but they're still in there, because they want to make a difference.[61]

The social work profession in the UK is changing to one where traditional ways of practice are being transformed by expectations of a more active participation by service users in the way they are perceived and supported. Whether this happening in a constructive way for all participants is not clear. Are the views of users matched by equally positive views from practitioners? The challenges for social work practitioners are many. A study of social workers indicated high levels of stress and vulnerability to physical attack at the same time as evidence of a workforce that continued to embrace change.[62] In the face of rapid change in expectations of the profession and challenges arising from organisational restructuring, practitioners who are confident in their abilities, skills and knowledge of their domain are in a stronger position. Having a capacity to reflect and learn from experience requires the opportunity and encouragement to do so:

> Social work is very susceptible to government wish lists about what they want done. . . . As a profession, we need to be more confident about what we can offer, and more certain about what we cannot offer.[63]

Echoing Fish's views, the effect of a lack of confidence and awareness amongst practitioners of the unique values and attributes of practice can be a diminution of professional autonomy and effectiveness. The imposition of externally derived targets and measures is an indication of the continued dominance of a technical rationality view of accreditation and professional development assessments and this strikes hard at the subtleties of practice and with it, the motivation behind practitioner commitment. Whether this applies in all professions is debateable and much depends upon the situation of practice and how much practitioners are under pressure to deliver services without being given time and support for reflection in practice.

The legal practitioner

[I]f they were applying reflective practice really well they'd be thinking about the areas where they haven't been trained. So not just the case law etc. but what am I like as a team worker, what am I actually like at client care in terms of my personal approach? Do I understand the business and finance?[64]

Legal practitioners practice the law under different remits and titles depending on their country of practice. For the purposes of this example I will use UK specific terms: solicitors and barristers both types of professionally qualified lawyers. A solicitor is a qualified legal professional who provides expert legal advice and support to clients who can be individuals, groups, private companies or public-sector organisations. A barrister generally provides specialist legal advice and represents individuals and organisations in courts and tribunals and through written legal advice.

The process of becoming a qualified practitioner varies considerably across different countries and within states and regions. The common feature is a set of rules setting down the pathway to full qualification required for admission or licence to practice.[65] There are also well-defined procedures for assessing professional development throughout the life of a practitioner and these are created and monitored by professional bodies with legally established roles. In the UK, the regulatory bodies for England and Wales are the Solicitors Regulation Authority (SRA), the General Council of the Bar, commonly known as the Bar Council and the Chartered Institute of Legal Executives (CILEx).[66] In recent years, the SRA has been at the head of initiative to reform the regulatory framework. One of the intentions of the change is to tighten up the relationship between the competence requirements and the set of skills the individual practitioner should aim for. In defining a framework for learning skills, the aim is to ensure that the target qualities and standards are made explicit. There is greater emphasis on the individual's understanding of their professionalism and what this amounts to in practice.

Reflection in legal practice

Until relatively recently, reflection in practice was an unfamiliar concept to practitioners in the legal profession. That changed in the UK in 2016–2017, when new regulations governing professional development, with implications for the renewal of practising certificates, were introduced. Previously the requirement was for accredited hours-based training which was not necessarily targeted to the particular needs of the individual. The new system has more flexibility and a wider scope which is intended to develop management, communication and leadership skills as well as technical knowledge of the law. Practitioners in law are now required to reflect on their role and professional competence and identify what further action is needed to improve performance according to specified learning objective.[67] The SRA has defined the new framework as 'continuing competence', a system where the process and effect of learning activities is undertaken for each individual solicitor. Under continuing competence, solicitors are expected to review their learning needs and address them within a framework of qualities established by the 'competence statement'.[68] They are asked to reflect on their own learning when dealing with clients and cases and look at ways they can incorporate this into their practice. This, in turn, should lead to a further review of any other learning needs. Competence is defined broadly as being 'the ability to perform the roles and tasks required by one's job to the expected standard'.[69] Requirements and expectations change depending on job role and it is acknowledged that an individual may work 'competently' at different levels. The motivation for change was designed to make reflection and learning fundamental to increased professional effectiveness and in doing so increase public confidence by addressing accountability and professional standards.

Embedding a continuous process of reflection, with the onus on the individual to keep a record and to learn how to reflect and learn from that process, is intended to inculcate the idea that continuous reflection is an integral part of a solicitor's professional remit. All this is relatively new to legal firms and practitioners alike and this has meant developing new ways of learning that involve individuals monitoring and assessing their reflections on practice. It also means that law firms have a responsibility to bring their learning strategies into line.

Karen Battersby is Director of Knowledge Management at national law firm Freeths where she is responsible for the training and development of firm-wide personnel, a role that involves ensuring everyone has the knowledge and skills that they need to fulfil the requirements of their job. Her remit includes implementing the changes in professional development regulations that replaced the existing continuing professional development regime with continuing competence. She previously taught the theory of reflective practice and reflective documentation as diaries using university assessment criteria on a Master's degree in Business Administration (MBA) in legal practice. Her teaching experience indicated that people need time to absorb, apply and think about the different ways that reflection could be incorporated as a continuous process rather than a piecemeal response to the last case completed.

In her interview,[70] Karen provides insights into the new regime for professional appraisal through reflection on practice and gave an indication of the potential impact the changes may have, stating:

> we are now having to say to them, you've got to do this continuous reflection – and to a lot of them it seems quite an alien concept because they've never

had to do it. Obviously, they are intelligent people and get the idea that they are thinking about how they need to develop but the recording element of it seems particularly tricky to some people and this is shared across other firms who are having to implement this.

Reflections on practice provided by the individual practitioners will provide a source of information about an individual practitioner's standard of service that could be consulted in the event of complaints:

> There's principle 5[71] which requires solicitors to provide a proper standard of service to the public. If say a solicitor had a complaint or negligence claim, they could look at the L&D reflection and say maybe the reason you did not meet principle 5 was because you hadn't developed yourself correctly.

The range of skills required of legal practitioners is expanding beyond legal expertise to business, client care and communication. Reflection in practice is intended to address deficiencies in expected professional competencies in skills outside of law. Whilst regulatory bodies are technically responsible for ensuring compliance overall, in practice, lawyers self-certify and their employers sign off having carried out their own internal checks. The individual solicitor has to make a declaration that they have reflected over the year and undertaken any necessary activity to improve skills. Many companies have competency frameworks in place based on the guidelines provided. Procedures for ensuring compliance with the new regime can, in theory, be checked anytime by the regulatory body and should be available in case of complaints. Many legal firms sign off their employees' records of reflections in bulk as documented in internal recording systems. On this basis certificates of practice are renewed.

Where a solicitor cannot produce evidence of reflection, they could have difficulty acquiring or renewing their practising certificate because they will not be able to meet their employer's internal procedures. Ultimately, the individual is the person responsible for ensuring the requirements of practice competence are met. Most firms make sure that all bases are covered and share an interest in supporting the compliance and continuous development of their practitioners. Practitioners are expected to set their own learning objectives within a specified range of professional attributes and evaluate their progress through reflection, as a form of self-coaching.

There are inevitably challenges and risks involved in transforming any well-established system that has been ingrained in the daily practice of a profession. Some practitioners, finding themselves free of the need to attend and record hours of accredited training courses, might be less inclined to make time for something as difficult to measure quantitatively as 'reflection'. There is a potential risk in the way that responsibility for compliance is shared between individuals and firms in that this might lead to inaction where each relies on the other to ensure compliance. It also relies on the integrity of all participants, a recognition of the value of the new approach and being prepared to take it seriously. For some less confident (and competent) people, the temptation to record plans, reflections and outcomes that never happened might arise. Obviously, this also relies on firms knowing their personnel well and having checking procedures in place, well before they are faced with a complaint. More important is the lack of prior experience of the reflective approach in the legal sector, implying a need for companies to establish supportive programmes for learning about the competences required and the standards expected.

By establishing a new culture of self-directed continuous learning, the hope is that practitioners will become more aware of what they have to do to deliver a proper standard of service. If reflection becomes a necessary part of professional thinking, this can bring benefit by accelerating the learning process. For less experienced practitioners learning from experience through reflecting and evaluating the way they behave could speed up the path to higher levels of professional competence – or so it is hoped. Experienced and highly skilled practitioners are that way because they have had years of facing new situations, solving new problems and learning from their mistakes. The capacity to reflect on one's actions, evaluate the outcomes, learn from the situation and apply the new knowledge is integrated into the best practice of the best practitioners.

The architectural practitioner

> Architects have operated between science and art- they have always sat between the two which means you have to be good at both and that is quite difficult.[72]

Architects sit at the boundary between professional and creative, and their practice shares attributes from both. Most architects work in private practices: in the UK for example a majority (80 per cent) of architects practice as 'sole traders', the rest working for larger operations. For the individual architect, working with clients means being involved throughout the construction process, adapting their plans according to budget constraints, environmental factors or client needs. Client projects come in many sizes from buildings large and small to minor alterations and major redevelopments. Architects use their specialist drawing skills and construction knowledge to design buildings that are functional, sustainable and aesthetically pleasing. They lead or operate in design teams, working closely with a range of other professionals from quantity surveyors to building services engineers. As such, an architect has to have a range of skills from personal communications and business acumen to a high degree of technical knowledge including planning legislation, environmental impact and financial controls. The pressures that affect the daily practice of an architect arise from meeting the requirements of business require exacting standards, for example, giving good advice about designs, materials, legal requirements, which are the very substance of practice. Where a client is not satisfied or the advice proves not to be correct, this can undermine professional credibility and personal esteem. Professional practitioners try to live up to the standards they set for themselves as well as what is expected of them by clients and society at large. It is a profession undergoing change as the world of the built environment changes as other contenders arrive to contest the space.

Reflection in architectural practice

The following draws on an interview with **Gregory Shannon**, Director of LTS Architectural Practice based in London. The full interview is available online.[73]

As with all professional practitioners, solving problems for other people is central to the architect's work. The challenges that they share with other professions arise from factors outside their control such as clients changing their minds or financial commitments. Architects are known to create their own challenges. This can be especially so with those high performing successful architects. In these cases, high levels of commitment and effort are made to create outcomes that meet exacting standards, standards that are set by the architects themselves. It is not unknown for architects to refine a design even at the last minute if they are not satisfied because they want it to be the very best thing they can do. As Bryan Lawson puts it in summing up key characteristics of outstanding architects he studied: 'Architects care enough to create their own crisis!'[74]

The architectural profession, as in medicine, law and social work, is expected to observe ethical codes of practice and operate according to legal frameworks that can be invoked where practitioners commit misdemeanours or make serious mistakes. In most countries there is a body established in law of registered practitioners entitles to be called 'architect'.[75] But what is the essence of being an 'architect' and what do they bring to the design of buildings and the spaces people inhabit that defines the professional?

The architectural profession has been steadily losing ground to other related occupations such as quantity surveyors and landscape design:

> Architects are less and less leaders of construction projects. If you have a construction project that's not led by an architect but by a building surveyor or a quantity surveyor or a project manager or a technician, then they are going to get to a solution in an hour because they are not trying to find something else in it.

It seems that the public understanding of what architects do is limited and sometimes dismissive. It is not always understood that they bring a distinctive value to the business of designing buildings and spaces including defining what problems need to be solved. The specialist surveyor or construction engineer finds solutions to problems that have been defined already within a specific brief. For the professional architect, every brief is a challenge that is open to many solutions but because it is a process in which it takes time to find the 'right one', it is frequently misunderstood. The architect looks for that 'something else', seeking the 'poetic' over prosaic, in a central cohesive design idea. This where the element of creative thinking comes into play and is crucial to the value that such expertise brings.

In any architectural practice beyond that of the sole trader, there are different roles and tasks to be undertaken some of which require more creativity than others. The architect who typically solves 'routine' problems such as sourcing information, filling in forms and producing legally viable plans that follow correct procedure has few opportunities to be creative. This kind of work usually falls to the less experienced practitioners, often the junior employees in a company, who take instructions and guidance from more experienced people. Taking on a more creative role requires an ability to think on one's feet in the face of complex briefs and unanticipated turns of events. Being creative involves an open and imaginative way of working seeded by curiosity and a drive for new forms, a process not dissimilar to the way artists think and work.

The process of architectural design is often very complex and developing solutions involves many iterations of proposed designs working with the clients. This requires a great deal of creative thinking and reflecting. It is through many iterations of designing, construction, and reflection that the architect practitioner arrives at the desired outcome. Reflective practice embedded in this way is vital because expert knowledge is not enough by itself. It is the ability to handle unexpected situations and events by distilling the key elements and dependencies through testing and reflecting that really matters. Having learnt from that process, it is then possible to identify ways forward.

One of the key challenges that Greg Shannon faces is having a clear vision that guides the ongoing design process and to which the design team can refer when compromises are proposed. He describes how that works in practice:

You constantly challenge yourself. If you take the design brief for the temple- in a half an hour you could arrange a series of compartments which fulfil that brief- temple hall, kitchen, car park, landscaping. You could come up with a functionable solution in no time at all. But that doesn't take you anywhere near far enough in terms of a solution. I think it's the difference between making something that's poetic and something more prosaic. You know when something has an idea at the centre of it and it's taking it to a conclusion rather than a shopping list of events that a possible. . . . [T]here's something in a project that just clicks when you get the components in the right place and the right relationship to each other. It's not just an aesthetical concern although that's part of it because there is some judgement about taste. You start at the beginning of a project that you can get to something that's going to make you happy, make your client happy. You've got it in your head- you don't know what it looks like but you know it when you see it and until you've seen it you can't rest, and you keep fighting it. And I would say that's what I would determine are real architects versus people who are just journeymen. You can't rest until you've found a solution that you think is good enough.

The idea that you move forward with in the project needs to be coherent and tough because so many things will erode it on the way. If you don't start with an idea that is complete and fully understood and justifiable, it will get eroded by budget, by planners, by client, by swathes of people.

You are using your senses as an architect and you are having to communicate in so many different ways on different platforms with different people during a project. You have to sell something to a politician, to a client, to a planner, to a building controller, to an energy specialist, to a hall full of angry neighbours. There are so many different people you have to use different nuanced language to drag the project to a conclusion.

As we see from the comments above, architectural practice is a continually moving, dynamic process that provokes reflection and in turn is guided by it. The key elements are creative thinking, testing and iterating through making drawings and what is more, effective communication through dialogue with multiple stakeholders. These are the kinds of challenges that Science Gallery London exemplified for Shannon and his team. Science Gallery London opened in September 2018 and is one of seven science galleries around the world. Its role is to being academic scientific research into the public realm by creating exhibitions made in collaboration with artists. The site for the gallery is a heritage building that was part of the original Guy's Hospital, opposite London Bridge Station. The multiple partners and interests meant this was inevitably a challenging brief, one that leant itself to finding creative solutions. Arriving at an agreed solution to a complex project with many stakeholders was achieved through an iterative process of testing and reflecting. The architect's role is to foster and facilitate that collaborative reflective process:

What does a building need to do to accommodate that? It needs to be very flexible because you cannot predict the contents from month to month. There are lots of access issues about multiple events happening simultaneously: you might have a lecture at one end of the building, dining at the other end, some retail somewhere in between and a show that weaves between all of those events starting and stopping at different times of the day. You have acoustic issues that are the consequences of those different events, traffic flows of people, different servicing demands.

What it all boils down to is you have to have a very robust, flexible building that is serviceable, mostly from the top in our case. You can drop anything down anywhere, fixing points, water, power, all of those things – very flexible, movable lighting.

The variants on reflective practice that are discussed next in Chapter 3 are to be found in the practice of the creative architect.

FIGURE 2.1 The Science Gallery London: LTS Architects

Source: Photos ©Peter Landers

Conclusions

The impact of Schön's ideas continues to be felt today in well-established professional development programmes that respond to the directives of new codes of practice. Introducing reflective practice into appraisal procedures can be limiting, however, and there is a danger of losing sight of the deeper questions that Schön raised with regard to how we conceive and interpret the kind of knowing that arises from, and is used in, real-world practice. Although his challenge to the technical rationality model of knowledge continues to be relevant, his case for addressing its negative impact on our better understanding of the true nature of knowledge in and from practice remains. As yet we do not fully understand the many dimensions of practitioner knowledge including the role of reflection in practice. By listening to the voices of the practitioners as they reflect on their work and observing how they expand their expertise through experience in practice, we can begin to ask the right questions about the nature of this 'knowing-in-action'.

The professional practitioners whose voices are heard, through verbal and written accounts, can tell us a great deal. We see that individual reflective practice takes place within a given context and very often in relation to group action; as such, it is not always amenable to broad generalisations. Another basic tenet of professional practice is how encountering unexpected events and problems is a normal part of practice and dealing with it effectively means embedding reflection in every thought and action. Reflective practice is a continuous and dynamic process and practitioners need time to absorb, apply and think about the different ways that reflection is incorporated in everyday action rather than a piecemeal response to the last case completed. From professional practitioners, we learn too about the value of understanding contemporary practice through the prism of earlier belief systems and that a historical perspective enables you to trace the evolution of finding the right solutions to seemingly intractable problems. For Schön the entire business of reflective practice, whether it is reflection before action, in the very moment of action or reflection sometime after the action, is central to the way practitioners deal with uncertain, unique, unstable, conflicting situations. They are most likely to initiate reflection when uncertain as to how to move forward, and the attribute that marks out the highly expert professional practitioner is knowing what kind of thinking process will help. These features are exactly why such an approach lends itself to other forms of practice including creative ones. Later, in Chapter 7, we consider the subject of learning reflective practice.

In Chapter 3 Reflective Creative Practice that follows, we take a look at creative practice and how reflection has similar features but with significant differences to that of professional practice. It is the differences that will be the main focus of attention.

Notes

1 Schön (1991) first published by Basic Books in 1983. The page references apply to the 1991 edition.
2 Schön (1991, p. 14).
3 Schön (1991, p. 21).
4 Schön (1991, p. 69).
5 Schön's contribution is the nature of knowledge in professional areas from health, defence, education, business, the law to building design and construction.
6 A frequently cited example comes from the UK 2016 referendum on whether to remain a member of the European Union. A government minister gave his unreserved support for basing one's opinions on anything but expert advice: 'I think people in this country', declared Vote Leave's Michael Gove, 'have had enough of experts'. Anti-expert sentiment was soon spreading across the land. 'Experts', snorted a caller on Jeremy Vine's Radio 2 show, 'built the Titanic': https://www.telegraph.co.uk/news/2016/06/10/ michael-goves-guide-to-britains-greatest-enemy-the-experts/ Deacon (2016).
7 ePatients are health consumers who wishing to be active participants in their medical care, seek knowledge via online communications. https://hitconsultant.net/2014/06/25/ rise-of-the-epatient-movement/
8 Citizen Science is 'scientific work undertaken by members of the general public, often in collaboration with or under the direction of professional scientists and scientific institutions': www.citizensciencealliance.org.
9 Cree and Davis (2007) bring together the voices of social work, both users of services and the practitioners who provide them. Practitioners were asked to tell their stories in response to questions about what motivated their entry into the field, their career history and examples of critical incidents that seemed to make a difference. They were also asked to reflect on the lessons they learnt that could inform future thinking about the direction of the profession.
10 Cree and Davis (2007).
11 There is increasing scrutiny of regulatory frameworks for professional practice particularly in health, nursing and social care. The Professional Standards Authority for Health and Social Care promotes the health, safety and wellbeing of patients, service users and the public by raising standards of regulation and voluntary registration of people working in health and care. It is an independent body, accountable to the UK Parliament. www.gov.uk/ government/organisations/professional-standards-authority-for-health-and-social-care.
12 Kinsella (2007, 2009): makes a case for this kind of due diligence arguing that the conceptual and philosophical basis for Schön's theory is stronger if, along with John Dewey,

we include the contributions of Graham Wallas, Nelson Goodman, and Gilbert Ryle. Kinsella situates Schön's thinking within the constructionist view, drawing on Goodman's idea that humans actively construct their personal realities and models of the world using available symbols such as words, images, sounds etc. Goodman's 'worldmaking' surfaces in Schön's account of the way practitioners shape their individual interpretations of their world, an analysis that becomes more explicit in a later book.

Ryle's challenge to Cartesian dualism of mind and body was that the mind's working is actually revealed through the body's actions, which presages the theory of reflection-in-action and embodied cognition Ryle (1949).

13 Schön's legacy: the contributions he made that may ultimately be considered to have the greatest value, such as his writings about the relationship between theory and practice and the role of intervention in learning should however not be forgotten. This work was undertaken in collaboration with Chris Argyris, himself a significant contributor to innovative theories of organisational learning. Schön and Argyris came up with new ways of conceptualising the 'learning society' and the theory of 'double-loop learning'. They devised highly original perspectives on complex, long standing problems that affected individuals and organisations at all levels.

14 Action research has been used to underpin a stream of research dedicated to improving practice and has, in combination with Schön's concepts of reflective practice, become an invaluable feature of ongoing practitioner research.

15 Argyris et al. (1985).

16 Dewey (1910).

17 Dewey (1910, chapter 1, p. 2).

18 Dewey (1910, chapter 1, pp. 2–3).

19 Schön (1991, pp. 68–69).

20 Schön (1991, p. 26).

21 Schön (1991, p. 280).

22 Schön (1991, p. 278): 'The action-present (the period of time in which we remain in the "same situation") varies greatly from case to case, and in many cases, there is time to think what we are doing ... for example, a physician's management of a patient's disease, a lawyer's preparation of a brief, a teacher's handling of a difficult student. In processes such as these, which may extend over weeks, months, or years, fast-moving episodes are punctuated by intervals which provide opportunity for reflection.'

23 See Schön (1991, p. 68).

24 Schön (1991, Chapter 2).

25 Schön (1991, p. 26).

26 Schön (1987a, p. 218).

27 'In the varied high ground where practitioners can make effective use of research-based theory and technique, and there is a swampy lowland where situations are "messes" incapable of technical solution' (Schön 1991, p. 42).

28 Noë (2015, drawing on Dupré (2001) says 'Scientism is committed to something like the idea that it is possible to describe the world as it really is in a way that is independent of our particular interests, needs, values or standpoint (p. 67). He also suggests that it was Descartes's view and that everything we experience is 'mere effects, in our minds, of processes that are in themselves, without colour and without sound (p. 68). Everything is pure matter, devoid of quality in other words, it is tantamount to 'reductive materialism'. Noë goes on to discuss how scientism has affected the way we approach questions of mind, consciousness and human nature and also the nature of art. Noë, pp. 67–71.

29 See chapter 6 for a discussion of the difference between 'evidence-based practice' and 'practice-based evidence'.

30 Schön (1991, p. 268).

31 Schön (1991, p. 269).

32 Schön (1991, pp. 272–274).

33 Schön (1991, p. 275).

34 Protocol analysis is a research method whereby data, in the form of verbal reports is used as the main source material for an analysis of the thinking processes of research subjects (Ericsson & Simon 1993).

35 Grounded Theory is the discovery of emerging patterns in data and the generation of theories from data (Glaser & Strauss 1999).

36 Schön's method is not as rigorous as many in the research world would prefer. Schön countered criticism by arguing that practitioner reflection-in-action, whilst different to scientific method, is nevertheless highly rigorous.

37 Schön (1991, p. 276): 'There is always a gap between such descriptions and the reality to which they refer . . . when a practitioner displays artistry, his intuitive knowing is always richer in information than any description of it. Further, the internal strategy of representation, embodied in the practitioner's feel for artistic performance, is frequently incongruent with the strategies used to construct external descriptions of it'.

38 This view is supported by an examination of the protocols used by Schön to illustrate the sources of his theory which reveal the dialogue between experienced and less experienced practitioners working through situations in a considered manner without the pressure of clients and service users hammering on the door for attention. Ixer also points out that the earlier 1974 theory of action research which established the link between theory and practice as a cyclical process of thinking and doing is a more plausible model for practice albeit less well founded in the protocol studies that came later (Ixer 1999).

39 Cognitive Load theory states that effective learning can only take place when the cognitive capacity of an individual is not exceeded. It has come to be used in everyday parlance but the relevance to creative actions in the moment remains unknown. Cognitive Load Theory was developed by Sweller (1988).

40 Eraut (2007, pp. 403–422).

41 Bengtsson (1995).

42 Schön (1987b, pp. 225–237).

43 Fish (1998).

44 Fish (1998, p. 12).

45 In most countries, professional associations award professional qualifications and define codes of conduct. Statutory regulations impose a framework for legal responsibilities. Green (2009) identifies four types of professional practice.

46 Candy (2012, pp. 57–84).

47 O'Sullivan (2016, p. 309).

48 O'Sullivan (2016).

49 Schön (1991, p. 62).

50 Evidence-based medicine is an approach to medical practice that use of evidence from research that is classified according to the strength of its methodological credibility, i.e. systematic reviews, randomized controlled trials. The use of the term has been extended to decision making that is used widely in health care referred to as evidence-based practice.

51 Theories-in-use: building on Argyris and Schön's (1974) theories of action, two types: espoused theory, that which the individual claims to follow; and 'theory-in-use' that which can be inferred from an individual's action and which are often 'tacit cognitive maps' which individuals use to design action (Argyris et al. 1985, pp. 81–85).

52 O'Sullivan (2016, pp. 200–201).

53 Marsh (2014, p. 155).

54 Cree and Davis (2007, p. 154).

55 In the UK nation and in the US state, organisations issue licences after which the practitioner is responsible for ensuring they are up to date. Registrants agree to abide by the Professional Code of Practice and there are different regulatory bodies depending on the country of practice. The training of social workers is framed by relevant laws in areas where social workers operate (e.g. in the UK the Children Act 1984, Community Care Act, Mental Health/Capacity Acts).

56 Denise Bate: the quotations and discussion come from several conversations since July 2016.
57 Cree and Davis (2007).
58 It is interesting to compare this with the situation of an architect whose building designs are there for life and against which life-long insurance must be maintained or the case of someone who takes over the designs of another and is criticized for life for not doing what the originator found impossible to achieve. Peter Hall completed the Sydney Opera House after Danish architect Jorn Utzon resigned. But he was pilloried for his efforts and died broken and destitute. www.abc.net.au/news/2016-01-31/peter-hall-architect-who-fixed-opera-house-after-utzon-departed/7127160; Peter Hall: www.sydneyoperahouse.com/our-story/sydney-opera-house-history/the-interiors.html.
59 Cree and Davis (2007).
60 Cree and Davis (2007, p. 31).
61 Cree and Davis (2007, p. 101).
62 Balloch et al. (1999).
63 Fish (1998, p. 159).
64 From an interview with Karen Battersby.
65 This usually involves at least five or six years of tertiary degree level study (undergraduate or post graduate as in the USA where the professional doctorate degree is known as a Juris Doctor – JD); the legal knowledge education is followed by vocational training in law schools and apprentice-like placements in legal practices. There are different routes within vocational training according to whether distinctions between different categories of lawyer exist: e.g. solicitor or barrister or chartered legal executive each requiring different kinds of certificates.
66 The Solicitors Regulation Authority (SRA) is the regulatory body of the Law Society of England and Wales: www.sra.org.uk/home/home.page. The General Council of the Bar, (Bar Council) is the professional association for barristers in England and Wales. It is a disciplinary and regulatory body through the Bar Standards Board: www.barcouncil.org.uk/about-us/.

   (CILEx) Chartered Institute of Legal Executives is the professional association for Chartered Legal Executive lawyers, paralegals and other legal practitioners in England and Wales: www.cilex.org.uk/about_cilex
67 Toolkit www.sra.org.uk/solicitors/cpd/tool-kit/continuing-competence-toolkit.page.
68 SRA Statement of Solicitor Competence: full details here: www.sra.org.uk/solicitors/competence-statement.page.
69 From the SRA statement of competence: www.sra.org.uk/solicitors/competence-statement.page.
70 Battersby's Interview appears online at: http://lindacandy.com/CRPBOOK /battersby.
71 Principle 5 SRA Code of Conduct: www.sra.org.uk/solicitors/handbook/code/content.page.
72 Shannon's words from his online interview.
73 Shannon's Interview: http://lindacandy.com/CRPBOOK/shannon.
74 Lawson (1994, p. 145).
75 The Architects Registration Board keeps the official UK Register of Architects legally entitled to use the name 'architect'. The title 'architect' can only be used in business or practice by people who have had the education, training and experience needed to become an architect and who are registered with ARB. www.arb.org.uk.

3

REFLECTIVE CREATIVE PRACTICE

In Chapter 3, the nature of reflective thinking in creative practice is explored and reframed drawing on the views and experience of creative practitioners. Creative reflective practice involves many interwoven activities, as practitioners search for understanding through making works of varied forms. We look at creative practice through the prism of the practitioner process – the activities. The outcomes – the 'works' – are considered insofar as they are integral to the process, but they are not the main focus of attention. Creative practice is influenced by situations that are different to those that typically face the professional practitioners discussed previously in Chapter 2 and this has implications for how reflection takes place. Variations of reflection in practice that provide a more nuanced picture of the reflective creative process have been identified and five inter-related categories are described. Practitioner observations about personal practice and the way they appraise and learn from making works appear as examples throughout the discussion. This is followed by individual profiles and interviews with practitioners currently working in a range of fields including visual and sound art, curatorial and collaborative art and projects combining traditional theatre and digital technologies.

Creativity has been characterised variously in terms of its contribution to novelty, originality and cultural value.[1] Csikszentmihalyi described it as a process that can be observed only at the intersection where individuals, domains and fields intersect.[2] It can be helpful to classify creativity into three types: everyday, exceptional and outstanding. Everyday creativity is valuable to the individual concerned but the outcomes may not be new in the world. Exceptional creativity may be evaluated (and valued) by others, usually a peer group but not necessarily by the wider public. Outstanding creativity is something that has stood the test of time to become widely recognised and valued beyond the lifetime of the creator.[3] The potential for creativity is shaped by factors that are both outside our control and within it. Research studies indicate that a combination of complex, interwoven factors contribute to success in creative work including genetic makeup, geographical location, social and economic resources, health provision and educational opportunity.[4] Overall, formative life-long experiences contribute in different ways to the scope for creativity that a person enjoys.

Creativity belongs to everyone but few live a life of creative practice. A life of creative practice can be an irresistible driving force that demands considerable expertise as well as the fortitude necessary for survival, often without rewards of any kind. There has to be a strong element of intrinsic motivation to keep on doing what you do in the face of indifference and puzzlement and even hostility. Nevertheless, for those who persist, the work can be engaging and fulfilling and the creation of new works has its own rewards and is often transformational for the self. The practitioners represented here have informed the discussion of creative practice and the forms of reflection in practice that take place.

Distinguishing creative and professional practice

I make a distinction here between professional practice (as discussed previously in Chapter 2) and creative practice. This does not imply that professionals are not creative and creatives are not professional. Clearly there are overlaps, but there are also differences. To be a creative practitioner you do not need a licence to practice whereas if you are a professional practitioner you are subject to legally enforceable code of practice and you have others to answer to for the way you practice. Neither of these things applies to creative practitioners — at least when it comes to choosing what to make and how to make it. The idea of making things to order, so to speak, is not a primary motivation for most artists, although being commissioned to produce a work for money, might fall somewhere in that direction. However, differences between the respective working practices, for example in the degree of creativity needed to solve a problem, are harder to categorise in absolute terms because each situation of practice has multiple factors that influence how the practitioner can work.

There are similarities and differences in the process of practice, whether in professional or creative contexts. Providing services that meet the needs of people is not an essential element of creative practice as it is for the professional practitioner. To be able to practice as an architect, lawyer, doctor or social worker, you have to comply with well-defined educational and training requirements that, on qualifying, will open the door to a right to practice your profession. For creative practitioners, the rules, expectations and opportunities are quite different. Whilst there are designated routes to becoming an artist, composer, choreographer, writer, director etc., these are not normally absolute requirements. However, whatever the chosen path, there will be hoops to go through, some more formal than others. In certain fields, like music and dance, early years training in physical skills is vital but beyond that phase, there is considerable variation. Practitioners can be musicians and composers without having specialised qualifications although they would be hard-pressed to gain a position in a good orchestra or as a teacher without recognised formal qualifications.

As far as legal requirements are concerned, artists, for example, do not need to hold certificates of practice to be able to make artworks or installations. However, in the case of public space art, artists as well as the architects and designers involved are responsible for the quality and safety of the works and this has legal implications. Depending on the nature of the public art commission, practitioners may be required to sign contracts and to take out public liability and professional indemnity insurances.[5] Because of a lack of binding codes of practice, the process that governs public art commissioning is not without its problems and public art producers can be frustrated by unwelcome constraints that are not made explicit. A case in point is illustrated by the rules for public art created by *Situations*, an organisation based in the UK that works in the public realm internationally. They found that the commissioning process often imposed heavy constraints on what artists could do as well as frustrating the aspirations of local authorities, community organisations, and other partners: 'the process was one of resistance rather than shared purpose'. Their strategy was to devise a set of rules that were consistent with the goal of expanding ideas rather than being shut down by conventional assumptions.[6]

Whilst there may be fewer formal requirements placed on the creative practitioner beyond the general rule of law compared to those required of the professional practitioner, there are other demands such as building up a reputation founded on track record and personal achievements. In some ways this can be harder than following an established career path. The conventional career route can provide security and opportunities for promotion but at the same time, it imposes constraints on time and energy to work creatively, which for practitioners can be a barrier to fulfilling their creative ambitions and dreams.

Although creative practitioners do not have to obtain a certificate to practice and have their practice legally validated, nevertheless, many find benefit from joining professional associations or trade unions whose role is to further the interests of your field of practice. London is awash with royal societies that have long and distinguished histories extending to all manner of scientific and arts fields in which they are highly active in promotion through awards, events, exhibitions and publications: e.g. Royal Society of Biology, Royal Society of Arts, the Royal Society of Sculptors.[7] If you want a professional career as an actor you become a member of Equity.[8] As a trade union it cannot guarantee you employment nor help you find any, but the Equity card you receive with your unique stage name stage will at least, give you a feeling of being a professional actor especially when you're starting out. In the USA, SAG-AFTRA- Screen Actors Guild joint venture with American Federation of Television and Radio Artists, has a stronger influence than in its UK equivalent; it is also harder to become a member and costs more.[9] Although the main aim of these, and similar organisations in other countries, is to negotiate pay and conditions, there is also the more general aspiration to promote the idea of professionalism in the creative industries as a whole in the way social work, law and medical professions are recognised.[10]

Historically, certain institutions have imposed judgements on what was 'acceptable' as art, such as the French Academy Salons.[11] Some artists wishing to be successful, court acceptance by the establishment, but there are those who reject the very idea of conforming to norms and conventions. Many practitioners have traditionally decried the stultifying influence of the academy on creative fields especially in visual art. This is because they have had a reputation for shunning those who challenge the status quo. The barriers imposed by the Paris Salon exhibitions were countered by the Salon des Refusés[12] which showed works of those who were refused access. Equivalent institutions today remain powerful arbitrators of success. National and international awards such as the Pulitzer Prizes,[13] the Turner Prize, organised by the Tate Gallery[14] and the Man Booker award for literature[15] can have great influence on a practitioner's prospects. Such public recognition propels an individual into celebrity status bringing greater opportunity to exhibit and sell works. The increased visibility alone is highly valued and can be very helpful in furthering a creative career. Having said that, being judged and valued in this way is only available to a small proportion of creative practitioners.

To some practitioners, even today, the contemporary versions of the academy represent too much constraint on creative work that challenges existing norms or merely does not fit with contemporary fashionable trends. Many practitioners look for alternative opportunities to further their practice and are adept at finding new models outside the established organisations. The internet is one such avenue that has afforded alternative ways of building networks and promoting work and there are emerging forms of collaborative collective groupings that provide support in different ways (see Chapter 4 on Reflective Collaborative Practice).

Universities also have a role in establishing training grounds for creative works at undergraduate and post graduate level. This is where aspiring new creators can learn methods and techniques for making new works and at the same time, sit at the feet of, or rather in today's inter-connected democratic world, rub shoulders with, the chief practitioners of the area and start to build up a network of their own. One of the practical benefits of academic training and familiarity with its rules and norms is the opportunity it can offer for employment. Working as a teacher or assistant as a way of supporting unpaid creative work has a long history that continues to this day. Many practitioners teach to live and, in parallel, make creative work. The benefits of this support for creative practice are immense and largely under-valued in the wider world, and dare I say it, even within the creative communities themselves.

Those aspects of creative practice that are intrinsic to its value and that motivate creative practitioners in what they do, are unlikely to be dampened by the kinds of judgement criteria imposed by established institutions as mentioned earlier. An exception is acquiring funds for making and exhibiting work when you have to adhere to a tightly specified commission or meet strict requirements for eligibility for a grant. Because creative practitioners are not accredited in the same way as professional practitioners, this leaves more room for flexibility in determining the kind of career path to follow. However, what differentiates a creative practitioner from a professional practitioner in respect of their thinking and actions goes deeper. By taking a closer look at the nature of creative reflective practice from the practitioner perspective some of these characteristics can be revealed. One of the first areas to consider is what motivates the making of works and what inspires the choices of subject and ways of working.

Reflection in the creative process

> Reflective time engages us intrinsically in a sharply focused attentive mode of functioning. Artists in particular give themselves over to virtually continuous reflective time placing reflection at the heart of the creative process.[16]

Artists are often asked where the seeds for new works come from. Do the ideas emerge spontaneously in a serendipitous way? Or do they emerge from chance encounters in the world or from committed social, environmental or political concerns? The answers are as varied as the art itself.

The sources of inspiration for creative works are often unspoken and not necessarily obvious at the time but emerge on reflection further down the line. For the creators themselves knowing *why* they do it is bound up with the doing itself. For artists, the many facets of creating a work of art are not revealed as a result of an explicit reasoning process, but rather the art making is itself a way of trying to understand what it is really all about. American artist, Robert Smithson expressed the puzzle that is being an artist in this way:

> My art is incomprehensible to me, and I wish somebody would tell me what it is all about. . . . On one level my structures might be parodies of obsolete science-fiction type architectures, and on another slippery forms and spaces. One could also say they have a 'non-content'. I really don't know what they are, that's why I do them.[17]

Like Smithson, many artists, faced with the all too frequent – 'what does it mean?' question find it difficult to answer. Often the 'meaning' resides in the questions the art provokes, what they have learnt from the making and how they arrived at new understandings. This is not easy to articulate, especially in advance of the doing. Once made, the creative works are readily accessible, are visible, open to scrutiny and reflection, and not only to the practitioner. For those outside the art making itself, but nevertheless fascinated with it, this has led to a focus on the art objects as sources for critical and historical commentaries. It means that there has been much less attention paid to the making process seen from the practitioner's perspective. This situation is changing everywhere as curators, historians, and practitioners alike are beginning to value the process of art making alongside the works. A change in perception about creative practice is also taking place because of the arrival of the practitioner researcher. This has made the creative process and the new understandings that emerge more available as a result of research articulated in written form.

This phenomenon occurs in areas of creativity where making artefacts and reflect-ing on them through research are inextricably inter-twined. This theme is taken up in Chapter 6, Reflection through Research.

The creative process requires conscious reflective practice as well as the 'intui-tive' processes of creativity and artistry. Serendipity is frequently mentioned but its role in coming up with entirely new ideas does not appear to be the mainstay of the creative process, but rather occurs as an occasional moment of unexpected insight. Ideas do not typically arise in isolation but emerge as part of a longer standing vision that guides a continual stream of creating works. For example, when asked about the origins of new works and where the initial ideas came from, the part played by prior work is frequently mentioned. The contemplation of an existing work might set in train ideas for an improved version of the original. Earlier works could also be triggers for a more fundamental change of direction that proves to be transformational to the practitioner's way of working. Reflection on existing works may influence ideas of the present moment in different ways. Are they seeds for inspiration in themselves or do they enable a practitioner to learn what to do differently? Is there a temptation to change the work, having thought of other ways of doing it? This is not unusual and there are anecdotes of composers never really finishing a musical piece but continually returning to alter or embellish it in some way. The fact that artists liked to re-visit their 'finished' paintings armed with brushes was enshrined in 'Varnishing Day' at the Royal Academy of the Arts when famously the English painter J. M. W. Turner would touch up his exhibited work, a tradition that continues to this day.[18]

What is evident across all creative fields is that the making of works is in itself an 'investigation' in which the practitioner explores and experiments with materials and forms. The idea of art making as investigation is one that is familiar to artists but is not necessarily understood by the art appreciating public for whom the out-comes themselves are typically the measure of art and the success of the artist.[19] The creative investigation is a process that can give rise to challenging questions that do not rely on achieving success in the world. The immediate concern is less about whether the work is a success and is much more 'Does this work take me forward?' Appraising works does not involve asking questions such as 'Is it beautiful?' but rather 'Does it help me understand where to go next?', or 'What have I learnt from this?' Often it is important to experience the unexpected, to be surprised. For some, this last is the main point.

In a life of creative practice, these investigations ultimately represent a continu-ing quest to understand the human condition, explored in sensory, psychological and social ways. At the micro-making level, the investigation includes asking ques-tions that will shape the thinking and making to follow. Nico Muhly, American composer gives a richly articulate account of his creative process. He begins by devising a map for the creative journey (he calls it an 'itinerary') that he is about to embark on before any musical notes are created. Essential to the creative process are the specific questions that direct him towards certain qualities he wants for a particular piece of music: for example, the dynamics or rhythmic complexity, the number of voices, or instruments, which in combination determine the quality of the sound.

> [W]hat are the textures and lines that form the piece's musical economy? Does it develop linearly, or vertically? Are there moments of dense saturation – the whole orchestra playing at once – and are those offset by moments of zoomed-in simplicity: a single flute, or a single viola pitted against the tim-pani, yards and yards away?[20]

As well as guiding the making music process, these questions establish the criteria he will use for assessing whether he has achieved his intended outcome.

Many practitioners are driven by a curiosity that breeds a state of restlessness and a compulsion to move out of their comfortable, familiar zones. This engenders a state of uncertainty and can be fertile ground for generating new questions in an ongoing search for greater understanding. By devising new frameworks, adopting novel methods or simply deciding to change materials, instruments or tools, prac-titioners create challenges that shift their perspective in the making process and open up more searching pathways. The desire for deeper understanding through self-imposed challenge is crucial to achieving a sustainable creative practice. Con-tinual reassessment takes place that is often an integral part of the process. Whether the approach is systematic or improvisational, it is not uncommon for changes to take place. Sometimes the reassessment occurs with hindsight having recognised that certain influences have taken them in a direction they no longer find produc-tive. Being open to change can occur at any time and for some practitioners, it is a normal part of practice. Others take years to hone a method to a level with which they are satisfied. Many are continually seeking new approaches and methods and in doing so bringing new ways of thinking into their practice.

For creative practitioners, being successful takes different forms. How they think and feel about the artefacts, events and other outcomes will be crucial. Whilst achieving a 'good' outcome is important, this is not the only measure of success. It seems as if the process as well as the product has to be good, although it's the prod-uct that matters ultimately for most. One reason for using a clear, even systematic, process is that it helps the practitioner to analyse where things worked well or went wrong. A process that is clearly visible retrospectively makes it easier to reflect on the activities that have taken place and learn from them. Some would contend that a process that is unclear to the point of not being 'visible' or fully 'knowable' does not lend itself to moving forward because, without transparency, it is difficult to learn. Repeating one's mistakes becomes a real peril. Nevertheless, many practition-ers work in a more 'reactive' rather than reflective way, being guided by serendipity and 'intuition'. This approach acknowledges that much of what is done creatively is not subject to systematic analysis but rather emerges from emotional and intui-tive origins that are embodied in the acts and artefacts in a mysterious way. The process is then less open to analysis. This topic is expanded later in a section called *Non-reflective action.*

Creative practice involves a continuous exploration of ideas, materials and tools both prior to and during the actual making process. Such 'investigations' run in parallel with the design and making of artefacts and installations and there is a continuous appraisal of whether something 'works' or not. These iterative processes are key to the way a practitioner creates and reflects. The process of making something can facilitate a form of 'thinking through making'[21] as the practitioner moves towards knowing how to move forward. Thinking through making, as a conceptual framework for understanding the nature of creative practice has not received the full attention it warrants. The study and practice of embodied cognition extends the scope of reflective creative practice further in the context of thinking through the body. This is discussed further in Chapter 5, Digitally amplified reflective practice.

Making a work and then reflecting on the process and outcomes, is a pathway to understanding some of the underlying questions and assumptions: we might call them 'working hypotheses' or 'theories in use'.[22] Typically, such questions have not been articulated beforehand. The role of reflection has proven to be highly effective in supporting this process. This is nowhere more evident than where the practitioner undertakes research in creative practice as discussed in Chapter 6, Reflection through research.

Andrew Johnston is a musician, digital artist and researcher. In his creative practice, he explores new forms of interactive environments for artistic performance. For his research, he made virtual instruments for live performances through which he developed a model of interaction and strategies for designing conversational interactive systems. Reflection in practice is embedded in his way of working as a maker of digital art systems as well as a researcher. His observations indicate how for him, there are a number of variants of reflection in and on practice that are not compartmentalised in a neat and tidy manner and yet are fundamental to the many dimensions of creative reflective practice.[23] He describes the variants of reflection in practice that pertain to his own work and which he observes in the practice of others:

> **Reflection throughout Creative Life**: I suspect that everyone engages in reflection-in and reflection-on practice continually in all aspects of life. In the work I do there is continual movement between reflecting on the immediate situation – and placing what we are doing in a larger context and 'reflecting-on-action'.
>
> **Reflection at a Distance**: I try not to evaluate consciously. . . . I will often be in the experience mode but other times there is an evaluation thing that comes in. As you are experiencing that you may find something that's getting in the way of you experiencing it fully and you'll try and identify why . . .
>
> **Reflection on Surprise**:. . . . like a happy accident. A serendipitous thing where you say well that wasn't actually as we rehearsed it but it worked.

It could be a little nuanced thing that I would notice because I know that it's not the timing we rehearsed. . . . That's why you do live performance.

Reflection through Research: There are times when you do sit down and say now I am going to rethink what's happening. Then there's a more formal process where I have the researcher hat on. This is where you are looking at your own practice and reflecting on that and you are looking at other people-reflecting with them, talking with them, interviewing them about their thinking and seeing that they had quite a different conception of stuff to what you had. And then you are writing that up and trying to make sense of it. I am quite interested in using discussions, interviews with others involved in these projects as a way of reflecting on action. When I do this, it helps give me new perspectives on what has been going on. This is a kind of assisted reflection or reflection from outside my personal frame of reference. I think that running these as 'interviews' helps by giving everyone 'permission' to ask the naïve, obvious questions which lead to higher-level reflection-on-action.

In his interview on page 73 Andrew talks about his creative practice and collaboration with Stalker Theatre Company.[24]

Reflection in creative practice is a multi-faceted and pervasive process that is embedded in the practitioner's way of working. The dimensions of reflection are varied and change according to the context and the stages along the way towards an eventual outcome. Practitioners exhibit all types of reflection in practice. I will discuss the variants of reflection in the sections to follow illustrated by practitioner voices whose interviews appear at the end of the chapter.

Variants of reflection in creative practice

From my many conversations with creative practitioners, it has become clear that reflection-*in*-and *on*-creative practice is a multi-layered phenomenon that has temporal constraints and dependencies that are contingent on the type of activity in hand and the particular scenario. By focusing extensively on creative practice from the practitioner perspective, I have come to understand that the divide between reflection-*in*-action and reflection-*on*-action as Schön characterised it[25] and as outlined in Chapter 2, Reflective professional practice, is too broad to account for the variety of reflective activities and situations in the creative process.

Amongst the practitioner accounts represented in this book, supplemented by studies in the broader landscape of creative practice, reflective thinking occurs at different levels of granularity during and after actions takes place. A number of categories of reflective thinking have been identified:

- Reflection-for-Action
- Reflection-in-the-Making Moment

- Non-Reflective Actions
- Reflection-at-a-Distance
- Reflection-on-Surprise

These variants on reflection in and on action happen throughout reflective creative practice. How and when particular types of reflection occur depends upon the nature of the activity, the point reached in the making process and whether different actions are needed in the light of lessons learnt. I call the first variant 'reflection-*for*-action' and discuss it in the following section.

Reflection-for-action

> Reflecting for is mainly about reflecting about what the constraints of a project are.

Reflection-for-action precedes action in the present moment as part of the intensive preparation required for certain kinds of actions.[26] It involves contemplating previous actions, thoughts and achievements in order to understand the implications of what has taken place and learn how and where to go forward. It includes reconsidering existing works and products and reviewing relevant knowledge with a view to determining ways of proceeding. Reflection-for-action is a regular feature of designer practice and an area of close similarity between design and art especially where the projects are of a larger scale and include requirements to meet public needs whether as prospective customers or audiences.

When making a physical form, a sculpture for example, there is the roughing out on paper, testing types of materials, building models, discussion with other people, and so on, during which conscious reflection takes place. There is a great deal of decision making to be done: 'I chose this material over this because it fits the purpose' or 'I'm going to work within this space because it is right for the piece', all of which involve deliberated rational thought. This is a pattern that pervades an individual's practice and not only in the moment: the practitioner is continually aware of their process and how it changes and develops over time. Past processes are bought forward into present projects and adaptations based on previous learning are incorporated.

A key element of reflection-for-action is the ability to identify the kinds of constraints that will have an impact on the anticipated work. Being faced with too many options can be paralysing and it is a useful skill to have a way of handling the complexities and conflicts before embarking on a new work. The results of the reflection-for-action may be returned to throughout the making of a work. If actions are to have the potential to move the practitioner forward, it is necessary to consider what has already been done and to assess the available options. This awareness makes it possible to reflect and learn from past outcomes and is preparation for future action. In the context of creative work, it represents the all-important preparatory activities that precede highly intensive actions taken in the present

FIGURE 3.1   Person interacting with *Just a Bit of Spin*, Powerhouse Museum Sydney 2007

Source: Photos by Brigid Costello

moment. (See *Reflection-in-the-Making Moment* to follow). An example of reflection for action in the practice of an artist with extensive experience in designing and making digitally controlled installations follows.

Brigid Costello is an artist working at the boundary of design and digital interaction to create participative art experiences. From her research into audience behaviour, she developed design strategies and a model for classifying different kinds of play that contributes to the fields of Games Design and Human-Computer Interaction. Her works bring objects to life through animation that relies on playful and rhythmic elements, themes which she explores in her book on this subject.[27]

The statement in the following box captures Brigid's perspective on reflection-*for*-action and the starting points and stages of creative reflective practice. Her need to identify constraints and reduce risk is a necessary element of making works for public spaces where the quality and robustness of the artwork is central to her creative process. For Brigid, 'reflection for' represents constraint identification and this is followed by 'reflection during' the making process and the highly significant role of 'reflecting after' all is completed, when what is learnt feeds into her understanding of what has been achieved artistically and, moreover, how this informs future works.

> For me practice often emerges out of theoretical thinking but I don't see it as a direct cause and effect relationship. The practice is not trying to represent the theory. It's definitely a more complex back and forth reflective process.
>
> **Reflecting for** is mainly about reflecting about what the constraints of a project are. At the start of a project you are faced with an array of possible approaches and that can be paralyzing. So, when you say 'I am going to make

something', you need to first make a few key decisions about practical constraints. For instance, is it going to be exhibited? How much time do I have?
Do I have to send the materials overseas? Who is going to install it?

Following that there is the process of **reflecting during** while you are
actually making the work. It won't end up necessarily as you have imagined
the work at the start because you definitely change your ideas as you go along.
The reflection during process is really about shaping the artwork to satisfy your
artistic intentions. During that making process, the work transforms into what
it will eventually be and then there's major **reflecting afterwards**.

Reflection about how successful you have been at preserving the spark
of your concept. Lots of learning goes on too. Finding out unexpected things
that work or don't work. Observing the myriad ways that people might interact or behave around a work. Often that feeds into other iterations of a work or
into future things that you might create. I think that is a form of reflection . . .
after the making process to reflect on what else can be done. And to generate
a desire to take your ideas further . . .

Reflection at a distance: I've spent many hours in gallery spaces observing and recording audiences for my own and other's works . . . those hours
have given me a much keener eye for noticing the detail of audience engagement. Of course, all that reflective thinking then feeds back into the things
that I create.

In her interview on page 78 Brigid expands on the relationship between thinking and making and the role of research.[28]

Reflection-in-the making moment

> I put the colour that I am thinking of putting on the canvass, onto the making
> tape so I can see that colour almost where it's about to go. It isn't perfect . . . so
> 'that is not going to work and I need to put a little more blue in it'. I can see it's
> too dark, needs to be a bit lighter.

Reflection-in-the making moment is a form of reflection-*in*-action that is characterised
by the immediacy of action during a closely inter-twined reflective thinking and
making process. It occurs as actions are being taken and can occur for relatively
brief moments of time. This kind of reflection takes place in response to a specific
action in fleeting pauses, sometimes in short breaks, sometimes brought about by
external interventions or interruptions. These moments make space for reflection
on the detail of a work in progress and involve working with the 'material' of the
situation whether it is paint, musical notes or computer code. The scale of the
activity is crucial and the timeframe, for example, in painting, from making a single

brush stroke to the finished painting, embraces many pauses and break points. The breaks in the process can happen at any point and for different reasons: the opportunity for reflection depends upon the trigger for the break. Questions crop up: Is this colour/line/position right? I wasn't expecting it to do this – what now?

An example of *reflection-in-the making moment* is in the mixing of paints. This is often a process of experimentation to find the right colour, something the artist is not always able to pre-determine exactly because of the effect of light and surfaces on visual perception. Only by actually mixing the colour, applying and testing it by eye can you to judge what works for that composition on a specific surface. The reflection is the process of assessing what the effect is each time a new colour is mixed and applied. A colour is assessed visually but note, not verbally. This is the 'deep looking' moment of painting in action when the artist is aesthetically aware in a perceptual sense that a colour seems to need a bit more 'something'. One way of putting it is to think of the paint and the colours 'talking back' to the painter's perceptual senses through the conduit of the eye. There is a fast turnaround in the practitioner's reaction to combining materials until a point of satisfaction is reached.[29]

There are multiple layers to reflective practice in the making moment. The reciprocal relationship between reflection and making is a key aspect of reflective creative practice. The materials, the tools, the technologies are important elements that facilitate and at the same time, shape the thinking and making process. Reflection in the making is closely intertwined and can occur in short turnaround moments as well as longer periods of time. The notion of an intertwining of what we see and how we express it through creative expression is a well-known theme in, for example, the philosophy of Merleau-Ponty.[30] From an anthropological perspective, Tim Ingold characterises 'making' as an inherently mindful activity in which things emerge from 'the correspondence of sensory awareness and material flows in a process of life'. He describes how learning takes place through a direct, responsive engagement with physical materials.[31] For example, using wood as a material, a craftsman requires a practical and physical responsiveness to create a well-crafted object. This analogy can be extended to apply to sound design and sonic art, and how sound works through its materiality and the process of understanding its properties.

The reflection that takes place as practitioners manipulate and shape materials is integral to that process and so closely intertwined that there is often no perceptible difference between making and reflecting. Artists experience the act of drawing as a way of seeing, as 'a kind of reflective conversation' with the materials of a design situation.[32] Through drawing, the artist sees what is there, draws in relation to it, sees the result, judges its quality, learns from it, and draws again. If, in this process unintended consequences are discovered and judged to be good, this has a key role in justifying another move. An important background point is that, because we have limited cognitive capacity, we cannot consider in advance all consequences of actions relevant to our reflection on the result.[33] That is why the process of iteratively drawing-seeing- drawing again is essential to the evolution of the practitioner's understanding. Reflective practice involves multiple iterations of making-seeing -> reflecting-> making again-> reflecting again'. The learning that goes on throughout the process advances knowledge in practice. This can help to build knowledge and foster the development of practitioner appreciative systems, for which conscious reflection is vitally important.[34]

For many practitioners, reflecting in the making moment is a significant part of their creative practice. Some practitioners devise and refine frameworks and methods for this over many years, which become deeply embedded in their working practice. 'Tacit knowing' of this kind is akin to habituation but has wider implications for the practitioner's working style. One strategy is to devise a rule or system that combines the tightly constrained with loosely defined options. The artist who devises a rule to follow may apply it carefully at the beginning but over time, the actions begin to take on a life of their own and the work 'paints or draws itself'. A rule is needed to start the process but is then allowed to run freely. In the example of music improvisation, the preparatory process for action may require a high level of immediacy: observing, listening and thinking about what other improvisers are doing and working out a way to respond before entering fully into the moment of making. The value of making tacit knowing explicit is reflective practice's contribution to discovery and learning. Nevertheless, in certain kinds of intense creative work at a critical moment, some practitioners develop ways to put conscious reflection aside.

Allowing the self to 'go with the flow' represents an experience that practitioners find compelling and at the same time, hard to disentangle from emotion and feeling. In creative work, there are times, for example, during group improvisation, when pausing to reflect is not appropriate or indeed, possible. Those who program computer code also recognise it as an absorbing and immersive experience. The term 'flow' has entered the language of creative people when trying to describe this state in the context of their own practice. Being in a flow state is when you lose track of time and your entire being is focused on the work; it is when you are balanced between finding the effort a challenge but at the same time very doable, something that many find immensely satisfying in itself. The concept of 'flow' conveys the experience when conscious reflection gives way to intense focused concentration and a sense of control combined with a loss of time awareness.[35] This is not to be equated with 'intuition' although it is a state that seems to bridge conscious and unconscious action, and therefore, has similar qualities.

In group musical improvisation, the idea of 'flow' has a particular kind of resonance because of the immediacy and responsiveness required. The sounds are made in the moment in response to sounds made by other performers. The action involves filling a space with a sound so other people can respond and that requires on the spot invention. That process is repeated for as long as the session continues. In such a situation, the process and the outcomes (the music) operate in a highly reflexive and integrated way such that the practitioner's awareness of time is altered. As he makes music responding to other musicians who are also responding to his sounds, if the improvisatory skills are well matched and the musical interaction develops well, it reaches a point when each performer ceases to look for how to respond and enters a state where conscious thinking is not needed. In a sense, it is like an animated conversation amongst close friends.

Roger Mills[36] describes the implications of the 'flow' state on his state of awareness during improvisation with several musicians who are playing across the Internet and therefore not in the same physical space. This improvisatory music making occurs only in the moment when there is no room for reflection. Moreover, it seems that what is made in sound can never really be experienced except in that moment. Listening to a recording of the same musical event inevitably provokes reflection because it reveals things that were not registered at the time. His reflections on the nature of flow in improvisation follows.

> Once I'm in an improvisation, at a certain point I get into what Csikszent-mihalyi describes as a 'flow state' where temporality becomes distorted and I essentially get lost in the music. Once you get to that point of completely locking into the challenge of improvising with other musicians, that's when you start to lose track of time and actually what you played . . . so listening back to the 'product' in the recording, you can hear things in it, sense things in it that you don't remember being there . . . you've actually gone into some sort of ethereal state. . . . In improvisation, what you capture as an artefact, as a recording in other words, is not a true reflection of what the performers and audience experienced at the time. That experience is actually more about the interaction between performers, in a musical or sonic moment, and you can't ever really capture that. You can only ever capture a recording of it, so there is always this sense that it is incomplete, although sometimes a recording will also reveal things you don't remember.

Improvisation in music performance is readily understood because we can easily appreciate the intense absorption and immediacy of response such an activity requires. A similar state also occurs in other types of highly focused creative activities sometimes where there may be different layers of thinking going on at the same time but none of which is directed specifically to the task in hand, for example in drawing.

In the interview on page 82 Roger describes his state of awareness during improvisatory playing across the internet.[37]

Esther Rolinson[38] is an artist whose carefully structured approaches to making art involve a high degree of preparation through reflection-*for*-action. This preparedness is a precursor to moments of making that require less conscious thinking. During the drawing process, when thoughts intrude, she notes – 'acknowledges' them but then consciously 'lets them go' as if in a meditative state, a form of reflection in the making moment. The mind is consciously prepared for the drawing actions in

FIGURE 3.2   Drawing and Maquette in 'Ten Thousand Thoughts' series

Source: ©Esther Rolinson. Photos by Linda Candy

the moments to follow. She applies simple rules for each line and direction that are repeated across the drawing space. This enables a more fluid process to take place by disassociating the drawing action from conscious thought. The drawings are the source inspirations for that sculptural installations that emerge as subtle and complex 3-dimensional shapes. The relationship between drawing and sculptural form is essential to the evolution of light and movement elements.

The drawing was made for the sculptural system 'Ten Thousand Thoughts'. It has a tension between order and motion that recurs in different forms throughout the artist's practice. The maquette was made for the installation 'Revolve' for Curve Theatre Leicester 2017. The work follows the rhythm of a straight line, a curved line and a twisting line. In her interview, Esther describes a state where from a starting point, an idea for a fluid shape, the drawing begins to take on a life of its own and gives back something unforeseen. Her awareness of things outside the creative activity is deliberately 'disallowed' in the interests of giving precedence to the drawing actions. It also can lead to surprise at the result, a subject I will explore later.

> I have lots of layers of thought at the same time. I might be thinking about people, anything really mulling things over. . . . You've got lots of other things in your head as you are drawing and I try to let go of them actually. I try to go well it's just weather coming- the thoughts about everybody until it becomes less and less. . . . I thought I am going to do a drawing and just stuck some paper on a wall very casually and I started to draw something . . . but it didn't look

> anything like I expected it to. And I felt really like the work was teaching me and that I had to let go of my ambition to make something and to forget about that and I couldn't predict anymore and be so in charge and I had to be quiet and wait for it to come to me. . . . [I]t's like you are allowing at that moment kind of unconsciously and consciously at the same time and so you can be unconscious and forget about yourself and all the things you might think about, the people all sorts of things passing through but then you have forgotten about even thinking. And then you think oh that's not what I had in mind at all!

Esther expands on her creative practice and the role of collaboration in her interview on page 86 and online.[39]

Non-reflective actions

> If I'm happy with it, I try to stop thinking and sink into the process. There is reflection up to a certain point, then 'go with it'.

Creative actions sometimes seem to come almost automatically from deep within, perhaps from emotional or aesthetically charged forces. It's an experience that is very familiar to most practitioners. The word 'intuition' is typically used to describe our ability to understand or act without having to reason it out analytically. Intuition is seen as something like a bridge between the conscious and non-conscious parts of our brains whereby we make successful decisions without deliberate analytical thought. Many people experience a phenomenon where they do something without being consciously aware, but the underlying reasons for this are hard to unpick. This is because we have yet to find ways of separating the phenomena from the particular context or scenario in which it occurs.

When we act intuitively, is it instinctive, inherited or learned? In nature, many animals know which fruits to avoid eating and where to find water or safe places to have their young. When threatened, animals, including humans, react very fast because their physical systems are geared to do so. How much of this is innate? How much is learned? Humans are learning creatures who absorb information for specific purposes, which then becomes implicit in what they do and think. High levels of knowledge arising from experience leads to expertise which is then hard to express explicitly but which nevertheless, is used in practice.[40] Unfortunately, research is not offering compelling evidence, at least so far.[41]

In relation to creative practice, for want of a better term, I have referred to this phenomenon as 'non-reflective' action, a category which includes actions arising out of habit as well as those referred to as 'intuitive'. There are a number of dimensions to this. A simple statement like 'I don't think about it. I just do it' expresses a familiar experience for many of us when we take an action coming out of nowhere, as if we are acting almost involuntarily. We have not consciously had a thought that says now draw these lines or play this set of notes; we have acted spontaneously, perhaps responding to the feel of the pencil moving on the cartridge paper or the touch of the ivory keys on the Steinway piano. Many creative practitioners irrespective of their field know the feeling of being immersed in the activities as if they were led by the instrument or material in use. In those kinds of situations, we might think of the 'I don't think I just do it' scenario as 'non-reflective'. We act but are not conscious of thinking about the minutiae of the specific actions. 'I don't know why I did it that way. 'Must have been intuition' is a frequently used expression for explaining this away. These moments are experienced as ones where the unconscious mind appears to take hold and acts independently of the rational conscious mind.

Actions that arise through habit and familiarity can easily be conflated with intuitive actions and they are almost as difficult to describe. It is important to distinguish between creative actions and habitual actions that are spontaneous, the last being ingrained by repetitive learning over time. Only in a superficial sense, are creative intuitive actions comparable to those habitual actions that we assimilate deeply through repetition. Many of our activities fall into the habitual category: driving a car, playing an instrument, singing a song, dancing the waltz, or cooking an omelette, and once learned have no need for conscious thought, and even less for creative thought. We are beginning to understand more and more how these ingrained activities reside deeply within the brain such that even when dementia sets in, they are retained in memory.[42] Different activities require degrees of attention, the habitual (driving on 'automatic pilot'), the spontaneous (dancing for joy), the responsive (the 'tingle factor'), and do not invite reflective thinking. They also allow us to do other things in parallel, for instance, driving while talking, cooking while listening to radio, etc. Habitual actions are basically learned repetitions that are necessary for effective and smooth processes to take place.[43] They should not be confused with creative actions.

Many practitioners would say that intuitive actions arise spontaneously during creative work when they are fully absorbed to the extent that they lose a sense of time passing, and there is little or no room for conscious decision-making. It is not possible to separate the thinking from the making, so demanding and intensive is the creative work. Indeed, at these times, pausing to think in a conscious considered way would get in the way of the action. Acting spontaneously in a creative way is what children do readily and easily and is a natural inclination in all of us. Just as the urge to draw, to sing, to write, to dance can arise at any time, so is the desire to create something new and the temptation is to 'just do it' and see what happens.

Referring to creative thinking as 'intuitive' is very appealing because it simplifies what is felt to be an elusive, probably unknowable, process that is near impossible to describe. The phrase 'sacred gift of the intuitive mind' captures some of the reverence with which it is associated[44] and exemplifies the mystical over rational explanation. Is this description of what happens adequate or even near to the truth of it? I suggest that there are other ways of looking at this widely held notion.

When people say 'I don't think. I just do it', it is a way of describing a moment of action that escapes definition but which is commonly used to explain away the apparently inexplicable. But is this notion adequate to convey what is happening in a vital part of the creative process? I suggest not. Because many believe that how practitioners think and act is hard, even impossible, to fully understand, giving it the label 'intuition' can be an attractive way of putting any further explanation aside. It suggests that understanding what is going on must always be hidden. This feeds the notion that the creative process is inevitably always mysterious- words like 'intuitive' and 'instinctive' convey this sense of the inarticulate unknowable. This belief is problematic when it comes to learning from the experience of creative practice.[45] In creative work, there is a strong element of appraisal. Taking an action is almost always followed at some point by a moment when you decide whether you like what you see or not. What is evident from hearing creative practitioners talk, is that the moments of 'non-reflective' action are those when everything has come together at critical points in the process, when the level of intense absorption is high. Whilst these actions may be important, without conscious reflection, the 'I just do it' action is hard to learn from.

The notion that *truly* creative ideas or actions must be intuitive flies in the face of the years learning through reflection that typically go into a life of creative practice. This is not to say that creative practice does not include time not thinking consciously about anything in particular so as to deliberately giving oneself time and space for incubating new ideas.[46] Some of this activity may be, on the face of it, trivial: for example, strolling about, making a cup of tea, staring out of the window at the sea or a landscape. This looks like doing nothing but for the practitioner, it is time for avoiding active contemplation of the work in hand. And yet, it may be exactly what is needed to prepare for considered reflection prior to taking an action. Many will testify to experiencing moments of inspiration springing out after fallow periods (and sometimes ascribed to 'intuition' or 'instinct'[47]) but which can have a significant influence on progress. These actions rarely take place in isolation and without some form of reflection prior to, during and after the process.

Today we have new avenues of theoretical and scientific research that afford opportunities to delve deeper into these hidden processes. Actions that appear to be automatic and not under direct control of the rational mind can now be better explained as cognitive neuroscientists are increasing our understanding of what this entails. The theory of embodied cognition has opened up new territory that is in the early years of systematic exploration.[48]

A related perspective comes from Barbara Montero's research. She holds that conscious thinking is not actually detrimental to successful expert performance but rather is fundamental to it. Thinking that might interfere with action is also the type of reflection that is necessary for an expert to improve upon his or her top performance. She argues against a strong so-called 'just-do-it principle', which maintains that for experts, when all is going well, optimal or near-optimal performance proceeds without any of these mental processes, which would, it is claimed, interfere with expert performance. She advocates the 'cognition-in-action principle' which asserts that for experts, when all is going well, optimal or near optimal performance frequently employs conscious mental processes such as self-reflective thinking, planning, predicting, deliberation, attention to or monitoring of actions, conceptualising their actions, and acting for a reason.[49] Montero's examples are drawn mainly from physically dominant activities like high performance sport and dance rather than artistic or scientific domains and therefore we should be cautious about drawing direct comparisons with all forms of creative practice. Nevertheless, her observations are highly relevant. Whilst Montero's position is contrary to the stereotypical view of intuitive and serendipitous creative actions to be found in much literature as well as in verbal accounts by practitioners, it accords well with my observations of how many creative practitioners work.

The 'I just do it' actions have an important place in creative practice but they represent only one part of the spectrum of actions that characterise the whole. Just doing it does not imply that there is no reflection. *Reflection-in-action- in the making moment* – can arise from different states of mind, prompted by emotional and aesthetic considerations not only ones fired by rational thought. Reflections *in the making moment* are often preceded by reflection *for action*, and as we will see next, reflections arising from distancing oneself from the action as well as reflections provoked by surprise and the unexpected.

Reflection-at-a-distance

> It is as if I am inside a puzzle and there cannot be coherent reflection until it is over and I am viewing it from a distance.

Reflection-at-a-Distance is a category of reflection-*on*-action that can occur when a degree of detachment from the process is warranted. The creative work will usually have reached a sufficiently developed state to allow for a change of space and viewpoint. There are different ways in which distance can be achieved: the first is to change the context of the work from the practitioner's perspective; the second is to expose the work to other perspectives outside that of the practitioner's own experience. In both cases, this is a way of stimulating reflection in the practitioner by breaking with the familiar existing status of the work either in progress or at completion.

The first audiences or viewers are the practitioners themselves. They are also the ones closest to the process and the outcomes. For those without ready access to willing observers, there are nevertheless, ways of achieving distance. By placing the work in a different context, the practitioner's perspective can be altered by seeing or experiencing it in a different kind of space: for example, changing the viewing environment by taking works out of the studio to a different location, or changing the form by transferring a hand-written text to a screen and then producing paper copy. This is particularly pertinent to visual art, although it can equally work with sound pieces if a composition is played using different instruments or through different sound systems. Altering the form and presentation of a work in progress can throw it into relief and reveal aspects not previously considered.

Another and more challenging way is by revealing or displaying the work to others: for example, by performing to an audience or exhibiting and offering works for sale. By placing creative outcomes in a different context and exposing them to the world, practitioners give themselves an opportunity to experience them afresh and through the eyes of others. It is hard to reflect when things are too close to hand-body-mind and the physical environment can heavily influence the experience of them. Factors such as the nature of the light or acoustics in a studio, the quality of the materials and how they are combined in different spaces and the sheer familiarity of the working environment affect one's appreciation and understanding of what is there.

Placing one's works into the public arena is more difficult to achieve and often the more problematic. It is not always easy to acquire a means of exhibiting or performing works to the world at large. In doing so practitioners open themselves up to uncertain and sometimes uncomfortable exposure. Nevertheless, many do this despite its potential impact on self-esteem and the effect of seeing your work through the responses of others, many of whom will have no idea what it took to get there. Reflection on the world's opinion is a tricky issue and often poses a dilemma: you want them to see, hear, feel, appreciate and understand what you have revealed but once it is out there you no longer are the only witness or judge. Having released your works into the world, they are now subject to opinions that can be hard to face. This is sometimes a painful, albeit illuminating, experience for many practitioners, especially those new to it.

The question of how creative intentions are influenced by the audience is a complicated matter. Many would say that in making a work, they do not take account of what an audience will say or how they respond. The work is appraised in progress and evaluated at the end but when it is revealed to other people, this is the moment when it is no longer within the complete control of the originator. Nevertheless, there are things to be learned from observing how the audience responds to a work. Reflection can be provoked by observing audiences and the ways people respond to the experience of the artworks. Audiences will have their own experience in their own way. If an artist makes a work with an intention to evoke a particular experience, they are inevitably going to be influenced by the ways in which people respond. It is also especially hard to avoid queries coming from other artists who are notoriously interested in the way things are made. As Nico Muhly[50] says at the start of his account of how he writes music:

> When I talk to my colleagues, I am of course happy to hear about their sex dramas and squabbles with their landlord, but what I really want is shop talk: what kinds of pencil are you using? How are you finding this particular piece of software? Do you watch the news while you work? I find these details telling.[51]

Some practitioners have clearly articulated hopes and expectations that their works will facilitate particular forms of response in people who experience it. Audience engagement takes different forms, and some artists conduct research by observation, survey or interview to understand what is going on in the minds of the audience as viewers or participants. The anticipated audience response to the 'Ocean of Light' series[52] arose from Anthony Rowe's fascination with movement and his desire for it to create some kind of contemplative effect or even a sense of awe in the more spectacular parts of the performance. The unexpected element was the way participants turned the outdoor space experience of 'Submergence' into an opportunity to party, take photos ('selfies') lit up by the work and even wrap the LED strands into hammocks in which they could lie. This behaviour was not anticipated when it first occurred and influenced what followed with the addition of public safety notices by the organisers. A general lesson is that the installation environment influences the behaviour of the audience and certain spaces encourage excitable behaviour rather than a contemplative response. See Chapter 4, Reflective Collaborative Practice for discussion of Anthony Rowe's work with Squidsoup.

The Squidsoup experience raises more general questions about what happens when an artist pays attention to audience reactions. Does the audience matter when it comes to creating works and should artists be allowing those kinds of considerations to affect what they do? Does negative or risky audience behaviour change the way the work is made? Or does it simply make the artist more inclined to work in some spaces?

The relationship between the urban environment and art has become an area of growing activity and it is these kinds of experiences that will inform future directions for that type of installation and performance. For many, the works they create are expected to stand for themselves and for the audience to experience it in many different ways. Many contemporary art installations are made with considerable research knowledge but that is not an explicit part of the viewer experience. When the experience is contemplative and relaxing for audiences, that is often a good outcome from the artist's perspective. Observation of and communication with audiences has been an important aspect of the feedback. There is always a sense of excitement when talking to practitioners who are in the middle of creating new works. It seems as if a crucial ingredient of living creative practice is never tiring of what happens when you reveal your work to the public and see it through their eyes and their behaviour. In the example that follows, the audience plays a key role in the artist's reflections on her creative practice and the installations she makes.

Julie Freeman's creative work explores the relationship between science, nature and how humans interact with it.[53] She experiments in transforming complex processes and data sets into sound compositions, objects and animations. Her focus is on questioning the use of electronic technologies to 'translate nature' by providing an interactive platform and using scientific techniques to manipulate an audience's senses. For Julie, the fascination is in the way the work has created a communication path between animal and human through the transformation of the animal data into a form that can be observed and understood by a human being. The artist's hope is that the work will provoke in the audience a contemplative almost meditative response to a natural phenomenon rather than an analytical one. She aims to create experiences that engender different states in those who participate, a form of *reflection-at-a-distance* that enables her to see her work in ways she has not anticipated through the way others engage with it.

> I was trying to understand from the audience whether they felt connected to the animals through the movement. Could they tell that it was 'life', from real-life, a biological system as opposed to a mechanical system? I think I have a very traditional approach to what my audience will be and I think (and it's probably not very fashionable) but I think that I'm making work that people could just encounter as they would from a more traditional art gallery. It's a process where I expect the audience to think about what they are looking at or listening to. It's always important that the audience responds to it in a – I can't hope for much more than a positive reaction- but ideally something that triggers a lot of thought for them about what's going on and why we're doing it. I know when I'm happy with a work but I really want other people to like it and engage with it in ways that I hadn't seen. . . . It's always important that the audience responds to it – I can't hope for much more than a positive reaction- but ideally something that triggers a lot of thought for them about what's going on and why we're doing it. I know when I'm happy with a work but I really want other people to like it and engage with it in ways that I hadn't seen.

Julie's interview appears on page 91 and a longer version online.[54]

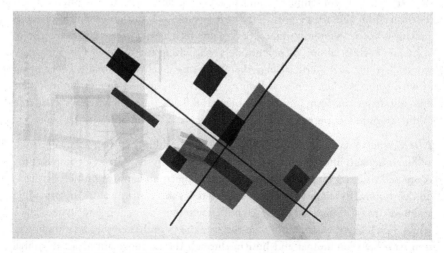

FIGURE 3.3 *We Need Us* 2014/2018, single frame from *Planet Four: Ridges* animation

Source: ©Julie Freeman

We Need Us is one of fifteen compositions from the animation *Planet Four: Ridges*. The sound and animation are informed by open data from the Zooniverse website representing image classifications of the polygonal aspects of the surface of Mars. The work was inspired by the altruism of Zooniverse users – that the work constantly animates indicates how people are willing to help scientists discover more about our planet and beyond.

Reflection on surprise

> What differentiates the ordinary practitioner from the creative practitioner is maybe that they are more unhappy with just repeating the same thing over and over again and they are looking for ways of disrupting, surprising themselves
> – *Stephen Scrivener*

> I think that makes a massive difference to how you view a surprise, how you view an unexpected event. The unexpected event for the professional is a problem to be solved, whereas for the creative person, not everyone, some may focus on the craft skills rather than the originality side of things- most of those who are interested in creating something new- they see that unexpected event, as a challenge, an opportunity.
> – *Benjamin Carey*

Reflection-on-surprise during a creative activity is a category of reflective thinking that affords a particular contrast with reflective practice amongst professional practitioners. This is not to say surprises do not occur in professional practice-of course they do, but they are not viewed in the same way as in creative practice and they are rarely welcome.

I want to make three distinct points about the nature of surprise and how practitioners respond to it. First, surprise comes in different guises and there are more kinds of surprise than Schön's categories of desirable and undesirable suggest. Second, practitioners may respond in different ways depending on the nature of the surprise and the context in which it is encountered. Third, some practitioners may engineer surprise in order to jolt them out of a familiar path into a new direction. The creative practitioner is frequently open to what a surprise might offer even where it means having to reject and abandon things already done. For artists, surprises are grist to the mill because they are a form of challenge, whereas for most professionals I think it is fair to say it is not something they necessarily go looking for. Unexpected surprises may pose new problems that have to be resolved and this usually implies a rethinking of established approaches and techniques. When that is the case, the busy and often demanding situations that professionals deal with on a daily basis make it hard to find time and energy to respond. More positively, in certain situations, the professional practitioner may find surprises useful for what they reveal: this can prompt them to respond to the situation at hand in a better way: for example, in consultations with clients or patients, unexpected revelations that increase their awareness and understanding may enable them to tailor their practice more effectively.

Is creative practice in itself a way of making surprises happen? Is it really all about creating opportunities for confronting ingrained assumptions and expectations?

When new ideas emerge as works are created, the results can give the practitioner surprises that are welcome as well as those that are not. In creative practice, those that displease can be disregarded or corrected whilst the pleasing surprises offer opportunities to explore unplanned avenues. For some, the natural response might be to reject an unexpected development in the work and start over whilst others may see it as an opportunity to follow the surprise into a new direction. Good surprise involves recognition and positive response to 'go with it' either trusting one's instinct or relying on own judgement, acquired through years of experience. A bad surprise can prompt reflection on what went wrong: how did that happen? How to move forward? Some artists consciously provoke or look for surprises, e.g. spill paint to see how it flows in a serendipitous manner, whilst others are more concerned to give themselves challenges in a different way, a manner that is less random but with a potential to throw them off course. The need is to come up with a challenge that is both stimulating and satisfying at the same time as learning something new from rising to it.

Experiencing surprise for the creative practitioner may evoke a variety of responses. For some, provoking surprise is intentional and using mechanisms to achieve this is part of their practice. Actions such as dropping leaves or string or paint splashes or introducing chance elements are familiar ways of bringing the unpredictable unexpected into a creative process. Marcel Duchamp and John Cage are well known examples of artists who exploited this notion in their work. Duchamp's method of research and reflection addressed the notion of invention- what was possible. When asked which work he considered to be the most important, he cited *3 Standard Stoppages* (1913–1914), a work that used chance as an artistic medium:

> In itself it was not an important work of art, but for me it opened the way – the way to escape from those traditional methods of expression long associated with art. I didn't realize at that time exactly what I had stumbled on. When you tap something, you don't always recognize the sound. That's apt to come later. For me the Three Stoppages was a first gesture liberating me from the past.

The idea of letting a piece of thread fall on a canvas was accidental, but 'from this accident came a carefully planned work'. Duchamp's interest in chance as a way of redefining conventional forms of artistic expression appears early on in his paintings and is tied to his interest in chess.[55] John Cage said that any part of a musical work is indeterminate if it is chosen by chance, or if its performance is not precisely specified.[56]

Another way of provoking surprise comes in a branch of generative art that uses models of artificial life. The basic idea is that the artist creates software that sets a process in motion in which each step relies on some rules and events that are not known in advance. Techniques have often been based on 'cellular automata', a mathematical system that can be thought of as a way of modelling living processes of birth, death and evolution, themselves unpredictable processes.[57]

There are types of surprise that can be unwelcome or have disturbing effects. According to Schön, new knowledge is acquired when practitioners move in a way that has a surprising outcome. He identified two ways in which the moves are surprising: 'desirable' and 'undesirable' surprise. Undesirable surprise can be negative because, having anticipated a particular result from taking an action, what occurs is not what you expected and is therefore showing that your ideas are unsatisfactory ('incomplete') in some way. To address this the practitioner is forced to come up with a theory as to why this has happened and then use that new understanding in the next action. For Schön, desirable surprise did not pose such a problem because if the outcome of action is both surprising and desirable, the practitioner has no need of re-thinking what they have done.[58]

But does 'desirable' surprise have *no* place in creative practice?

Artist theorist, Stephen Scrivener thinks it does. He sees the potential for creative thinking in the 'desirable' surprise that Schön considered unsuitable for reflection because you don't have to attend to it in any way. Responding to it positively allows the practitioner freedom to explore where it leads without reflecting on why it happened.

> I understand now that desirable surprise is a crucial aspect of practice . . . you do something and that produces an unintended outcome, but you can like it, you can find it appealing and you can just go with it, follow it.

Stephen expands on this theory and his creative practice in an interview available online.[59] He has discussed the evolution of his thinking on surprise in the context of changes to UK policy on art, design and research.[60]

When faced with an unwelcome development in a work in progress, the initial reaction might be, not unnaturally, to check to see if what was seen was really there and then wait some time before working out what to do next. How an artist responds to unforeseen situations is crucial to an understanding of that individual's working practice. In particular, it provides us with insights into how initial intentions are altered by engaging in a creative process that involves appraising the outcomes as they emerge from the making itself. The very experience of seeing or hearing something unexpected in a work that does not 'feel right' has the potential to stimulate reflection about the making method itself.

Ernest Edmonds is a painter and maker of computational generative art.[61] He gives an example of an unintended outcome that gave rise to changes at the micro level of making a visual artwork. Having transferred four separate elements to a single canvas, this introduced an unexpected new point of focus. He changed the background colour to help retain the appearance of separation between the elements but the effect was to create a new point of focus in the painting. As this was not pleasing to him aesthetically, in order to mitigate its effect, he added edges to create a window. As he says:

> I hadn't expected it. The only way is to experiment with some possibilities. I can say maybe this would work. Maybe if the outer boundary was not the width of the bar in the middle but was much bigger, more of order of or related to the size of the four images themselves. It began a field in which these things floated. Now, if you think about it, I am starting to explore something which I hadn't conceived in the first place at all.

This shows one of the ways of combining the four images, in this case without a border at the outer edge. Ernest Edmonds discusses his art practice and the nature of his reflective process in an interview available online.[62]

FIGURE 3.4   *Shaped Forms 4PH" 2014*

Source: ©Ernest Edmonds

A surprise or unexpected outcome that is appealing to the practitioner can also be a way forward in creative practice. In creativity, where surprise is a driving force, it extends beyond making of works. If practitioners like what happens, they can proceed along the line suggested by the pleasing outcome without having to reassess it. This can be simply a matter of following through or repeating the same process to see what happens next. It is seldom talked about when it comes to reflecting on finished artworks and yet a practitioner's ability to learn and become better at what they do may depend upon how they respond to different kinds of unexpected surprising events arising from their actions whether pleasing or not.

It is natural that most of us are ready to discuss our successes but it is sometimes the case that we learn better from the mistakes that surprise us. Over time when something 'goes wrong' and lessons are learnt, it can have the effect of turning the practitioner in another more fruitful direction and shifting focus towards something new and more positive. In achieving a better grasp of the consequences of certain actions, the true value of 'hands on' experience becomes manifest. Something that does not work as planned can develop into an exploration of ideas that would not have been thought of otherwise. Reflection on surprise can be a very important element of the thinking through making creative process.

Conclusions

Creative reflective practice is a richly varied process. People are driven by curiosity and a desire to set challenges that take them out of safe and comfortable ways of thinking. We learn from practitioners that living creative practice involves strong motivation, determination and an ability to manage uncertainty and take risks. Reflection in creative practice facilitates the practitioner's investigations and enables them to move forward though the making process. In this way, reflection plays a vital role and enables the practitioner to learn from the process and its outcomes. Creative reflective practice takes various forms:

- *Reflection-for-action*: extensive preparation takes place, including constraint identification and devising structured approaches before the main event begins.
- *Reflection-in-the-making-moment*: sometimes reflection is prompted by external factors such as interruptions or more frequently, pauses imposed by uncertainty of what to do next. Sometimes conscious reflection is seen as undesirable because the practitioner is striving for a different state of mind when brain and body work in unison. To achieve this, practitioners devise ways of setting aside conscious reflection using techniques devised for that purpose such as rules for drawing.
- *Non-reflective actions*: arise spontaneously during intensive creative work when the mind is fully absorbed and it not possible to separate the thinking from the making.
- *Reflection-at-a-distance*: this happens when the process is sufficiently developed state to allow for a change of space and viewpoint. It can be provoked by

observing the ways people respond to the experience of the artworks and this raises questions about the role of audiences in influencing creative practice.

- *Reflection-on-surprise* affords a particular contrast with reflective practice amongst professional practitioners. Some creative practitioner welcome surprises and respond to it depending on whether or not they like the outcomes of the unexpected by trusting instinct. Unwelcome surprises can prompt reflection on what went wrong and lead to new ideas and directions of travel.

In the interviews to follow, we hear from practitioners in art, design, music, and digital technology about how they practice and the role of reflection in making and appraising their works. To meet space limitations, the interviews have been shortened and longer versions are available online.[63]

Practitioner interviews

[64]Andrew Johnston: Interaction Designer and Performer

> I suspect that everyone engages in reflection-in and reflection-on practice continually in all aspects of life. In the work I do there is continual movement between reflecting on the immediate situation – engaging in the 'reflective conversation' with materials and situations and placing what we are doing in a larger context 'reflecting-on-action'.

Andrew Johnston is an interaction designer, musical performer and researcher.[65] His creative focus is on designing systems for exploratory approaches to interaction, and the experiences and practices of the people who use them. He works with artists, theatre professionals and technologists to create public performances in parallel with developing innovative interactive systems for dramatic experiences. The process of creating these works involves exploring the interactive possibilities between live performer and digital technologies. He has worked with colleague Andrew Bluff on Stalker Theatre performances: *Encoded*, and *Creature: Dot and the Kangaroo*, directed by David Clarkson as described further in Part 4 ahead. The collaborative teamwork required for public performances with radically new forms of technology presents challenges to individual creative practice. The stimulus for that individual practice comes largely from the interactions with the team.[66] Although that team has a leader in the director, the success of the whole collaboration depends on satisfying the artistic integrity of all parties. The sheer scale of working with a team of fifteen to twenty people compared to a small group not only brings stimulating new perspectives but also imposes the reality of real-world performance from time constraints to tight budgets. His reflections on the collaborative experiences of the technological and theatre team including the interaction designers, the actors, choreographers, dancers, directors and technical crew reveal the importance of having clear strategies for keeping everyone working to exacting standards and tight deadlines.[67]

Reflection in practice is embedded in his work as a designer of interactive experiences facilitated by digital technologies. His research influences the degree to which the reflection is carried through into a more formal mode which give rise to written reflections in articles and books.[68] At the heart of this process is the dialogue that comes with close collaboration with other practitioner researchers and audiences. In the following interview, Andrew describes the different kinds of reflection in practice that occur in his own work and which he observes in the practice of others. Reflection in practice is embedded in his way of working as a designer, performer and researcher. His observations indicate how for him, the variants of reflection in and on practice are fundamental to the many dimensions of creative reflective practice. These variants happen throughout the creative process as *reflection in the making moment, reflection at a distance and reflection on surprise.* His reflective practice is informed throughout by research.

In the extended version of the interview,[69] Andrew discusses his ongoing collaboration with Stalker Theatre.[70] In the following extract, he talks about his personal creative process, his views on reflection and writing software.

Q: *Can you say something about your current creative work?*

A: Right now, it is mostly interactive systems that performers interact with, dance with, and the system produces animations in response to their movements. It is team work, in that we are working with the director, choreographers, performers, musicians and production crew. Right now, the current work is more about using the existing systems we have already got and customising them for a particular project. So we have these interactive fluid simulation systems for example and over the years we have added more and more stuff to them. We've got these 'big instruments' that we are deploying in different ways, exploring different approaches, projecting on different surfaces, using different screens, using different ways of tracking performance movement, working with musicians so that sound might interact with the fluid simulation rather than movements . . .

Q: *What does it mean to be cutting edge in this context?*

A: Using interactive technologies in new ways. Interactive technologies in themselves are still quite new in the broad history of performance practice. The cutting-edge bit comes in with not just the technology but really how the technology is changing practice. So, we are asking: 'can we change the practice using this technology?' And there is a dialogue going on there. We can see what they [artists] are trying to do with it which we hadn't anticipated they would do, and because of that we change the software or pursue a new avenue.

Q: *Do you see software writing as a creative process?*

A: Yes. It's a different kind of creative process though. . . . Usually I have a clear goal. So I want to do this masking thing, for example, I want to put a white circle over the top of a starry background and see the stars revealed through that white circle. And I might do that in a creative way. I might say, 'Well I've found a new way of making a circle.' It is creative but in a different way to visualising interactions and imagining someone moving in front of the system and what it looks like afterwards. That's really a more open creative process, I think. In this process you are finding the creative 'problems' or constraints for yourself – the goals are more open to being changed.

Q: *Would it be possible for things to happen in an unexpected and interesting way?*

A: Yes, that's the dialogue with the materials. You have that defined goal making the white circle and the stars. You actually make a pink circle on stars and that's a bug, but it turns out you really like the look of that. That's the materials 'talking back' in a way.

Q: *Would you say you are a risk taker when it comes to trying things?*

A: This question's really hard to answer- there's always yes and no. I'd like to think that aesthetically I take risks and enjoy exploring something new and experimental. I'd like to think that I'm into that, but also I don't like watching works that are based on technology that simply doesn't work. People fluffing around in front of a computer, sounds coming out from a computer and graphics coming out from it but really there are no connections, no meaningful connections between what the person's doing and what the computer's doing. I find that boring and so I want things to work- typically. I don't want the technical stuff to be risky. I want the technical stuff to be as 100 per cent reliable as it can be. So we set this thing up, put the projectors here, put the cameras here, do all the lighting, setting everything up carefully and thoughtfully. It's part of being a professional, like being a professional musician, so when the performance happens, all that stuff just works. So, I try to minimise the risks associated with that.

Q: *What does reflection in and on practice mean in your creative work?*

A: I suspect that everyone engages in reflection-in and reflection-on practice continually in all aspects of life. In the work I do there is continual movement between reflecting on the immediate situation – engaging in the 'reflective conversation' with materials and situations – and placing what we are doing in a larger context and 'reflecting-on-action'. The key thing is reflecting – only the scale, and possibly the time between action and reflection, makes the distinction between reflection-in and reflection-on action. It's like Schön says: he gives the example of the architect looking at a site and calling it a 'screwy' site. In our case you walk into a theatre and you look around and say, 'These walls are a disaster, we can't project onto them,' or 'It's a big space with a 'boomy' sound.' You are looking around and getting a sense of the possibilities of it – what it affords and practical things like where you could put your projectors so they will work, where you could put the cameras and track people effectively, etc.

Q: Is reflection on action something that happens after you have done something? Whereas reflection in action is as you are doing it. Do you see it like that?

A: Well, broadly yes, but I don't think it is as tidy as that necessarily. You don't walk out the door and say 'it is time to reflect on action'. When you are there in the moment and trying to see the software doesn't break and responding to the immediate situation, another part of you is always storing this stuff away and semi-consciously comparing it with other things you have done. But it might not be consciously happening all the time.

Q: Are you aware of a time when you stop and take stock of where you are?

A: Yes, that does happen too. There are times when you do sit down and say, 'Now I am going to rethink what's happening.' You are writing a paper often. And then there's a more formal process where I have the researcher hat on and I am interviewing people as well. This is where you are looking at your own practice and reflecting on that and you are looking at other people- reflecting with them, talking with them, interviewing them about their thinking and seeing that they had quite a different conception of stuff to what you had. And then you are writing that up and trying to make sense of it.

Q: Do you think there is a difference between testing things out and reflecting?

A: Well it's a continuum. You don't suddenly say, 'I am going to reflect on action'. Reflecting happens while you are testing things out, while you are seeing the results of the test as well as afterwards at various time scales.

Q: I've talked to artists who sometimes say that too much 'thinking' gets in the way of their work. They feel that sometimes they just have to (they use this phrase) 'let it go'. Can you relate to that experience?

A: As a trombone player I can, but not really as a digital artist. As a trombone player you often need to get out of the way of your own tendency to over analyse things. One difference is that as a digital person – at least in the context we're currently working in – by the time you get to the performance stage you are not really performing in the moment in quite the same way as you are on the trombone. By the time you get to the performance stage, it's mostly been decided: the show has a specific structure, and the behaviour of the interactive systems has been decided from scene to scene. Having said that, in performance there will always come a time when you have to let the work go, because the curtain is going to go up – we don't get to rehearse and develop for ever!

Q: What about writing the software? Is it possible to think that once you have done your program design and you've worked out what's going to happen, is that always constantly analytical or methodical? Or do you sometimes find you let it go?

A: To me it's a completely different mode of thinking. There's the problem-solving way-I'm writing code and I need it to do this. Sometimes you can just solve it and everything's fine and sometimes it's quite tricky and it's not working the way you want and you need to put it aside, go do something else and come back to it. So, there is a 'letting go' in a more problem-solving kind of way.

Q: *And at the end, when you see a performance, are you able just to enjoy it? Or are you still evaluating it when it's out there?*

A: I try not to evaluate consciously – with any performance of anything. I think it's a bad habit to get into. I'd rather just experience it. I will often be in the experience mode while watching but at another time there is an evaluation thing that comes in. As you are experiencing that you may find something that's getting in the way of you experiencing it fully and you'll try and identify why. It might be that a particular animation is not going smoothly enough for example, so that would be something to fix . . .

[71]Brigid Costello: Artist Researcher

> Reflecting in the process of making? I don't think anyone is capable of embroidering a sampler or making a loaf of bread without thinking about the quality of what they are creating or thinking about the intention of what they are trying to design. Being reflective makes you judge your work differently.

Brigid Costello is an artist and a researcher in equal measure who works in new media, web and game design.[72] Her research centres on interactive design with a particular focus on playful experience. Her recent book on rhythm, play and interaction design expands our understanding of this area through art and practice-based research.[73] The making of interactive artworks is central to Brigid's creative practice and the relationship between her practice and research is integral to the making process. Having completed a PhD[74] she has developed a systematic approach to art making that produces practice-based evidence that informs her ongoing art making.

In her interview, Brigid expands on the relationship between thinking and making and the role of research.[75]

Q: As far as your creative practice is concerned, what would you say was the central work?

B: My work is definitely centred on human computer interactions and thinking about and experimenting with ways that they can be designed and the types of experiences they can produce. Another thread you can see if you look back at my artworks over the years is that they often involve experiments around the tradition of animation and different ways of bringing things to life. That focus has led me to my current obsession with rhythm and play. I make interactive installations. Installations that usually need audience interaction to complete the work. These artworks will generally involve some kind of visual output, often a screen, and some kind of audio output as well. But it is the audience who animate the audio-visuals, the audience who bring them to life. For example, I made a work called *Just a Bit of Spin* where the audience had to spin a disc in order to bring forth visuals and sounds: the spinning of the disc was a metaphor for political spin. When the audience spun the disc they heard different phrases and trigger different animations based on the speeches of politicians. Another recent work was called 'Blown Away' and, unusually for me, this had no audience interaction. This work was a 3D data visualisation of a year's worth of pollution data from a weather station in Sydney Australia. In this case, the bringing to life was done by the computer which animated falling cubes in real-time based on each day's wind patterns and pollution particle count.

Q: *How much of a work changes as a result of the reflecting process?*

B: In the case of the work 'Blown Away' I started from a position where I gave myself the constraints of working with a specific pollution dataset and making the work using a 3D gaming engine. I also decided I would use only black and white. The first major change was that I let grey scale in. That was because I quickly realised I needed more gradations of tone to represent the fine-grain of the dataset. This project was also the first time I'd worked with 3D rather than 2D. So that was a very new aesthetic for me. And because I am interested in how the tools of making can affect the creative process, I was also constantly reflecting on what did a 3D aesthetic mean? To be honest in the past I hadn't liked 3D aesthetics that much. There are a lot of them I am not very keen on so I was thinking 'Where's my place in this 3Dness? What does this tool do well?' and What do I need to do to take advantage of what this tool does? What am I ruling out with this tool? I could have used it in a 2D way but I didn't. I wanted to explore 3D.

The other changes made during the process were a result of this reflection about 3D aesthetics and were more about the detail of what the work looked like. I originally had this idea that because of what 3D is the work had to look realistic in some way. My particles looked like little lumps of coal falling down and I got to a certain point when I thought, 'No. I am being influenced by everything else I've seen in 3D. 3D has this link to realism and I don't need that'. I went more abstract and used cubes to represent the pollution particles. Interestingly, this change process was made really obvious because I was working pretty close to the bone with the deadline and had to generate some publicity images before the work was finished. When I look back at those early images they are way too representational. I much prefer the abstract look I ended up with.

Q: *What does it mean as a creative practitioner to reflect? How is it different from making?*

B: I don't know that you can separate those two words out – making and doing, because the making is everywhere. Let's keep with the same piece, 'Blown Away'. I knew I wanted the level of pollution to change the colour of the cubes so I had a surface that was made up of a grid of small cubes, and then the pollution particles were falling as small black cubes from the sky. The direction they fell from was based on the prevailing wind of that day and the speed was based on the strongest wind gust of that particular day. They would shoot in from different sides of the screen – north, south, east, west – depending on the data. The cubes would hit the surface and where they hit the surface it broke away- revealing layers going from white to black with shades of grey in between. As more and more pollution landed, the surface got darker and darker but it also got eaten away.

There were two aspects to that. First, the colour shift as the surface got eaten away, thinking about the patterns of that colour shift and where they appeared on the surface. That was one thing to experiment with. The other thing was the wind speed and how to translate that speed into the cubes' movement as they fell. Related to the speed was deciding the point that the cubes dropped from and where that point was in space. These two things (colour and speed) were separate and were experimented with in different ways. And so, there's the *making* moment where you could be coding in say the target point where this cube drops from. But to me the 'making' happens in the whole process. It's in seeing what it looked like with the target point here and finding that wasn't right for a particular reason and deciding I should move it further to the right and then having a go and seeing if that worked. And that thinking and experimenting is all part of the making not just the single moment where you type in the code to put the cube at a particular coordinate. It's a complex interconnected web of multiple experiments, reflections and decisions that cycles iteratively until the work is complete.

Q: *As you are doing that thinking ... did you note the reason? I don't like that because ...?*

B: I did. And one thing you would see if you looked in my project folder on my computer is I do a lot of saving versions and going back to an old version and saying was that really better? Because you can sometimes go down a cul-de-sac where you end up ruining it completely. A painting analogy would be putting too much paint on. You can ruin it completely and it is a good idea every now and then to look back at an earlier version because you might suddenly go 'you know what I have over complicated things and it was much better when the work was doing that'.

Q: *When you look back do you see it differently in the light of what you have done subsequently?*

B: Perhaps. I suppose an earlier version might shine more in contrast to something later that doesn't work. The crucial thing is that you can't take the *doing* out- you can't just think about it: that won't work at all. The ability that you have to reflect on an earlier version and the quality of those reflections is influenced by all the doing and making that has occurred since.

Q: *Did your post graduate research change your reflection processes?*

B: Yes, definitely. Mind you I don't think anyone is capable of embroidering a sampler or making a loaf of bread without thinking about the quality of what they are creating or thinking about the intention of what they are trying to design. I would say that post graduate research gives you a more systematic way of doing it *and* makes you value it more. I know from speaking to other people that often when people come into post graduate research they are a bit suspicious about reflective practice and what it might mean for them. I definitely was. There is possibly a fear that too much thought can ruin something, a fear they'll go too much into their disembodied head and lose the power of their making. For many people the impetus and knowledge that something is 'right' happens in a less conscious way and that's how they like to work. I found the experience of post-graduate research enhanced my practice. It especially gave me a way of connecting with, communicating to and thinking about my audience that was very valuable.

Q: *It sounds to me as if reflecting during making (process) and the results of that making are very tightly bound together and the reflecting is a way of making it satisfy some kind of criteria. . . . Is that right?*

B: Yes, and maybe that is where we go back to that electrifying bodily tingle that a good concept can have. To satisfy a work's internal criteria is about keeping the spark of that concept alive. It's about maintaining the original concept's energy and liveliness in a way that hopefully allows that spark to also be felt by the audience. Reflection is about how successful you have been at preserving the spark of your concept. Lots of learning goes on too. Finding out unexpected things that work or don't work. Observing the myriad ways that people might interact or behave around a work. Often that feeds into other iterations of a work or into future things that you might create. I think that is a form of reflection . . . after the making process to reflect on what else can be done. And to generate a desire to take your ideas further . . .

Q: *Is there a negative side to it in terms of the creative work in being too reflective?*

B: If being reflective holds you up from making more work I think that would be a big negative. All creators are also harsh judges of themselves. You have to be brave and to keep on putting your work out there in the face of this self-criticism. But I think reflecting has actually helped me here. Unlike some artists I tend to make artworks that are quite different from each other in terms of theme and execution and I often criticise myself for this. I wonder if I do this because I don't have faith in what I have created and so want to always move on to something quite different and not stick with the same thing. In reflecting, particularly in the systematic way that I did during my post graduate research, I have started to see that on the surface the artworks I create don't look the same but there are still themes that run between them. Since the PhD my art practice feels more connected. I would definitely say that the more systematic processes of reflection I learnt to do through research have had a positive impact on my practice.

[76]Roger Mills: Composer and Sound Artist

> For me reflection could be best described in a spatial and temporal way. There might be a momentary reflection on what you have just heard or what you have played, which might become a reflection on the formulation of future responses.

Roger Mills is a composer, musician, sound artist and educator whose creative practice and research focuses on electro-acoustic and networked music performance, improvisation and experimental radio.[77] His work includes large-scale international network collaborations, composition and sound design, studio albums and radio production. His sound works have been exhibited at the Prague Quadrennial and the V&A, London as well as ViViD Sydney.[78] From the mid 1990s, he was involved with a stable of Bristol based musical groups and then started to work collaboratively, first with the here_nor_there collective and then Furtherfield, a London based Net art organisation, a path that led him to found the intercultural network music ensemble, Ethernet Orchestra.[79] He is a classically trained trumpet player whose exploration of extended playing techniques has led him into novel sonic territory in free musical improvisation. He improvises sound with musicians across the Internet, first listening, reflecting on what is heard and responding and often when each player finds they meet one another's musical challenge, a state of flow is experienced. Whilst collaborative musical improvisatory performance is at the heart of his creative practice, research based in that practice also plays pivotal role. Through his PhD and subsequent writings,[80] he has developed an understanding of how to generate new knowledge by channelling and interpreting existing information through appropriate theoretical frameworks. The contributions he has made to new knowledge include ways in which 'qualities of sound can evoke cultural representation in the mind of a musician' as well as in collaborating musicians and lessons about methods for performing music with traditional instruments. The research also elucidates the crucially important role of digital technologies in a field where collaborative performances across different locations and different cultural contexts are 'intrinsically networked'. This 'inter-cultural tele-improvisation' enables its participants to experience and absorb cultural differences through creative performance practices.[81]

In the interview that follows, he describes his state of awareness during improvisatory playing across the Internet: a longer version is available online.[82]

Q: *Could you say something about your current work?*

R: The creative work I do has most recently focused on telematic improvisatory music making: that is improvisatory music performed through the Internet. It involves conceptualising what it is to play with other people in different locations and cultures, and the methodological and creative and cognitive components of doing that. Creating new work as improvisations spontaneously, with people in dispersed parts of the world. It is collaborative networked music performance but not necessarily to an audience...

I think the creative process is the outcome with improvisation. The artefact or recording is a copy of that process that doesn't necessarily contain everything of the original rendition . . . In improvisation, it's often thought that what you capture as an artefact, as a recording in other words, is not everything that was experienced at the time. You can't ever really capture the interactive components of an improvisatory musical or sonic moment in a recording. You can only ever capture a snapshot of it, so there is always this distinction between listening back to a recording, and what you actually experienced during the performance. For instance, the last album my duo Nada released, *Mirror* Image was a recording of a live improvised concert that when I originally listened back to the recording brought up things for me that weren't there at the time or I don't remember. I am quite interested in that perspective as a musician because I often listen back to recordings, particular those to an audience, and I think 'Oh I don't remember playing that.' Sometimes I think 'I didn't know I could do that!' so in a way, playing to an audience is a *process that enables* you to extend yourself in a way that you don't if you are playing a solo by yourself or in a studio environment with other musicians . . . Once you're in an improvisation with other musicians, I often find that I get into what Csikszentmihalyi describes as a flow state, where temporality becomes distorted and I get totally absorbed in the music losing track of time and space. He describes it as the moment when your skill level meets the challenge at hand. Performing with other players, I find I get to that point of completely locking into the music and I lose track of time. So, that becomes part of the process as well. Listening back to the 'artefact' or recording, I often hear things in it, sense things in it that I don't remember. This scenario is particularly interesting in telematic improvisation in which geographically displaced performers are spatially and temporally separated by time-zones and geographical distance.

Q: *Does the word reflection have a particular meaning for you?*

R: For me reflection could be best described in a spatial and temporal way. There might be a momentary reflection on what you have just heard or what you have played, which might become a reflection on the formulation of future responses. Maybe a way to describe it is when you are reflecting on something a musician has just played, you perceive what they have done and simultaneously how you will respond from a point within your immediate consciousness. That's what can happen in the moment-to-moment interaction of improvisation. It is different from reflecting over a longer period of time when listening to previous recordings, reflecting on what you have just played and thinking 'How could I do that again because I really liked what I did there?' 'I liked that texture, I wonder what other scenarios that could be used in.'

In improvisation, my reflection is often focused on what other musicians are saying in sound. I am not only responding to what they contribute but how they are responding to me. I see it as having a reciprocal nature. As I also play notated music, I would say that it happens with composed music as well. There is the initial sight reading that takes place but once familiarity with the musical patterns set in, a synchrony of sound and pattern recognition takes over. Once you become familiar with a piece your eyes start to just float over the notes guided by sound. There is something about the embodied nature of sound, whether it's guiding you over the musical structure or the experience of the sound you can quite easily find yourself in a semi-meditative state. This example is another illustration of the flow state, i.e. once the musician's skill level is matched in the difficulty of enacting the written music, it is quite easy to experience a sense of flow in your consciousness.

Q: *In the improvised situation, isn't that different insofar as you are doing active invention of sound in the moment in response to other sounds?*

R: Yes, someone has to fill that space initially with sound, so other people can respond and that in itself necessitates spontaneous invention Now, whether that is qualitatively more active than interpreting notes on a score, I am not the one to answer that. I love improvising, because on a personal level it provides me with more challenges.

My understanding of reflecting on practice is that it is on-going. It is not a static thing and constantly surprises me. That's what I find the most exciting and the most challenging because sometimes it can highlight things I find difficult, but sometimes it can also provide possibilities for the future work in terms of how I can use the reflection I do in my research. My practice involves a number of different disciplines (improvising, composing, writing and teaching) and I reflect in a different way in each of those scenarios. That is probably the most important thing to me; reflections are different in different scenarios. When I listen to a recording of an improvisation I have participated in, I can find myself listening back to sounds that are more complex than I imagined I could create and that is both exciting and unexpected . . .

Q: *If improvisation gives you more challenge, does it also give you more surprises?*

R: Yes, it does. One thing that I really love about it, particularly in a collaborative context, is its dialogical nature. It can be very conversational, which metaphorically can include arguments, or consensus but it is ultimately about listening and sharing a social experience with your fellow performers and an audience. In this sense, improvisation is a social practice in which layers of meaning are embodied in sound that act upon us through the knowledge of what it is to physically produce those sounds. This is where the surprises emerge, as it can lead you down some very unexpected musical paths. Recent examples of this are the performances Ethernet Orchestra have been doing as part of the Bauhaus anniversary[83] in which we are interpreting Wassily Kandinsky's *Improvisation* series paintings as graphic scores to lead the online improvisation. Kandinsky was quite vocal about his belief that improvisation is the true reflection of an artist's inner thoughts and feelings. Our improvisatory interpretation of his abstract, paintings, have led to some intriguing results. He uses dense texture and big dramatic lines, which have an almost physical dynamic. While listening back to these performances, and my part in them, it is as if they reveal my inner thoughts and feelings in a way that I was not overtly conscious of at the time. As with the previous example with my duo Nada, there were parts in my performance that were genuinely new and surprising elements. There were techniques that I haven't heard myself do before and moments of complexity where I thought 'I didn't know I could do that!'.

Doing a PhD gave me an understanding of the importance of a theoretical perspective in which to interpret information, and how you can construct knowledge from looking at information through a particular framework. Previously I did not have a basis on which to interpret what I was doing myself or hearing from my fellow musicians. I would say that new practitioner knowledge that has emerged from my practice-led research is in understanding. I would categorise these as follows:

1. Knowledge – This is what I learnt from analysing and evaluating the case study performances in my thesis. An example of this is what emerged with the Mongolian musician, e.g. the ways in which qualities of sound can evoke cultural representation in the mind of a musician. And how these same qualities produce analogous feelings in the collaborating musicians despite them being unaware any specific cultural representation they may have triggered. This occurred repeatedly with reference to other musicians' culture specific representations, the resulting interactions, and their verbalised reflections on those interactions.
2. Methodology – thinking about how my practice as a musician (when I compose or improvise) develops new knowledge, and I immediately go back to the sense of this being methodological e.g. approaches to playing particular passages such as manipulating breathiness in the production of a tone, or designing soundscapes by different recording methods, placement of microphones, setting up a mood through harmony or dissonance. This practice-based knowledge is achieved through a process, and purpose of, developing a work, which can be a performance, recording, sound design, installation etc. It is often trial and error in that it focuses on achieving a desired outcome for the work at hand. The evaluation of which changes each time and is dependent on the context in which the work is being developed.

[84]Esther Rolinson: Artist

> Initially I allow myself to draw instinctively. As the work develops I start to
> reflect on it but from lots of different disjointed perspectives at the same time.
> It is as if I am inside a puzzle and there cannot be coherent reflection until it
> is over and I am viewing it from a distance.

Esther Rolinson makes remarkable light installations which have been shown
national and internationally.[85] In 2016, she won the Lumen Prize Sculpture & 3D
Award[86] and first prize at Art CHI Exhibition[87] for 'Flown' a cloud-like form made
up of over 800 hand folded acrylic pieces illuminated with moving lights, developed in collaboration with artist researcher technologist Sean Clark. At the heart of
her creative practice is drawing itself from which sculptural works emerge into subtle and complex shapes.[88] The relationship between drawing and sculptural form
is essential to the nature of the light and movement elements in the works. In the
drawing process, she explores sensations, structures, movements and connections.
She uses simple combinations of lines in repetition to build up complex forms. Her
creative process moves though felt experience, into drawing, and eventually into
three dimensional structures in varied combinations of materials. She has always
ranged through different mediums from drawing to sculpture and digital technologies were a natural extension of this.

Esther's drawings and sculptural installations are systems of forms and movements
that employ digital technology to realise her vision for the final works. Because
she recognises the value of collaboration to her art, she is continually in dialogue
with other artists, architects and lighting designers as well as computer programmers. In the 1990s, Esther joined the COSTART project[89] and in this emerging
art-tech arena, she evolved an approach to digital technologies in her art which
has continued to this day. She was quick to recognise how the sensitive nature of
programming could be used to control light and movement and collaborated with
a team of technologists in the design and construction of the system necessary to
realise her artistic vision. The concepts and technological solutions were arrived
at through a collaborative process in which hand drawings, computer generated
images and prototype lighting behaviour interfaces played key roles.[90] As an artist
seeking new challenges, her ideas and outcomes feel ever fresh. What stands out is

the consistency of her practice and the total coherence of the artworks that emerge. That process is open and exploratory, a continual search for the exact structure and materials to make extraordinarily evocative sculptural forms combining movement with light. Her drawing in particular involves a high degree of preparatory reflection-*for* action structured approaches that enable her to follow through in a fluid manner during the execution itself. Her interview here touches on these and other aspects of her reflective practice and the role of collaboration.[91]

Q: Can you say something about your past and current creative work?

E: I have always made things. A key moment was in finding my practice again as my children were growing. I had just two hours a week to myself. Time was so precious. I took away all the rules and expectations. I started with a little bundle of stones that Leon, my son, had given to me from the beach. I threw them on the plate and drew them and the next week I threw them again and so on. I worked with them in Photoshop and saw them as shapes and forms. They became the pieces 'Splinter and Thread'. I can see now that I was using a system to guide myself back into my work . . .

Q: What kind of materials do you prefer to use?

I do not have a loyalty to any particular material, my approach is to find the best fit for each work. I try out all kinds of things to find out how they function. There is an effect or sensation that I'm trying to achieve and I am drawn towards a material that expresses that. This might be consciously or quite instinctively. I often buy bits and pieces of materials that I like but have no use for. When I feel that this material is right then perhaps it is the thing that starts to influence other aspects of the work. . .

Over the past couple of years my practice has become clearer to me. The work starts in drawings. Some are very measured, others are instinctive. In the drawings, I am uncovering structures and movements and at a certain point there is a clear place or object I can see to make. Then it moves into a different phase where I take the work out into the world. I need others skills to do this so there is always a collaborative relationship or team of people to negotiate. This expands the work to go beyond my own boundaries.

I have started some new drawing. There is a comfort in paper and pencil after the intensity of making an installation and collaboration. I started drawing something and had a strong sensation of what I it was going to be, but what came out on the paper was completely different and I was surprised about that. When I have completed it I often recognise it to be an event or experience that I have had that has been transformed into an object. This is not premeditated and I do not know what will come next.

Q: Why was it surprising to you?

E: I was playing with an idea of what I want to make next and started to draw but it was not what I expected. I felt like the work was teaching me and that I had to let go of my ambition to achieve something. The work teaches you about itself and perhaps to let go of expectation. I try not to predict what will happen and wait for structures and patterns to emerge. To do this I have to quieten my mind.

Q: Did you become aware of this surprise in the work afterwards or during the drawing itself?

E: I had a sensation of wanting to draw this very 'softly' thing . . . very soft. Even the way I draw it, I sit close up against the paper on the wall, it's very quiet. I was going to draw very fluid shapes but they weren't at all and I started thinking this is something different. Sometimes I would say I am drawing sensations and following them rather than leading. I might even start with the conscious decision to use a method that repeats, but gradually conscious thoughts about people and all sorts of other things pass through and seem more distant. It's as if I am listening to them in an upstairs room.

Q: Let's take the drawing: Do you consciously think about it in a reflective way?

E: Initially, I allow myself to draw instinctively. As the work develops I start to reflect on it but from lots of different disjointed perspectives at the same time. Some might be practical about possible materials for instance or ways structures fit together and also sensations and memories. It is as if I am inside a puzzle and there cannot be coherent reflection until it is over and I am viewing it from a distance. Perhaps some parts of the process do not immediately benefit from scrutiny. As if too much attention will shape them before they come into existence. There is always time to ask why later and experiments that don't work are obvious. I find this more difficult in commissioned work as the reasoning is required up-front and that, for me, is creatively incoherent, it's a pressure.

Q: Would you say that typically you reflect during the process?

E: There's reflection when I set up a repetitive drawing and I question 'is this working? If I'm happy with it, I try to stop thinking and sink into the process. There is reflection up to a certain point then 'go with it'. There is also practical reflection: for example, I am doing a big pastel drawing . . . I have done a metre of it and I have decided the paper is too 'slippy' and I don't think it will stick to the paper so I'm not going to carry on. Some things are difficult technically and require proper concentration. I might do a difficult drawing for a while and feel I can't do any more but instead of stopping I'll move on to an easy drawing. I generally feel the best forward is to treat them all as just a process, then at the end ask 'what do you think of this? I ask my trusted people what they think and I get one or two comments. It does spur me on. As my drawing process develops I notice different types of works. Some are measured and require concentrated effort. When I am setting these up I might try several different rules or techniques to establish a system of work and I'm reflecting very actively. When I can see the system works then I reflect less and sink into a more meditative process. Other drawings are easy and instinctive. I might use them to figure something out or simply as an activity to do in between working on the more difficult pieces. I also use these drawings as a way to settle my mind and come into a non-verbal space . . .

Q: *Would you say that you take risks?*

E: I take risks in numerous ways. I find being an artist requires the risk of sharing my personal self. Then there are everyday creative risks, perhaps to continue into a work to understand more although it ruins what you have already done, or to use a material in an unusual way. In making larger scale works there are practical risks when all the elements are brought together in the installation. I minimise these by testing out every aspect I can and planning. I walk through the process in my mind, the order of events and clarity about each person's role is important. Every installation, however rehearsed, will require responsive action and negotiation. It is important to have someone with me who knows my plan and helps to ensure everything is being carried out. I find an interesting relationship to risk in work made using a system. To use a system directs the possibilities, but it does not limit them. I find using a system serves to contain the experience of risk whilst paradoxically allowing me to take them.

I also experience risk in collaboration as I move from the security of total ownership into the tantalising expansion of the work through dialogue. The latter wins. I feel the risk is the trust in other people to bring what you've asked them to bring. There's risk in allowing them into your process and sharing with them. I feel like that is a risky sort of business and you've got to be prepared to give something away as well. I have collaborated with lots of people, much more before these recent pieces of work and with some people you can be really open hearted and they probably feel the same. You are reflective of each other I would say. But occasionally you can be open hearted and somebody else will just take most likely innocently because they are driven in their own process. . . . If I view the shared territory as a finite space then it becomes a battle ground, I can win but I, and most likely the work, are diminished by the process. If I view the shared territory as infinite then every outcome is possible and all ambitions can be met . . .

Q: *Is collaboration with others important to you?*

E: To use programming like many other materials I need to collaborate. I work with other practitioners including manufacturers, artists, consultants and programmers. The dialogue can be on different levels and time spans. When I visit a factory or workshops I often meet skilled makers and thinkers. Creativity is in so many processes, but not necessarily recognised. I relish the moments discussing how to use tried and tested skills, perhaps slightly differently. If the other person is curious and willing it is our shared enquiry that achieves the work. Collaboration can lead to the physical, technical and conceptual expansion of the work. There is risk in negotiating all kinds of things. It is not possible to predict how this will play out. The questions must always be: 'what does the work need?' not 'what is best for me?'

My experience is that I am not diminished by connection and there is no real loss of my creative space. If there is conflict I can negotiate or walk away and make something else. It is not possible to take art from me as a person, it exists in me. In my current collaboration with Sean Clark we are exploring our mutual interest in complex interconnected systems. Our current work is in deciphering movement patterns inside the drawings that can be brought back into physical objects through light movements. We have mutual interest viewed from different perspectives so we fit together well. At the same time our collaboration calls for 'right' boundaries where we identify our differences and work in our own creative practices to their fullest extent. For our overall system of collaboration to exist we must maintain our own core. I learn from the recognition of ideas in conversation and I hope to have a deeper understanding. I have also learnt to recognise the collaborative dialogue as only one aspect of a much larger field of work.

The collaboration requires you to 'step outside'. I feel that my part of the work is largely made in isolation through drawing. From there I project what it might become and develop an ambition for how this might happen. When I have carried out all that I can myself, I then engage with others. However, in working with Sean there is more cross over there is a more fluid sphere of influence I carry out the drawing process on my own but I am listening to many external influences from inside my own creative space. I see our conversation and the exchange in the hinterland between two private worlds. The desire to create immersive experiences brings me into collaborations. I have a drive to absorb the audience in the 'drawing' space with me, to envelop them in the experience. I aim to bypass decision making and thought so the viewer might float in the work like a river. The installations I make require such a variety of skills that I could not construct them alone. When the work is complete, I try to step away to allow them their space. The process for me is over and the work is no longer mine. There is a theory called 'relationship as teacher'. The premise is that the nature of the relationship teaches what you most need to learn and how to proceed in the relationship. I think this is a very good way to approach collaboration. Rather than pushing for a desired outcome you see what emerges. It may not be what you expect or find comfortable but it also might lead you to go beyond what you could foresee . . .

[92]Julie Freeman: Artist Computer Scientist

> Reflection-in-action seems to acknowledge the moments when you 'know' that something is right. These moments of decision making are hard to describe but they are essentially built from layered and various past experiences that coalesce in a single moment. Reflection-on-action suggests to me using an action as a focus and exploring it from a number of perspectives.

Julie Freeman is an artist and computer scientist whose work explores the relationship between science, nature and how humans interact with it.[93] She is deeply curious about the natural world and at the same time fascinated by the interactive possibilities of digital technology. Her artistic focus is on how to deploy that technology to 'translate nature'.[94] Her pioneering work 'The Lake' used hydrophones, custom software and advanced technology to track electronically tagged fish and translate their movement into an audio-visual experience.[95] She has a PhD in Media & Arts Technologies.[96] Julie translates real-time data generated by wildlife into soundscapes, animations and other visualisations. In this way, she uses the unpredictability of data to give audiences different kinds of experience: 'a contemplative experience of nature – through data – in which I try to evoke a similar effect as watching the sea, or other mesmerising natural motion'.[97] Combining art and technology and research is central to Julie's creative reflective practice. For her, the role of digital forms and methods for construction through coding is a pivotal underpinning to the character of her art, which involves the transformation of large complex data sets into objects and animations. She believes that for artists who use digital technology, learning to program computer code is essential. Observation of and communication with audiences has been an important aspect of the reflective practice that raises questions about the impact on artistic intentions. Julie aims to create experiences that prompt people to different states of contemplation, a form of *reflection-at-a-distance* that brings greater understanding of her work.

In her interview, Julie describes the various ways in which she engages audiences and at the same time retains control of her artistic vision. There is a longer version available online.[98]

Q: Can you describe the kind of creative work you do?

J: My work tends not to have a distinct narrative or obvious message, although all the works are grounded in a lot of research that can be taken or left by the audience. It is up to them to dig deeper to look for my intention or inspiration or observation. If there is a spectrum of contemplative←——→spectacle my work is at the former end. Projects like The Lake, We Need Us, and A Selfless Society are all created as pieces that you can spend a long time with, works that hopefully provoke meditative thoughts or encourage relaxation as nature itself might – a similar feeling to looking at the sea or a flock or birds or clouds over and over again, and for a long while. If my work can trigger even an element of this feeling, it would be an honour.

The dynamic aspect to my works which use real-time or live data has become more important to me over this past decade. It's a fundamental reflection on life and death, the concepts of reanimation, of animacy in inanimate objects, the desire to pull biological life into our increasingly digital lives . . . it's about flux and change. I've been describing the data within my work as an art material, something malleable, transformable, and time-based – this way of thinking about data has freed me from harder constraints and precision of academic data science (as we see on a daily basis that data is a tool in the post-truth society I've inserted the word academic here to refer to precision, accuracy and repeatability). It has also encouraged me to think about the nuances and variations of data, aspects of data which we need to describe more accurately. An encounter with art using real-time data is very different to art using static data, the meaning shifts with a 'living' data-feed and the experience becomes heightened, more urgent.

Q: Tell me about your interest in data?

J: My interest in data has always been in the fact that it is the communication channel between things: machine to machine, animal to machine, machine to human. No matter where you look in the digital realm, there's always a stream of data connecting us to everything. For me this idea of using data as an art material seemed like a no brainer coming from a technology and art background – how can you make art about a digitally affected society without considering one of the most pervasive subjects around? I have been looking at data below information and knowledge, further down the triangle, data at a level beyond discrete values and toward an amorphous material, malleable, changeable, time-based material: something that changes over time but obtainable, something constantly moving like small bacteria or another cellular organism. In the paper[99] on a taxonomy of data, I describe how we use data as a broad catchall phrase even though each set has loads of different properties, for example whether it comes from a biological source, or a mechanical source like an aeroplane or car, whether it's real or synthetic. My interest initially is in this idea of a material that will bring dynamics and vitality into my work instead of me programming it in. I'm also interested in trying to work out how we begin to think of data as not a single thing but as lots of different things which allow us to connect to different parts of our world in different ways (#notalldata).

Q: *It's often said by artists: 'I don't think about it, I just do it. It just happens.' I wonder if you have any thoughts about that.*

J: Some bits I don't think about, like I don't sit down and think I am going to make a piece of work, I am going to come up with an idea today. That never happens. The idea to do something will come from a random moment from somewhere else. I'll have an idea and then the conscious thinking starts when I try and work out how I am going to make this happen. But that very beginning bit obviously comes from a whole lifetime of experience, from reading things you are interested in and from making random connections and being interested in a diverse set of things, some will fuse in your head but is often really difficult to pin point and explain. The old idea that if you could explain a work fully enough you wouldn't need to make it springs to mind.

Q: *How do you make decisions when you are making something?*

J: Sometimes that's really easy because it's a technical decision (it has to work on a certain platform in a certain way) or it will be 'I want to use this new technology, because I haven't used it before and this is how we are going to do it in the future'. Some of the decisions are dictated by the direction global technology is taking – I'm fascinated about where we are going next, and which technologies will shape our world. For instance, The Lake used bespoke tagging and animal tracking systems but now (14 years later) these technologies are off the shelf and are helping conservationists protect endangered species. My work with soft robotics is also an early tech – it won't be long until Boston Dynamics produce an organic looking robot that resembles a soft giant hairless critter. Non-technical decision-making, aesthetic ones, are harder to unpack. From early in the project I'll work with visual inspirations and notions – for A Selfless Society the work of Ernst Haeckel was important, and the idea of creating a pencil-like digital drawings. That steered many decisions to make lines softer, and the palettes were synthesised from a combination of his drawings and photos of the animals. This colour palette technique is one I use a lot, but this time I built a tool to semi-automate it – an example of my process changing even if the original notion exists across artworks.

Q: *Are you thinking about the audience during the process of creating a work?*

J: I am thinking about myself as the audience. What I want to have at the end is something I want to see and hear and experience. I think I have a very traditional approach to what my audience will be and I think (and it's probably not very fashionable) but I think that I'm making work that people could just encounter as they would from a more traditional art gallery. It's a process where I expect the audience to think about what they are looking at or listening to. I like placing work in unusual places such as a lakeside or in a festival, but I guess I have an expectation that it will be treated as art, and not advertising or entertainment.

Q: What does the term 'reflective practice' suggest to you?

J: I would say that it suggests a practice in which the practitioner is continually aware of their process and how it changes and develops over time. That past processes are brought forward into present projects and adaptations based on previous learnings are incorporated. Prior to reading a summary of the theory, I would have possibly limited the reflection to practical and intellectual considerations and not emotional ones. However, it is clear to me that many of my choices within my practice (who I work with, how I work, where I work) are driven by emotional experiences. For example, over time I have learned when to walk away if things feel wrong, I've also learned that I struggle letting go in certain ways so I need to be alert to this. A question that occurs to me about 'reflective practice' is whether any artist practices without reflecting and evolving their work or processes?

Q: What do the terms reflection-in-action; reflection-on-action suggest to you?

J: Reflection-*in*-action is the term that I find most interesting because it seems to acknowledge the moments when you 'know' that something is right. These moments of decision making are hard to describe but they are essentially built from various and layered past experiences that coalesce into a single moment. We see this with very skilled and experienced makers. The 'in-action' element suggests that the reflection is happening at the same time as the activity, which is in opposition to the more usual way of thinking about reflection as looking back on something that has happened. Reflection-*on*-action suggests to me using an action as a focus and exploring it from a number of perspectives – practically, conceptually, emotionally – plus the variety of impacts it may have had. In my work I would say that I often instinctively perform reflection-in-action, not always and not consciously. There are moments of risk-taking that sit outside of my experience which are important in keeping new work exciting, which are harder to reflect on at the time or, dare I say, reflecting too hard would steer me away from doing things if they echo any failure from the past.

Q: Which is more interesting to you, the process of getting there or the object and how the audience responds to it?

J: The process is my practice. Yet, it's always important that the audience responds to it – I can't hope for much more than a positive reaction – but ideally something that triggers a lot of thought for them about what's going on and why we're doing it. I know when I'm happy with a work, but I really want other people to like it and engage with it in ways that I hadn't seen.

Q: Do you like to be surprised by their reaction?

J: And also, I get surprised by the work. Because I am working with real-time data, with animal data in particular, I can never predict the data flow, the rate of change and all of that that comes with it. There are elements that I can control within my system and there's elements that I can't control. The latter makes me really happy because sometimes I can sit and listen and be with my own work for a really long time, and it can still surprise me as it's changing and shifting in ways I can't predict. I just want to be with it. I've made static works in the past, but I don't feel that they have a sense of life and change within them, so they are more transitory. With my animated work, I never tire of it and that's what I want the audience to experience.

Notes

1 Boden (1990) proposes two categories of creative ideas, concepts and artefacts: those of historical creativity (H-creative) and those of psychological creativity (P-creative). In the former case, the distinction applies to those ideas that are novel with respect to the whole of human history, that is, ideas that are first credited with originality such as Newton's Law of Gravity. Psychological creativity, on the other hand, occurs within the individual mind: any person may generate an idea and perceive it as fundamentally new, whether or not others have had the same idea.

2 Csikszentmihalyi (1996, p. 6).

3 Models of evaluation in creativity are proposed in Candy (2012).

4 A comprehensive guide to creativity research may be found in Sternberg (1999).

5 Artists making Art for Public Spaces: Depending on the nature of an art commission, artists sign contracts and take out public liability and professional indemnity insurances. Artists do not always have the expertise in insurance policies and the cost and risk increases according to the success and failures of other projects they have insured. There are no defined public art codes of practice to follow as would be the case for other professionals involved in public art projects. For example, landscape architects have the Landscape Architects Institute's code of practice. From an artist's point of view, tighter restrictions imposed by not having a clear code of practice to refer to and abide by mean that the work is very likely to be over specified. The bottom line is that a public artist cannot remove themselves from being the first in line as the point of contact if a project goes wrong. If they specify something incorrectly and there is a consequence then they may be able to prove that this or that was directly the responsibility of another consultant or manufacturer, but nevertheless they are the first point of call. In UK public art work, sometimes other parties, such as arts consultants, define the insurance levels required; this is often stipulated as a requirement to be agreed to before applying for the project. In some cases where the risk is high, as in public festivals, the insurance levels are set higher than normal. Any work that is taken, for example, from the UK into the USA requires an increase the insurance levels.

6 The New Rules of Public Art: Twelve rules designed to break with conventional assumptions about the nature of public art: www.artscouncil.org.uk/case-studies/new-rules: see Rule 12. Get Lost: Public art is neither a destination nor a way finder. Artists encourage us to follow them down unexpected paths as a work unfolds. Surrender the guidebook, get of the art trail and step into unfamiliar territory.

7 Royal Societies: https://royalsociety.org/science-events-and-lectures/2018/summer-science-exhibition/proposals/what-does-the-royal-society-do/; https://londonist.com/london/history/a-royal-society-for-everyone.

8 Equity UK is a union of entertainment practitioners, mainly actors but also singers, dancers, designers, directors, stage managers and other performers. Its main function is to negotiate with employers on pay and recognition rights fair terms and conditions in the workplace and but it also lobbies government in relation to relevant legislation and campaigns on behalf of its members and the creative industries and creative professionals more generally: www.equity.org.uk/about/.

9 SAG-AFTRA – Screen Actors Guild joint venture with American Federation of Television and Radio Artists represents approximately 160,000 performers and media professionals across the United States working in film and digital motion pictures, television programs, commercials, video games, corporate/educational and non-broadcast productions, new media, television and radio news outlets, as well as major label recording artists: www.sagaftra.org/about/mission-statement.

10 When comparing Equity with SAG-AFTRA's structure is far better in terms of protecting their members and providing value to their actors. American actors' union who are not members of SAG-AFTRA have significantly less work available to them from big productions. That is not the case with UK Equity where the rules, benefits and restrictions are less strict. https://actinginlondon.co.uk/equity-british-actors-union/.

11 The Salon was the official art exhibition of the French Academy of Fine Arts (Académie des Beaux-Arts) in Paris. For 150 years, the Salon was the most prestigious annual art event in the world. It upheld the traditions of academic art, and over time became more conservative and was very hostile to the avant-garde.

12 The term 'Salon des Refusés' refers to an art exhibition held in Paris, in 1863, to show paintings that had been rejected by the selection committee of the 'Paris Salon' – the official annual showcase of French art. The French Academy organised the annual Salon exhibition, for which works were approved or rejected by a jury or committee of reputable, usually conservative, artists, typically drawn from members of the Academy. The jury tended to vote against any artwork which was unconventional. Subjects were ranked according to a Hierarchy of Genres, and lower ranked genres were regarded less favourably. In terms of style, idealized, true-to-life realist painting with no traces of brushwork were preferred. The exhibition legitimized the newly emerging forms of avant-garde art and paved the way for Impressionism. More Salons des Refusés were held in 1874, 1875 and 1886.

13 The Pulitzer Prize (www.pulitzer.org): is an award for achievements in newspaper, magazine and online journalism, literature, and musical composition in the United States. It was established in 1917 by provisions in the will of American (Hungarian-born) Joseph Pulitzer who had made his fortune as a newspaper publisher. It is administered by Columbia University New York City. Prizes are awarded yearly in twenty-one categories.

14 Turner Prize: Tate Gallery (www.tate.org.uk/art/turner-prize): an annual prize named after J. M. W. Turner, presented to a British visual artist and organised by the Tate Gallery. It began in 1984 and is the UK's premier art award for all types of media.

15 The Man Booker Prize: https://themanbookerprize.com/fiction: is a high profile literary prize awarded each year for the best original novel written in English and published in the UK. The winner achieves international recognition and the prize is of great significance for authors and the book trade more generally.

16 Burnard and Hennessy (2009).

17 Robert Smithson Handwritten Note: University of Queensland Art Gallery Exhibition 'Time Crystals 2018'.

18 'Varnishing Day' at the Royal Academy of Art London was the day in which artists could varnish their paintings before the official opening of the Summer Exhibition. It was also a private viewing in which artists, journalists and celebrities could meet and discuss the paintings before the exhibition opened to the public. According to reports, Turner not only used Varnishing Day to put finishing touches to his works but also to make significant changes or even finish incomplete paintings.

19 See Dewey (1934), Sullivan (2010). Noë (2015, pp. 29–30) argues that art is a tool that that we make to investigate ourselves. His distinction between first and second level

activities is relevant because the reflective practice this book is concerned with is at the second level- that is when creative activities lead to what counts as 'art' in its many dimensions.

20 Nico Muhly (2018).

21 Thinking through Making as a conceptual framework for understanding the nature of creative practice has not received the full attention it warrants. Dewey is helpful here: in his 1934 book *Art as Experience*, he considers the question as to why art is so bound up with making (1934, p. 48): 'Art denotes a process of doing or making' And on page 50: 'Man whittles, carves, sings, dances, gestures, moulds, draws and paints'. Noë asks the question *where* do we think, and makes a case for extending the landscape from the brain into the body and into the world beyond (Noë 2015, Chapter 3, pp. 27–28). As he puts it: 'Thinking is more like bridge building or dancing than it is like digestion' (p. 27). The study and practice of embodied thinking that is discussed in a subsequent chapter extends the scope and explores this subject further in the context of thinking through the body (Shusterman, 2012).

22 'Theories in use can be made explicit by reflection in action but reflection itself is governed by theories in use' Argyris et al. (1985, pp. 82–83). There are two kinds of theories of practice according to Argyris: 'espoused theories' versus 'theories-in-use'. According to this view, there are two kinds of theories of action (in practice): espoused versus theories-in-use. Espoused theories are those that (when asked) a person claims to follow, for instance, 'my theory rests on the principle that design should always meet client's requirements', but these are not necessarily what they actually do. He argues that although people often do different things to what they claim to do, theory exists that is consistent with what they do – a 'theory in use'. For example: meeting the client's requirements might mean bending them to match those needs as perceived by the designer.

23 Johnston (2014, 2015).

24 Andrew Johnston's longer interview: http://lindacandy.com/CRPBOOK/johnston.

25 Reflection-*in*-action: (Schön, 1991, pp. 68–69) Reflection-*on*-action (Schön, 1991, p. 26).

26 In the context of developing curricula and models for action in learning, Killion and Todnem (1991) proposed an expansion of Schön's original model to include the concept of reflection *for* action.

27 Reflection-at-a-distance and the role of Audiences Costello (2018).

28 Brigid Costello's longer interview: http://lindacandy.com/CRPBOOK/costello.

29 How this takes place is described in relation to painting by Ernest Edmonds: http://lindacandy.com/CRPBOOK/edmonds.

30 Maurice Merleau-Ponty's philosophy of perception and the unification of our affective, motor and sensory capacities; for Merleau-Ponty, 'perception' is an expressive and creative instance intimately linked with artistic practice (his focus was painting). He wrote that 'it is the expressive operation begun in the least perception, which amplifies into painting and art' (Merleau-Ponty 1951/1993, pp. 106–107). In other words, while perception is the origin of both the act of making art and its end-product, 'amplification' denotes the specific, important changes that occur in the 'translation' and 'extension' of perception into the physical process of art-making. See 1952 essay in 'Indirect Language and the Voices of Silence' Johnson (1993).

31 Ingold (2013).

32 Schön and Wiggins (1992, pp. 135–156): working from protocols in architectural design and drawing on the Quist and Petra protocols (elaborated in Schön, 1983) drawing is presented as an experimentation in which there is a close interplay between making and seeing: the process overall is described as an interaction of making and seeing, doing and discovery.

33 Drawing on Miller (1956) and Simon (1969) Schön and Wiggins remind us that because of limited cognitive capacity or what they call 'information processing' we cannot consider all consequences of making a move relevant to the eventual evaluation of the result. Cognitive Load Theory (Sweller, 1988).

34 Schön and Wiggins (1992).
35 Flow experience: Entering flow depends on establishing a balance between perceived action capacities and perceived action opportunities (Nakamura and Csikszentmihalyi 2001; Csikszentmihalyi 1990, 1996).
36 Roger Mills Website: www.eartrumpet.org.
37 Roger Mills interview: http://lindacandy.com/CRPBOOK/mills.
38 Esther Rolinson's Website: www.estherrolinson.co.uk.
39 Esther Rolinson: http://lindacandy.com/CRPBOOK/rolinson.
40 I am grateful to Jonathan Michaels for his insights into this area: 'These would seem to be unconscious cognitive processes, the accuracy of which have the potential to be tested experimentally. For example, the surgeon who makes an intuitive spot diagnosis of appendicitis may be calling upon a variety of conscious and unconscious triggers to recognise a pattern. There has been quite a bit of work in healthcare comparing 'intuitive' expert decisions to computerised expert systems, the earliest I know of was work by de Dombal in the 1980s regarding computer aided diagnosis of appendicitis. In fact, I think a lot of the examples are related to pattern recognition, often picking up a set of triggers that allow us to understand something or make decisions that are cognitive in nature, but which we may not be able to articulate. This includes common activities like facial recognition, examples like Schön's description of a fireman who senses that a burning building is about to collapse, the way that an experienced psychotherapist may pick up unspoken projections from a client, or personal experience of sensing that someone is upset or being untruthful' (Personal Email Communication: 20 November 2018).
41 Research that claims to provide evidence for the existence of intuition: Lufityanto et al. (2016).
42 Despite the level of brain impairment and severity in dementia, certain activities remain preserved in most instances and are very resistant to decline. These include activities such as pedalling an indoor bicycle, enjoying music, dancing, and throwing a baseball. The person doing these activities may not know who you are or who they are, but the activities were learned and engrained in younger years and remain. The memory for this is called Procedural Memory. Memory for events, knowledge, and reasoning, called Explicit Memory gradually disappears as dementia worsens. This subject is explored in Devere (2017).
43 Habit and Habituation: once an activity has reached a certain level of competence, it can become a largely habitual act carried out without much conscious reflection. As we walk in familiar streets and wish to cross the road we do not have to think about how to do that: if there is a pedestrian crossing we know how to press the button and what signals to wait for before heading off. We do many complex things without having to think or analyse beforehand because we have an embedded a set of rules to draw on. If we are in a different country, all that changes: the street furniture is located differently and it is all too easy to trip or collide with something; the device to cross the road may operate by sensor or not as the case may be: visitors waiting for lights to change at a pedestrian crossing by an alert device that has not been pressed is a familiar sight to locals in London. Some of the older trains in the UK require you to open the door window and lean out to press the handle and if you are not aware of this, you may find yourself still standing there as the train moves out of the station. In these situations, we have no prior knowledge that we can automatically use and suddenly we find ourselves having to study the environment and work out a new solution to whatever 'problem' faces us. Going through process in a reflective manner leads to understanding which allows the person to move on. The ability to move out of a habitual frame of reference and deal with unexpected events (surprises) is the mark of a proficient professional practitioner. Once something is learnt it becomes part of our habitual actions but if we encounter surprises we learnt something new: creativity involves generating surprises that disrupt habitual thinking and actions.
44 'The intuitive mind is a sacred gift and the rational mind is a faithful servant. We have created a society that honors the servant and has forgotten the gift'. A saying often

ascribed to Albert Einstein but highly contentious given the religious connotations and the fact that Einstein was an avowed atheist.

45 Schön was sceptical about the notion that intuitive understandings limit the ability to reflect in action. He argued that the remedy to the mystification of practice and the constriction of reflection in action is the same, 'a redirection of attention to the system of knowing-in-practice and to reflection-in-action itself' (Schön 1991, Chapter 9, p. 282).

46 Incubation is one of the four stages of creativity, which are preparation, incubation, illumination, and verification. It is defined as a process of unconscious recombination of thought elements stimulated through conscious work at one point in time, resulting in novel ideas at some later point in time. Incubation is related to intuition and insight in that it is the unconscious part of a process whereby an intuition may become validated as an insight. Incubation substantially increases the odds of solving a problem, and benefits from long incubation periods with low cognitive workloads. See Finke et al. (1992)

47 Intuition covers a number of different processes. Instinct is different insofar as it implies something innate not learned; there is some sort of innate or inherited knowledge that allows us to act intuitively. Animals know the difference between nutritious and poisonous plants, predator and prey, and undertake complex reproductive behaviours, such as finding remote breeding grounds that they have never visited. It is not easy to determine which human knowledge is inherited rather than learnt but whether it comes from inherited knowledge or early socialisation, we must have a stock of fundamental knowledge that can be called upon for intuitive decision-making. Another kind of intuition that people refer to is the tacit or experiential knowledge of the expert – unconscious cognitive processes, the accuracy of which have the potential to be tested experimentally. For example, the surgeon who makes an intuitive spot diagnosis of appendicitis may be calling upon a variety of conscious and unconscious triggers to recognise a pattern. A different kind is value, moral or preference-based knowledge (from Jonathan Michaels).

48 Traditional theories in psychology place all the responsibility for generating our behaviour in the brain; perception is the input to a computational, representational system that mentally transforms the input into motor commands. Many researchers treat embodied cognition as the idea that the contents of these mental states/representations can be influenced by the states of our bodies. This supports the view that reflective thinking is influenced by the emotional and embodied elements of the creative practitioner's deliberations. We are not just a thinking brain encased in a frame of flesh and bone but a whole being whose behaviour, including what we think and do, is the result of the complex interaction between bodily, nervous and neurological systems. Contrast with Descartes's dualism 'there is a great difference between mind and body, inasmuch as body is by nature always divisible, and the mind is entirely indivisible ... the mind or soul of man is entirely different from the body' Descartes (1637) published by Hackett 1998).

49 Montero (2016).

50 Nico Muhly is an American composer of contemporary classical music: http://nico muhly.com

51 Muhly (2018, pp. 38–39).

52 Ocean of Light-Squidsoup: www.oceanoflight.net/grid.html.

53 Julie Freeman: Translating nature: www.translatingnature.org/about/.

54 Julie Freeman: http://lindacandy.com/CRPBOOK/freeman.

55 For a detailed exploration of Marcel Duchamp's contribution to artistic research see Molderings (2010). Duchamp's interest in chance as a way of redefining conventional forms of artistic expression appears early on in his paintings and is tied to his interest in chess (Kuh, 1962, p. 81).

56 Cage (1961, pp. 260–273). Indeterminacy 'the ability of a piece to be performed in substantially different ways'. He called it chance composition. Any part of a musical work is indeterminate if it is chosen by chance, or if its performance is not precisely specified. The former is called 'indeterminacy of composition'; the latter is 'indeterminacy of performance' (Simms 1986, p. 357).

57 Generative art that uses models of artificial life: Christa Sommerer and Laurent Mignonneau, Paul Brown https://vida.fundaciontelefonica.com/en/2013/07/24/on-interactive-art-and-artificial-life-christa-sommerer-and-laurent-mignonneau/; https://en.wikipedia.org/wiki/Artificial_lifewww.paul-brown.com/WORDS/STEPPING.HTM.

58 Schön (1991, p. 153).

59 Stephen Scrivener: http://lindacandy.com/CRPBOOK/scrivener.

60 Scrivener (2013).

61 Ernest Edmonds: www.ernestedmonds.com. For a book on his generative systems art see Franco 2017.

62 Ernest Edmonds: http://lindacandy.com/CRPBOOK/edmonds.

63 http://lindacandy.com/CRPBOOK.

64 Photograph: Andrew Johnston, reproduced courtesy University of Technology Sydney.

65 Andrew Johnston's Website: http://andrewjohnston.net.

66 Johnston and Bluff (2018).

67 Johnston (2015).

68 Johnston (2009); Johnston (2014).

69 Andrew Johnston's longer interview: http://lindacandy.com/CRPBOOK/johnston.

70 www.stalker.com.au.

71 Photograph: Brigid Costello.

72 Brigid Costello https://sam.arts.unsw.edu.au/about-us/people/brigid-costello/.

73 Costello (2018).

74 Costello (2009).

75 For an extended version of the interview: http://lindacandy.com/CRPBOOK/costello.

76 Roger Mills Photograph: Linda Candy.

77 Website: www.eartrumpet.org; Mills (2014); Mills and Beilharz (2014).

78 Recent work includes the sound scores for stereoscopic animation, Aquatic Movement by Holger Deuter at the UTS Data Arena 2019, flow#1–3#fließen an immersive multiscreen animation by the tranSTURM collective exhibited at the Galleries, Sydney, for VIVID2016, and the acclaimed studio album Mirror Image by his duo Nada 2015.

79 Ethernet Orchestra are an internet music ensemble that explore new methods of intercultural improvisation, https://ethernetorchestra.net/.

80 Mills, (2014) PhD title is *Tele-Improvisation: A Multimodal Analysis of Intercultural Improvisation in Networked Music Performance.*

81 Mills (2019): This research monograph explores the rapidly expanding field of networked music making and the ways in which musicians of different cultures improvise together online. It draws on extensive research to uncover the creative and cognitive approaches that geographically dispersed musicians develop to interact in displaced tele-improvisatory collaboration.

82 Roger Mills interview: http://lindacandy.com/CRPBOOK/mills.

83 Homage to Kandinsky is an improvisatory networked music performance to celebrate the life of Wassily Kandinsky during the 100 the anniversary of the Bauhaus design school – https://ethernetorchestra.net/homage-to-kandinsky/.

84 Photograph: Linda Candy.

85 www.estherrolinson.co.uk/portfolio.html.

86 Lumen Prize Sculpture & 3D Award: https://lumenprize.com/newsarticle/2016-lumen-winners-announced.

87 ArtCHI Award: www.estherrolinson.co.uk/wordpress/flown-at-art-chi-2016/.

88 Rolinson (2018).

89 COSTART: http://lindacandy.com/COSTART/pdfFiles/COSTARToverview.pdf.

90 Candy (2018).

91 Esther Rolinson: http://lindacandy.com/CRPBOOK/rolinson.

92 Photograph: Bret Hartman/TED.

93 Julie Freeman: Translating nature: www.translatingnature.org/about/.

94 Art and Science – Julie Freeman's artist profile. In *Materials Today*, Volume 12, Issues 1–2, January – February 2009, p. 48.

95 *The Lake* is featured in Art + Science Now, 'How scientific research and technological innovation are becoming key to 21st-century aesthetics', Wilson (2010).
96 Julie Freeman Defining Data as an Art Material: http://qmro.qmul.ac.uk/xmlui/handle/123456789/31793.
97 The Artist who Paints with Data www.accenture.com/gb-en/blogs/blogs-artist-paints-data.
98 Julie Freeman: http://lindacandy.com/CRPBOOK/freeman.
99 Freeman et al. (2017).

4

REFLECTIVE COLLABORATIVE PRACTICE

In Chapter 4 we examine collaborative practice and its implications for reflection. A picture of the world of collaborative creation emerges in which different patterns and structures influence how practitioners think and make. The terms 'pattern' and 'structure' are used to differentiate types of collaborative practice at the individual and the group level. A 'pattern' refers to recurring ways in which events happen or actions are undertaken by collaborating practitioners in any given domain or area of creative work. The term 'structure' denotes the groupings adopted to organise co-creation in any given context. Collaborative creative practice is a fluid and dynamic process that undergoes change depending on the type of work, the ethos of the group and the different roles of each participant. The sources for the patterns and structures include art, science[1] and journalism studies,[2] research which complements earlier observational studies of interdisciplinary collaboration.[3] Research on organisations working collaboratively, including artistic collectives, news media operations and design companies have provided valuable examples of real-world collaborative practice. Above all, interviews with artists, designers, curators, entrepreneurs, musicians and technologists who collaborate extensively have been invaluable. Together they represent a broad spectrum of co-creation that provides the foundation for the discussion of co-reflection which follows.

The landscape of collaborative practice is wide and complex. Collaboration involves individuals working together towards a shared goal through exchanging ideas and expertise. It spans conceptual and practical activities within the cultural, political and social contexts that shape its character. Group working in partnerships and teams is a positive, even necessary, aspect of contemporary enterprise culture. These groups operate within formal and informal structures that are designed to achieve creative and commercial goals. Creative practitioners are everywhere seeking out partners and forming groups, teams and collectives. Working with others is normal practice for many. It has, perhaps, always been that way. The art world[4] has, for a very long time, consisted of networks of people who combine their expertise in order to produce exhibitions and marketable outcomes. For many practitioners, the attraction of collaboration is in having a genuine dialogue based upon difference and drawing on that difference. They benefit from exchanges between people with differences in outlook or 'world view', differences in ideas and beliefs and differences in working practices. This is where the interdisciplinary element, a key aspect of collaboration, plays a crucial role.

We begin with a short discussion of collaboration in relation to individual creative work followed by initiatives for fostering interdisciplinary ventures.

Collaborative creativity and the individual

The vital place of collaboration in creative work is widely recognised, but nevertheless, when it comes to assigning credit, individual ownership remains the norm. Historically, people of exceptional ability who created highly prized artefacts, have garnered most attention. The unique position of the master artist as thinker has been observed in cultures as diverse as China and Japan, the Americas and Europe. The Chinese were the first to raise the status of the painter from that of a low status craftsman to the equivalent level of the inspired poet. Art making and the role of meditation were thought to be inextricably connected. The idea of fixing the mind on an idea for many hours of contemplation in a spirit of reverence became an integral part of the painting process. Devout artists began to paint water and mountains, not as mere decorations or to teach mastery, but as Ernest Gombrich puts it, 'to provide material for deep thought'.[5] Artists as deep thinkers, not just makers of art works, raised their status and gave them a special place in society.

That the individual is given credit over the collective for new discoveries and master works might have a great deal to do with the way the stories have been told. Historical accounts have traditionally been written around memorable individuals and the landmark events in which they play key roles. Art history is a record of the lives and works of highly prominent artists who have exercised great influence on the way we understand the nature of art. The story of art has been told through the prism of exceptional individuals who stamped their signature style on future generations by creating art that broke with tradition and forged new ways of thinking and making.[6] This version of events has forever masked the stories of sharing ideas, techniques and resources, and diminished the importance of contributions to authorship from colleagues, friends and family members.[7] It is not surprising therefore, that individual responsibility for creating works and developing new knowledge dominates contemporary thinking. It is relatively easy to seek out a star performer and focus on his or her achievement rather than take account of those behind the scenes who are indispensable to success. Even in those industries where team work is acknowledged to be the norm, such as film or theatre productions, there are, nevertheless, individual names, usually the creative/artistic director and lead actors, who receive most attention. In many ways, creative enterprises such as these exemplify the need for achieving a balanced view of the role of the individual and the collective if we are to better understand the true nature of collaborative creative practice.

There are complex historical, social and cultural factors that determine value and recognition for achievements. The impact of theory on cultural perspectives is also interesting to consider. Jean Piaget and Lev Vygotsky were significant theorists who represented very different views about the role of the individual versus the collective in human cognitive development.[8] For Piaget, the focus was almost entirely on individual development whilst Vygotsky took a more social perspective. He proposed that the child's capacity for thought, and the resulting development of knowledge, is highly influenced by interaction with others:

> [A]n essential feature of learning is that it creates the zone of proximal development; that is learning awakens a variety of internal development processes that are able to operate only when the child is interacting with people in his environment and in cooperation with his peers. Once these processes are internalised, they become part of the child's independent development achievement.[9]

This is important in the context of co-reflective practice because he addressed the issue of the impact and contribution of others to an individual's cognitive development. By extension, collaboration seen as a process of social interaction is fundamental to the development of human cognition throughout life.

The idea of the inspired mind that gives rise to great steps forward has strengthened our belief in the importance of the individual in creating original works and making new discoveries. The legacy of this enduring notion is with us even in today's rapidly changing collaboration-oriented world. By the 1990s, in psychological research at least, there was a shift of attention towards acknowledging the role of social and cultural factors in creativity. Mihaly Csikszentmihalyi produced new wide-ranging perspectives.[10] In the conclusion to his essay on the 'Implications of a Systems Perspective', he called for a change the direction of creativity research:

> [C]reativity cannot bring forth anything new unless it can enlist the support of peers. Instead of focusing exclusively on individuals, it will make more sense to focus on communities that may or may not nurture genius.[11]

Although the tide has turned, nevertheless, the fascination with individual minds continues. With advances in brain scanning techniques and a consequent increased capacity for obtaining measurable results, the focus on the individual has deepened, often tied to a desire to impart techniques for improving individual creativity.[12] Notwithstanding the fluctuations in fashion over time, many factors have influenced the territorial claims of individuals, groups and communities when it comes to assigning credit for new works. Giving Oscars and Nobel prizes are prominent, high value ways of celebrating ground-breaking achievement but too much focus on individual names inevitably loses sight of how essential collaborative partnerships are to that success.[13]

There are, of course, innumerable instances of achievements by individuals, working largely without extensive collaborative networks, that have changed the course of the arts, the sciences and other areas of creative work. Individual effort and collaboration are both necessary and give value in different ways. What is more, individual work combined with collective effort can be a powerful force. If there is a balance to be found in the thinking around individual and collective responsibility, a fruitful place to go looking is in creative practice that combines individual initiative and enterprise with collaborative effort. In co-creative practice, the question of who does what takes visible form. A lead person or prime mover may give vision and drive to the processes involved but that individual expression is only able to find its full realisation through the contributions of others. Later in this chapter, we explore the roles that practitioners take in different patterns of collaboration.

The long standing and persistent attention to individual creative processes can be set against emerging changes in attitudes to collaborative working that are transforming the nature of creative practice. In architecture, design, drama, engineering, film and science, collaborative working is so normal as to be unremarkable and, whilst the role of outstanding individuals remains significant, it is the collective outcomes of the teamwork that assumes primary importance and achieves maximum impact. Beyond constructed collaborations, many of which are sustained over the lifetime of the people involved, there are ideas-based connections that come together around a particular project. What begins informally through incidental events can be fostered through funding initiatives and commissions that support the collaborative ventures. Nowhere has this been more apparent than in the impact of funded programmes for interdisciplinary art and science collaboration.

In the next section, we consider some initiatives that laid the foundations of interdisciplinary collaboration and fostered the growth of a community of practitioners for whom working across disciplines is a normal part of their creative lives.

Interdisciplinary collaboration

This is an age when collaboration has come to be recognised as a necessary aspect of creative practice. It is also a time when the value of exchange across different disciplines has assumed a high level of importance. In architecture, design, film making, theatre performance and dance, the co-existence of different disciplines and areas of expertise is a normal and necessary part of the core business. The barriers to collaboration across disciplines that C.P Snow found so limiting to mutual understanding have been eroded.[14] There has been a transformation in attitudes to interdisciplinary work across the arts and sciences such that collaboration has become part of the new cultural fabric. Learning how best to collaborate across disciplines, nevertheless, remains a challenge and there are no simple recipes for success.

In creative work, collaboration and interdisciplinary activity go together. From the late 1950s through the 1990s, there were moves to bridge disciplinary cultures between artists and engineers. In New York, E.A.T. (Experiments in Art and Technology) arose out of a series of leading edge technology-based creative performances held in 1966 called *9 Evenings: Theatre and Engineering*. E.A.T. was led by engineer Billy Kluver, in collaboration with artists Robert Rauschenberg and Robert Whitman. Early explorations in computers in art were shown at *Cybernetic Serendipity* held at the Institute for Contemporary Art in London in 1968.[15] Events like E.A.T. and Cybernetic Serendipity still resonate today as forerunners of the evolving relationship between artists and technologists and were key to expanding the role of artists in developing ground-breaking work in an era of new ideas and interdisciplinary events (e.g. Fluxus[16]).

Another different but as enduring event was the arrival of the international journal Leonardo, established in Paris by artist and scientist, Frank Malina in 1968.[17] It concentrated then, as it still does today, on interdisciplinary work across the arts, science and engineering and is a highly successful channel of communication amongst creative practitioners. The art, science, technology relationship has been consolidated in the following decades until interdisciplinary collaboration has come to be an established form of creative work.[18] On the way towards that situation, a number of key initiatives brought financial and expert assistance to the doorstep of creative practitioners in Europe, North America and Australasia. Funding opportunities were critical to the development of interdisciplinary collaboration, without which the many examples of exciting and innovative creative work might never have happened.

The role of far-sighted initiatives, born of different intentions and goals and in widely different contexts, was a crucial element in the growth of interdisciplinary collaboration. In the 1990s, the Xerox PARC laboratories in California went in search of innovative organisational strategies intended to encourage new ideas and products through a series of artist residencies called the PAIR project.[19] Because collaboration between scientists and artists was nowhere more evident at that time that in the large digital media creative communities operating around the world, the PAIR programme aimed to provide an environment in which the interdisciplinary intersections could be explored and facilitated using the advanced technological tools available at the time. Reflecting on his experience, Stephen Wilson, artist participant, and later author of the book 'Information Arts'[20] observed that his contact with scientific researchers made him see that artists and technologists were working at the cutting edge of both art and technology. Most importantly, it opened his eyes to the role of art in research and how working with world class researchers could help him develop his ideas.[21] Following the PAIR model, the COSTART project[22] encouraged artists to take the lead in defining the projects. From studies of the artist-technologist residencies, categories and attributes of collaboration were identified. A partner model was characterised by complementary interests even where the outcomes by each participant differed. One of the most successful ongoing partnerships operated in such a way as to serve convergent interests but, at the same time, produced quite distinct artistic outcomes. In this way, the partners achieved benefit but nevertheless, retained ownership of their individual achievements. This required the participants to share control over the whole process and be willing to compromise at critical moments. Having differentiated but complementary roles was best suited to achieving such mutual benefit.[23] The COSTART research provided the foundational ideas for *Beta_Space*, an inter-organisational location for interdisciplinary developments in the creation and appraisal of public art based in the Powerhouse Museum Sydney, now MAAS.[24]

In the UK the SciArt programme,[25] a major initiative in interdisciplinary collaboration acted as a catalyst for change in artists' practice.[26] Whether or not artists and scientists benefitted equally from such collaborations has been hotly debated. Stephen Webster, in his research on interdisciplinary art and science, asked what effect collaboration with artists had on the work of scientists and concluded that it affected their thinking and working practice rather than producing immediate scientific results. He also questioned the view that it is art that benefits most from art-science collaboration and that science has little to gain. In practice, there is benefit to both artists and scientists and experience suggests that artists can have a technical influence on science and that artistic thinking has a role in the development of theory.[27] Australia too has been at the forefront of providing public and charitable funding to support interdisciplinary work.[28] In fostering collaboration between art and science and between disciplines within the arts, is driven by a belief that interdisciplinary work has the potential to create new knowledge, ideas and processes that are beneficial across all fields. The success of the ViVid Sydney festival has demonstrated public appetite for novel arts experiences and vindicates the interdisciplinary collaborative initiatives that make it happen.[29]

Interdisciplinary collaboration initiatives have the potential to change the way practitioners think about how they work.[30] The precedents outlined earlier were important in demonstrating the potential benefit for creative interdisciplinary work. Moreover, they seeded the growth of a community of practitioners working across art, science and technology. Opportunities for interdisciplinary creative collaboration continue to flourish. Many organisations and networks are supported by public funding initiatives especially where opportunities for technological innovation are also possible. The challenges of the 21st century have increased the need for new approaches that are made possible through collaborations across different disciplines and different ways of thinking. To that end, the European Union launched the STARTS programme, focusing on innovation across Science, Technology, and the Arts.[31] The landscape is changing and lessons have been learnt and the enthusiasm for interdisciplinary collaboration continues as demonstrated by recent experiences of an alliance of leading science organizations and cultural institutions in the field of digital art.[32]

Establishing an interdisciplinary culture is necessary for solving complex problems. That complexity extends to collaborative creative projects which present new kinds of challenges. Large or small, these endeavours require novel methods and technologies in a continual search for innovative outcomes and new knowledge, often appearing as new connections in existing areas of knowledge. Those who partake in interdisciplinary collaboration are all too aware that the advantages reaped are founded on the existence of discrete disciplines. The boundaries between disciplines and domains are, of course, inevitably subject to change and new delineations are continually drawn. Nevertheless, disciplines serve important purposes in creating opportunities for building deep layers of knowledge. People who partake in the 'well-aired clamour for interdisciplinarity'[33] are advised to remember the value of disciplines. To reach across those disciplines in a *cross, inter, multi or trans* manner is meaningful in no small way because of the legacy of specialised knowledge acquired over many years.

Interdisciplinary thinking provides insights into the way that working across disciplines can influence reflective practice. We will now explore the different ways that practitioners work collaboratively and consider what influence this can have on the way that creative works emerge. In order to uncover the complexities of co-reflective practice, we will look into some of the identifiable patterns of collaborative creative practice. Before that, a reminder that behind novel initiatives are people with commitment and drive to make change happen.

Ken Arnold has been a leading figure in the interdisciplinary scene and a prime mover of the SciArt programme since its inception in the exhilarating and energised city of late 1990s' London. Ken's main body of work is expressed in the initiatives and exhibitions that he has created over many years of facilitating interdisciplinary collaboration. His support for interdisciplinary work notwithstanding, more recently, he has been reflecting on the essential underpinning that separate disciplines give to cross disciplinary activities. Realising imaginative exhibitions and events happens best Ken believes, when people of different disciplines and experiences devise sometimes 'quirky' ways of reimagining a subject. At the heart of this is a long-standing commitment to bringing distinct perspectives into the mix. At the same time, he is mindful of the dangers of having to ensure all stakeholders sign up to the idea. Giving voice to independent and sometimes contrary views is essential for effective co-production in which truly innovative experiences can be created, carried through and co-owned without the debilitating effect of a consensus driven imperative.

One of the things that is so obvious is that there is no such thing as trans or multi interdisciplinary practice unless there are disciplines. If everyone became multi-disciplinary, by definition multi-disciplinary would disappear because we wouldn't have the disciplines to draw on. . . . [A] lot of interdisciplinary projects have within them people who started in one place and ended up in another and carry with them that sense that maybe the world doesn't have to be looked at just one way.

If you're multi-disciplinary the opportunity for surprise often comes because one small group of people are not surprised because they've spent their whole lives living with it but then they meet up with another group of people who've never seen that before and somehow, it's the surprise of the second group that in turn surprises the first group.

Ken's interview appears on page 144 and online.[34]

Patterns of creative collaboration

Patterns of collaboration evolve over time and are shaped by the context in which they take place. Of the many possible ways to categorise collaboration, John-Steiner's four broad patterns are a valuable springboard for considering the influences this has on the nature of creative reflective practice.[35] Her categories of *distributed, complementary, integrative and family* patterns are drawn from historical and contemporary cases and are associated with different roles, values and methods. The divisions do not imply a rigid set of situations but rather a continually evolving and dynamic state of play. The patterns are useful starting points to examine how different patterns of co-creation enhance or inhibit reflection in practice. They also provide a framework within which creative practitioner perspectives are included.

Distributed collaboration

In *distributed* collaboration, those involved have similar interests but do not necessarily share the same goals. The distribution is reflected in the separation of the participant's projects, whilst at the same time, making connections over areas of common ground. The starting point is often simply keeping in touch with current ideas and new techniques, a sufficient motivator for many creative practitioners. The collaborations are frequently transitory or begin as temporary arrangements that develop into something more sustained. They span informal as well as highly organised partnerships. Distributed collaboration in the sense of taking place in distant locations, is facilitated by online communications and is a frequent pattern of informal and formal collaboration across many fields and organisations. It brings with it the advantage of access to highly skilled people wherever they happen to be in the world but sometimes there is a price to pay for working long-distance. Strategies for overcoming the disadvantages are needed if coherence and unity of purpose are to be maintained.

In the creative industries and in creative practice more widely, distributed collaboration often begins with groups of like-minded people coming together informally to share ideas for projects. People meet for a conversation over coffee or tea to exchange ideas about putting together a proposal for funding, writers set up regular meetings where poems and stories are shared and discussed, and artists have working sessions around using new digital techniques led by a local expert. Distributed collaboration occurs in artists' groups where a loosely defined sharing of interests in workshops or short projects can lead to group exhibitions. For some practitioners, exchanges with people who stimulate them to think differently are even more valuable than having skill support. Participating in distributed collaboration can provide a stimulus to reflect on what *could be* not just what *already is*.

The distributed pattern of collaboration is to be found in journalism and news media operations where participants create their content separately and then share it. In this case, the creative process is itself distributed. The advantage of having a distributed pattern of co-creation is that participants are able to work in their unique creative cultures but at the same time, are able to access additional opportunities for sharing and, in that way the dissemination of news stories is increased. The downside is that the potential for skills transfer is minimised and participants are not directly exposed to new ways of thinking. By adopting a different model whereby content is created jointly, the potential for transforming organisational culture and the kind of reflection employed is increased, but the risk of conflicting priorities is greater. That risk can be mitigated through a climate of trust and personal rapport between the participants.[36]

Distributed collaboration is very common in academic circles and research initiatives. In science, whilst the rewards of outstanding achievements are often seen as the provenance of extraordinary individuals, behind the celebratory prizes such as the Nobel laureate, are multiple layers of distributed team work and organisational systems that support the complex processes involved. The success of such collaboration depends on having access to systems that underpin the ability of people to exchange ideas and methods. Large enterprises such as the Higgs Boson discovery at CERN''s Large Hadron Collider are dependent on distributed collaborative efforts by thousands of people.[37] A belief in the importance of collaboration for both individuals and organisations lies behind initiatives such as 'Together Science Can'[38] which aims to connect people distributed in locations far and wide internationally and geographically.

For distributed collaboration to evolve into something more sustainable, shared commitment and group rapport are needed. These are some of the characteristics of complementary collaboration discussed next.

Complementary collaboration

Complementary collaboration is a pattern in which each participant's role is different and a division of effort based on distinctive expertise. The participants negotiate goals (which may be different) in the interest of reaching a common outcome. In many types of complementary collaboration, the practitioners are equal in status but embrace quite different ways of working. There may also be differences born of training in unconnected disciplines relevant to thinking styles: for example, visual, mathematical, kinaesthetic, spatial ways of thinking which translate into different ways of representing ideas.

Disciplinary boundaries between practitioners are reflected in the distinctive contributions each party brings to the collaboration. The value of each individual's contribution is based upon how well the level of skill, specialised knowledge and differing perspectives supports the shared endeavour. Some complementary collaborations, as with the distributed kind, are transitory, whilst others develop into longer term mutually beneficial and inter-dependent operations. Working with people with complementary attributes can lead to a greater confidence on the part of each practitioner and a consequent increase in ambition for the work in hand. In this way, the group is able to extend the range of possibilities that an individual working does not always allow.

Complementary collaboration is to be found in organisations such as museums, theatre and film companies and news media operations as well as in established artists' groups. In-house teams are selected to address major projects on the basis of complementary roles and skills. How collaborative projects bring together complementary attributes is influenced by the particular field in which they operate. For the creative curator, film director or theatre producer, collaboration can present particular challenges. The stimulation to new thinking that arises from interactions within the team can often lead to contending proposals and viewpoints and there can be an uneasy balance between encouraging active participation and commitment and agreeing on a single way forward. Although the team usually has a leader, the director or chief curator in theatre, film production or museum projects, the success of the whole collaboration may depend on satisfying the artistic integrity of all the main parties responsible for creative contributions. Working with teams of twenty or more people compared to a small intimate group not only brings new perspectives but also imposes the reality of real-world performance, from time constraints to tight budgets. In these scenarios, success depends on the kind of collaboration that facilitates and enhances the creative practice of everyone in the team. That practice is enhanced by having greater opportunities for active reflection on the work as it progresses towards a final outcome.

For the practitioner, complementary collaboration requires access to extensive personal networks bringing with it a knowledge of people and what they can offer. Complementary attributes that work well together, offer the possibility for more enduring relationships. The complementary trajectory is made possible by numerous factors, including the trust and rapport necessary for overcoming conflicts. We should not, however, under-estimate the power of success in the wider world. When a group achieves recognition in the public realm, this can give momentum to ongoing collaboration that increases the demands on the participants. The ability of a collaborative group to withstand pressure and keep true to their creative goals depends upon mutual trust and effective leadership.

Squidsoup is a group of visual and sound artists with extensive design and technological expertise. The group's considerable success in producing powerful digital and interactive media experiences has achieved international standing.[39] Squidsoup works in both distributed and complementary patterns of collaboration with each member of the group playing different roles using expertise in vision, sound, design and technology. The early beginnings were dependent on key individuals working in a distributed manner, a pattern that is ongoing as participants move across the globe. Sometimes new people are imported into a particular project to supplement the efforts of the core team. In a case such as this, where the work undertaken is in a very real sense 'distributed', that is, the parties work in far distant locations like London and Sydney, a close acquaintance with each person's personal attributes and skills is vital if the work is to be successfully achieved. Working in a complementary pattern has enabled the creation of innovative novel forms of responsive audience experiences in light, movement and sound. The collaboration is dependent on highly skilled participants who are able to interpret one another's requirements even while reflecting alone and at a distance. The group's public art works are ambitious, both artistically and technologically, and whilst the preparatory work is often done from remote locations, when it comes to bringing the final production together, face to face contact on site is essential.

Anthony Rowe, founder of Squidsoup, inspires and manages the co-creation process. High levels of commitment are needed to achieve this kind of technologically advanced public art. Anthony's goal is to harness each team member's differences without limiting their creative scope:

> I am the lead and this particular project was my idea but nevertheless, there are huge amounts of it that haven't come from me. I think that's a positive thing. It has a lot more in it than if it had just been me. . . . [W[e have a much more democratic and positive approach to the whole creative process anyway. We are equals. I want people who will challenge my ideas and come up with better ones. . . . There is also a fair amount of compromise- it's not one person's singular vision that governs the whole thing.
>
> Each one of us has got a core skill whether it is music, coding, graphic design, interaction design. . . . But also, you need a whole bunch of other qualities: you need to be creative, you need to work with a team, you need to be able to fit in which not everybody can into the kind of structure where there isn't really a boss.
>
> Working at a distance can be frustrating – Skype can only capture so much, especially on limited bandwidth. If one group has one idea and the other has another, reconciling the two can be troublesome.
>
> We all think in different ways and come up with different approaches and ideas.
>
> We often want different things from a project and so you end up with multiple assessments.

Anthony Rowe's interview appears on page 149, and a full version is available online.[40] In a recent article, Anthony reflects on lessons from Squidsoup's collaborative practice over many projects.[41]

A partner in Squidsoup is Oliver Bown, a creative technologist and sound artist with grounding in several disciplines from social anthropology and music to computer systems and interaction design. Whilst programming is a largely solo activity, Oliver nevertheless values the stimulus that working collaboratively gives him. Working up ideas with other people he quipped: '*I feel so much smarter having two brains.*' The success of the collaboration in Squidsoup depends upon long standing relationships built on trust and mutual respect for the skills and expertise each individual brings to the ventures undertaken most of which are complex and challenging. Oliver discusses his approach to programming and collaboration in his interview available online.[42]

FIGURE 4.1   *Submergence at Winter Lights* 2019, Canary Wharf, London

Source: ©Squidsoup/Rikard Österlund. Photo by Nunzio Prenna

An example of Squidsoup's work is 'Submergence', an immersive, walkthrough installation that consists of virtual and physical components all with interactions that are manifested in response to the presence of one or more people in the space.[43] The installation transforms space into an environment where virtual and physical worlds coincide. The result is a highly immersive experience where the space responds in real time to the movement and position of visitors.

Integrative collaboration

Integrative collaboration is characterised by creative closeness accompanied by the suspension of differences in order to achieve a common vision. John-Steiner suggests that integrative collaboration is motivated by a conscious desire to radically change the field in which the participants sit and to upend conventions.[44] In such cases, the participants are empowered through their joint endeavour to think in far-reaching ways. For collaborators with highly ambitious goals, this pattern can enhance the process of converting creative ideas into successful outcomes provided they can agree on the way to achieve this. Overcoming conflicts requires a willingness to give time to work it all through as well as valuing each other's capability as creative practitioners. An example of integrative collaboration is that of Pablo Picasso and Georges Braque.[45] Having achieved their transformative work together, each carried its legacy forward but in different directions. We can only guess, but it seems reasonable to assume that in the integrative stage, Picasso and Braque shared their reflections whilst working and talking together.

Transforming the art world (or design or science for that matter) may come about because what the practitioners do has significance of an order they did not imagine when they first began the endeavour. In science, many thousands of small steps take place carried out by different people. For most scientists, everyday practice is dominated by mundane activities and few are consciously driven by a mission to change the world. Sometimes a flash of inspired thinking connects the work of many together and a breakthrough emerges and only then does the wider world take note. If transformation of a discipline or field does take place, it is likely to come about as a result of dedicated, sustained commitment over many years. The ploughing of a deep furrow is equally likely to be the way it happens as the effect of an inspired idea or vaulting aspiration. The impact of ground-breaking work is very often only recognised many years after it takes place. In the case of art, it may take a hundred or more years of obscurity before the artist achieves recognition. If the work is appreciated at the time, that comes mainly from people working in a similar vein who have the knowledge to understand its significance.

Moving between patterns of collaboration is perfectly normal as relationships develop and the reasons for working together ebb and flow. Practitioners who have come together on the basis of complementary skills can, in certain circumstances, find themselves working in a more integrated pattern as their relationship strengthens. Over time, the works produced being successful and challenging enough, it is entirely possible that the boundaries between the respective contributions begin to blur. This is not to say what they offer is not differentiated but rather there is so much inter-change and sharing that such distinctions seem to matter less and less. This can be problematic if the collaborative relationship is unbalanced in some way, for example, if one partner offers more to the physical making process than to the visionary conceptual level.[46] When partners develop a shared vision for the work, this can indicate how far something that began as a complementary collaboration might be moving towards the integrative pattern. In certain cases, where there are different layers of collaboration, the complementary and integrative patterns coincide as in the example that follows.

Collaboration is a key feature of **Shona Illingworth's** creative practice.[47] Those with whom she collaborates have, in the main, two kinds of roles in her creative process: the first is that of the 'participant' who is often the inspiration for the art; the second is that of a 'specialist' whose expert knowledge informs the artist's understanding of her chief preoccupations. Both roles involve close involvement in the co-creation but the artist retains overall artistic control. The participant's experience can be an inspiration to explore and develop new ways of expressing her concerns about humanity's relationship to memory: for example, Claire, whose sudden loss of memory due to a disease that left behind permanent brain damage, and who then found herself in unchartered personal territory, is at the heart of the work, *Lesions in the Landscape*.[48] The process of working with people who have experienced trauma deepens the artist's reflections on the interior (inner) worlds we live in as individuals as well as the exterior (outer) worlds as social beings. This finds form in different artworks each of which is just one aspect of a highly integrated process.

The artist's reflections on her works are influenced through working closely with specialists such as Martin Conway, an expert in trauma memory.[49] Although their working processes are different, there is, nevertheless, an impetus to share a common space and gain benefit and value from it. By working in partnership with a genuine sense of parity, this enables the artist to engage in more adventurous thinking, something that has a profound impact on the evolution of the artworks.

Their experience is, in a way, a way into the subject of the work. Often that experience, perspective way of being in the world is very hard to communicate, I try to find a way of working with them to articulate that experience which requires finding new forms of expression.

In a way to give their experience agency. To think about its value for how it may cause us to think differently. An example would be how do we understand the loss of memory? What are the consequences of that? How does it affect the sense of being able to pass through time? How does it affect a sense of self?

What I like very much about working with Martin is that there is definitely a sense of parity and there is a kind of organic movement, where one might lead sometime sand then the other. . . . He is an open and a creative thinker, very imaginative, very sharp very intellectual and informed. In a way there's a kind of parity there.

Shona's pattern of collaboration sits on the integrative end of the spectrum of co-creation punctuated by instances of complementary collaboration. The relationships with scientific experts occur across the development of different works giving rise to a sense of interconnected coherence over time. The role of the expert is not merely one of gathering information that is part of the research necessary to make a film or installation. An essential part of the creative process involves engaging in conversations and participating in meetings and events. The relationship between collaborative dialogue and reflection is a stimulus to ongoing exploration and a deepening of the collaborations. Both participants and specialists are integral to this practitioner's process.

Shona expands on her collaboration with participants and experts in an abbreviated version of her interview to follow on page 154. The reader is urged to read the full version online for a more detailed account of her practice.[50]

Because partnerships in science involve sharing large-scale equipment, John-Steiner implies there is an integrative kind of inter-dependency that does not apply to artistic collaboration. However, I would suggest that this assumption is based on a particular view of artists typically working mainly solo. The attributes of integrative

FIGURE 4.2 *Lesions in the Landscape* 2015, installation view, FACT, Liverpool

Source: ©Shona Illingworth. Photo by Jon Barraclough. Supported by the Wellcome Trust

collaboration could equally apply to Anthony Rowe of Squidsoup and Shona Ill-ingworth where in both cases, the nature of the collaboration is based upon parity of esteem coupled with complementary contributions. In large public art or major projects involving architecture and digital technologies, comparable conditions to those of science projects exist that require complementary types of collaboration. Making public artworks and interactive installations involves bringing in specialised skills, materials and resources. The co-construction of large-scale works requires more than shared vision: it requires division of labour, expensive and complex equipment and multi-disciplinary teams such as that necessary for film work, thea-tre, major design and architectural projects.

Family collaboration

Family Collaboration is a pattern of collaboration in which roles are flexible and may change over time. Goals, interests and projects may change but the core fam-ily entity remains fairly constant. A family group works sufficiently closely as to be able to support each other's roles and assist with any transitions that are needed over the length of the work. Family collaboration implies longer term commitment during which there is a tendency to develop a culture unique to the group. This might take the form of a coded language or terminology or adopting distinctive customs and dress styles. Within the creative performance world, there is often a strong element of the family pattern. Theatre, film and dance companies require flexible team working practices in which multiple disciplines are essential: actors, directors, designers, technicians and others contribute in different ways to the ideas and organisation of a performance. A well-known example of intensive family style collaboration was that of the Group Theatre founded by Harald Clurman in which a conscious strategy for creating and maintaining shared values was adopted and a common approach to life was fundamental to the strength of the collaboration.[51]

Becoming a successful collaborative team takes time and where a 'family' of practitioners already exists, joining that group requires a clear role and skills that complement the group. The joint work between Stalker Theatre and the University of Technology, Sydney has been ongoing since 2011 and a number of successful performances have increased in scale and complexity over time.[52] The strength of this collaborative relationship is indicated by its evolution into a named collective of artists, technologists. Together they are creating environments for large numbers of people to participate in playful, imaginative and social experiences facilitated by advanced interactive digital technologies.[53] Interactive technology designed and made in parallel with the choreography and drama is combined with dance and acrobatics to create powerful immersive experiences for audiences of all ages. The future of the company's creative practice is dependent upon continued research into how best to integrate digital technologies with performance.[54] The success is due to the opportunities created by the team for a continuous process of shared activity, feedback, response and action. The ethos is akin to that of an extended family:

> Being back in that group was kind of like family in a way, and collaboration gets deeper and more real in that kind of circumstance because you know everyone and there are shortcuts through conversation and levels of trust where we know one another's work. And we needed it because there was such a short time to get that show together with so many complexly relating pieces.[55]

Just like every functioning family unit, this brings with it an ability to handle a certain level of conflict. In the professional context of theatre production, it is essential to challenge each other's ideas in order to find the best solution for the production. Just like family members, the practitioners may have had their differences and rarely hold back any criticisms, but with mutual trust and respect, criticisms can be constructive.[56]

Family style collaboration between digital artists and dance and theatre performers illustrates certain key ingredients for creative practitioners from very different but complementary disciplines to make new art forms, in the Stalker case, to transform traditional theatre into highly interactive digital performance art. The design and construction of the digital systems and the movement choreography took place through workshops and improvisational scenarios in the build-up to the final performances. This kind of collaborative working practice lends itself to highly innovative outcomes. However, making such complex collaboration work well does not happen by chance and there is much to learn from the way the practitioners act and reflect on the processes involved. The thinking, talking and reflection were enabled by the trust and mutual understanding across the various partners to the enterprise. Constructive criticism taken to the conceptual (and creative level) implies a deeper commitment to collaborative work and the co-reflection that is an inherent part of it. Reflections on how that situation came about and the key ingredients for collaboration of this nature have been articulated in a number of published articles.[57]

Learning how to empathise with practitioners of a different discipline is a basic requirement for sustainable and robust collaboration that can weather difficult moments. Having complementary skills that can solve problems is not sufficient on its own to create opportunities to develop mutual respect and trust. Designing interactive digital systems involves understanding how they will be used and working hand in hand with the performers who will be interacting with it. In the case of the Stalker Theatre-digital artist researcher collaboration, the parallel working went further because the design of the system and the design of the movements were interdependent. The digital team was able to construct a 'palette of pre-set states' which worked with the choreography as the dance movements evolved. This close coupling of movement and system design depended on sensitivity to the principles and practices of a discipline other than one's own. It meant that the technologists were aware of the performers' specialism and at the same time, opened their own area of skills and expertise to the performers.

Andrew Johnston and Andrew Bluff, creative technologists reflect on their experience of this kind of co-creation:

> the collaboration in our case is based on an unusually high degree of what we might term cross-domain 'sympathy'. The digital artists have a strong sense of aesthetics and an understanding of performance and art history ... The creative director, David Clarkson ... has a strong sense of the essential aspects of digital technology – what it is good for, and where its limitations lie.[58]

Second, changes in the technical work took place immediately and rapidly in response to feedback from the movement work. The interactive system was altered as the dance movements were being explored and defined. This was made possible by locating the work in the same physical space:

> [O]ur sensitivity to movement came about largely through being present during warm ups and rehearsals, and this co-location was critical. While a large amount of technical preparation, coding and design work took place before workshops there was still a significant amount of technical work to be done in the room, as performers developed movement strategies and skills. This had immediate concrete benefits ... but also had longer term benefits in terms of digital artists and performers developing an understanding of one another's working methods, challenges, skills, limitations and artistry.[59]

David Clarkson, artistic director of Stalker Theatre, is a team builder who leads his collaborative projects from the ground up. Developing theatre practice goes hand in hand with encouraging an inclusive and empowering culture within the team. Each performance is an opportunity to strengthen and extend artistic practice and repertoire. This includes cross-cultural ventures in which he invites performers from other worlds to choose their own themes and from which shifts in thinking occur. This kind of intervention encourages the kind of reflection that comes from direct experience and the creation of works that drive learning. His role as a prime mover extends to facilitating and guiding his teams through different kinds of performances and events.

> I think one of the main things I do is build artistic teams but I also build artistic practice and approach to practice. One of the main approaches that Stalker uses – to devise a work – it's very much a collaborative effort from the team.
>
> The family feel comes and goes. I think that's a little bit to do with my willingness to run teams, my usual warmth on the floor, my inclusiveness. . . . I try and keep an empowered team and that possibly leads to the family feeling. Families can be awfully inefficient and there's arguments and dis-function as well.
>
> The golden rule is if you smell something's going wrong, you talk to it, you don't pretend it's not there. If there's tension between people, if there's something that you go 'Oh god that could fall into a hole. I'll deal with that next week', it's better not to deal with it next week, it's better, especially with conflict around people, to go 'how are you feeling? What's going on? The sooner you deal with those things the more efficient the team is, and the healthier the team is.
>
> I think the best artistic results can come out of artists if you give them the space to be the best they are and to draw forth their own creativity. If I'm saying to someone 'I want it done like this', you've got no choice in the matter, it's my vision not yours, that's a one- way conversation which may be very good in a commercial pipeline because it's efficient, but it doesn't necessarily lead to innovation and satisfaction in the team.

David Clarkson's interview appears on page 159 to follow. A longer version is available online.[60]

The collaboration between Stalker and the technology researchers exemplifies a family pattern of mutual support and cognitive empathy[61] combined with complementary thinking and practice. The practitioner performers co-reflect with the practices and knowledge of the theatre: the practitioner researchers co-reflect with the practices and knowledge of digital technology. Because the researchers work is based upon an empathetic relationship with the theatre group, there is a strong element of the Relater role in the collaboration (see Roles and Co-Reflection in Creative Collaboration to follow). The benefit comes through dialogue and

FIGURE 4.3   *Creature: Ms Kangaroo meets Dot.* June 2016, Out of the Box Festival, Brisbane

Source: Photo by Darren Thomas

mutually agreed activities leading to novel, leading edge works. In theatre production, it is essential to challenge each other's ideas in order to find the best solution
for the entire production. The pattern of collaboration is complementary as well as
family style. The family pattern depends upon a high degree of trust that underpins the co-reflection so necessary to achieving their shared goals. Complementary
working enables people to expand their reach into new practices and outcomes.

In this performance by Stalker Theatre of *Creature: Dot and the Kangaroo*, the
fluid simulation graphics are responding to the actors' movements.

Evolving and overlapping patterns

The patterns of creative collaboration described previously are not fixed in stone
with well-defined boundaries. Changes occur depending on the particular circumstances of the project in hand and there are variants that combine features of
the others. Highly integrated and complementary patterns of collaboration are
needed to produce complex innovative works for public audiences. This is particularly so where the work involves developing entirely new systems that are
integral to the creative work and which have to be created during the preparation
and on site, as in the case of the Stalker theatre performances and the Squidsoup
installations. In these circumstances, there is a need for teams that vary in size and
composition according to the particular event or project and this inevitably has an
effect on the team ethos and cohesion. Size and composition of collaborative team

work inevitably varies according to the scale of the works and available time to completion.

The pattern of collaboration changes again when parties meet infrequently and develop components separately compared to situations where daily contact is needed. These changes represent a spectrum of co-creation that is responsive to the needs of the project and the people concerned. It is vital that the collaboration retains a high degree of flexibility in order that unexpected events and surprises, as well as the inevitable technical hitches, can be handled without derailing the whole enterprise. In his reflections on the Squidsoup development experience over many years Anthony Rowe puts it this way:

> All of the collaborations discussed above have spawned surprising synergies, affordances, abilities and opportunities, and surprisingly often through misunderstanding and unexpected developments . . . looser creative collaborations can foster an increased likelihood of serendipitous and unexpected benefits. Flexibility is needed to capture these possibilities . . . it is always a balancing act. Too little flexibility and creativity and serendipitous discovery suffer, too much flexibility can easily have an adverse effect on the artistic integrity of a project.[62]

If we turn our sights to integration at the structural or organisational level, there are significant differences in the way integration operates and that has implications for the co-creation process. The structures of journalistic collaboration often develop out of successful temporary projects into permanent arrangements. Success and the positive experience and learning that goes with it can have extended benefit. The organisations benefit from content sharing whilst maintaining a high level of autonomy and independence. However, fully integrated organisational collaborations are rare, perhaps a reflection of the novelty of this practice in this context. Although fully integrated collaboration is a relatively unusual condition, there are some circumstances when it is not only present but actively sought as part of the rationale for the collaborative venture. In the world of the creative collective, individual identity is set aside and partnerships are formed that merge visions, ownership and working processes. In these situations, the integration of the creative process is reflected in a conscious decision to subsume individual identity and ownership even to the point of adopting a common name. See the section on collective collaboration in Structures for Creative Collaboration to follow.

Structures for creative collaboration

In the previous section, I discussed patterns of collaboration amongst individuals, this section focuses on structures for creative collaboration at the organisational level. 'Structure' here refers to ways of combining people as distinctive entities under umbrella identities or organisations. These groupings may be called 'collectives', 'co-operatives', 'colonies' or 'societies' depending on the cultural or commercial context in which they are formed. We begin with a review of the well-established tradition of the artistic collective followed by examples of two contrasting kinds of collectives: an online creative colony and a design business that is a collective of companies. Finally, different structures adopted by distributed media companies that involve intra house groupings as well as external ones are described.

Collective collaboration

In the 20th century world of art practice, the emergence of collaborative partnerships or groups has frequently taken the form of the collective. Movements dedicated to changing societal and cultural norms, including challenging the conventional art world, have taken a variety of forms. Despite barriers to acceptance as collaborative entities, the march of the collective creative enterprise has been irresistible as artists seek informal and formal ways to establish unified identities.

Collectives are very varied in character, sometimes taking a single named identity (e.g. Assemble, boredom research, Christo) or using individual names (Eva and Franco Mattes, Gilbert and George), designations that are intended to shift the attention to the unit by weakening the separate identities. If there is one noticeable feature amongst the work of many collectives, it is in the notion of art having a point to it, a rationale, beyond the aesthetic qualities of art as an end in itself. For such collaborations to work successfully over time, it is necessary for the participants to work through differences and conflicts through dialogue. That there is a continuing drive to choose this collaboration route of sharing ownership and identity with all the intensity and commitment it implies, is a clear recognition of the value of close creative relationships.[63]

There is a pattern of integrative collective collaboration that has its own unique form of expression called the manifesto. In the early 20th century, artists as individuals and groups began to adopt the manifesto, a form originating in the political arena. Groups of like-minded people sought to distinguish their art from what had preceded it and what was contemporaneous. To a large extent the art manifestos that appeared then and now envisage art as a political tool. The role of the manifesto is to challenge contemporary culture and existing forms of art as well as to set out alternative values and paths. It can be a significant document that is referred to in the present time, and historically, for its record of the thinking at the time. Manifestos were sometimes intended to be works of art in their own right, sometimes to be performed publicly as a new genre that, in the words of Alex Danchev, amounted to 'an adventure in artistic expression'.[64]

Through the manifesto, groups of artists differentiated themselves from the mainstream and, at the same time, established the ground rules on which the movement was founded. In effect, the manifesto has a dual role: internal within the group and external to the world outside. It can be used as a means of name calling or remonstration against everything that the group opposes or alternatively, can be used to embrace the work of others. Historically it is the name calling 'merde' that has been more frequent than the accolades 'rose', famous juxtapositions from Apollinaire's

L'Antitradition Futuriste of 1913, a document solicited by and transformed by F.T. Marinetti into manifesto form. Marinetti, who is credited with both the founding of the Futurist movement and the idea of the art manifesto,[65] believed that Apollinaire's words would cause controversy with the futurist group, which was exactly what he intended to happen. In this way, the manifesto was used to provoke controversy about ideas and practices between the various members of the group.

Most manifestos are purely text, although some have included pictorial or diagrammatic elements. Manifestos challenge widely held assumptions about artists as people unable to articulate ideas verbally. As Barnet Newman, the American painter wrote:

> The artist is approached not as an original thinker in his own medium, but rather as an instinctive, intuitive executant who, largely unaware of what he is doing, breaks through the mystery by the magic of his performance to 'express' truths the professionals think they can read better than he can himself.

Artists as thinkers who also write give the lie to those who would confine them to the 'intuitive-expressive' box:

> Making manifestos engages the thinker-practitioner. . . . Art and thought are not incompatible after all.[66]

As these testimonies indicate, manifestos indicate that artists too are capable of more than one form of expression, but perhaps even more importantly, they act as mechanisms for exchanging, provoking and promulgating new ideas in an integrative collaborative way. The manifesto is a tried and tested mechanism for co-reflective practice. It embodies a rejection of strident individualism, embraces a shared world that integrates thought and action and heralds an awakening of collectivism in creative work as in the case of the De Stijl movement led by Theo Van Doesburg. As founders of the new plastic art, De Stijl declared its belief in collective experience and a desire to achieve universal values by taking a stand against 'the domination of individual despotism'.[67]

By their very nature, collectives are designed to subsume the individual voice into a conjoined whole and the role of each person's reflection is inclined to be masked by the stance taken. This unified entity out of multiple contributors inevitably means it is hard to know much about the individual reflection that takes place. Within each collective there may be many intensive discussions but gaining access to that private world is dependent upon a willingness to articulate and reveal innermost thoughts and intentions.

Creative colony: a new kind of creative collaboration

The notion of the collective is evolving and there are new ventures on the contemporary arts scene, often combining location-based activities with global reach through the Internet. An example is **Baby Forest,** an online creative commu-nity[68] that embraces difference in an open interdisciplinary way between people from distance places. The manifesto proposes a common vision with shared val-ues.[69] The collective enables participants to promote their work within a financial and legal framework tailored to their needs. The term 'colony' suggests coming together to explore new territory with the goal of building a culturally meaning-ful identity. Historically, artists' colonies were places where practitioners lived and worked together gaining value and stimulus from close exchanges with others working in a similar vein. In Baby Forest, the collective has been re-imagined in a 21st century digitally enabled collaborative context. The colony is a 'collective' in the sense of being a shared space, a platform, where creative practitioners of many kinds connect, collaborate, exhibit, promote and sell their work. It is different from other kinds of collectives in the sense that each member has a personal space that they manage independently without interacting with others on the website. The colony enables them to share and discuss their ideas and reflections on practice when they wish to do so. Because they can choose when to relate to the com-munity, this fosters an open and fluid ethos. In this way, maintaining a balance between creating a supportive structure and the freedom of individual members to choose their own level of engagement is achieved. The colony facilitates distrib-uted collaboration but with the potential for other patterns such as complemen-tary co-creation.

Sue Crellin-McCarthy and Tom McCarthy are the founders of *Baby Forest.*[70] As artist entrepreneurs, they embody the complementary-integrated-family patterns of collaborative practice.

We aim to build a multi-disciplinary colony of talented creators. . . . Our aim is to create a model, a two-way conduit, where the member, audience, con-sumer, user, has direct access to creators and their worlds – their work, their inspirations, their thinking, their personality, every aspect of a creative life that a creator wants to and feels comfortable enough to share. . . . [M]y artis-tic practice has mainly been put to work in these areas – which has been immensely useful as being an artist really means being able to visualise the 360 picture – it's not enough just to output work – an artist really needs to be able to deliver, envisage and manage the whole package.

[W]e hope we can unite as creators to inspire other creators – they do have the opportunity to take things into their own hands and produce remarkable and meaningful events, and we are now seeing some of our members doing the same within their own local networks.

Sue and Tom reflect on their collective and individual experiences in the inter-view available online.[71]

FIGURE 4.4   Heart of the Forest Film Installation. *I Am All Things*. Collaboration between Rob Monaghan/Tom McCarthy and Phyllis Akinyi

Collective commerce

In the business world, a collective can have quite distinct characteristics because it is driven by commercial values as well as the demands of available human capital. Here a collective might be an association of companies that deliver different but related products and may be steered by the single vision of one individual or a small group. This kind of organisational structure facilitates interdisciplinary activity at the same time as maintaining a depth of skill and knowledge within the domains of each affiliated company.

Vince Frost has created an innovative commercial collective known as *The Frost Collective*.[72] Vince believes that design underpins every aspect of the world that human beings make, as he makes clear in his book 'Design Your Life'.[73] The collective consists of six separate but inter-related companies that perform different functions but operate as one to fulfil the mission of deploying design thinking across a range of domains. The aim is to transform the business design process approach by bringing different kinds of expertise under an umbrella organization that permits flexibility in tandem with autonomy. The individual companies are set up so as to ensure a high level of specialist expertise in, for example, business strategies for diagnosing problems, developing policies, develop solutions and team action plans. In creating a collective of six separate but inter-related companies that perform different functions, Vince's goal is to develop strategic thinking based upon measures of success. As an entrepreneur with high ambitions, he is a prime mover in creating environments for co-creative ventures.

> I decided to create stand- alone businesses within the Collective. I grew a business and continually learnt and experimented with the business and projects and designed a business around helping people in terms of the breadth of people's needs. . . . I try to find people who are going to share my vision and values and direction. I want them to thrive. I deliberately create the environment for people to thrive in. I want them to be proud and confident, I want them to enjoy, to grow, to be inspired, question, challenge. . . . I want us to become better at designing businesses, experiences, customer journeys, user experience. . . . We want to be deliberate, we want to understand how people think, how they engage with things and design to create that. Like intuition is great and we can use the experience in doing things . . . but I want to be focused on hitting that target . . . spot on. I believe our responsibility as an ideas business designing success is that we have to recommend the most accurate solutions, the most accurate experiences.

Vince expands on his mission for making design integral to life and work in his online interview which took place at the Frost Collective in Redfern Sydney in January 2018.[74]

Co-creative journalism

In journalism, different structures have been adopted by distributed media companies involving intra house groupings as well as external ones. In the 20th century, competition between news organisations was the dominant working model even though individual journalists often collaborated in the course of creating news content. In the early 21st century, however, driven by the arrival of novel forms of digitally enabled coverage, an era of networked news sharing is underway and challenging the traditional role of the journalist.[75] Alan Rusbridger, former Guardian editor, describes a new type of 'open journalism', taking a positive view in the face of an existential challenge, is to put professional expertise to work by mediating citizen news content.[76]

In professional news media, a study of organisational collaboration identified six types of collaboration between news organizations for creating content.[77] Two factors are relevant to our previous discussion of patterns in creative collaboration. First, the matter of *time*: that is how temporary or sustained the duration of collaboration is, whether one-time or finite (temporary) or ongoing or open-ended (permanent). The second key factor is *integration*, that is the degree to which the writing of news stories and the creation of publicly distributed material, is carried out jointly. The degree of integration operates at three levels: a) completely separate content creation but shared distribution; b) individuals work together to create content using separate resources; c) co-creation with sharing of all resources at the organizational level.

Of the different structures of collaborative projects studied (referred to as 'models' in the study), several fell into more than one category and some evolved into different models over time. Temporary projects put together with a finite duration differed in the way new material was created: in one case, participants created news content separately and then shared it, whereas in another they created the content together. The first model is a pattern of collaboration best suited to first time smaller group participants who are looking to extend their reach into high interest subjects and generate better products. Where problems were identified they were mitigated by collaborative practices that addressed differences in working 'cultures' and shared scarce technical expertise. On the negative side, there was less opportunity for skills transfer and learning new techniques. This type of structure lends itself to people wishing to test the co-working water and if successful, provides a bridge into more integrated collaboration. Where participants co-created new content, a closer, more coordinated collaboration takes place but this process requires more resources than the case in separate creation.

Co-creation can lead to conflicting priorities because of different organisational cultures and practices but a pre-existing level of trust and good rapport between people can overcome this. Overall, the study found that co-creation leads to a better product than could be achieved working separately in the context of today's news sharing in collaborative journalism. A third type of structure is of one-time projects in which partners share content, data and resources at the organizational level. The level of integration involves close co-ordination and regular contact. An example of one off integrated collaboration is the production of 'The Panama Papers'[78] whereby participating organizations had access to the same data and software but wrote different stories unique to the outlet that produced them. Each participating organisation gained from the shared resources and expertise but was able to provide content to their own readership in their own way. Having multiple inputs and being able to create multiple outcomes gives flexibility in collaborative situations where enforcing a uniform product could otherwise cause conflict. The benefits of the integrated single project are high including acquiring additional skills and expertise, sharing data but principally in extending the organisation's reach by producing high quality outcomes for more outlets. However, the study also suggests that negative factors such as having unequal power dynamics, disparate levels of technical expertise and different cultures are unlikely to be mitigated by the fact of collaboration itself. Thus, whilst the benefits are higher than other structures for collaboration, the risks are greater. What it does suggest is that in the context of single discipline professional work, organisational integration has distinct advantages for collaborative working. In more interdisciplinary work, there may, however, be advantages in retaining a looser form of connection, in other words, adopting a complementary over integrated pattern of collaboration.

The structures for journalistic collaboration with more permanent arrangements or having evolved from temporary into ongoing projects, are of particular interest in co-reflection and creative collaboration as this is where relationships between practitioners are supported by organisational frameworks. A common feature of these collaborations is that the organizations benefit from content sharing, whilst at the same time maintaining a high level of autonomy and editorial independence. Where the collaborations are both open ended and co-creating, more coordination is required to organise regular meetings and ensure communication between the various organizations involved. It is a more integrated process than the previous kind but not as much as that of an ongoing *and* integrated collaboration in which participants co-create content and the organizations share resources. Collaborative journalism seen through a lens of optimism envisages fully integrated co-creation as a cornerstone practice that can support future sustainability. The structures offer instructive lessons for ensuring success.[79] For the purposes of our interest in co-reflective practice, the focus on integration at the co-creation level is relevant because of the increased exposure to different perspectives and the potential for stimulating reflection to which this can lead.

In the following section, we explore how co-creation offers a pathway to co-reflection. Certain features of co-creative practice enable and encourage, indeed provoke different kinds of reflective thinking. The discussion is illustrated by practitioner statements from the interviews that follow this chapter as well as from related research studies.

Co-reflection through co-creation

When people collaborate creatively, they learn from one another as they are exposed to each other's ideas and actions. The creative works that arise from such exchanges are the physical forms of ideas materialised by joint effort. Reflection on the process and outcomes is as necessary in co-creation as it is in solo work. In the discussion to follow, I suggest that certain features of co-creative practice have a role to play in encouraging, and indeed provoking more reflective thinking.

By making artefacts, events and performances, individual practitioners create tangible outcomes to contemplate, appraise, evaluate, reassess and revise: in effect, they are mechanisms for reflection. The creative work enables greater reflection because working together invites dialogue. Co-creation gives the collaborating participants opportunities experience each other's thinking and working methods both during and after the activities. Participants are able to reflect on the similarities and differences in their respective responses to what they have created together in an open and constructive manner. It is a test of the quality of collaboration whether this is indeed possible. Whether the experience is positive or not, it is likely to contribute to the development of each individual's reflective practice through the stimulus and challenge that come from interacting with other people.

Factors that foster and provoke reflection are discussed next in the context of co-creation, given impetus through the challenges and tensions of collaboration, the stimulus to new thinking, and the role of dialogue.

Challenge, conflict and tension in co-reflective practice

Working with someone who has a different way of looking at the situation in hand encourages a kind of creative tension which can influence the way reflection takes place. A key element of the way practitioners work creatively is in making challenges for themselves. This is a very effective way of provoking self-reflection. Both self-reflection and co-reflection arise from the challenge posed by close working within teams. In venturing into collaboration, practitioners expose themselves to uncertainty, often because they are travelling into unfamiliar landscapes. This very uncertainty can provoke reflective thinking. Viewed this way co-creation becomes a reflective process that supports directional change.

There are many challenges to forming successful collaborations that often stem from deep-rooted assumptions and prior experience. In the creative world, seeking out collaborators for the express purpose of having access to specialised expertise may involve working with people who share little common ground. Many misunderstandings can arise and problems occur because underlying assumptions are not made explicit and individual agendas conflict. In an art-science collaboration, for example, the artist may assume that the scientist has no interest in the artistic side of the work but is happy to play a limited supportive role. Then when it becomes apparent that on the contrary, the scientist has strong views about his or her own creative capability and is keen to assume active co-ownership of the artwork, this can pose a dilemma for the artist. Such points of conflict can impact the harmony of the collaboration unless there is a genuine preparedness to give and take and, most important, resist personal grand standing. Some practitioners make a deliberate choice to view the creative ground as shared territory, a result of learning from experience of the negative effects of conflict.

By viewing co-creation as a limitless ground that can be occupied equally, creative practitioners can achieve much more for themselves. At the same time, differences can emerge which lead to positive outcomes. Collaboration between participants with different expectations and experiences can lead to a kind of creative tension which influences the direction of the work and opens up unexpected routes to novel outcomes. Creative tension may offer a promise of something different to old patterns of thinking and thereby give rise to opportunities for expanding horizons and active reflection on ideas and approaches that would otherwise remain unchallenged.[80] For this to work, much depends upon the participant's capacity for self-reflection and a willingness to accept criticism.

The effect of creative tension on reflection raises the question as to whether collaborators need to share values or viewpoints in order to work together successfully. Previous cases suggest that partners can benefit from collaborative relationships in which the participants do not share the same beliefs. For example, siblings who were rivals, Heinrich and Thomas Mann, argued from very different standpoints[81] but at the same time, were able to appreciate each other's ideas and endeavours.[82] On the other hand, shared opposition to another belief system that collaborators consider faulty can strengthen the bonds. For example, Hubert and Stuart Dreyfus together challenged the unbounded optimism of the artificial intelligence community of their day whilst coming from very different philosophical positions.[83]

Co-creation, new thinking and risk

Schön argues that the most agile practitioners are those who are adept at reflecting on their 'knowing-in-practice' whether in the immediate aftermath or over a longer time frame. This means they have in built ways of breaking out of overly familiar routine ways of working and can handle unexpected events better. Practitioners who may not have learned to reflect on their practice to the same extent as the more experienced, need certain forms of stimulation to help them respond to the unfamiliar. In the creative context, this applies especially when the vision or intention is new and has implications for methods and materials.

In creative practice, the impact of collaborative working can prompt reflection in several ways. One way is in dealing with the limitations imposed by familiar ways of thinking that can happen in solo practice when there may be little opportunity for sharing and articulating one's ideas during the process. Some practitioners seek collaboration solely to exchange ideas with people from different backgrounds. They may anticipate that their exposure to different ways of thinking will be stimulating and enable them to break out of self-imposed constraints. Others may be drawn to collaborate by opportunities to take part in speculative initiatives that bring funding and resources. This may lead to involvement in unfamiliar worlds that can be both stimulating and productive, but at the same time, risky. Co-creation invites, indeed encourages, practitioners to step outside their 'safe zones' and embrace the uncertainties that come with working closely with others. It can involve surrendering control and sharing risks that would not have been entertained working solo, as confirmed by John-Steiner:

> Transformative contributions are born from sharing risks and challenging, appropriating and deepening each partner's contribution. Individuals in successful partnerships reach beyond their habitual ways of learning, working and creating. In transforming what they know, they construct creative syntheses.[84]

The notion of risk in collaborative creative work is unlike risk in many other contexts. An artist may deliberately open up an internal world of creative practice by inviting a collaborator into a process that is exploratory and full of risk and uncertainty. In doing so, there is a possibility that the situation will not be respected and there might be unintended consequences in the future. Having someone to share your ideas with can be stimulating but at the same time, just when you are beginning to formulate your vision of a future work, this can lead to difficulties because the need for trust is implied. There is a need to trust your collaborators on a number of fronts, the first of which is the question of who 'owns' the original concept or whose name is attached to the ensuing work. Moving from the security of single ownership is an expansion of responsibility, not only for the eventual outcome of the collaborative effort but for the longer-term implications for one's reputation.

For some, the risk is worth it because of the potential for expanding one's thinking and expectations of what can be achieved. It is wise to be aware of the risks and, moreover, be prepared to lose something in the process.

There is an inevitable balance between risk and trust: the participant has to assess the risks and what is gained from risk with what they stand to lose. It is a finely judged decision to trust in another without losing your sense of yourself. Revealing yourself can be a raw experience as so often the making and exhibiting of artwork implies.

Co-reflection through surprise

Intersecting with people from different disciplines can lead to surprise via the stimulus of contrary perspectives; in the words of Ken Arnold on the way surprise for one discipline provokes surprise in another:

> If you're multi-disciplinary and you've got lots of different things you are working with then the opportunity for surprise often comes because, one small group of people are not surprised because they've spent their whole lives living with it but then they meet up with another group of people who've never seen that before and somehow, it's the surprise of the second group that in turn surprises the first group.

In the case of an artist working with a scientist, the impact of bringing unexpected, surprising thoughts into a well-established frame of reference- the knowing-in-practice'- can be to break through the barrier of what Schön refers to as 'over-learning' that is, patterns of practice that are inflexible. Everyday terms used to describe over learning include 'burn out' and 'boredom'. This arises through repeated experiences that lead to developing a set of expectations, and techniques that work well if all cases are similar and there is less and less surprise leading to a 'knowing in action that is more tacit, spontaneous 'unthinking' action.

Reflection through surprise can lead to new directions for the creative practitioner. This is not always a pre-planned, deliberate act but can arise as a result of happenstance. What can seem like chance at the time of a surprise encounter may happen because of pre-existing factors, as the story of the origins of 'The Curious Economist: William Stanley Jevons in Sydney' exhibition illustrates.

Matthew Connell is a Physics graduate who first worked in geophysics exploration and then as a research technician in Microelectronics. He became the curator of Computing and Mathematics in 1991 at MAAS, the Museum of Applied Arts and Sciences Sydney (formerly Powerhouse Museum Sydney). Working as part of in-house teams demands a great deal of reflection through dialogue and communication in a constant search for new ideas and exciting connections. Exploring what others do and how they do it is a fundamental part of Matthew's co-reflective practice. In his interview, Matthew relates the story of the origins of an exhibition he curated about William Stanley Jevons.[85] He first became interested when his attention was caught by Jevons's invention of a 'logic piano' around the time he had acquired a piece of Charles Babbage's Difference Engine[86] for his museum. But it was a chance meeting of a colleague and friend in the street that was to prove highly influential in expanding Matthew's ambitions for the Jevons project. Simply following the research on this subject, as fruitful as it was, would not have been as innovative as the project turned out to be but for the conjunction of two people's mutual interest and the dialogue that ensued. Not only was the exhibition a revelation about the importance of Jevons but the collaboration brought about significant changes in his own creative practice, as his new passion for photography demonstrated. Matthew describes his experience:

> I am very interested in new practices, in innovation across the board. I'm interested in the fact that innovation often occurs in the new connections that are made in existing areas of knowledge. But I am also aware that inter-disciplinarity doesn't mean anything if you don't have disciplines. People sometimes forget that you need strong disciplines to have interdisciplinary anything. Disciplines of course do change but they emerge for reason and those reasons shouldn't be forgotten.
>
> That's a case where I'm following one thing and I uncover another thing when I realise that this man sat at the conception of a number of the most important discourses of our time.
>
> Then I started thinking well how do they all work together? How do they intertwine? And then I bumped into a friend at Market City. I was going for some noodles and saw an old friend who was walking and as it turned out thinking about Jevons whose photography he loved. I didn't know Jevons was a photographer, an amateur photographer. I then started talking with Lindsey Barrett, the Friend and colleague. He didn't know that Jevons had been a logician and we started to talk and we ended up doing an exhibition called William Jevons: The Curious Economist. It wasn't huge but it was rich. Every bit of research we did, we discovered something. We were reflecting the whole time. And there was serendipity too.
>
> . . . bumping into Lindsey was ridiculous! He was interested in economics and photography and Jevons tied the two together. I was interested in logic and as it turned out I was interested in mathematics and economics. I wasn't a great reader of photography before this came along and Jevons photos taught me to read photographs and drew me into the history of Australian photography which I knew nothing about prior to that. Now I am completely captivated by it.

For Matthew collaboration implies listening and learning from one other as he explains in the context of his creative curatorial work: see his interview on page 164 to follow and an extended version online.[87] Surprise as a feature of reflection in practice was discussed previously in Chapter 3.

FIGURE 4.5 *The Curious Economist: William Stanley Jevons in Sydney.* The Powerhouse Museum, October 2004

Source: Reproduced courtesy of the Museum of Applied Arts and Sciences

Conversations and co-reflection

Reflections need to be explicit in order to be shared and for that to take place, spoken articulation and the written word play a vital role in the co-creative process. The value of shared reflection through dialogue is that it can bring to light the tacit assumptions that exist when practices have become routine and are unable to respond to unusual situations and unexpected events. Creative practitioners can find themselves struggling to move forward either because they have run into arid patches or finding effective methods and materials has proven difficult. This is where co-creation offers stimulus to reflection and learning through the conversations that take place between practitioners.

The interaction of thought and speech is an important feature of co-reflection and its role in stimulating creative thinking. Co-creation demands communication in a continual search for novel ideas, practices and outcomes. Thinking with others is based upon various types of dialogue: informal conversations, talks with feedback and questioning, exchanges about ideas and expertise, critiquing or appraisal exercises, interviews with visitors and audiences, not to mention presentations to commissioning bodies and funders. Encounters with people at all levels can be a fruitful opportunity for trying out ideas and gaining feedback from those not directly connected to a particular project. As Matthew Connell puts it:

> You just know that one conversation that's brought some of it to the surface and another that's raised something else and a third one that's amalgamated that, and it does feel as though there are definitely bits of it that I can find my voice in. But that voice only makes sense because it's been part of a congregation, part of a communal activity.

But does dialogue of itself promote reflection in co-creation? Is the mere act of speaking sufficient to provoke new thinking between people working together?

As most of us are aware, when we engage in conversation, often new ideas emerge during the exchanges as if out of the blue and we can surprise ourselves with such serendipitous moments of inspired comment. Thinking and speaking often feels indistinguishable as new thoughts arise during active speech. In the heat of debate, there is little time for careful preparation and, if you are someone who 'thinks on their feet', as the phrase goes, you are well placed to get your ideas on the table. Some people are stimulated best by having others to bounce ideas off and many discover the benefits that talking with others provides.

The conjoining of thought and speaking aloud is considered in some societies to be a natural phenomenon. However, this is not universal and there is evidence to suggest that it is a culturally determined aspect of discourse. A research study compared Asian Americans and European Americans thinking aloud while solving reasoning problems. Participants' beliefs about talking and reflecting were correlated with how talking affects performance. The study demonstrated that talking impaired Asian Americans' thinking performance but not that of European Americans. The researchers suggest that cultural difference in modes of thinking can explain the difference in the effect of talking.[88] My own first experiences of cultural differences came on a visit to Japan in the late 1980s when, during exchanges between fellow researchers, I noticed that the hosts paused for at least two to three seconds before responding to my observations. In subsequent exchanges, whilst some of us were mindful of the differences, others were not, and there were occasions when the Japanese researchers sat waiting patiently whilst the Westerners followed a familiar pattern of rapid fire exchanges, oblivious to the fact that it was necessary to pause for breath in order to allow our hosts to enter the conversation.

There is considerable discourse in the area of dialogical thinking which is relevant but in a tangential way to the themes explored here in respect of co-creative reflective thinking. For our purposes, it is perhaps sufficient to note that a dialogical process is one in which multiple approaches are able to co-exist and has been proposed as key to understanding group identity. Compared to dialectics, a dialogic exchange can be less competitive, and more suitable for facilitating cooperation. Dialogical thinking is open-ended and pluralist and therefore, perhaps, ideally suited for collaborative creative work. Dialogue can also provide a means of making sense of unexpected events or phenomena and enable such awareness to have a positive benefit through creativity and reflection. This resonates with Virginia Woolf's account of being able to explain, to find a reason when faced with a 'shock' experience, a capacity that she believed made her a writer. As a writer, she turns the shock into 'a revelation of some order' and putting it into words makes sense of a surprise experience that enters the mind unexpectedly and turn it into a positive experience.[89]

Roles and co-reflection in creative collaboration

Within the various patterns of collaborative creative practice, individual practitioners adopt different roles linked to particular patterns or combinations of pattern.

The particular creative context can influence the roles adopted which in turn may depend on the pattern of collaboration. Collaborative patterns and roles are ever changing because it is a learning process and dynamic in character. Being collaborative is often much more than bringing useful skills to the process and there is often a need for individuals in a team to assume a particular role that requires certain personal qualities: for example, an ability to attune oneself in a way that chimes with the context or ethos of the situation. Sometimes, this means taking the right initiative at the right time or being able to work without continual direction and contact with other team members. Being sensitive to environment, especially in highly critical setting requires an understanding of the demands and special conditions of the context in which the work takes place. In this view, a collaborative role requires skills that work to bridge prejudice and negative preconceptions. This is often the case when artists are encouraged into scientific fields and it is sometimes necessary to counteract existing assumptions and prejudice about what artists do and the way art practice works. Whatever the situation or demands of the creative work in hand, the people involved may find themselves taking on tasks and responsibilities that require them to step outside their usual way of working individually.

Drawing on the studies that have informed the previous discussion of patterns and structures of collaboration and the experiences of the practitioners represented throughout this book, a set of key roles have been identified and are discussed in this section. The roles have been assigned labels for ease of discussion as follows: *Relater, Partner, Facilitator, Prime Mover*. They are discussed in relation to collaborative patterns where they have been identified. Naturally, the presence of particular roles is not assumed to apply to one pattern of collaboration only and people may move between different roles depending on the situation.

The relater

The *Relater* role is so named because it is one in which the participants in a collaboration develop relationships that are built on trust and a desire to learn from one another. This applies even where they do not share the same intentions or visions. A willingness to trust the other in the interests of mutually beneficial exchange even where priorities differ, relies on knowing your collaborator reasonably well and this implies working together over a reasonable length of time. The Relater role offers much more than practical assistance but is partly driven by an awareness that each has much to learn from the other. It is a different relationship to that of teacher and student or indeed, mentor and mentored. This is a relationship of equal status where the very differences provide the basis of the collaboration. Rather than simply focusing on achieving a tangible outcome such as a new artwork or a new discovery, there is continuous dialogue that may or may not have a specific goal but is nevertheless rewarding in itself. Although it arises from quite different standpoints, given sufficient opportunity and determination, it may become a longstanding relationship. This kind of exchange involving contrasting perspectives, knowledge and expertise is one that can prompt the participants to reflect and to learn from one another. However, this often depends upon the individual forming a relationship that is responsive to the particular situation, something that is closely connected to a capacity for listening and interpreting sympathetically. For this purpose, the Relater role can be especially effective and often crucial in enabling a distributed pattern of collaboration to work in bringing different priorities and skills together for a common purpose. The following example is of a collaboration which involves two people who both take a Relater role in their ongoing co-creative and reflective practices.

Esther Rolinson and **Sean Clark** have worked together for a number of years. Both are artists with distinctive styles and practices who also work with others on complex art installation projects. The collaboration was initially intermittent and based on a need for technological advice from Sean for the construction of programming systems for Esther's light sculptures. Gradually a closer common ground emerged and together they developed a piece by Esther called '*Flown*' for which Sean was an important part of the technical development and installation process. They decided to enter the finished work in an international exhibition competition and were awarded first prize.[90] They went on to win the 3D and Sculpture award in the Lumen Global Digital Art Prize 2016,[91] gaining success in both the USA and UK in the same year. The various artworks they have created together reflect an ongoing evolution of shared concepts. At the same time, they see the world of art and art making differently and whilst their 'art systems' interconnect, they nevertheless remain distinctive. Such relationships require more openness and a readiness to allow unexpected and unplanned things to arise.

In their reflections on their collaborative relationship, Esther and Sean demonstrate the benefits of having shared goals but aiming for different outcomes. Their experience indicates that having a continuous dialogue has enriched their individual practices at the same time as extending what they can do through co-creation:

> E: There is a broad spectrum of collaboration between us, with some shared goals and also different desired outcomes. The dialogue gives me greater understanding of my practice which is a fundamental benefit beyond sharing of skills. Sean has great digital expertise and his understanding of the connections and flow of activity through living things identifies something I express non-verbally in my work.
>
> In my collaboration, we are exploring our mutual interest in complex interconnected systems. . . . I expect my drawing process to be influenced by the output of the digital drawings and vice versa. The nature of the relationship also teaches me about interconnected systems.
>
> S: despite our very different creative histories, we had a great deal in common. In particular, there was a shared interest in systems and the relationships between 'parts' and 'wholes' . . . [T]his process is continuing beyond a single piece of work and consequently issues such as attribution and ownership of work raise themselves. Our solution to this is to maintain a creative dialogue that gives us space for individual and joint practice.[92]

As these statements from their own writings indicate, the ability to reflect on one's own work in relation to a different frame of reference opens up new possibilities that might not have otherwise have been encountered. Instead of viewing her artworks as a discrete set of drawings and sculptures, by working with a collaborator who makes artworks as inter-connected systems, this has revealed synergies within Esther's own work and opened up the opportunity to learn from new influences arising from the works themselves. This relationship of artists co-creating in a sustained reflective way has been documented. Observations about the nature of successful art-technology collaborations are discussed with reference to the conclusions from previous research.[93]

The facilitator

An important role in a complementary collaborative team is that of the *Facilitator*, a role with different characteristics depending on the context in which the creative work takes place. The Facilitator may be needed to manage the communications between participants and coordinate the process so as to achieve outcomes according to time constraints. This applies especially in the kind of collaborative performance work where time zone differences are a factor. In certain situations, the Facilitator observes the exchanges between the participants as well as the contextual and environmental factors that influence what can be achieved in order to arrive at an understanding of what might be feasible and desirable. Having reflected on all the constraints and potential risks, the facilitator is then able to mediate between what the various creative practitioners seek to do and prompt new reflections in them about the intended process. This is especially important in situations where the presence of an artist is unfamiliar and there is uncertainty about what will happen: for example, when an artist is 'embedded' in an environment that is distant from the artist's own and where the inhabitants are unfamiliar with artistic intentions and practices such as a hospital. Left to his or her own initiative, the artist might be able to establish a direct relationship with a patient or clinician without difficulty, but often it is also necessary to gain the prior agreement and acceptance of others in order to facilitate that presence in the first place.

The Facilitator role involves reframing or 'interpreting' the role of the artist to non-artists: for example, medical clinicians. Until they have actually seen for themselves how an artist works, it is hard to judge whether something positive is taking place that might benefit their patients. To ensure this happens is the responsibility of the Facilitator who understands that the really difficult part is convincing people to allow 'intrusions' to happen in the first place on the basis that first-hand experience is the best way to accept risk. The first step for the Facilitator is to find a place for the core creative work. This is often very hard at the beginning especially where the environment is sensitive because of critical conditions. Creative practitioners who venture into this kind of situation are giving themselves genuinely difficult challenges because of the implications for the people involved. The Facilitator can act to reassure and explain when the occasion arises. That elusive 'something' can happen through listening carefully and adopting an empathetic stance by way of responsive conversations initiated by the artist as well as the facilitator thus encouraging more reflective responses. In any such collaboration, it is important to value the work of the other party to the collaboration. The Facilitator acts, in effect, as an enabler of both individual and co-reflection.

Anna Ledgard facilitates long-term partnerships between professional artists, healthcare professionals and patients. Operating in a distinctive manner, she facilitates creative partnerships in challenging interdisciplinary environments in her role as mediator between artists and other people. These relationships are established in settings where working with artists is an unfamiliar experience. She makes sure that non-artists, for example, clinical professionals in the health service, can observe and understand how artists work and how that relates to their own situations. This requires an understanding of the differences as well as areas of common ground:

> My role is to make sure we facilitate the situation in which they can observe an artist at work and be convinced . . . what I am doing very often is providing the frame for that to happen. . . . It is my role to weave the web of collaborative relationships with individuals and organisations, to gather the resources and build the dialogue and organisational structures which are essential to the success of this work.
>
> I think through the reflection back to the context is an exchange of knowledge – which is why I talk about it as learning. Those encounters are all about us learning about each other.

Anna Ledgard's interview appears on page 169 and online.[94] She has written about shared, paired and individual reflective practice.[95] She is currently working on arts and science public engagement projects with artist Sofie Layton[96] (see Figure 4.6).

The partner

The *Partner* role exists in co-creativity where both complementary and convergent interests co-exist and is found mainly in integrative and family patterns of collaboration. Partners are able to designate their works as common property as in the case of the collective or agree to retain ownership of individual achievements whilst acknowledging their mutual benefit from each other's work. Full partnership may, as in the case of the collective, involve the relinquishing of individual control to the extent of giving a single name to the outcomes of common work.[97] Having a respect for differences in methods is a feature of the partnership style: this means, for example, acknowledging the way differences in approach can benefit one another. In studies of artist-technologist collaborations, co-creativity in art and technology was characterised by complementary interests even where individual outcomes differed. One of the most successful partnerships operated in such a way as to serve convergent interests but, at the same time, produce quite distinct artistic outcomes.

FIGURE 4.6 *Making the Invisible Visible* 2016 and *The Heart of the Matter* 2018

Source: ©Sofie Layton. Photo by Stephen King

In this way, the partners achieved mutual benefit but nevertheless, retained ownership of their individual achievements. To be able to enjoy such mutual benefit, requires the relinquishing of individual 'control' of the creative process. Having differential, but complementary, roles appears to be best suited to achieving that end.[98]

The role of a partner is vital to realising the full possibilities of co-reflection. Long term partnerships can act as mirrors to one another in a type of reflection that relies on each person understanding the preferences and thinking style of the other. Differences in modes of thinking can create opportunities for expanding creative ambitions. The person who thinks verbally and works with words will benefit from the one who thinks spatially and works with diagrams and drawings. In the field of architecture, for example, this is especially important because of the need to produce high standards of both verbal and visual information that are critical to the success of the business. The demands of creative architectural practice include giving good verbal and written advice about materials, building and planning regulations and also creating visually exciting and accurate drawings and diagrams. This means that to be successful the team should include people who think and reflect in various ways. Having variants in team thinking styles applies in many other domains.

Co-reflective practice offers a way of stepping back to view one's ideas from a different perspective. Being one's own critic is hard, especially for someone early in their creative life. Even when the person is experienced, it is not always possible to see through one's own considerable efforts to the elephant in the room or to give attention to the niggling problem grumbling away in the back of your mind. This is where light touch collaboration can offer significant support as a reliable sounding board. Even better, those who work together over a period of time can maintain the dialogue in the face of serious setbacks. Constructive criticism encourages reflective thinking. Critiquing as a method for provoking reflection in creative partnerships has a distinct role in advancing the creative work itself. It is not enough to give generalised feedback on work in progress but to show close awareness of the kind of goals the practitioner has in mind. To be truly constructive, the response to a collaborator's work needs to help develop the ideas further. This is often best achieved by partners with common interests and commitment to the joint work As James Stigler says: *it is much more special to have someone who is going to try to take your idea and help develop it.*[99] Critiquing means more than pulling apart someone's idea but rather helping them see another way forward. This is likely to be found in the integrative pattern of collaboration discussed previously. Perhaps even more important, successful partnerships depend upon an explicit commitment to shared interests and achieving goals that serve both parties.

Sue Crellin McCarthy and Tom McCarthy of Baby Forest exemplify the partner role.[100]

The prime mover

The *Prime Mover* is a lead person whose vision and drive motivates the collaboration. This person is often the one with the original idea although that is not always the case, particularly where an external body commissions a project and provides funding and resources. The Prime Mover may actually determine which pattern of collaboration is appropriate for requirements of the situation. The role is critical to a successful outcome, something which often depends on team building amongst people with very different backgrounds and working methods. Prime Movers do not rely on promoting self-regarding grand schemes for success and, whilst putting forward the driving vision for a project is vital, it is nevertheless essential to bring people along with you and to encourage a consultative ethos. For that to work, it is important to acknowledge what each member of the team can achieve and give them scope to do what they do best.

A relatively democratic and positive approach to the whole creative process seems to be fundamental to forming strong collaborative groups where everyone feels equally valued. The freedom it brings encourages people to challenge incumbent ideas and produce innovative ways of solving problems. A Prime Mover who values the 'push back' from the team benefits from the sense of shared endeavour it can bring. The compromise that takes place in long-standing collaborative groups is an important reason people continue to work together over length periods of time. They are then able to get to know one another's strengths and weaknesses and are better able to ride difficulties and come up with satisfactory outcomes no matter how hard the direction of travel proves to be. The reflections that the Prime Mover engages in are often about the dynamics of the team and the co-reflection process itself. Getting the most out of individual contributions within a collaborative context often requires imaginative thinking on the part of the Prime Mover. This is especially so where they do not have complete freedom of choice in selecting people for the projects: for example, in organisations such as large museums, the team members are usually drawn from in-house specialities such a design, publicity, editorial sections.

The Prime Mover role usually involves seeing a project all the way through from the initial concept to the final outcome, making sure that the result is high quality. The role is critical for creative work that is subject to external deadlines and limited resources. The label applies to those practitioners whose activities span everything from making the work to finding the funds to support others. It is found in those situations where the individual practitioner has a singular vision that transcends the overall endeavour. In the case of the creative practitioners in this chapter, a majority have at some point in time taken a prime mover role that is ongoing and essential to the success of their work and the projects they initiate and carry forward.

Examples of Prime Movers are Ken Arnold, David Clarkson, Anthony Rowe and Roger Kneebone.

Roger Kneebone explores the crossing of domain boundaries, whether discipline or culturally based, through unconventional perspectives. In many cases, he sees parallels with his own search for understanding through applying different kinds of lenses to existing phenomena and scenarios. For example, as a teacher of surgical practice, he took an unusual perspective on his field by locating it within craft and performative science as opposed to its usual place in medical diagnosis and treatment. By viewing surgery as something that surgical teams 'act out' rather than as a mechanism for solving a physical problem, he was able to throw new light on the nature of surgery as it happens in the theatre. In doing so, he drew attention to the gestural, non-verbal forms of communication involved and identified similarities with other kinds of performance such as the fine motor skills, the uniqueness of each performance and the close team work required.[101]

In Roger, the trained mind of a scientist, the knowing in practice of a clinician and the imagination of an artist come together in a life of exploration, action and reflective thinking. Amongst his many innovative projects, he has brought the public into close contact with the inner world of the operating theatre through simulation workshops. He works in ever more novel and inspirational ways that rely on a drive to connect people from different disciplines. Bringing practitioners, scientists and members of the public together to share their perspectives – a process, as he says of *'reciprocal illumination'* is key to making connections between practices that might appear to be very different but on closer examination have surprising areas of similarity. Puppeteers, potters, musicians, tailors and surgeons not only perform their tasks using similar hand gestural patterns, they also work to tight timings in close partnership with others. The public events, the writings, the talks and the *Countercurrent* podcasts[102] together reflect Roger's passion for revealing and promoting greater understanding of the intersections between disciplinary boundaries and the synergies between clinical practice, biomedical science and the performance arts:

I started to think that in the world of medicine – I think we are invited . . . to see ourselves almost as applied scientists – as people who apply scientific and medical knowledge to make individual sick people better. . . . But I think there are other ways of looking at it as well and I think medical care, particularly clinical care and especially surgery, but not only, you can also see as having elements of performance, and elements of craftsmanship and all sorts of things- team working. Then

I started to think what might come into view if we looked at other people who did things in those more general categories, even if what they did was very far from the application of scientific knowledge.

In his interview online, Roger Kneebone gives an account of his role as a prime mover of unusual and illuminating intersections between unlikely areas of practice.[103]

Conclusions

Creative collaborations happen for many reasons. Going solo remains a preference for many practitioners but it is not always possible to achieve everything oneself and collaboration is sometimes a pragmatic choice. Having extra hands to save time when faced with a work overload is useful, and sometimes essential when deadlines loom. The move towards collaboration can be a sign of growing confidence as practitioners introduce new challenges and start to work with unfamiliar materials and technologies. The more ambitious a project is, however, the greater the need for collaboration can be and when practitioners venture into unchartered territory, as the risks increase so does the need for contributions from other people. Working with people outside your own field can stimulate unexpected insights and new understandings that contribute much more to the project than a piece of computer code or a customised electronic circuit, as essential as they might seem at the time.

Collaboration is often talked about in generalities but rarely understood as the multi-dimensional, dynamic phenomena that it is, one that is becoming the norm as globalisation and digital technologies transform the world of work in many professions and fields. For artists, curators, designers, musicians and performers, collaboration means opportunities for working with people outside their own fields and benefiting from their skills and expertise. This implies not only learning the language of interdisciplinary communication and alien working practices, but also how to gain benefit without sacrificing your own vision. The solo practitioner has the freedom to make choices without having to agree them with others, but that liberty can be daunting especially when venturing into new territory. That is where working in partnerships, groups or teams can be an advantage.

Creative collaboration is not a single track, one off process and the duration and continuity can be highly varied. Some collaborations are started in order to provide additional resources, skills or expertise and finish once an outcome has been achieved, whilst others develop into more lasting relationships. The exchanges take place on many levels and have different degrees of intensity and productivity. In any given collaborative scenario, people may continue working together over the longer term, but it takes time and determination to establish significant and enduring relationships. For a collaboration to survive through the inevitable difficulties that occur especially in demanding, complex projects, personal qualities such as empathy and trust are vital to sustain momentum and commitment. We learn from wide-ranging studies of collaborative practices from art, design and science to writing and music, that wholly solo work is, in reality, a rare phenomenon.

By looking at the different kinds of relationships whether formal or casual, personal or professional, occasional or sustained, it is apparent that no one size fits all situations and that proposing definitive guidelines for conducting collaborative work is in all probability a waste of time. Nevertheless, how practitioners create and reflect in collaboration is revealing and instructive. By considering what happens through the different patterns, structures and roles, we can see how the context influences the reflections. Both self-reflection and co-reflection arise from the challenge of working within teams especially where the leaders are open to challenge and make opportunities for others to engage with the creative aspects of the work.

In the interviews to follow, we hear from practitioners in art, curating, theatre, performance, producing and science about how they practice and the role of reflection in making and appraising their works. To meet space limitations, the full interviews are available online.[104]

Practitioner interviews

Ken Arnold: Creative Curator

> A lot of interdisciplinary projects have within them people who started in one place and ended up in another and carry with them that sense that maybe the world doesn't have to be looked at just one way.

Ken Arnold is head of public programmes at Wellcome Collection, London and creative director at the Medical Museion, the University of Copenhagen. His role in establishing the original SciArt initiative[105] was pivotal.

Two key elements of his creative thinking are first, the primacy he gives to turning familiar time-honoured knowledge into 'mysterious' unknowns from which new discoveries arise; and second, the method he proposes of adopting a narrow focus as an initial constraint from which larger ideas can be derived. Underpinning Ken's practice is a commitment to the idea of museums and galleries as participative 'living laboratories'. By placing his kind of co-produced multi-disciplinary exhibition into the museum space, the public's encounter with them, 'turns the curator's multi-disciplinary a la carte menu into some truly trans-disciplinary nourishment'.[106] Keeping open his capacity to generate fresh ideas is vital for his mission to revitalise the role of museums as active public spaces for discovery. For this to happen, he believes that curatorial programmes require flexible processes that reflect a balance between materials and makers seeking cultural engagement that resonates with the visiting public. Finding ways to collectively source, connect and synthesise ideas and then transform them into the tangible objects and artefacts of striking exhibitions is a hallmark of this vision. His record of innovative curatorial projects is outstanding: for example, in 'The Identity Project,[107] the topic of genetics became one of identity and the space of possibilities was expanded into asking what influences our sense of who we are. This meant that rather than focussing what geneticists could tell us, the topic was open to other disciplinary viewpoints. In 'Brains: Mind as Matter',[108] by asking not what brains do to us, but what we have done to brains, the attention was focused on the bodily presence of the organ rather than the neuroscience.

A shorter version of Ken's interview follows and is available in full online.[109]

Q: *Where does a new idea for a work, event, performance come from?*

K: I am almost sure that the best ideas I am involved with almost by definition can't be traced to where they come from. I think that the best things we've done next door (at Wellcome Collection) and the best things I've been involved with are about bits of ideas coming from different places. That's one aspect of it . . . just being alert enough, being interested enough, not in swallowing everything hook, line and sinker that you're presented with, but finding the thing in it that might be latched to something else. The other answer is – and this is something that is under-explored in the meta thinking about creativity – is how people come up with interesting topics. And one of the things we got right quite often at Wellcome Collection was to find subjects that seemed so ludicrously broad . . . and then finding a way of turning something that seemed very big into something quite narrow. Or alternatively finding something that seems quite small – often in material culture and focusing on them and then beginning to derive some rather bigger ideas. But that thing of 'how do you find the topic and how do you find the question within it', I suppose there is a bit of an art to that.

I am really interested in the role of museums and public spaces have in creating new ideas. We aren't here to get the best art ever, we are here to hopefully get artists interested in what we are interested in and then leave them alone enough so they can do the best they can within their own practice . . . there is something very powerful about encouraging these people to operate in the public domain . . . In a world so used to the idea of access and interaction and in finding things easily, it's the slowness and the awkwardness of what goes on in museums that is important. The other thing is that many places now welcome the notion that you are using lots of different intelligences. There is a sense of using lots of different type of modes of enquiry – an audio, a visual, a movie.

I think the world divides into people who say what they think and other people who think what they say. The people who are fairly quiet and compose what they are going to say and then they say it because they know that's what they think. Whereas I often don't know what I think until I hear myself say it. People have asked where did that idea come from for that exhibition and I always think 'I don't know really!'. . . . You just know that one conversation that's brought some of it to the surface and another that's raised something else and a third one that's amalgamated that, and it does feel as though there are definitely bits of it that I can find my voice in. But that voice only makes sense because it's been part of a congregation, part of a communal activity.

Q: *What do you think of John Dewey's characterisation of reflective thinking?*

K: I suspect, for me, it might be a little more muddled than Dewey suggests. I get the sense of going around in circles sometimes, but somehow moving on a little while doing so – certainly repeating thought processes with variations – practicing something till you nail it. Thinking about (and frequently talking about) the same thing time and again until one time it just seems/feels a little different and you know you've got something new and more vibrant.

One of the interesting things I have been reflecting on recently is the role of disciplines – trans, cross, multi etc.; how much of it is lining up disciplines in parallel, how much of it is really squashing them together. One of the things that is so obvious is that there is no such thing as trans or multi interdisciplinary practice unless there are disciplines. If everyone became multi-disciplinary, by definition multi-disciplinary would disappear because we wouldn't have the disciplines to draw on. I think a lot of interdisciplinary projects actually have within them people who started in one place and ended up in another and carry with them that sense that maybe the world doesn't have to be looked at just one way.

Q: *What are your main aims in relation to facilitating interdisciplinary collaboration?*

K: It's creating new experiences . . . it's a legitimate question that could be asked at any stage of what I've done- and my sense is that I'd probably give a different answer. It's not always been 'this is what I'm trying to do and I've finally managed to do it'. Wherever I am it would probably be different. I think that what seems to unite all of this is an eagerness to find interesting ways of finding things out. I think that my core interest is in enquiry, both the things that are being enquired into (e.g. an exhibition about the heart) and then because I am very methodologically interested, it's new knowledge discovered in interesting ways. The background of all of that- the politics of it- is a sense of who is doing the discovery. There are interesting ways of making that more and more democratically accessible.

Q: *In interdisciplinary work, what is needed most to make it happen successfully?*

K: I think I do have a kind of recipe. It's primarily about people, places and things. And having the right resources to get the right people, places and things means that you need some money and the activity of putting things together. In my solipsistic world, some like me who can puppeteer it all. People is the obvious thing but for me it's the curators on the one hand and the participants, the visitors. I don't go in for this 'there shouldn't be any hierarchy: some are paid to do it and they are experts; others go there on a Friday afternoon. I don't think we have to pretend they are all providing the same amount but each need each other and the whole things would be meaningless if neither of those group were there. So yes, good people at the top and good people overall helping the work. . . . We are totally reliant on good people- good scientists, good artists.

And to complete my trio – the places and things: I am convinced it needs to happen in a forum where people come; these are public activities in my mind. A location? A real place. I don't think it's accidental that these things largely happen in public institutions. It's almost axiomatic for how artists and scientists get together. I am a museum person but I am really intrigued about how much of this stuff – I suppose it goes together with places; places have tangible things by and large- even though they can be a vehicle for imagination (and the digital is just another form of imagination). In that way bringing the stuff and the places where that stuff can be thought about and examined.

Q: *Does interdisciplinary working have an impact on within discipline working?*

K: Yes. I've often thought that interdisciplinary is almost the narrow bit in the hour glass. You start with your separate particles above and then they go through a tunnel in the middle and then they come out at the other end. I'm not sure that interdisciplinary is an ongoing state as much as a phase you go through. The ideal is then you end up back in sort of a new discipline but with added layers or with open questions. The other thing was to make sure by and large, that whatever topic we tackled wasn't entirely owned by one discipline . . . for us it was much more interesting to say let's do an exhibition about identity that would be woefully incomplete if we didn't tackled genetics, than do something called genetics and make a passing gesture towards identity. Because with identity, theologians, artists and geographers have a lot to tell us about identity, whereas if you just do something on genetics, I'm afraid that wonderful as some geneticists are, you are only going to get one voice.

Q: *Do you find that you have to find a consensus or can you go for left field projects?*

K: In this organization, it was easier than one might imagine not to have to get considerable buy in and consensus . . . finding one or two, ideally two, or maybe three people to be the people to make it real and not to ask them to make sure they bring forty stakeholders along with them; but to give them the licence to be as self-propelled as they wish. We did this exhibition on brains but the genius of the project was to say we're not so interested in brains and what comes out of them but it's not what brains have done for us but what we've done to the brain. Coming at something that every museum in the world that's interested in science might do an exhibition about, they would be telling us about neuroscience whereas we've we telling about weird people who'd stolen Einstein's brain and chopped it up into hundreds of pieces and started analysing it. I'm fond of that idea that we take things that you think you know well and make it clear that they are much more mysterious that you thought they were in the first place.

Q: *Can you think of projects that have gone in a direction that is surprising?*

K: I think there is an ingredient of surprise in every project. If you're multi-disciplinary and you've got lots of different things you are working with then the opportunity for surprise often comes because, one small group of people are not surprised because they've spent their whole lives living with it but then they meet up with another group of people who've never seen that before and somehow, it's the surprise of the second group that in turn surprises the first group.

The surprise can happen when you let the public in. An unvisited exhibition is oxymoronic really; it's got all that potential energy but until someone crosses the threshold and starts thinking the thoughts, it's entirely mute. Because museums are active spaces, there can be a very different sense of what the exhibition is all about. . . . We did a fantastic project largely down to the artist Neil Bartlett.[110] He had a great idea for sex surveys- let's create a new survey inspired as much by poetry art as by statistics and science, and the way to incorporate the visitors in this project would be to have the last question in his printed survey, as 'what question do you want to ask the rest of the public?' And then choose one to replace one of his original questions. He did this repeatedly so that by the end of the exhibition the entire questionnaire had been composed by visitors. In that way, the form was unsurprising because it was understood from the start. . . . It was less a revelation than a strategy for making sure that continual surprise and discovery and activating that notion that a visitor to an exhibition if it captures an interesting idea that someone had just at that moment, that can be a way of making sure there is surprise continually fed into a project.

[111]Anthony Rowe: Installation Artist

The end is to create ambiences and emotions.
I'm interested in movement and flow and presence.

Anthony Rowe is an installation artist who leads Squidsoup a highly successful group responsible for creating powerful immersive experiences. These works have been installed in a range of public spaces from art galleries to concerts and open-air festival events. He was inspired by a video work by Jim Campbell called Running Falling (2004), from which he learnt that the human brain needs quite minimal information in order to be able to construct a full picture. The work of Rafael Soto, a Venezuelan artist whose tactile works 'Penetrables' introduced him to the potential of physical interactive spaces was also very influential.

Over ten years his personal aesthetic surfaced as a preference for abstraction over narrative style. He has the training and skills of an engineer, a mathematician, a designer, a technologist, and a researcher. This 21st-century artist was moulded by transformations in education, science and culture sitting on top of the rise of modernism in the 20th century. His is the voice of a quintessentially contemporary artist whose creative practice is steeped in reflection informed by deep levels of research exemplified in his PhD[112] and influenced by the collaborative process. He sees the role of digital technology as critical both as an enabler as well as 'a source of inspiration', a trigger for creative reflection. Nevertheless, he recognises its limits in determining what the final artwork will be and affirms the vital role played by 'artistic priorities'. Without this, art that employs technology risks being perceived as a showcase for the technology over the art. Invisible to audiences but essential to the art is technology that facilitates the experience of encapsulated movement in light and sound. The disguise is intentional in order to directly engage the senses and emotions of the audience and to avoid provoking the rational intellect to respond.

Anthony talks about his work with the Squidsoup team and the way he sees reflection and collaboration: from a discussion in November 2016 at St Pancras Station London.[113]

Q: *Can you describe how 'Submergence' came about?*

A: In 2002 I saw the work of Jim Campbell (low res video work) in a show in Japan in Nagoya. I just loved it aesthetically . . . and the way he blurred it with Perspex's and so on was really exciting. And I started thinking, could that be done in 3D? . . . The first version of 'Submergence' was built very quickly. . . . The first week we put the thing up and got the lights to come on. It was entirely new technology to us, and until we actually flicked the switch we didn't know it was going to work at all. 'Submergence' was built in five days, five very long days and 5 days of extreme work . . . but because these volumetric media are pretty new, it's not until you are in it that you know what works anyway. You can do as many sketches as you like beforehand and come up with as many ideas as you like, it's not until you are actually there in the space, tweaking it. . . . The whole Ocean of Light-Submergence, I see not as an art work but as a medium. This is a way of placing a digital virtual architecture in a physical space in a way that you can spatially interact and coexist with it. In that way, it's got huge potential that we have only just begun to tap. . . . The idea came from a vision of what I wanted to experience myself. Technology has been a limitation but as a limitation it allows you to go in certain ways more than others . . . but I wouldn't say it was a driving force. it's a necessary evil if anything! It's all re-appropriated technology that reconfigured and restructured to do what we want it to do.

Q: *Is evaluation or appraisal or assessment a part of your creative process?*

A: Definitely. Our work is very iterative. 'The Ocean of Light' project has been going for ten years. The process of creating a work, and then evaluating it -in the field, in itself as compared to the initial vision, aesthetics, effectiveness, immersiveness, audience responses and feedback feeds directly into the next iteration of the project. The interaction designer in me is really interested in creating spaces and environments in which people can reflect themselves and can apply their own meaning to what they see. We are creating these things that are boiled down to the bare minimum so you can create whatever you want with the little information you're given. I am not trying to make cinema. I am not trying to tell people what to think but nevertheless I am trying to evoke these abstract powers. I remember the first time we got to walk through thing running in this gallery – 'Submergence'. We hadn't even run through any code in it just turned on the lights and thought 'Oh Yes! This is going to work!' The whole building lit up!

Q: *What does the phrase 'reflective practice' or 'reflection-in-practice' mean to you?*

A: I would say that reflection is very integrated with the practice and it's very much a feedback loop. I am talking primarily about my own practice here and the work with Squidsoup. Our work tends to be very iterative so we take an idea and the first time we do it it's a total nightmare because so much of it is new but then we refine the bits of it that don't work so well. Each iteration is a result of the reflection of the previous one: so for example, the Ocean of Light projects, like Submergence, the first one of those we did in 2007 but we have done about fifteen iterations since then and each one is very much looking at what we did before and how we can improve it, but not only how we can improve it but also what else we could do with that idea.

Q: Does the reflection come from the making process?

A: Yes, but not only. It comes from the making: you come up with an idea, you try and make that idea and as you are making it something else may emerge: the idea for a variety of reasons sometimes through practicality some of them to do with inspiration. That initial idea in our case may change, or develop, before it's finished. That's a result of reflection on other things but also the result of practical limitations and so on. But then we look at the final work and use those observations as inspirations for further projects – so that's reflection on the practice and the work.

Q: How much change goes on during the process?

A: Quite a lot quite often and that's because we're fairly pragmatic in a lot of ways, in that we have an idea of what we want to do and how to get there but as we start building it, other opportunities appear and they may be a short cut to where we are trying to go but the result of taking that short cut might put a different inflection on the work. And then we have to reflect on whether we want that or not. It's a constant balancing act and this is happening all the time.

Q: And then you have the audience. Was it surprising how they behaved or did you antici-pate that?

A: I anticipated I suppose the feeling of awe – the strong experience. My hope was that people would go in and say 'Wow!' – the sense of being sensorially immersed and being engaged with it – not looking at it analytically but just feeling it and being affected by it. I anticipated that kind of response. I wasn't antici-pating the whole party thing, the fact that it sometimes turns into an impromptu party space. We didn't anticipate that and also we didn't anticipate the whole selfie thing- the fact that you're in a bunch of lights that are quite close to your face and it becomes a very photogenic experience. That was a surprise!

Q: Has that sort of behaviour, and the risky behaviour (wrapping LEDS into hammocks) changed the way you make the work now?

A: We warn the client that it needs to be invigilated properly. That's always going to be the case in a piece, especially if it's outdoors, because in public spaces, people feel more free. If it's in an art gallery there's a certain amount of implied respect and you treat it differently to if it's on the way to Old Trafford, for example, where people see it as more of a challenge! But you live and learn. The only other thing I'd add is that in order to get an audience to respond emotionally or affectively rather than logically and analytically, is by getting rid of any reference to technology as much as possible. . . . the sensor is discrete in a corner, there are no computers in sight, all the power supplies and the cables, the tech is hidden.

Q: *Is it a team effort to do the software and hardware as well?*

A: Yes. It is hard to break down. . . . There is also a fair amount of compromise-we are a group so it's not one person's singular vision that governs the whole thing. I am the lead and this particular project was my idea but nevertheless, there are huge amounts of it that haven't come from me. I think that's a positive thing. It has a lot more in it than if it had just been me and my very reductionist minimalist tendencies. I can't tell people what to do because there isn't enough money for me to pay them properly; if I don't pay them properly I can't tell them what to do. But also we have a much more democratic and positive approach to the whole creative process anyway. I don't want minions. We are equals. I want people who will challenge my ideas and come up with better ones.

Q: *From your point of view, what kinds of skills . . . qualities are necessary in your team?*

A: Well, each one of us has got a core skill whether it is music, coding, graphic design, interaction design, whatever . . . and you bring that as a basis. But also, you need a whole bunch of other qualities: you need to be creative, you need to work with a team, you need to be able to fit in which not everybody can into the kind of structure we were talking about earlier you know where there isn't really a boss, you are expected to come up with ideas on your own and you do all that kind of stuff- and for no pay! We have been playing around with these things for ten years.

Q: *What are the hardest things to deal with working collaboratively?*

A: Working at a distance can be frustrating – half our team on our most recent project is based in Australia. Skype can only capture so much, especially on limited bandwidth. If one group has one idea and the other has another, reconciling the two can be troublesome.(*and in the public arena?*) The weather, and the public: two unpredictable and destructive forces!

Q: *Is collaboration essential to your creative work?*

A: It means that as many aspects of the production as possible are made by people involved creatively. And more heads are good – it is a filter and an amalgamator. We all think in different ways, and come up with different approaches and ideas. I think the end results bear this out. I think the end results bear this out.

The trick is to know when to say 'that's it— we are doing this'. Otherwise, the possibilities become endless.

Q: How does working with others affect the way you assess or evaluate what you do?

A: I assess it in my way, colleagues do it in their way. We often want different things from a project and so you end up with multiple assessments. This is then discussed and poured back into the pot for the next cycle.

[114]Shona Illingworth: Artist Film Maker

> What's interesting, looking back, reflecting across a practice is how certain pre-occupations seem to re-appear all the time, they configure in different ways but there are these very central preoccupations running through the work.

Shona Illingworth's preoccupations embrace an interplay between individual experience and the wider cultural, social and political dimensions. Her film works probe the many layered landscapes of human experience. One of her key concerns is the exploration of human experience as we see ourselves in relation to the exterior material and physical world we inhabit. Amongst the many forces at work that connect us to and between those worlds is the major factor of memory. She describes the role of memory as an 'active agent' that dynamically constructs the present and shapes our capacity both individually and collectively to imagine the future. This re-envisioning of memory as a constructive and dynamic process, rather than simply as a repository of past events stored away until triggers act to restore elements of it to our present minds, is a distinctive feature of her art. She makes artworks that explore individual human experience of trauma founded in scientific knowledge about brain function and interleaved with cultural, political and social dimensions.

Collaboration is a key feature of Shona's art practice challenging hierarchies of knowledge through establishing alternative networks of dialogue and exchange.[115] In her interview, Shona expands on her preoccupations and the way collaboration with participants and experts is at the heart of her creative work. The reader is urged to read the full version online for a detailed account of her practice.[116]

Q: What does the phrase 'reflective practice' suggest to you?

S: I think it would suggest that you learn through doing: where the process of making is central to an ongoing process of both critical reflection and discovery. So that thoughts and ideas and concepts come into being through practice in ways that could not possibly happen otherwise. For instance, I make a lot of 'sound drawings' while creating sound compositions that interact moving images. This allows me to integrate the development of spatial composition and an aesthetics of sound, such as varying intensities and atmospheres, with concepts, ideas in order to create a multi-layered dynamic that activates not only an intellectual but also a critical aesthetic and emotional response to the work.

Q: *Is there a dominant narrative within your mind – something you are trying to disrupt in your own thinking or does it come from somewhere else?*

S: It's often a social or cultural construct that is specific to a particular work. One example would be a video and sound installation called *The Watch Man*, which I made with my father, David Illingworth. My father was one of the first British soldiers to enter Bergen Belsen when it was liberated in 1945. The resulting trauma memory for what he witnessed affected him deeply throughout his life but he never spoke about it. I made The Watch Man with him when he was in his late seventies. During that time, I was working in dialogue with cognitive neuro-psychologist Martin A. Conway and we were talking a lot about trauma memory and how it impacts on the experience of the present. . . . *The Watch Man* explores the disjuncture between the deeply affecting and fragmentary nature of trauma memory, the persistent and disruptive pressure it exerts on the present and the need to create a coherent 'life story'. It explores this in the context of society's inherent need to create coherent narratives about the past and how in those processes of history making dominant narratives are constructed that do not account for a multitude of experiences, including those that are complex, traumatic and very difficult to articulate or share.

The Watch Man was developed through a series of sound drawings made alongside the edit which also intersects with and is informed by diagrammatic drawings made by Martin in conversation with me to capture scientific understanding of complex processes underlying trauma memory. The sound world that was created is explored and developed through an ongoing exchange between these drawing processes and the editing process, which involves working simultaneously across sound, voice and moving image. For instance, in the edit, discordant sounds of a spinning lathe or escapement break through the intense focus on the intricate and highly skilled work of mending clocks to impact viscerally on the viewer's body, voice becomes fragmented – it becomes embedded in the everyday in a way that's uncomfortable and difficult. The work resists the trope of the cinematic flashback and uses sound to evoke the sense of constant pressure of traumatic memory pressing in on the present with an intensity that's difficult to contain. Composing sound is an essential element in creating a structure and underlying conceptual framework for the work. I think what's interesting, looking back *reflecting* across a practice is how certain preoccupations seem to re-appear all the time, they configure in different ways but there are these very central preoccupations in the work.

Q: Can you say what those central pre-occupations are?

S: A major preoccupation is how does one think about − and this is very general − the intersections and relationships between the material world, the physical exterior world − and one's interior world, where one begins and the other ends is not clear cut, and we also need to consider the multitude of forces at play across, between and through these worlds. I think of memory as an active agent in this, both in the present and shaping our individual and collective capacities to imagine the future, it is not just past orientated . . . the way memory is constantly being changed and updated. It is a process of constant construction that's incredibly complex and in some sense, involves thinking about those intersections between how you experience the world as an individual, how you are situated in a social, cultural, political, phenomenological, spatial context; how those relationships are not fixed, they are constantly in motion, thinking about those dynamics. Often, I work with people for whom some event or something has caused a major shift in that relationship. . . . Working with people for whom that experience of the world and the ways in which they navigate the relationships between their interior selves and the world around them has changed so significantly has been incredibly important to me as it has enabled me to think much more deeply about what I would call 'invisible architectures' − the complex social cultural, political 'architectures' that we all somehow inhabit, and to challenge the hierarchies of knowledge that structure or dominate thinking about human experience and the world that we live in.

Q: What is the final form you are heading for?

S: I would see my practice as involving a set of ongoing dialogues with people with different expertise, experience and perspectives, some over many years. So, while when I am in the final edit phase of making a video and sound installation or a film, this is often an intense and solitary process in my studio, there are a wider set of conversations that run through, across and beyond individual works. Often these have very long trajectories and cross through and inform practice often resulting in multiple interconnected bodies of work being produced. I make a film or a video and sound installation or body of works for exhibition yes but in the process of making that I might run a whole series of interdisciplinary forums or events. These are part of the practice, as part of the ongoing work; I don't see them just as a research element.

Q: Are they co-creatively doing things with you or is it simply a dialogue distinct from the creation of a work?

S: I would say the dialogue informs both my practice and their practice. The dialogue isn't just oriented towards the production of a series of artworks. I would say that the questions and challenges of making an artwork help to shape a dialogue in a way that wouldn't exist without that practice. Generally speaking the central driving force of the work, the thing that I find a voice through, that is multi-layered and has a kind of inherent set of complexities that drive me and preoccupy me is working with image and sound. So essentially, making film works, and often making video and sound installations, where sound and moving image are further spatialised to create a more immersive experience, using multiple channels of synchronised sound and multiple projected moving images. Someone described it once as creating an 'affective geography'. There are a lot of different things to talk about here. One is intimacy. So, if I am working with someone like my father or like John Tulloch, who is a survivor of the 7/7 London bombings who I worked with on a work called *216 Westbound*, or Claire, there's a level at which I want the work to create an intimacy with the way that person experiences the world without that person becoming exposed.

Q: Are these people an integral part of the work?

S: I generally work with people over many years and their experience is, in a way, a way into the subject of the work. Often that experience, perspective way of being in the world is very hard to communicate, I try to find a way of working with them to articulate that experience which requires finding new forms of expression. But in that process the focus of the work isn't biographical — I don't want to expose them as individuals. I don't want you to have a privileged access to personal aspects of their lives.

Q: What is it you are trying to do — to re-create their experience?

S: In a way to give their experience agency. To think about its value for how it may cause us to think differently. An example would be how do we understand the loss of memory? What are the consequences of that? How does it affect the sense of being able to pass through time, live in time? How does it affect a sense of self? How are questions of agency played out if you can't access memory of your past? How do you locate yourself in time, place, culture. . . . How can you imagine the future if you can't remember the past? There is always a focus on the individual in the wider social, cultural, political landscape. In that instance, I am looking for a way to think about memory loss and amnesia through an individual experience. And how that might enable us to think about cultural amnesia and cultural erasure differently.

Q: When you have made recordings, how do you then progress the work?

S: I then start to work with that material in an edit, I may not be able to do that straight away though, I may need to listen to many recordings again and again to really listen to what is being said, I often need to transcribe speech, then also listen to emotional tenor of the voice, to really try to listen — and by that I also mean reading transcripts — to the recordings with different sensitivities I might still have other filming to do. It might be something connected to what they've said: because I also listen a lot to tone of voice. I'm trying to capture something that goes beyond a linguistic account or representation. So, when I've made those recordings, it might be that there's a lot of material that isn't there yet- it could be a set of images, sounds . . . those recordings cannot be anticipated and they also shape the work. A good example would be working with John Tulloch on *216 Westbound* I could talk about *Lesions in the Landscape* too but I'll talk about this first. John Tulloch is a media sociologist and professor, who was on the Edgeware train sitting opposite Mohammed Sadique Khan when Khan's bomb went off. He was injured but survived and when he emerged out of the Tube station, the media took his photograph. The image of him became one of three iconic global images of that attack. Subsequently his image was used by the Sun newspaper on the front page with the words 'Tell Tony he's right' next to his mouth as part of the Sun's campaign to support of Tony Blair's proposed 90 days without charge terrorism legislation bill. This was legislation that John vehemently opposed. and this appropriation of John's image both denied him voice and agency, with an appalling disregard for his sense of self and identity. . . .

Q: *Dialogue is an area I'm fascinated by − the relationship between the talking and the thinking and how far that contributes to new thinking, new ideas.*

S: *Lesions in the Landscape* is important in this respect, that work generated a lot of new thinking, approaches and ideas for both myself and cognitive neuropsychologists Martin Conway and Catherine Loveday whom I worked with. Central to this was the dialogue with Claire, and her experience of amnesia. Out of this work came new questions and thinking about the impact of amnesia caused by brain injury on the ability to daydream and the vital importance of the relationship between memory and imagination in both remembering the past and being able to imagine the future and how this could introduce new ways of thinking about impact of cultural amnesia and erasure. The consequences of being locked in the present moment, of a kind of petrification of memory, that comes with a loss of that dynamic interaction between memory and imagination opened up new thinking about landscape - social, cultural and political landscapes- the complex intersections between lived experience and neuropsychological models for understanding amnesia developed in the work introduced perspectives that resist a more conventional linear time-based approach to historical narratives and Cartesian approach to mapping. That for me is fascinating.

David Clarkson: Artistic Director

> I build artistic teams but I also build artistic practice and approach to practice. . . . I think the best artistic results can come out of artists if you give them the space to be the best they are and to draw forth their own creativity.

David Clarkson is the artistic director of Stalker Theatre originally founded in 1985 in New Zealand with Rob McClaren and Bruce Naylor and re-established in Sydney in 1988 with Emily McCormick and Rachael Swain.[117] David has been directing and performing with the company for the duration of its existence. His roles include devising new events from the ground up, planning the production models, raising finance, working on storylines and building the collaborative artistic teams for each show, a process that involves developing a distinctive artistic approach to practice. David is a prime mover who inspires and teaches at the same time as introducing challenging interventions into the field of theatre practice. Nowadays this take place through investigations into how complex interactive technologies can be used to extend the range of human experiences both as performers and audience participants. The technology is a way of enabling the performers to expand the scope and quality of their practice. However, his express approach resists the kind of domination of the human element that introducing new forms of technology can often bring. The impact of partnering so closely with technological tools is he acknowledges still unknown and it will take time and research to understand more clearly what has been achieved for good or ill.

In his interview David discusses his role in facilitating and guiding his teams through different kinds of performances and events. A longer version is available online.[118]

Q: Before you were the director of the company were you a performer yourself?

D: I was a director and a performer simultaneously. I have embraced both roles. I was the founding member of Stalker theatre way back in 1985. Back then I was a performer and artistic director. For many years we ran a model where we would conceive works and then invite directors in to direct us. For many years, initially there was a core team of artists, more like an ensemble. In that way, there were multiple directors. We would invite directors in to direct shows but we would conceive those shows. Then the company morphed into a two-artistic-director model for many years. Each block was about a ten-year block. That was two artistic directors running two separate strands of Stalker. And then more recently, I'm the sole artistic director of the company.

Q: *What does your role entail?*

D: Conceiving shows from the ground up, planning the production models for those shows, helping raise the finance that makes those shows possible, building the artistic team, working on storylines with the team. I think one of the main things I do is build teams. I build artistic teams but I also build artistic practice and approach to practice. One of the main approaches that Stalker uses – in theatre terms you talk about 'devising' – and to devise a work it's very much a collaborative effort from the team. There is an initial template, or a sketch or a thought that is continually refined by a group of artists as we work towards the final vision.

Q: *Thinking about the collaboration is there a particular kind of pattern in your operation that seems to manifest or that you encourage?*

D: I think that relates to what I was saying about the devising process really. But to be clear I build each team and each relationship to each project. What tends to happen- there's usually a several-year cycle, maybe it's as big as a ten-year cycle, where there is a group of artists I work with, that gradually people come and go, but there is a semi-core team that exists usually for several shows. With the *Creature* installation, there was a team of about twenty; with *Frameshift*, there was probably around twenty-five to thirty. With some of my smaller shows maybe there's a team of ten. It really varies from project to project.

Q: *Does the size of the team change the pattern of collaboration?*

D: I think part of the flexibility is being able to operate in a number of ways depending on the situation – situation ethics maybe, or situation's practice. Something both Andrews and I were commenting on is, at the moment as we move into this technology work and as we build our aesthetic, and our complexity, the teams necessarily become larger. So, at the moment, in regards to the shows we're making, we are in a period of expansion. And I've been in periods of expansion before: periods of expansion come to an end and you usually go through a period of contraction so you may have a vision to make a very large work like my next work *Big Skies*, which could have a team of probably forty or so artists but then the show after that, in theory, could be a contraction where we go OK let's refine an aesthetic, let's scale down, let's achieve the goals we need to achieve. So, with each show often we rely on consolidated artistic platforms and we are also developing artistic platforms or artistic expression. So, you can't make a show that is totally new from scratch, you always use some existing components but what those components are changes for each work.

Q: I'd read that some of the people involved describe it as like being part of a family. Do you agree with that? And what does that mean in reality?

D: The family feel comes and goes. I think that's a little bit to do with my willingness to run teams. . . . I think the best artistic results can come out of artists if you give them the space to be the best they are and to draw forth their own creativity. If I'm saying to someone 'I want it done like this', you've got no choice in the matter, it's my vision not yours, that's a one–way conversation which may be very good in a commercial pipeline because it's efficient, but it doesn't necessarily lead to innovation and satisfaction in the team.

Q: If you don't impose your vision, is, there nevertheless a unity of purpose and aesthetic?

D: Yes. It's a moot point around imposition. Some people might feel imposed upon but I can make decisions, I will ask people's opinions but at the end of the say if it's 'Is it 'A' or is it 'B'? I will decide, let's run with that because it's my job. But then sometimes other people might feel they are the final arbiter. I try and keep an empowered team and that possibly leads to the family feeling. Families can be awfully inefficient and there's arguments and dis-function as well. . . . I've done a lot of conflict resolution and the golden rule is if you smell something's going wrong, you talk to it, you don't pretend it's not there. If there's tension between people, if there's something that you go 'Oh god that could fall into a hole. I'll deal with that next week', it's better not to deal with it next week, it's better, especially with conflict around people, to go 'how are you feeling? what's going on? The sooner you deal with those things the more efficient the team is, and the healthier the team is.

Q: If you bring in people from other groups from outside (like the collaboration with the Korean dancers) does that have an impact on the way the rest of the team works?

D: It has a huge impact because you are not only talking about another team you are talking about a cross-cultural collaboration. I've done a number of cross-cultural collaborations, a huge amount internationally. Often our works have toured to non-English speaking countries. I like to think I am not an imperialist or a colonialist. Every culture has its weaknesses and strengths as Australia does, as do Western styles of thought. I try to be as inclusive as possible and as pluralistic as possible without leading to a cacophony, if you know what I mean. Often when people ask to collaborate with us internationally, they have things they want to learn from us and the question for us is, what are we learning from them? That can be a slightly grey area at times but there is always a cultural learning that is a reciprocal process.

Q: *Can you think of situations where a member of the team might shift your way of thinking about something?*

D: It happens continually. For instance, say with the piece we are about to do *Pixel Mountain* in Bogota. We made that about five years ago in Korea. Korea is an interesting country. . . . It has a huge glass ceiling for women in particular, a huge income disparity between men and women, high suicide rates — all the normal fracturing you'd expect in a country that has gone from a village mentality to a highly industrialised nation within a generation. I could make all kinds of statements and lectures about that but, in the first instance, I went to the Korean dancers and said, 'what comment would you like to make? What's an aspect of your culture in regard to the disparity that are going on in your society as you perceive them? What would you like to make a scene about?' And they wanted to make a scene about ritualised female suicide which is a very strong topic!

It was of interest to them because there is a tradition in Korea that women cannot have a voice. The only voice they can have when they are dissatisfied in a marriage, or in a work situation, is they ritually commit suicide. They dress up in their bridal outfits and they go and hang themselves in the middle of the living room. It's a shocking and very telling point. So, we made, in part of *Pixel Mountain*, which was a journey of culture from a pastoral way of being to intensely commodified industrialisation and a reflection on that — there is a scene where there is a ritualised suicide. It's a dance work so how much of that is graphically understood by the audience, is a moot point, but the symbolism is there. I never knew about ritualised Korean female suicide, did you? (No). With every piece we make, I personally learn. People say they learn from me; they learn from me artistically but they also learn from me about process and communication and aesthetic. I think that's what I pass on.

Q: *If you could cast your mind back, were there particular barriers to bringing in the new type of technologies and to make it acceptable to the team?*

D: There were several people who were key to my journey at that stage. My nephew Sam Clarkson was a gaming designer; he was doing very interesting gaming design working with photogrammetry. That was my initial link. I looked at what he was doing and saw the bridges between theatre practice and some of the gaming practice he was doing. I was particularly drawing parallels with masking and the Greek practice of 'masque' — creating a mask related to notions of masking the body or masking space. That gave me the beginning of the template for *Encoded*. I then started working with Andrew Johnston. Kate Richards came in and helped me with my dramaturgy towards the integration of digital technology.

We took it very slow. We were fortunate to receive some funding from the Australia Council which allowed my research and development to proceed in stages. I built the palettes up in conjunction with the Andrews. We generated states, we had conversations, we did a lot of research. I think that then gave me the confidence to move into these other works: there has been research and development in each of the works, but particularly that grounding phase- it was a year of solid research.

Q: *What was the impact of bringing in the technology on your theatre practice?*

D: We'd need to talk through the evolution of each show really. *Encoded* was the first work. I'm trying to think about the relationship it had to the preceding work which was *Mirror Mirror*. There are commonalities with each work I make but there's also progressions with each work. The first work I made with technology had tracking in it, and fluid simulations and live projection and that was fundamentally different from the previous works. My catchall was to not let the pixel dominate the human: the humanity has to be complemented – and really the pixels must support the humanity. I want to use technology to make pertinent comments about the human condition.

Q: *Some say the technology is just a tool, other say it's a new medium, some take it further and say it's much more of a partner relationship. How does it feel to you using those terms?*

D: It has been one of the dominant fields of enquiry. Theatre has many components when you deliver a show. The technology aspects for the last five or six years have been one of the major fields of enquiry. It has been extremely fruitful and rewarding; it has allowed for an increase in aesthetic, a deepening of understanding of the human condition . . . since the industrial revolution, technology has been either the blessing or the curse of humanity. How we use that technology to make comment in theatre shows is an interesting question. For many years I stripped back and made comment on the human condition with minimal technology, if you like. Now we are moving into increasingly high-tech worlds, you can use that technology to make social commentary or you can just that technology to be almost invisible but spectacular. . . . I think there needs to be considerable time figuring out what the impact of that technology is on performers. . . . I think to create a 3D immersive space that is not VR, but in some way, has the ability to be physicalized, will make a profound difference on staging and what staging is. That needs research and development and no-one has done that yet, I think.

[119]**Matthew Connell: Curator**

> The best ideas come when everyone feels they have a say and we get to agree on what works best.

Matthew Connell's creative practice ranges from building collections of unique and resonant artefacts to creating innovative exhibitions that transform public museum experience. From such work, stories emerge that open new windows into old worlds and make connections with present and future aspects of human lives. An important element of Matthew's thinking is how in the contemporary museum context, new theories and forms of knowledge are created and how different disciplines feed into that process. He shares a strong interest with Ken Arnold in interdisciplinary thinking but with a caution that being interdisciplinary is founded on a disciplinary bedrock: The exhibition 'Out of Hand' which he curated, exemplified his commitment to bridging disciplines in its exploration of the interplay between materials, technologies and processes through the work of outstanding practitioners connected across time and place.[120]

Reflective practice for Matthew is an evolving process of exploration and experimentation. Reflection as an integral way of working has developed over his professional curatorial career: as he says: *Reflective practice is helped by time*. However, reflecting solo is not the norm in contemporary curatorial work where collaboration is essential for success. Working as part of in-house teams demands a great deal of reflection through dialogue and communication in a constant search for new ideas and exciting connections. Exploring what others do and how they do it is a fundamental part of Matthew's co-reflective practice. Thinking with others is based upon various types of dialogue: informal conversations, formal speeches with feedback, exchanges about ideas and expertise. Encounters at all levels of his own organization and outside it too, provide vital opportunities for trying out ideas and gaining understanding from many sources and disciplines.

As he explains in the following interview, collaboration for him implies listening and learning from one other. The complete version of the interview is available online.[121]

Q: *What is your view about curating as a practice?*

M: Firstly, this museum has a particular approach to curatorship. We are collecting curators so we are the people who make decisions about what will be acquired into the permanent collection of the museum. Also, we are the people who propose exhibition subjects and develop the content in conjunction with a project team to then design those exhibitions. So, we are exhibition curators and collection curators. . . . Recently, and I think it's a continuation of the impact of information technologies, there's been a move towards interdisciplinarity and cross disciplinary practice. A lot of it started with changes to the way the research was understood – the move away from discipline-based research to interdisciplinary research and cross-disciplinary research which I think has some fantastic aspects to it. Like all changes we love to rush over to the other side of the boat from time to time. . . . I do see the curatorial role as being an epistemological role: we are engaged in it at a high level.

I am very interested in new practices, in innovation across the board. I'm interested in the fact that innovation often occurs in the new connections that are made in existing areas of knowledge. But I am also aware that inter-disciplinarity doesn't mean anything if you don't have disciplines. People sometimes forget that you need strong disciplines to have interdisciplinary anything. Disciplines, do change, of course, but they emerge for reason and those reasons shouldn't be forgotten. It is an interesting point that people come in and say we have to rethink the purpose of the museum and one of the things that people say is 'we are an agent for social change'. I always put up my hand and say 'sometimes we are an agent for social change but sometimes we are an agent for social stability'. It depends on what is required at the time because not every occasion calls for a change and sometimes our job is to resist change or remind people of the implicit values, those taken for granted, that might be under threat.

Q: *How much scope do you have for being creative?*

M: I feel I have a lot of scope to be creative . . . one of the things we do here is we write a collection policy that demonstrates that we are going to collect in a way that is rationally determined and free of bias or subjective which is not possible. If you go back and look at our collections, and the objects we collect are meant to reflect the values, views and beliefs of the cultures used to produce them- that's the basis of our practice, that's why we collect and that in some way those values and beliefs can be viewed in those artefacts. There's another side to that and that is that the values and beliefs of the person who collected are also very evident in the collections. As a curator, I feel it is my job not just to sample: we sample history- there's no other way of doing history, of collecting everything so we take bits and we invariably create some stories. My view as a curator is not to manipulate that to our own advantage; we do acquire this material as primary source material that gives you a window into the past. We can't avoid bringing in our personal biases into our collecting so we should acknowledge that and be conscious how easy it is to collect with a confirmation bias. . . . To me the creative element is in building a collection. . . . The other thing is that if I collect something, that will lead me to collect something else. Just as when I take the artefacts and put them together in an exhibition such that they tell a story, I collect along that way too. As I collect the artefacts speak to me and start to represent things and then I find myself looking for the other pieces that go with it. I don't see an artefact and go 'how does that fit?' I look at how it fits into a story, how it fits into our policy but I also identify stories that I feel are emerging.

Q: Is that what happened with the 'Out of Hand' exhibition?

M: Yes. We developed a new iteration with the advice of the Museum of Arts and Design in New York in 2013 who did the original exhibition curated by Senior Curator Ron Labaco. I changed it to reflect the story of our institution or our message which, because of its longevity which is represented through its collection, I believe there are longer term stories in stories of innovation that are important to understanding innovation. I have a particular view that the very term innovation is so over-used that it is almost rendered meaningless. For me, innovation and creativity arise from a cultural bed. You create conditions where that happens: our job is to help create those conditions, to help create a culture, a sustained culture where the conditions of innovation are always in place.

Q: When you start on a project, where does that come from usually?

M: I carry ideas all the time and it spills right outside of my work hours. It comes from my reading and from my conversations and from my networks. It's really important for me to go to the edges of my fields of interest. Ideas come to me from the collection, from what is in the ether in various other media, from conversations with colleagues, with visitors, from other museums. A lot of the ideas come directly from conversations with other people. For the practice itself, I get an enormous amount of excitement. What happens if I do an exhibition is I have an idea, I have a way I want to go but I never see it all. Something new is revealed every time. Every time I do an exhibition I get surprises, new things come up.

Q: Can you think of an example where a surprise makes it turn in a different direction?

M: I did an exhibition once about a guy called William Stanley Jevons[122] who I was following because I had acquired a piece of Charles Babbage's Difference Engine at auction for the Museum and then attended to the publicity that went with spending so much money. I was also reading and learning a lot about Babbage and telling everyone else about him and uncovering things he had done. Fortunately, he had done lots of things and everything he's done seemed to have a resonance with things happening in the world today. Flush with the success of that, I started mining the 19th century for precursor computing ideas and inventions. I learned about a machine called a logic piano designed by a guy called

William Stanley Jevons. I went, 'A logic piano sounds great! Who could resist that?' I just knew enough about computers being logical machines to know that it was an area to explore. I knew that symbolic logic had had its origins in the 19th century. I found this guy Jevons had built this logic inference machine and that it still existed at the Oxford Museum of the History of Science. I then was reading about logical machines and diagrams. I read that William Stanley Jevons travelled to Sydney and discovered that he had been an assayer at the Sydney Mint. He'd come as a 19-year-old to work at the Sydney Mint. He was already a polymath who had the scientific gaze that he cast his scientific gaze upon everything that he saw and not just Nature . . . (*see full interview for rest of story*).

That's a case where I'm following one thing and I uncover another thing when I realise that this man sat at the conception of a number of the most important discourses of our time. Then I started thinking well how do they all work together? How do they intertwine? And then I bumped into a friend at Market City. I was going for some noodles and saw an old friend who was walking and scratching his head and, as it turned out, thinking about Jevons whose photography he loved. . . . He didn't know that Jevons had been a logician and we started to talk and ended up doing an exhibition called *William Jevons: The Curious Economist.* . . . Every bit of research we did, we discovered something. We were reflecting the whole time. And there was serendipity too.

Q: Can you say what reflection amounts to in relation to your creative practice?

M: Thinking in the moment is where ideas arise or crystallise but I do a lot of reading and talking and reflecting on what we have done, what works, what I would do again, what I would do differently. New technologies, new audience expectations, new administrative environments, new cultural priorities all have their impact on what we do over time. I try to be conscious of what is happening around me or at least check in from time to time.

I like to experiment, I like to work with people from outside curatorial, outside the museum. I like to look at what other curators and museums do. I work with a lot of other professionals especially academics and I like understanding the different approaches we have to the same subjects, issues and concerns. I think a lot about how exhibitions work as a communications medium and that the craft of the curator is to better understand that medium. I look for things that work well especially unexpected things. I look for little success to carry through to another exhibition – iterate. I look for clichés in form and content. (to draw from my lexicon) I also try to stop and look at how successive projects work together over time and how collection development and research and exhibitions work together across the museum. I do some writing and a quite a bit of speaking about curatorship which gives me the opportunity to reflect upon what I/we do. I speak to a lot of students who make me think. I have also had the benefit of having been a curator for a long time. Reflective practice is helped by time.

Q: What kind of collaborations are you engaged in?

M: For me collaboration really important because I don't think with a blank piece of paper, I think when I am talking to somebody else. I have a close group of friends I talk with a lot but any exhibition takes me into other areas. From an ideas' perspective, I really have to talk out loud. There are the people I work with here: they are not all curators. They're 'sounding board' people who I have spoken with over long periods of time who either validate or not the things I am saying and are excited by the same things but also have other areas of attached connections. I am interested in ideas; they arise out of conversations and I don't care who delivers the idea. I like everyone to engage in the story we are telling and how we might tell it. . . . The best ideas come when everyone feels they have a say and we get to agree on what works best.

Q: Do the people you work with challenge you?

M: Yes, they challenge me and sometimes they challenge me just over design issues which is why I insist they engage with the content. I work very closely with editors when I'm writing and we have great editors here and they're talented writers- and they definitely challenge.

Q: Do you want your team to be as creative as you are?

M: I like to think so. To acknowledge people and to give them opportunities. We work in a big museum, we have a big team, there are assistant curators, designers, graphic designers, writers, marketing specialists, registrars who look after objects, conservators, technicians. They are all bright people; the museum attracts such people. They might have very technical skills but nearly everyone is interested in bigger ideas. That's probably why they signed up in the first place. The exhibitions work when people bring their particular skills to bear on an idea that they like. Sometimes we work with curatorial teams and curators take responsibility for different sections: that can be fine but it is really important at some point that someone steps back and checks that the exhibition works as a whole. Team need to be teams.

[123]Anna Ledgard: Creative Producer

> It is my role to weave the web of collaborative relationships with individuals and organisations, to gather the resources and build the dialogue and organisational structures which are essential to the success of this work.

Anna Ledgard[124] is an award-winning producer, researcher and educationalist who works across the arts and bio-medical sciences to facilitate long-term partnerships between professional artists, healthcare professionals and patients. She works with artist collaborators and a team of sound, digital media and performance artists; past projects with artist Mark Storor, include *The Barometer of My Heart*[125] and *For the Best*[126] Winner of the TMA Theatre Award for Best Show for Children and Young People of 2009. Recent arts and science public engagement projects within the NHS have been with artist Sofie Layton and bioengineer Giovanni Biglino: *The Heart of the Matter* (2018)[127] and *Milk* (2017/8).[128] Her work is grounded in a belief in the capacity of the arts to tell powerful stories which can build resilience and connect and engage communities and individuals. Collaborating partners include Guy's and St Thomas' NHS Trust; Evelina London Children's Hospital; Great Ormond Street Hospital; Bristol Cardiac Institute and the Freeman Hospital, Newcastle. Anna was Chair of the Wellcome Trust Large Arts Awards panel 2010–2014. Her work has been produced in collaboration with Artsadmin where she is an Associate Producer.[129]

A combination of reflection and learning are key principles in Anna's collaborative practice that she brings to bear throughout her long-standing relationships with artists in a series of successful creative projects. In her interview, Anna describes some of her creative projects that facilitate innovative artistic experiences in highly critical and demanding environments, a learning process that involves sharing knowledge.

Q: Which word best sums up what you do?

A: Facilitation is very close. I would say now that I facilitate collaborations very often in settings where the presence of an artist is not the norm. It's a big issue, the nomenclature, for me, because actually the producer role, which is what the outside world now calls me (and I used to say Oh I don't like that descriptor, it doesn't encapsulate the complexity of the role) but I now understand that the outside world needs a name and producer kind of fits. But they know that with *me* I have this research process interest so that very often the role of self-evaluation comes with producing in our projects. I am just a complete anomaly but I would say (and this is important to your research) that my background skills learnt as a teacher in the classroom in my 20s and early 30s, fuelled what I do every single day and are the backbone of my practice now. And those principles of inclusive learning, principles of reflection – Schön, Stenhouse – it was drummed into us in the 80s as trainee teachers. I think those principles and values are absolutely central to the way I work with the artists – and I only work with a very small group of very particular artists and we return to each other constantly.

Q: *Is there a core part of your work that is the creative part for you as an individual?*

A: I think I see the first meeting when the artists and I and the clinicians sit in a hospital meeting room with a whole load of people whom we do not know and we begin a conversation about what we bring and then we ask them what they need, what are their current priorities. It starts always in this way if possible – and we might be being a bit manipulative in that situation, I'm not being disingenuous – and that for me is a hugely creative moment. So my definition of the creativity is far broader than the making of the work of art. It's about the facilitation of the conversation in a way that brings in everybody's voice. I think some of those meetings or encounters have been some of the most creative moments. So that is one aspect of it. Another moment I would say, I call them the 'at the bedside moments', the moments which very often are not about what happens at the end when there's a big public outcome, but they emerge from the process where we are working, artist, myself, the patients, the nurses in a hospital context and people are beginning to tell their stories. Those for me are the most powerful moments of creativity. And that's when I think absolutely this stuff is unparalleled in its power in a sense because it has the capacity for people to share their experiences meaningfully.

Q: *What do you think are the critical issues for making successful partnerships?*

A: Listening . . . this is the thing I am constantly asked to talk about. I think those principles from my early work as a teacher are really important here. What makes the partnership work is the sense that everyone feels they are as important as everyone else. Now it isn't like this at the beginning, so our job, because we sometimes have to do a lot of convincing initially, because your busy clinician doesn't see why an artist should be where they should be. However, by the end, or by the middle actually, they do, if we've worked our magic well.

Q: Is that part of your job to enable the other participants to understand the role of the artist?

A: Yes. It's all of our role but I suppose my role particularly is to make sure we facilitate the situation in which they can observe an artist at work and be convinced.
In a sense I don't think it's important to ask the artist to do anything other than
what they would do. So what I am doing very often is providing the frame for
that to happen and making sure that the people who need to see it in action
can be convinced themselves of it in action. I think there's a 'call and response',
responsive conversation going on and that is obvious to everybody. It involves
responsiveness and empathy, a sensitivity to the setting. They understand very
quickly, when they watch the way that we work, that we are really careful about
how we are in a space. Of course, you have to be when you are in an intensive
care unit. So yes- the listening, the responsiveness. . . . Things like having external
funding . . . we are considered legitimate and we behave like legitimate people in
that setting. Often, we are counteracting a lot of understandable prejudice about
what the artist does. There has been some bad practice.

In each project it's different, so for example . . . the practice has slightly
changed. Initially when we were working with hospitals- the very first projects,
I went to the hospital school because I knew I could talk the language of teaching with the school. The approach is always that we bring a pretty open artistic
process, what are your priorities?

*Q: I can imagine that some partnerships go better than others. Have you got a feel for what
makes the most successful kind of partnership?*

A: I think they do go better than others at times. The beginnings of projects can be
very challenging because the artist has to find a place . . . for example, we have
been invited into the intensive care unit at Guy's and St Thomas' hospital where
we are working at the moment. S. and myself are working with mothers of
very tiny very ill babies. We are with them; she is doing little footprints of their
children's feet and she is beginning to work with them about singing lullabies
and putting sound into the incubators. But it has been hard for the artist: it's a
difficult situation to find a place physically and emotionally for herself in a very
busy intensive care baby unit.

All of our environments are challenging. All medical. Some of the most difficult medical situations- the last one with M on erectile dysfunction, a really
complicated subject. The issues around the end of life and dying, that's another
aspect of my life which is quite separate to this but I am an end of life carer and
have had training. That is quite important to understand the situations that people may or may not find themselves in. The difficulties, the challenges are often
at the beginning and the setup.

Q: Where does the idea for something originate, what gives rise to a new project?

A: It's a really good question because what I am very passionate about is not so
much the content (*muses- is this right, maybe not right?*) but the nature of, or the

place that creativity can have in enabling somebody to express something that maybe very difficult to express. That's from my roots as a drama teacher – all of that understanding. Whilst we set a broad context, for example, with *For the Best* our context was what's best for children in a hospital context, that was as broad as it was but very quickly as the work and the conversations started to emerge, we realized part of it was about children's thinking about death, because they were not allowed to express it anywhere else.

Q: *Can we now move on to what reflective practice means to you?*

A: I don't think you can have a creative practice without reflection.

Q: *When you are being creative and reflective, how do you know the difference?*

A: Mmm . . . a really good question – how *do* you know the difference? I don't know if I am going to answer it. If I'm creating a conversation with a group of people that would lead to a project, the reflective bit is that everyone has to be listening and responding and then thinking about what it means together. That is both reflective and creative. I think I am probably quite a reflective person but so are the others. And that has to happen because what we are dealing with essentially is bringing people with different contexts into our conversation. In our situation, the world that somebody is bringing, the world of the nurse specialist, for example, is very different to my world or the world of the patient. I think through the reflection back to the context is an exchange of knowledge which is why I talk about it as learning. Those encounters are all about us learning about each other. Once we've understood something that can be shared in the middle- and that's what art does – then we can move on to the next step.

Q: *Do the reflections feed into the evaluation?*

A: They feed in but all the time we are trying to make that an iterative process. I will be logging shifts in our plans, for example, we say we are going to work with 8 children or whatever and it becomes clear that that is not a context we can work in and we are going to have to approach this differently for this reason – those are really important shifts to log. So, when our intention has had to change because we are being responsive to our situation. . . . I am interested in why. . . . an interesting one where we have had to think differently about what we bring into an intensive care setting. The simple fact that the child wants only to use tissue to work with, which at the time might seem insignificant, can inform an entire piece of the work. That has happened – a little boy who tore paper and tissue constantly and made a mess around his bed (which frustrated the nursing and teaching team). But what he revealed through the work was that, as many renal patients do, his eyes were failing and the tearing tissue was a tactile act which he loved. He then created a whole piece about this. And actually, it was about him having some control of his situation.

Notes

1 John-Steiner (2000) for example, has explored patterns of collaboration drawn from history.
2 Stonbely (2017) draws on collaborations involving over 500 newsrooms and other news providers. Collaboration is defined as: a cooperative arrangement between two or more news and information organizations, which aims to supplement each organization's resources and maximize the impact of the content produced.
3 For example, Candy et al. (2018).
4 'Artworld' embraces more than the term 'art market'. It is defined as a 'network of people whose cooperative activity, organized via their joint knowledge ... produces the kind of art works that art world is noted for' Becker (1982).
5 Gombrich (1972, pp. 109–110).
6 Names of artists like Rembrandt, Monet, Duchamp, Picasso, Kandinsky, Rothko, Hockney and scientists like Newton, Faraday, Darwin, Bell, Einstein, Hawking, Berners-Lee are more familiar to the general public than their many collaborators.
7 The authorship of Marcel Duchamp's Fountain (1917) is disputed: he wrote to his sister 'One of my female friends under a masculine pseudonym, Richard Mutt, sent in a porcelain urinal as a sculpture' which contradicts his later story. Elsa von Freytag-Loringhoven, a Dadaist was reputed to be that friend: see for example, www.nrc.nl/nieuws/2018/06/14/famous-urinal-fountain-is-not-by-marcel-duchamp-a1606608.
8 Piaget's ideas on child development put forward in the 1920s, did not gain significant traction until the 1950s; Vygotsky's work on 'The Psychology of Art' 1925, was not published in Russian until 1965, and in English in 1971, long after his death in 1934. Although a contemporary of Piaget working in the same field but in distant locations, his ideas had no impact at the time. Much later he was acknowledged to have made a significant contribution to the role of social interactions.
9 See Vygotsky (1978, p. 90).
10 Csikszentmihalyi (1996).
11 Csikszentmihalyi (1999, p. 333).
12 Andreasen (2006, pp. 131–132) argues that we are all capable of achieving advances in our intellectual abilities and a greater capacity for innovative creation given more knowledge and the right methods.
13 Jeremy Farrar, Director of the Wellcome Trust: www.theguardian.com/commentis free/2017/sep/30/we-hail-individual-geniuses-success-in-science-collaboration-nobel-prize; international collaboration: www.togethersciencecan.org.
14 Snow (2001) [1959]
15 Cybernetic Serendipity (Reichardt, 1968) curated by Jasia Reichardt: 'The Computer in Art' Reichardt (1971)
16 Fluxus: an interdisciplinary group of artists, composers, designers and poets formed in the 1960s and known for experimental art forms. Artists in Fluxus: Joseph Beuys, Hansen, Dick Higgins, Alison Knowles, Yoko Ono, Nam June Paik.
17 See www.leonardo.info/history: Leonardo: Where Art, Science and Technology Converge.
18 Reflections on collaboration by significant innovators in this field may be found in Candy et al. (2018); Candy and Edmonds (2011); Candy and Ferguson (2014).
19 Harris (1999)
20 Stephen Wilson, was artist and writer died in 2011. His computer mediated art works were concerned with interaction with invisible living forms, information visualization, artificial intelligence. He explored the role of artists in research. Wilson (1999), Ch. 10, pp. 187–208.
21 Wilson (2002)
22 COSTART was funded by the UK's Economic & Physical Science Research Council-EPSRC: http://research.it.uts.edu.au/creative/COSTART/overview.html, Accessed May 28, 2017.
23 Candy and Edmonds (2002a).

24 Connell and Turnbull (2011).
25 Set up by the Wellcome Trust in 1996, SciArt was run by a consortium between 1999 and 2002 of the Arts Council of England, the British Council, the Calouste Gulbenkian Foundation, the National Endowment for Science, Technology and the Arts (NESTA) and the Wellcome Trust. From 2002, the programme was run independently by Wellcome.
26 Glinkowski and Bamford (2009).
27 Webster (2005, 2008).
28 The Australia Council formed the Art and Technology Committee in the late 1980s, out of which the Australian Network for Art and Technology (ANAT) grew. The Art and Technology Committee merged in to the Hybrid Arts Committee in the early 1990s and supported a fusion of art forms. Thenceforth, the Creative Nation arts policy of 1994 had a very strong focus on digital technology initiatives. The Australia Council seized the opportunity to establish its support for new practices through the New Media Arts Board, formed in 1998 and charged with responding to the growth and interest in electronic art, seen as a key point of change. In 2013, the Inter Arts Office was merged with the experimental arts section.
29 www.vividsydney.com: where art, technology and commerce intersect.
30 See Poltronieri et al. (2018) for a more detailed account of this history.
31 STARTS: https://ec.europa.eu/digital-single-market/ict-art-starts-platform. It funds residencies of artists in technology institutions and of scientists and technologists in artists' studios.
32 Stocker and Hirsch (2017, p. 9). Through artists' residencies at research facilities such as the European Organisation for Nuclear Research (CERN), the Ars Electronica Future Lab Linz, the groundwork for mutually beneficial collaboration is being laid down. The aim is to develop a culture of interdisciplinary collaboration by involving experts whose role is to facilitate the process and disseminate outcomes to audiences.
33 Arnold (2017, p. 6).
34 http://lindacandy.com/CRPBOOK/arnold.
35 John-Steiner (2000, pp. 196–204).
36 Stonbely (2017, p. 26).
37 In 2012, CERN's Large Hadron Collider teams announced they had each observed a new particle. The Nobel prize in Physics was awarded to François Englert and Peter Higgs for this work: https://home.cern/topics/higgs-boson.
38 Together Science Can: https://togethersciencecan.org: for promoting the value of international collaboration in science.
39 Squidsoup: http://squidsoup.org: an international group of artists, researchers, technologists and designers.
40 http://lindacandy.com/CRPBOOK/rowe.
41 Rowe (2018).
42 http://lindacandy.com/CRPBOOK/bown.
43 Ocean of Light series: Submergence (2013–16: www.oceanoflight.net/blog/portfolio/submergence/.
44 John-Steiner, p. 70, on integrative collaboration.
45 Pablo Picasso and Georges Braque: in 1909, they began to work together on painting that came to be known as Cubism.
46 The conceptual and craft elements of creativity rarely are seen as being on an equal footing.
47 http://shonaillingworth.net/about.
48 http://shonaillingworth.net/lesions-in-the-landscape.
49 www.city.ac.uk/people/academics/martin-conway.
50 http://lindacandy.com/CRPBOOK/illingworth.
51 Clurman (1975).
52 Stalker/CCS collaborative works: Encoded' (2012), 'Pixel Mountain' (2013), 'Frameshift' (2016), 'Creature: Interactions' (2016) and the children's event 'Dot and the Kangaroo' (2016): www.stalker.com.au/.

53 www.boxofbirds.net.
54 Stalker is a multidisciplinary Australian theatre company: www.stalker.com.au/about/.
55 Johnston and Bluff (2018, p. 349).
56 Johnston and Bluff (2018, pp. 341–351).
57 Johnston (2015); Johnson and Bluff (2018).
58 Johnston and Bluff (2018, p. 344).
59 Johnston and Bluff (2018, p. 344).
60 David Clarkson: http://lindacandy.com/CRPBOOK/clarkson.
61 Cognitive empathy: a capacity to understand how others work, what they are feeling, what gives them satisfaction or dissatisfaction. It is different from emotional empathy in that whilst the person grasps what the other is feeling, this does not equate to feeling the exact same thing. It is essential for making good judgements as in this case, where being able to understand the way the performers worked, to have a grasp of how their minds work in performance, was essential to meeting their needs in the design of the digital system. Bloom (2018), Smith (2006).
62 Rowe (2018).
63 De Wachter (2017)
64 Danchev (2011, p. xix)
65 Marinetti (1909) http://bactra.org/T4PM/futurist-manifesto.html. See Norbert 1994.
66 Danchev (2011, p. xxvi).
67 Danchev (2011, p. 216). The De Stijl group was dedicated to bringing art, design and architecture together in an early 20th century manifestation of interdisciplinary thinking.
68 BabyForest https://babyforest.co/who: What is Baby Forest?
69 BabyForest Manifesto: https://babyforest.co/manifesto.
70 See https://babyforest.co/hotfexhib.
71 Sue and Tom of BabyForest: http://lindacandy.com/CRPBOOK/babyforest.
72 The Frost Collective: www.frostcollective.com.au/about.
73 Frost (2014).
74 Vince Frost interview: http://lindacandy.com/CRPBOOK/frost.
75 It began in the mid-2000s, when publishers, journalism scholars, and foundations began to look at the opportunities made possible by digital networking (Benkler, 2006).
76 Rusbridger (2018, Chapter 17, p. 204).
77 Stonbely (2017).
78 The Panama Papers was a very large journalistic collaboration as a result of a leak of 2.6 TB of data to the German newspaper Süddeutsche Zeitung, from a Panamanian bank (Mossack Fonseca) that laundered money and served as a tax haven for billions of dollars belonging to politicians and elites from around the world. The collaboration was coordinated by the International Consortium of Investigative Journalists (ICIJ), along with flagship legacy news organizations Süddeutsche Zeitung (Germany), The Guardian (UK), BBC (UK), LeMonde (France), and LaNacion (Argentina).
79 The Stonbely study proposes four elements of successful collaborations:

- Have trained themselves to think from the beginning about framing stories in a way that is useful for partner outlets
- Have someone who manages the nuts and bolts of the collaboration at least part-time
- Have a level of trust and goodwill among participants
- Learn new practices and process through inter-newsroom, inter-medium, and inter-generational observation and sharing

80 See Becker 1982 in Artworlds Berkeley UCP, p. 25.
81 John-Steiner (2000, p. 32).
82 John-Steiner (2000, p. 36).
83 Having a different basis for discourse is not a barrier to a common viewpoint when there are other factors, in this case, a family relationship facing opposition from the outside world (Dreyfus and Dreyfus, 1988).
84 John-Steiner (2000, p. 96).

85 William Stanley Jevons FRS (1835–1882) English economist and logician who worked as an Assayer at the Sydney Mint.

86 Charles Babbage (1791–1871) designed two classes: Difference Engines and Analytical Engines. Difference engines are strictly calculators. The Analytical Engine marks the progression from the mechanized arithmetic of calculation to fully fledged general-purpose computation. www.computerhistory.org/babbage/engines/.

87 http://lindacandy.com/CRPBOOK/connell.

88 Kim (2002).

89 Schulkind (1985, pp. 71–72) for Woolf's account of how different kinds of memories are transformed through writing.

90 Flown: http://art-chi.org/flown 1st Prize Art CHI 2016 San Jose awarded by ACM SIGCHI

91 Lumen 3D Sculpture Award 2016: Flown by Esther Rolinson and Sean Clark: Flown is a scalable collection of parts that can be reconfigured to suit any location. The system animates the structure and illuminates the geometric haze with waves of light.

92 Rolinson (2018, p. 326); Clark (2018, p. 330).

93 Candy (2018, pp. 309–318).

94 http://lindacandy.com/CRPBOOK/ledgard.

95 Ledgard (2006).

96 The Heart of the Matter: https://shop.rwa.org.uk/products/the-heart-of-the-matter; Milk 2015–2018 http://annaledgard.com/participatory/milk/.

97 De Wachter (2017).

98 Candy and Edmonds (2002a).

99 John-Steiner (2000, p. 51).

100 http://lindacandy.com/CRPBOOK/babyforest.

101 Kneebone (2016, pp. 3–4).

102 *Countercurrent* podcasts: https://rogerkneebone.libsyn.com.

103 htpp://lindacandy.com/CRPBOOK/kneebone.

104 http://lindacandy.com/CRPBOOK.

105 SciArt: https://wellcome.ac.uk/sites/default/files/wtx057228_0.pdf.

106 living laboratories' Alfred Barr's 1939 invitation to the public to involve themselves in MOMA the Museum of Modern Art is a laboratory: in its experiments the public is invited to participate. www.moma.org/momaorg/shared/pdfs/docs/press_archives/4249/releases/MOMA_1969_Jan-June_0082_56.pdf.

107 https://wellcomecollection.org/exhibitions/identity-project.

108 https://wellcomecollection.org/exhibitions/brains-mind-matter.

109 Ken Arnold: http://lindacandy.com/CRPBOOK/arnold.

110 https://wellcomecollection.org/whats/would-you-mind.

111 Photograph: Erik Johan Worsøe Eriksen.

112 Rowe, A. (2015) see PhD list.

113 Anthony Rowe: http://lindacandy.com/CRPBOOK/rowe.

114 Photograph Mark Sealy.

115 http://shonaillingworth.net/about.

116 http://lindacandy.com/CRPBOOK/illingworth.

117 The Stalker Theatre Company website: www.stalker.com.au.

118 David Clarkson: http://lindacandy.com/CRPBOOK/clarkson.

119 Photo: Ryan Hernandez. Reproduced courtesy of the Museum of Applied Arts and Sciences.

120 Connell (2016): see interview https://maas.museum/inside-the-collection/2016/09/21/an-interview-with-matthew-connell-curator-of-out-of-hand-materialising-the-digital-exhibition/.

121 Matthew Connell: http://lindacandy.com/CRPBOOK/connell.

122 William Stanley Jevons FRS 1835–1882) English economist and logician worked in Sydney as an Assayer at the Mint. See Barrett and Connell (2006): www.rutherford journal.org/article010103.html.

123 Photograph: James Runcie.
124 http://annaledgard.com.
125 www.artsadmin.co.uk/projects/mark-storor-the-barometer-of-my-heart.
126 For the Best: http://annaledgard.com/participatory/for-the-best/.
127 The Heart of the Matter: www.artsadmin.co.uk/projects/the-heart-of-the-matter, www.insidetheheart.org.
128 Milk 2015–2018 Sofie Layton: http://annaledgard.com/participatory/milk-2015-2017/.
129 Artsadmin: www.artsadmin.co.uk.

5

DIGITALLY AMPLIFIED REFLECTIVE PRACTICE

We live in a world permeated with digital powered devices large and small, from mobile phones and domestic appliances to communications satellites and transportation vehicles of every kind.[1] Practitioners everywhere are amplifying their creative processes and the artefacts they make with digital technologies. In creative practice of this kind, the technology is often the material of the creative works as well as the means by which they are made. It can enable a vast range of aesthetic qualities as well as facilitate different kinds of audience experience. Chapter 5 explores the nature of reflection in creative practice amplified by digital technology. We focus on four kinds of amplification in which the digital role is differentiated as tool, mediator, medium and partner. The discussion is informed and illustrated by the ideas and works of creative practitioners for whom digital technology is integral to the way they work. In order to provide context for the amplified practices described, foundational research and theoretical concepts of augmented and embodied cognition are introduced.

Digital technology resides in creative works of enormous variety, be they visual images made with drawing or painting tools, dance and theatre performances mediated by sound and motion capture systems, sculptural forms embedded with moving light and sound, or musical performances in partnership with digital instruments. Powering these creative works is the programmable computer, a mechanism that has the potential to simulate a multitude of different processes existing or envisaged.[2] All forms of digital technology are underpinned by sets of instructions called algorithms made active as software. In his 1984 Scientific American article, Alan Kay draws an analogy between understanding software and clay in order to underline the significance of the versatility and abundance of what computers can do. It is the software that gives form and purpose to the programmable computer,

> much as a sculptor shapes clay. To understand clay is not to understand the pot. What a pot is all about can be appreciated better by understanding the

creators and users of the pot and their need both to inform the material with meaning and to extract meaning from the form.[3]

If we wish to understand the qualities of an artefact such as a clay pot or a Bach musical score or a digital image, it is not enough to know *what* it is made with, i.e. the material, the notation, the software. Instead, if we wish to be able to appreciate the significance of any form of art, we need to understand *how* it is made, by whom and for whom: in other words, the whole creative process. This embraces the practitioners who make digital artefacts as well as the viewers and participants who experience them and, in doing so, give meaning to the material.

The future that Kay envisioned has already become the past and with each day that passes, practitioners are pushing the boundaries of creative work as digital technology opens up new opportunities. People going to galleries and museums are frequently invited to make direct contact with artworks in any number of ways and are no longer 'viewers' but 'participants'. Making digitally enabled works has developed into the highly productive and innovative area of new media art.[4] The layers of formative influences that have shaped the development of contemporary digital arts derive from pioneering art systems, key advances in digital technologies and landmark cultural events. This is underpinned by a fertile landscape of theoretical and conceptual thinking that can be traced to the impetus that digital technology has given to the augmented and embodied cognition research.[5]

There is a spectrum of amplified creative practice that varies according to the design of the tools and systems and the uses to which they are put. Since the mid 20th century advances in digital technology, creative practitioners have worked with software systems and devices to develop new ways of generating sound and visual experiences, often combined. This has become a significant and well-established community of practice. Practitioners operate in a variety of scenarios depending on their motivation, knowledge and skills. Some explore the facilities for capturing and transforming photographic images into visual artworks using dedicated software applications whilst others write computer code that can partner with them in interactive performances where the human and the technology appear to have equivalent agency. The practices are range from using an existing software package (designed and constructed by someone else) for making a video or sound piece, to writing entirely new computer code that embodies and activates the practitioner's vision for a creative work.

Digital technology is continually evolving as new applications and devices appear on the market. Nevertheless, the software and hardware available rarely does exactly what the creative practitioner requires. This is because very often there are no 'off the shelf' technological solutions that match the requirements of leading edge creative practice. If this is the case, and it often is, where such technologies do not exist they have to be created. As a result, emerging forms of digitally amplified practice are breaking new ground and making something new technologically is often as much a part of the creativity as the concepts and visions that drive the practice. Inevitably this practice becomes a research process where innovation in the art and the technology are closely intertwined and, for the practitioner, can feel as integrated as a unified whole. Together, practice led research drives innovation in technology and technology facilitates the making of novel art forms. The role of research in creative practice is explored further in Chapter 6.

Understanding how creative practice is amplified through digital technology involves talking about new kinds of relationships, often complicated ones. The technological artefacts and systems that we humans have created are increasingly assuming identities and roles in our lives that extend well beyond earlier expectations. This is illustrated by the language we use to characterise our relationship with them. The very meaning of words is changing in the face of sustained interaction with ubiquitous digital technologies, a situation that is deepening our connection to them and, at the same time, raising concerns about the impact of such a pervasive influence on our social and cultural lives.[6] We have extended the meaning of the word 'think' because our notions of thinking have changed as a result of our experience of what computers can now do.[7] We still consider that humans have a unique capacity to think in the usual way, but what has changed is that the computer produces outcomes that give the appearance of being the result of human-like thinking. In the beginning, it was relatively easy to understand them as very fast calculating machines that could outperform human beings on the basis of speed and accuracy. As time has gone by, those capabilities have been extended to many kinds of complex and sophisticated activities, from the mastery of chess to diagnosing medical conditions and assessing legal cases. We have become accustomed not only to 'thinking' digital technologies, but talking, listening, sensing, forecasting and even creating ones.

As will become clear as this thread is developed in the upcoming discussion, how we use words reflects the kinds of influences and the changing experiences we encounter with new forms of digital technologies. The way we use language is continually on the move, and, in these days of ever faster communication via text messaging, email, social media and the global reach of online mass entertainment, the extent of change is hard to under-estimate. Attributes that we have customarily ascribed only to fellow humans are now accepted as appropriate for machines. Artificial intelligences have advanced to the extent that we see no surprise in the claim that not only can they execute routine tasks but they are equally capable of producing creative outcomes.

Today's creative digital comes in many forms from the camera on our phones with facilities for image transformation to the programming systems for making and controlling interactive art installations. The range of possibilities is vast and the role the technologies play depends upon the decisions of the people who create and use them. Far from having a unified set of features, the assemblage of digital technologies available to practitioners is complex and continually evolving in response to demand and use. Artists were amongst the first to see the potential of the digital for creative purposes and they continue to lead the way.[8]

How digital technologies shape and influence the nature of creative reflective practice is the main focus of what follows. We consider questions like: how do creative practitioners view the technologies they use: as tools for making objects, as mediators between thinking and action, as media for making or as partners to interact and perform with? Or perhaps, a combination of one or more of these categories? What do these terms tell us about how creative practitioners think about their relationship to the digital in their practice and the influence on reflection in action? How we think about the different roles that digital technologies play in creative practice gives clues as to how the relationship is perceived. Today, terms like 'tools' and 'medium' are commonplace but increasingly, 'mediator' and 'partner' are being used as practitioners explore what it means to enlarge and add to their thinking and making.[9]

Whether digital technology acts as a tool, mediator, medium or a partner, digital technology has the potential to amplify the creative process, but, as we will see in the following discussion, this happens in very different ways. Next, we will explore the how these differing relationships appear in the amplification of creative reflective practice with digital technology.

Creating with the digital as tools, mediators, media and partners

In most developed countries and in many emerging economies throughout the world, digital technology is ubiquitous and all pervasive in everyday life. The generation born since the year 2000, has known nothing else and learning to program computers is part of a normal education. Even so, for a majority of people, how the various manifestations of digital technology are designed and constructed remains a mystery. Being able to customise one's personal devices is possible but usually at a relatively surface level. Digging deep into the software and hardware is a skill that only a minority possess. This means that the extent to which practitioners can control the technology to suit their needs is often limited. This has implications for the type of relationship between human and machine and how we think about the role of the digital in practice. That sense of control over the technology is different if people are able to design and construct the tools for themselves. For many creative practitioners, this is the preferred path because their ambitions for their artworks cannot always be satisfied using ready-made systems. But let's begin with the digital as a tool and consider the characteristics of its role in creative practice.

The digital as tool

> [I]t has completely changed the way I think about creating art. It's extraordinary to think that this is just the beginning and where this technology could go in the future.
>
> – *Anthony Marshall*

When a piece of digital technology is seen as a 'tool' its role is to carry out a particular task. A tool is a device designed precisely for a purpose, like a file to shape your nails or a drill to make a hole in wood or plaster. Many tools have been refined over time so as to be highly effective and efficient. However, they can be somewhat inflexible for turning their use to other purposes, although of course that is possible: a chisel can be used to cut food instead of shaping a piece of wood but it will not work half as well as a knife. Digital applications that are specially designed to modify images or sounds could be said to fall into the tool category. We have tools for improving the images taken with our smart phone cameras that are so familiar as to be hardly noticed. We can draw, design spaces and make movies on our everyday devices using easy to use tools that take no time at all to learn. Software tools such as Adobe Photoshop[10] are designed to work best with photographic images, and, although you can apply it to drawings and paintings, its features are not designed for that purpose and there are better options. If you wish to work with photographs to make art pieces, for example, there are plenty of alternative tools available, as artist Anthony Marshall found when he began to work with the iPad and discovered a multiplicity of mobile software applications (apps). There was, however, no single tool that could do everything he wanted and so he set about identifying a set of image blending, enhancing and combining apps that together served his purpose well: see Anthony's interview on page 205.

Tool effectiveness relies on the degree of skill the human user possesses. As an example, consider the difference between using a mechanical typewriter and its digital equivalent, the word processor, both machines for writing characters similar to those produced by printer's movable type. Typing was once a valuable skill that was essential for employment as a secretary or office clerk. To be proficient required considerable training in speed and accuracy and much effort went into classes for that purpose. Without training, using a typewriter for your personal writing as an untrained amateur, was a laborious process subject to copious amounts of Tippex correction fluid[11] to remedy mistakes. The plain typewriter functions best with an operator trained to make minimal errors. It is a tool for writing neat type face instead of by hand, but the quality of the writing content and style depends on a user's skill. The typewriter's 'qwerty' keyboard lives on in the contemporary equivalent, the word processor, a tool which enables easy correction of mistakes and is very attractive to those without training in typing.

Is the word processor a tool in the same sense as the typewriter? The answer is 'yes but . . .' and I suggest there are important differences which centre on the role of the user and the tool's capacity for additional functions to give support to the writing tasks. If we write a story using a basic word processor, doing the task well is largely dependent upon our ability to turn our imagination and linguistic knowhow into a narrative shaped by good sentence structure and style. Functions that enable you to correct spelling and grammar offer more support than the early standard typewriters but the ideas and stylistic quality are determined by the person's ability as a writer. If, on the other hand, the word processor makes suggestions about content and how to structure the text, it is then contributing more actively to the writing process. The tool is becoming more of an assistant. And there are even more options for writing support available today as the simple word processor is developed into a multi-functional assistant and even one with autonomous capacities to write for itself.

Advanced natural language systems can produce texts and analyse existing ones going well beyond the facilities provided by a standard word processor. These kinds of technologies have been designed to operate in particular contexts, for instance, generating textual weather forecasts from weather prediction data.[12] Recent advances in machine learning are now producing documents which could have been written by a human being. Having a digital system write an essay for you is a tempting solution when faced with deadlines but so far at least, this is not a generally acceptable practice. Nevertheless, there is plenty of room for digital systems that offer suggestions and prompt different ways of approaching a writing task. Searching for information online as we write is commonplace now and better assistants are becoming available.[13] Where there is support for the thinking process rather than just the mechanics of producing accurate text, then the relationship between human and technology is inevitably altered. Support for the cognitive and affective elements of creative work begins to edge closer to a one of 'facilitator' or even 'partner', as discussed later in this chapter. For now, let's focus on practitioners who began with digital tools for creative practice.

David Hockey, the artist, is well known for his openness to new methods and techniques. He was an early experimenter with the *Quantel Paintbox* software which introducing him to 'drawing on coloured glass' as he called it.[14] It was cumbersome to use but he recognised its potential for his art. That was in 1985, when such systems were costly and not made for domestic use. Later, he tried other applications as software and hardware design improved, but the mismatch between the colour that appeared on screen and the printed version of it was a serious disadvantage as it would be for many artists. It was not until the iPhone appeared in 2007 and later, in 2010, the iPad,[15] that these more usable and portable digital devices became a part of his working method and were pivotal in expanding the kinds of artworks he was able to produce.

Hockney saw the technology as a powerful tool that enable him to expand his capabilities. As he said: 'Technology is allowing us to do all kinds of things today. . . . It wouldn't have been possible to paint this picture without it'.[16] He exhibited his 'iPad art' in the 2012 Royal Academy London exhibition, *A Bigger Picture*.[17]

The iPad was Hockney's first encounter with a digital technology that offered fluid and natural ways of art making. More important, it provided facilities that could not be replicated by conventional media and his practice was amplified as a consequence in several ways. Digital technology in the form of tools for production were vital to the pragmatics of preparing for an exhibition. He used digital photography for instant reproduction and then digital printing for creating very large paintings in ways he was unable to do before. By building up the work from individual prints this enabled him to see the full scale in overview. This process freed him from the limitations of painting 'en plein air'.[18] What he thought was impossible proved feasible and, because he had the artistic imagination as well as considerable resources, he was able to deploy the technology beyond his earlier expectations. He used digital tools to paint a 'bigger picture', the subject of a film by Bruno Woldheim.[19]

The conversations with Martin Gayford into Hockney's journey as he advanced his art with digital tools, are full of fascinating insights. We learn that once he had an iPhone, he was never without one to hand. Moreover, not only did he discover new ways of producing works, but being able to replay his drawings and watch himself performing a drawing enabled him to reflect on his art making in a new way. When asked if looking at his drawing process gave him new insights, he replied, 'I think I could be more economical'.[20]

Hockney's experience with the drawing replay tool is an example of how reflection in the moment can be facilitated by seeing an action immediately after it has taken place, and in real time. Recording the pen movements as they happen and then replaying the action afterwards, can stimulate reflection as the artist sees himself drawing and can observe what is happening close to the action, but at arms' length, so to speak. In a sense, he is coming as close to *reflection in the making moment*[21] as you can get when making a drawing, a process which usually leaves little room for stopping to reflect in a considered way.

Hockney's experience with the value of digital technology came to prominence on account of his status as a celebrated living artist but discovering its potential for amplifying art practice was not new at the time. This kind of experimentation with digital tools has been taking place since the 1960s and there have been significant initiatives and research programmes that both promote and investigate the area of art with digital technology, some of which were discussed in Chapter 4.

In the late 1990s, while working on the COSTART project[22] the artist Michael Quantrill, was exploring the relationship between people and digital technology through a study of his drawing process. He developed a tool for drawing manually with a pen on a so-called 'Soft-Board' which had the appearance of a conventional whiteboard except it was digitally enhanced with a laser matrix that enabled the data of the pen movements to be transmitted to a software application on a computer. Drawings with different coloured pens were recorded and could be replayed instantly. The artist was able to draw freehand to draw without an awareness of the constraints typical of drawing software that existed at the time. However, it was discovering the rapid playback facilities that amplified his capacity to reflect on its implications for what he refers to as 'human–computer integration'. Reflecting on this experience, he observed:

> I believe digital technology offers new ways to translate and transform. . . . My approach is to use drawing as a gateway to exploring these possibilities. I am using it to explore the notion of human-computer integration. The idea is to use the properties of computing machines to enable forms of expression that are unique to a human-machine environment where the human is the focus, but the expression is a composite of both human and machine.[23]

Quantrill's artistic search for a better understanding about the nature of drawing was bound up with his research into the potential of digital tools for investigating the drawing process in what was, at the time, an innovative way of working. This process was taken a step further in the artist residency of Fluxus artist, Yasunao Tone.[24] Tone used the same digital tools as Quantrill but with a major difference: new software was written in order to create sound works from marks made on the whiteboard. The augmented tool was designed to convert pen movements to sound directly, creating in effect, a new kind of instrument for performing an artwork.[25]

Amplifying creative practice with digital technology usually requires research to find what you need to make your visions come to life. Identifying new technologies that bring enhanced possibilities for making works is at the heart of what many creative reflective practitioners today are about. The practitioner will search for and select options and then experiment until the right solution is found. But that is rarely the end of the story and often its influence on the practice has unforeseen outcomes. What starts as trying out a new digital tool can end by transforming the way the practitioner works, as the example of artist Anthony Marshall demonstrates.

Anthony Marshall is an artist/photographer whose use of digital tools for making works has enabled him to amplify his practice in a highly effective way. Over several years he researched different digital options for turning photographic images into visual art and identified a set of essential tools to cover his needs. The impact on Anthony's creative practice has been significant, particularly in the way it enables him to experience an immediacy that promotes a fluid and improvisatory way of making works. Previous experience with software applications designed with maximising functionality as first priority rather than ease of use, had left him feeling frustrated and unable to exercise the level of control he needed to work effectively. All that changed with his adoption of the iPad when the sense of unity between hand, eye and brain that he now experiences, is not only more effective but open to improvisation in response to changing light conditions.

> Although my work starts with a photograph I think like a painter. My compositions are minimalist and use the visual language of shape, form, texture and colour. They are created using a very fluid intuitive technique of image capture, improvising with the light on any given day, then making composites by blending two or more images.
>
> The most important aspect about working with the iPad is that it allows you to develop your image ideas in a less complex digital environment. Working with software like Photoshop, Painter, Lightroom and others became increasingly complex slow and cumbersome. Every time you have to stop to think through the next series of technical moves within the software this is detrimental to your creativity, by breaking the fluidity of the moment. It's now about continuing the improvisation letting your unconscious mind take over to intuitively concentrate on your own creativity.
>
> . . . there is an immediacy because the hand and the eye work closely together, whereas before, with the old systems you used to have to type in

> lots of things and use lots of buttons. Now there is a sense of unity between hand and eye and your brain. The appeal of the iPad is that there's no barrier between the close connection between the eye and the hand.

Digital tools have transformed Antony's making process by enabling him to keep many options open at once until such time as he is ready to decide on a final composition. Iteration is essential to his exploratory and improvisatory way of working. His art making is amplified with digital tools that have been designed for ease of use as well as specific functions and this has influenced his reflective creative practice more generally including teaching other artists how to do the same for their own practice. An interview with Anthony Marshall follows this chapter and a longer version is available online.[26]

The digital as mediator

> [T]he assemblage of people plus technology alters how we sense, feel and act.... Technological mediation can open up amazing possibilities to augment and extend how this basic material is experienced.
>
> – *Sue Hawksley*

As well as acting as very effective tools for carrying out specific creative tasks, digital technology can also be used to enable a more complex relationship between people and machines. We can think of this as being the difference between using the

FIGURE 5.1A   *Water Reflections.* Exploring the properties and movement of water

Source: ©Anthony Marshall

FIGURE 5.1B   *Architectural Abstracts.* Exploring reflections in glass and steel

Source: ©Anthony Marshall

technology as an instrument (like a sewing machine) and a facilitator for creating an experience (like a cinema). Digital technologies can enable mediation between a practitioner and an environment. Mediation implies a relationship between two or more parties. The parties participate, interact, experience, inhabit, enact within a set of conditions or constraints. To facilitate mediation between performer and digital system, the key ingredient is interaction. To enable the interaction, you need suitable technologies to create the appropriate conditions, environments and spaces. Mediation technology enables interaction between different parties whether as practitioner-performers or participating audiences, co-located or distributed, real or virtual. They can be used to contribute to the creative process as we will see in Sue Hawksley's interactive performance with a dance colleague and also as key elements of audience experience in George Khut's body sense detection inter-active works. Interaction as an experience is very variable, ranging from simple to multi-layered exchanges that alter over time: from the immediate ('attracting') to the prolonged ('sustaining') to something that develops into an ongoing con-nection ('relating') with the system.[27] The degree of flexibility and responsiveness determines how far the role of mediation can develop into a sense of partnership as perceived by the practitioner. The art of interaction[28] and the nature of creative engagement with digital technology[29] has been the subject of extensive research in the interactive arts over many years.

Digital technology as mediator is at the heart of the interactive digital arts and is particularly relevant to creative practice where 'thinking through the body'[30] has become fertile ground for new initiatives in audience experience and research. When sensor, multi-touch and mobile technology technologies arrived in the 1990s, all kinds of interactive experimentation were unleashed, particularly in body-based experiences. For many artists, new technologies that were capable of detecting movement, heartbeat and breath opened up the opportunities for making the human body central to the art experience. The potential for innovative crea-tive practice seemed unlimited. Interactive art, such as the examples that follow, can facilitate a deeper kind of bodily awareness that offers new roads towards truly embodied audience experiences at the same time as extending their engagement within it as full participants in the art experience.

Practitioners engaged in embodiment research through art have distinguished between sensory perceptions that are understood cognitively (e.g. saying 'it reminds me of when . . .') from those which are embodied (e.g. 'it feels as if I am inside the womb'). Where these are prompted by image sensations, the first are associated with memories or past experience whilst the second can be deeply felt so as to be transformative.[31] These practitioners are making audience experiences which draw attention to the 'inner landscape' of the human body where imaginative and trans-formative states are located. This practice explores states of awareness by creating the conditions for mediated interactive experience; this 'somatosensory state' is one in which bodily perception and sensation is transformed through various mecha-nisms and techniques: e.g. sensory manipulation and digital/analogue stimuli. In these cases, the role of the artwork is to facilitate sensory experiences that confront conventional expectations and pose challenges to audiences faced with the unexpected demands of such interactive works. This provides a path to achieving an immersive state that can prompt reflection about the experience. It can also be witnessed by others and thereby facilitate both individual and shared reflections.

There is a highly active group of practitioners for whom digital technology as mediator amplifies their creative reflective practice. **Sue Hawksley, Sarah Fdili Alaoui and George Khut** and are significant players in embodied interactive art performance that is highly innovative and experimental in form and content. They are all practitioners with reflective research practices that are giving rise to new understandings about the role of the body in thinking.

Sue Hawksley's dance artistry affords new insights into creative thinking and making through the mediation of digital technology. The amplification to her practice that this approach brings allows her to better understand the embodied experience of dance, both as a choreographer and a performer. Technology designed to capture movement or speech data from the human performer can be a very effective way of enriching the system's knowledge but, whilst this may serve the purposes of developing a better, more autonomous system, it can afford less opportunity for taking control on the part of the performers. For practitioners who are unaccustomed to working with digital technology, this can feel somewhat alien at first. Sue Hawksley describes it as being 'extrinsic' to her intentions for her choreographic design. On the other hand, where technology acts as a mediator in a performance environment it can be more integral to the experience of the practitioner such that it can alter how she feels and behaves in the moment of action: *'I was intrinsic to the system'*. Similarly, the transformative effect of mediated performance can extend to the other performers and the audience.

There are inevitably constraints that have to be handled. Working within constraints is not unfamiliar to creative practitioners, indeed it is generally seen as something that can be beneficial to creativity, although this inevitably depends upon the attitude of the individual practitioners. Sue puts it this way:

I would argue that accepting the constraints affords different possibilities that can only occur because of the mediation, so it's a case of weighing up whether it's a price worth paying. I know a lot of dancers who feel oppressed by technology, but often it's because it is new and unfamiliar. They are usually so used to dealing with other constraints, such as stage dimensions, the tempo of the music, the demands of a choreographer's movement style, awkward set and costumes etc., that these become invisible to them. I personally like to set constraints in all my work, such as delimiting and then systematically reducing the performance space or defining specific improvisation tasks but leaving lots of choice about how they are employed.

In the work *Crosstalk (2014)*, the manner in which the technological and human elements interact within the system are seen as 'equivalent' and each has attributes that another does not. There is no technical difference between the way the algorithm treats the people, the texts, graphical objects and sounds. However, this does not imply they are the same and in the performance environment, the two dance performers have a stronger influence on how the work evolves. The intention is to enable awareness of their agency which may lead them to form intentions while performing. But the technology does not have its own intentions and its responses are generated through a complex ecology of system interactions.[32] Mediating technology of this kind affords sufficient sense of personal autonomy throughout the making and performing of a work with the potential to amplify the process. It extends the idea of an agent that acts on your behalf to one closer to a partner who brings independent thought and action to the collaborative mix.[33] If it is a true partner as far as the practitioner is concerned, this will depend upon the ability of the technical system to respond in ways that are appropriate to her intentions but at the same time contribute in unexpected ways.

Sue describes her dance practice and research in embodied cognition on page 209 to follow and online.[34]

Sarah Fdili Alaoui is a dancer and choreographer as well as a computer scientist, through which she discovered the area of movement analysis. Her research and practice centres on representing movement qualities using simulation and particle systems, embodied interaction and reflective somatic practices. Digital mediation is a vital part of her creative experimentation. In dance performances, she creates experiences for herself and other dancers that break new ground both technically and artistically. Digital technology is seen as an extension of the body and its role, as a tool for mediation and as a partner that can inform the dancers about the qualities of movement during performances, is central to Sarah's practice and research.

In my research on embodied interaction, technology is considered as an extension of the body and the integration of the technology as a support or a partner for moving is what I study and write about.

They are media, instruments, tools- they are partners that have their own decision-making process. It is very strong in one of the works I collaborated in called 'Double Skin Double Mind'[35] where I used physical simulation and particle systems to represent abstractly what these movement qualities are in the body. Such an interactive feedback informs the dancer on her movement qualities rather than directly reacting to the postures or shapes or trajectories of her body while having their own behaviour and revealing some unpredictability. This type of relationship is perceived by the dancers as a partnership rather than a control which is very valuable in dance learning and performance.

FIGURE 5.2 *Crosstalk*, 2014. Performance at Arizona State University Art Museum

Source: Photo by Simon Biggs. Dancers: Sue Hawksley and Angel Crissman

FIGURE 5.3 *SKIN*. Interactive dance piece by Sarah Fdili Alaoui and Tamara Erde

Source: Photo by Angélique Gilson

In her interview to follow on page 213 and online,[36] Sarah reflects on how the digital as mediator and partner contributes to her understanding of her reflective embodied practices. She also describes how this is an integral part of her practice related research, an area that is discussed in Chapter 6.

George Khut makes art as embodied experience and studies the process through sensor-based interactive digital systems.[37] Digital technology has been integral to George's practice and underpins his thinking, making and evaluation of different sensor based interactive and embodied experiences. He created a tool for programming, testing and modifying the art installation under construction. He wears the sensor apparatus that mediates the various elements in play — the breath, movement, reflexes, heartbeat, as he searches for what works best to connect body senses and mind states. By paying close attention to his own inner body experience, the creative practice is amplified, in particular, it enhances his capacity to judge what to change in order to transform the mind-body experience. This personal part of the making and testing process is characterised by reflection in the moment of action. Other people are also part of the testing and evaluation process and this can have a profound impact on how he perceives the behaviour of the work as it evolves. Observing others provides opportunity for reflection at a distance when a more analytical assessment can be made. Reflection in embodied creative practice can be a highly intensive experience in itself. This kind of reflection works alongside reflection before and after the body focused action, A combination of reflection in the moment and a distanced form of reflection bring the benefits of embodied and analytical thinking together.

With the body focussed interactions I want to draw people's attention inwards, and to frame these very subtle changes in nervous system orientation that can be difficult to notice. To develop the form for these works I have to pay a lot of attention to these changes inside myself, and then reflect on how the dynamics of the sounds and visuals can reflect this felt experience.

You actually shift your understanding of what that work does through that process of evaluation and reflection.

I think it's more a question of how we can include an understanding of the ways in which thinking is influenced and supported by the rest of the body, and then also how certain practices that focus attention on body and mind – can provide us with unique and otherwise inaccessible perspectives on what it is to be alive in this world.

George talks about the process of making embodied interactive art experiences to facilitate audience engagement in an interview on page 217: a longer version is available online.[38]

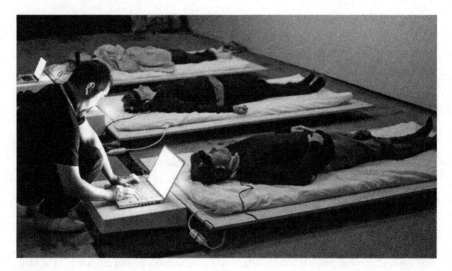

FIGURE 5.4   AlphaLab, alpha brainwave-controlled soundscape and neurofeedback event.
Collaboration with James P. Brown and Trent Books. ISEA 2013, Sydney

Source: ©George Khut. Photo by James P. Brown

Embodied cognition and interaction research

The examples of creative reflective practice previously described draw on embodied cognition and interaction research. There has been a fundamental shift away from the mind-body dualistic theory[39] towards a focus on the inter-relationship between body and mind that is more in tune with creative reflective practice.[40] In creative digital practices, the conceptual sources are diverse: from cognitive science, psychology, neuroscience and engineering comes augmented cognition research, an area that was to be foundational in developing augmented reality systems. From human-computer interaction comes experience design and interactive systems research;[41] from choreographic and movement methods come 'somatic' frameworks for thinking with the body.[42] As was discussed earlier in Chapter 2 in relation to Schön's contribution to reflective practice and knowing in action, writings from the pragmatist school of thought, established philosophical precedents, exemplified in John Dewey's case for seeing the function of art as making aesthetic experience an integral part of living. The march of ideas has been steadily expanding towards new perspectives on the audience and art participative relationship and radically different approaches to the art making process.

Whilst many mediated creative practices are underpinned by theories in embodied cognition and interaction, it is fair to say that practitioner approaches are very varied and patterns of ideas from theory interleave with rich and diverse creative practices. In parallel, new digital technologies are being developed that are integral to new forms of art where the technology mediates between practitioner and artefact; sometimes the audience are participants in the mediated experience. For those who wish to go further, there is much more to explore starting with the conceptual groundwork for the arts and social sciences in relation to the experience of art, that was laid down within pragmatist philosophy and its intellectual roots date back to 20th century philosophers such as Maurice Merleau-Ponty: Consciousness is a lived experience, where 'to be a body is to be tied to a certain world . . . our body is not primarily in space: it is of it'.[43] For the science and technological disciplines, models of mind owe much to Heidegger's exploration of the relationship between mind, body and knowledge.

In the 1970s and 1980s, the idea of the mind as a computational machine began to be questioned and ideas about embodiment gained ground.[44] The role of the body in thinking has emerged from a number of parent ideas: for example, Richard Shusterman extended Dewey's concepts of aesthetics into the cultivation of the body through somatic practice. He believed that amplifying the awareness of the living body was a mechanism for enhancing artistic appreciation and creation.[45] There are several variants on embodied cognition theory: for example, Mahon suggests that the mind must have something like a clutch which allows thinking to proceed unencumbered by representations of our body and the world. He concludes that it is the independence of thought from perception and action that makes human cognition special because it emerges from the real-time interaction between the body's nervous system with an environment that offers opportunities for behaviour. This implies that the brain is a part of a broader system that involves perception and action.[46]

As time has gone on, ideas about embodiment have become established in theories of language to the point where the role of body senses and perceptual and nervous systems are seen as integral to cognitive processes. Embodiment has profound implications for the relationship between body sensory and brain processes. The transformation of the established dominant model of human cognition from one of brain-bound mind power, to one where, not only is the physical body implicated in thinking, but the tools we make and even our interaction with the environment, the very world we inhabit and shape, are now considered to be fundamental to the way humans think and act. Exploring the biological basis of consciousness has over the last twenty years yielded new insights into the brain-body relationship.[47]

For a mind to work effectively in giving every human being full consciousness of the world around them, it is grounded in physiological systems that together construct experiences. As Anil Seth says:

> [O]ur most basic experiences of being a self, of being an embodied organism, are deeply grounded in the biological mechanisms that keep us alive. And when we follow this idea all the way through, we can start to see that all of our conscious experiences, since they all depend on the same mechanisms of predictive perception, all stem from this basic drive to stay alive. We experience the world and ourselves with, through and because of our living bodies.[48]

These theories and others have a long history in the philosophy of ideas, a story that has been told elsewhere.[49]

The digital as medium

> The medium informs the work: skill with the medium determines the quality of the work. This is a very unpopular point of view at present and considered a legacy of high modernism's . . . 'truth to the medium'[50]
>
> – *Paul Brown*

As the previous examples demonstrate, digital technologies as mediators can amplify the creative process and change the way practitioners think and make artworks in transformative ways. The practitioner uses a software tool to help perform a task and such tools can be utilised to implement digitally enabled environments for mediated performance and experience. There are other kinds of creative digital practices that involve an entirely different approach to the exploration of the technology. Artists talk about 'truth to the material' by which they mean exploring a raw material such as wood, metal, canvas and exploiting its inherent properties in the form and structure of works they make. A poem written in Chinese does not translate as the exact equivalent of a poem in French because the linguistic structures and sounds of the two languages are entirely different. Just as natural language influences the form, structure and style of a poem, so the medium and the way it is used determines the nature of any artwork. Digital technology can be seen as a raw material that is explored and exploited in a similar way as a medium for thinking and defining the artwork. Seen as a medium, an algorithm determines the visual appearance, sound, movement – how the work 'behaves' give the mechanism for delivering it: the type of screen, canvass, aluminium base or the environment into which it is conveyed.

In the world of the digital arts, those who use software tools as 'productivity enhancers'[51] and those for whom the algorithm is a medium for the art making, sit in very different artistic camps. For artists working with digital technologies, there is often a distinction between their core creative medium and the tools they use for performing supplementary tasks. The main medium for making an artwork may be computational, that is, the artist creates it by writing a computer program. The computer code is not just an instrument for making something but it is also the very material of the work itself. At the same time, practitioners for whom the digital is the main medium also use tools for associated tasks, as discussed previously. Media and tools are used in parallel depending on the type of artwork. Over time, artists often change the technologies they use when more effective programming languages and software applications become available. How they think and act within the creative process using different media remains a little understood process and further research is needed.

A small cohort of artists has been pioneering the role of digital technology in art from the mid 1960s. Paul Brown is one of the first of the British computer artists.[52]

Paul Brown is an artist whose pioneering work in computational systems as a medium for the visual arts has endured for fifty years. His early interest in generative forms stems from systems art influences and the arrival of the digital computer which, in turn, brought art and technology together in his art making. A recent review of his 2018 exhibition at the National Academy of Sciences in Washington, DC,[53] documents the evolution of his art from early prints in 1968, the year of the ground-breaking ICA exhibition Cybernetic Serendipity,[54] to the present day time-based art. The 'art that makes itself' – artworks that are generated by computer code as a medium – have emergent properties that can bring surprise to the artist even years after they have been created. Paul writes the computer code that generates his artwork and also uses a number of software tools for the supplementary tasks. His visual artworks change shape over time according to the instructions embedded in the algorithm. Where 'A-life agents'[55] are used it is impossible to predict what will come next giving the works a sense of continual change and unexpectedness.

Paul's creative practice includes sketching initial ideas for works on paper, an important thinking and selection phase of a preparation process for developing his digital works. Drawings that show potential are developed further either with more drawings or using the Adobe Illustrator application to develop the shapes more precisely. If this work progresses well, it is then time to start coding the software for displaying 'time based' works. His computational explorations began in the mid 1970s and continue to this day. After using Director, a multi-media software application for a number of years he changed to Processing, a language[56] which was created for visual and new media artists and designers. The advantages included automatic image resolution handling which meant it was more flexible (portable) for displaying works on different kinds of screens.

Paul describes some aspects of his creative computational practice in his own words:

> For me drawing is a form of thinking. Occasionally a sketch will show potential for an animated work and I'll do some more related drawings to see how this may be implemented. If it looks promising I'll then move to Adobe Illustrator to work the ideas out more rigorously . . . it gives me all the coordinate information for the shapes (and the tangents if Bezier shapes are involved) which I can use later in the code.
>
> Eventually if this all continues to show promise I'll start to code – now using Processing (Java) in the old days using Lingo (Director). Problems crop up. A simple example is visual priority, something that can easily be solved by breaking shapes into several parts and rendering them in the order they need to be seen on screen. However, some problems are more complex and these require a fairly intimate relationship between me and the coding agency. An example was when I had to identify how many individual composite graphic elements were on screen at one time in order to ascertain how many colours

would be required in the next time cycle. The solution was an elegant recursive function of which I'm very proud!

My knowledge of computers and coding (and together with A-life and AI) has had a direct influence and is an integral part of my work. Also, because the works have an emergent property I can be surprised by their behaviour – even years after I have completed them. In the past, I have written about this intimate relationship of the artist with their media and comparing it to traditional media like oil paint.

Another example of an early pioneer digital artist is the late Harold Cohen who made a significant contribution to creative computing. Harold's achievement was to make his own cognitive and artistic knowledge explicit in the computer program he wrote called AARON. AARON is art making software that consists of a set of

FIGURE 5.5   *Untitled*. Computer assisted drawing, 1975

Source: ©Paul Brown/Victoria & Albert Museum. Plotter Drawing: Ink on Paper, 10 × 10 in.

rules and a database that enable it to produce artworks in the style of the creator, without the need for human intervention. As a practitioner who exploited the digital medium in an original and ground-breaking way, Harold's use of the digital medium moved through several stages: first, he developed an autonomous drawing system which produced printed drawings which he could then colour with paint. Then he used the medium to make a painting system that could colour works itself. He built another drawing machine with a six-foot display with touch sensors and custom software that allowed him to mix colours and paint with his fingers directly on the display. The finished images were printed on canvas. Cohen made art with AARON but he was always careful to keep control over its development. The digital medium of software made AARON a tool for the artist to think about what makes an image and how colour and composition work.[57] Some of the issues that Harold Cohen grappled with over his long career in art with digital media are explored in the discussion of digital as partner that follows later.

Many different forms of digital technology can be used as creative media. One example that is significantly different from that of Paul Brown and Harold Cohen is to combine the digital with physical spaces and in this way, exploit this combination as a medium for art and amplify audience experience. Augmented reality (AR) art is one such area of new media art practice.[58] AR refers to superimposing digital (virtual) images onto a view of a physical (real-world) environment. A typical AR scenario might be visiting an art gallery and viewing paintings through a mobile phone camera to see information texts or images overlaid on the screen image of the works. AR has been made possible by the development of tools for image recognition, motion capture, sensor detectors and wireless location. These technologies are familiar to most users of mobile phones and motion-based games software devices such as and Nintendo Wiimote and the Xbox Kinect.[59] Adding digital elements to what we see of the physical world as if it is part of the real environment can alter how we view that environment. Virtual Reality (VR) by contrast, simulates the real world and replaces it in the viewer's experience. A variant on this is mixed reality which combines VR and AR and refers to the coverage of all possible variations and compositions of real and virtual objects.[60] Research in the practice of AR art has explored the relationship between physical and digital objects and raised questions about how this changes the way that we think about the interplay between these different states.[61] Rather than directly amplifying the practitioner's process, AR provides a live view of a physical, real-world environment whose elements are 'augmented' by computer-generated information.[62]

The digital as partner

> There is artistry and design on two separate levels; there is artistry in creating an interesting entity and then there is artistry in partnering with it to create an actual artwork.
>
> – *Andrew Bluff*

Digital systems that work with humans in creating live 'real-time' performances and interactive installations function in ways that extend the practitioner's expectations beyond the use of tools and as mediators of interactive experience discussed earlier. As far back as 1960, Joseph Licklider, a computer scientist and psychologist speculated that a symbiotic relationship between human brains and computing machines would prove to be complementary to each to a high degree:

> The hope is that, in not too many years, human brains and computing machines will be coupled together very tightly, and that the resulting partnership will think as no human brain has ever thought and process data in a way not approached by the information-handling machines we know today.[63]

When we speak of digital technologies as 'partners', this raises questions about what it means to be a 'partner'. The word is widely used in personal and social contexts and seems to imply some form of parity between the parties even if it does not assume sameness. Is this any different, however, when it comes to human and machine partnerships? For example, from the human point of view, does being partners imply that there must be agency on both sides? Does a partnership require a demonstration of autonomy in thought and action? Is it enough to think of a partner as the other half of a due engaged in the same activity?

I think that whilst there is no simply answer to those questions, we can nevertheless begin to understand why we are asking it at all by considering current developments in 'intelligent' machines and humanoid robots. If digital technology comes in the form of a machine that looks, moves, behaves and speaks in a human-like way, does this give it equivalent agency to that of a human? What characteristics does a simulated human need for it to be considered a candidate for this kind of relationship? Can such a system, or any machine for that matter, ever be sentient and if we humans think it is so, what does that imply?

How do the forms of digital technology that simulate human behaviour provide insights into the human computer relationship? What do they tell us about ourselves? When artists embrace these developments what are the implications for their art and for art in general? Within artificial intelligence, the digital systems range from human assisted to semi-autonomous and fully automated. Artists are working at all points in the spectrum. In creative practice amplified by digital technologies, human and machines play different but complementary roles.

In imaginative writing, there have been many fictional beings that are man-made but yet occupy a place in human relationships that goes beyond their mechanical make-up. From the 19th century fictional Frankenstein[64] to Nadine[65] a 21st-century human-like robot, people have imagined and constructed creatures that not only have qualities of feeling but are now looking and behaving like us. Nadine is based upon her creator Professor Nadia Thalman who, with a team of scientists at the Nanyang Technological University in Singapore, believe that this robot will be able to relate to humans in a companionable way. Since Nadine's creation there have been even more claims for sentience in human-like robots as the technology advances and large amounts of investment is poured into research into future artificial intelligence systems.[66] There is insufficient room here to explore this fascinating issue in depth, but perhaps it is enough to say that like 'thinking machines', the notion of what constitutes a partner will be decided by the human side of the relationship — for now at least.

But what does it take for a digital system to be more of a partner than a mediator?

In contemporary digital practice, the sense of partnership has evolved to a degree that even far-sighted pioneers did not fully envisage. What is more, this relationship is dependent on how the systems have been designed to interact. If their role is to assist the human in completing a task, this will elicit different behaviour than with a more responsive 'symbiotic' relationship, and here is where the word partner can seem more apt.

Amongst the many different activities that take place in the creative process, there is room for different ways to envision, design and construct a work. A tool for capturing ideas might be a camera from which images are transferred to a computer with functions for blending, structuring and sequencing the images that are then printed onto paper or canvass. Three instruments or devices – camera, computer and printer in combination – are all the tools a practitioner needs to achieve the desired outcome. Each tool has a specific job and whether they are used well depends upon the skill of the user. So far so straightforward. But let's imagine a different scenario, in which a practitioner wishes to create an image and combine it with other images so that when someone walks by, the image changes colour and the sequence begins to speed up and slow-down in rapid succession[67]; or perhaps, the practitioner is a musician who is playing a saxophone or trumpet and at the same time, a computer is producing sounds and as they continue to exchange musical notes, it sounds very much as if human and machine are improvising together. These scenarios are examples of the ways that practitioners and digital systems are engaged in creative exchanges, and what is more, the software has usually been programmed by the practitioners themselves.

Digital media that are designed to be highly interactive and responsive have the potential to become partners in creative practice. Not only that, they provide prompts and provocations for reflection during the making process. What makes interaction with these types of digital systems effective from the human artist or performer's point of view is not a simple story and research studies of these processes reveal how delicately balanced it has to be to stimulate and satisfy the practitioner. For example, Andrew Johnston (see interview on page 73) created and evaluated an interactive sound instrument that was used by musicians playing conventional instruments. He identified three modes of interaction with the instrument: instrumental, ornamental and conversational which gave him insight into what were the most desirable forms of interaction from a practitioner's perspective. Conversational interaction was a partner like relationship between musician and system: when the musician let go of control, the system 'virtual instrument' was able to change the course of the shared performance. This research indicated that, for a system to be effective in partnering with a performer in a conversational manner, it needed to facilitate the other two modes of interaction as well. Finding a balance between control and complexity was a key issue in facilitating the different forms of interaction.[68]

A practitioner who works with digital technology in today's tech world is unlikely to be developing the soft and hardware systems from scratch although, of course, that goes on apace in the companies that serve the tech industry. There are different programming languages that have been designed for sound and visual works or more usually, combinations of both and digital practitioners are attuned to the latest research developments. They typically work with software environments consisting of suites of tools, libraries and 'plug in' applications. For complex installations in sound, vision and motion capture, electronic circuits and chips as well as streams of computer code are necessary parts of the design and construction process as well as wires, cables and gaffa tape.

In *Andrew Bluff's* creative practice, programming digital tools plays a central role in exploring new ground for both technology design and for art making. When designing software, his reflection is a self-generated reframing of problems during programming, a process undertaken solo. In the art, which is highly interactive, his reflections are prompted by participants who experience the work in action. Using digital technologies can affect the way practitioners who work with them think and act creatively, but Andrew can exercise closer control over the software capabilities because he programs it himself. He believes that creative programming is where his strengths lie. Bringing his own thinking style together with coding skill is fundamental to creating creative interactive art systems. At the same time, as he observes, it is a two-way street: '*you also shape the program you are making to adhere to your own unique way of thinking*'. It is as if the software he creates to suit his needs becomes a collaborator in making a work. This imbues the human to computer relationship with a sense of partnership, but one in which the human has freedom to create in whatever way he wants, by contrast with the restrictions of ready-made tools.

Then the software application that comes out of this coding, does act like a creative partner in an artwork. There is artistry and design on two separate levels; there is artistry in creating an interesting entity and then there is artistry in partnering with it to create an actual artwork. When you are heavily involved in both stages, the trick is to spend at least as much time partnering as you do creating. This provides a richer knowledge of what might be interesting to add or change in the creation stage. I think an artist will always use or 'partner' with a software application in a slightly different way than the creator imagined, even when it's the same person doing both. I think it's important to be open and to embrace this.

You have the control to create whatever you want and that's what I love about it. So, if you are using one of these digital tools, you don't feel like you've got complete control to do what you want to do. They've got very hard restrictions that make it easier to do whatever the tool is designed to do whereas if you go into more low-level coding you can create whatever you want to create . . . it gives me freedom.

Bluff discusses writing computer code and partnering with digital technology in his interview to follow on page 221. A longer version is available online.[69]

Benjamin Carey created *_derivations*, an interactive digital system for partnering with a performer in musical improvisation.[70] The system 'listens' to a performer and uses this information to respond in a musical dialogue as happens when human musicians improvise together. Benjamin's ability to investigate, evaluate and alter his interactive system gives him more scope for exploration – more creativity. This kind of generative digital instrument is programmed to produce responses that are not easily predictable but nevertheless reflect qualities that are compatible with the expectations of the performer. The interactivity is crucial because without it, the human has less capacity for achieving a satisfying outcome. With a non-interactive system, one that for example, generates 'pre-set' responses, the performer can control the start and stop moments and the system responds in an entirely predictable manner. The kind of digital instrument that is an obedient accompanist is often to be found providing sound tracks for musical performances in concert halls and on the street.

FIGURE 5.6   *Entangled in Stalker's Creature Interactions*, Sydney

Source: Photo by Andrew Bluff

There is of course, an important difference between the performance with a digital instrument and programming it yourself. Benjamin Carey does both: he writes the code that defines the system's behaviour (as a digital medium) and in performing with it (as a digital partner), he is able to evaluate whether it responds appropriately. The fact that he writes and tests the computer code does not mean, however, that he can anticipate exactly how it will respond to his own playing. And this is interesting ground to consider what makes an interaction with a digital instrument become more of a partnership than a slave master relationship. A software system that responds in an unpredictable way too often does not feel right because its human user has a sense that this is purely random and therefore not very engaging. Finding the perfect balance between responding in a way that is consistent with previous actions and yet occasionally producing a 'desirable' surprise, is achievable through an iterative design, evaluate and modify process governed by design criteria devised by the creative practitioner.

The qualities Benjamin finds most effective for a musical partnership require the system to have a measure of autonomy. This means that how the system behaves is not easy to predict and yet at the same time it should be responsive to what the human performer presents it with in a way that feels right and is interesting to work with. Interestingly, Benjamin's wish for a measure of predictability-what he refers to as 'coherence'- was stimulated by his experience of unpredictability and the dissatisfaction this led to about the performance qualities he could achieve. This is a feature of musical improvisation where a creative tension arises as you respond to sounds heard in a musically intelligible way but also look for and make sounds that are different to what came before. The music is constantly changing but the style should be consistent so that features such as timing, dynamics and timbre are recognisable to the performers. If, on the other hand the human performer cannot relate to what is coming from a software performer that continually produces surprising responses, this feels too randomised and it is difficult to improvise satisfactorily with such a fickle partner.

Generative systems can be really complex and interesting on their own. As soon as you put a human in the loop, it completely vitalizes that whole situation . . . you also don't want it to go off on its own tangent and not be able to relate to things it's heard or to be able to provoke something that's in the style or context of what is going on now. If I'm testing it and a surprise happens, and then another surprise happens, and another and there's no consistency between the algorithm's output then it becomes random . . . I might try and provoke it to do different things . . . if I've been playing quite quietly, and interacting with the system in that way and the system has been quite quiet, and we seem to be in some kind of coherent dialogue and then it spits out something unexpected and seems out of context, there's one of two things I can do: I can try and play even quieter and move into a different area or I can start playing as if it has provoked me to play louder.

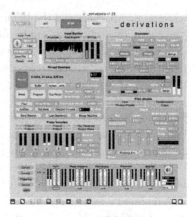

FIGURE 5.7 Album cover for _derivations: human-machine improvisations (2014, Integrated Records)

Source: ©Zoé Nelson-Carey (photo) and Holly Philip (design/layout)

FIGURE 5.8 Screenshot of the _derivations software, version 1.08 released in 2013

Source: ©Benjamin Carey

Benjamin Carey talks about reflective practice, research, writing software and creating a digital partner in the interview on page 226 a longer version is available online.[71]

Conclusions

The role of digital technology and how it affects the way practitioners work is a key issue for any examination of reflective practice. For some practitioners, the technology is a tool to make an image or a sound or to create an environment for mediated experience; for others, it is a medium that defines the very nature of the work; for others, it is a partner defined by the quality of the exchanges between human and machine. As the examples discussed previously illustrate, the reflection is influenced in different ways depending on the type of technology and the practitioner's relationship with it. An open-ended exploratory use of digital technology can lead to major changes in the way practitioners reflect on making works. New tools can amplify the creative process in ways not previously experienced by the practitioner. That digital technologies can add to the artist's capacity for drawing and painting and print production, we know well, but they also can bring new insights into creative work by stimulating ways of seeing the process differently and provoking new reflections.

Across the range of creative activities, there are variations in intention and purpose which can have a profound effect on the practitioner's thinking and making practices. This extends to the many different ways in which digital technology manifests itself and performs interactively. The role of technology as a mediator and partner in the amplification of creative practice raises a number of issues about the relationship between the machine and the human. The balance between limits imposed by the demands of the technology and the freedom to act or perform in a way that feels natural is one of them. Digital technology that defines interactions too tightly restricts the practitioner's scope for creative activity and a deeper, more sustained reflection.

What is clear is that the more deeply ingrained the technology is in the material and the process, the greater control the practitioner needs over its design and functions. To succeed in this, computer programming skills are essential, not just knowledge of how software applications work, and that may mean upskilling or collaborating with a creative technologist. In order to exercise maximum flexibility and control over how a technological system contributes to creative work, the practitioner needs to have a full grasp of the materials and tools just as a painter working with traditional media need to know canvas, brushes and oils in intimate detail. And it is not just being able to make the software and hardware more aligned with your needs as a practitioner that matters. Having a full understanding of the materials affords greater opportunity to create new forms of technology at the same time as amplifying creative practice. The medium itself can be transformed from that of an assistant to one that has the capacity to become a partner in creative exploration. Whether assistant or partner, reflection on the new practice and often the research that has to be done, is stimulated by the activities and learning experiences.

A journey from the digital as tool or mediator to medium or partner is not uncommon as practitioners explore and experiment with new technologies that amplify and often transform their practice. The amplification also comes with difficulties and disappointments. Many find the constant need to be alert to new developments, the frustration of finding something does not work when it is transferred to a different computer system, not to mention the relentless upgrading required of all types of software, a significant overhead on their efforts and are often tempted to return to more conventional 'non-mediated' methods. Nevertheless, it almost always is the case that creative practitioners, having found their practice amplified by digital technology will be drawn into expanding their digital knowledge in a quest to meet the challenges as well as the opportunities the technology affords. It might mean a continual quest to find the best available tools for completing the tasks need to produce visual images for exhibition; it might mean experimenting with different levels of agency in a digitally mediated performance environment; it might mean exploring different programming languages for combining sound and images for an interactive installation; it might involve creating your own digital partner whose characteristics complement or disrupt the performance or are designed to satisfy and extend the repertoire of possibilities. Over the lifetime of a practitioner, digital technologies will be absorbed into creative practice in different forms and perform a large variety of functions depending on the degree of amplification they bring to the process and is highly dependent upon the intentions of the practitioner.

In the interviews to follow, we hear from practitioners in visual and interactive art, dance, choreography and music about how the role of digital technology in amplifying their reflective creative practice. To meet space limitations, the full interviews are available online.[72]

Practitioner interviews

[73]Anthony Marshall: Artist

> Working with the iPad has completely changed the way I think about creating art . . . it's about fluidity and the direct connection between my brain and fingers letting your unconscious mind take over.

Anthony Marshall has been a professional artist/photographer for over thirty years. He has undertaken numerous art and design projects with multinational companies, national and private collections including Laura Ashley, Hallmark, Epson, Chatsworth and RIBA. His artwork has been exhibited in painters' galleries around the UK and sold in over fifty countries. His first exhibition, a photographic exhibition in Sheffield in 1980, was widely seen and well received; however, he was astonished to receive a number of letters from artists disputing the very idea of presenting photographs in an art show. The realization that creating with photographs as art was not accepted by all was to have a profound effect on him and it took time before he became comfortable with the label 'artist'. Anthony draws inspiration from the physical world he inhabits, both natural and man-made. His work embodies natural elements such as the quality and movement of water, botanical elements such as plants, flowers and trees and the urban environment of contemporary architecture. Constantly seeking out these elements provides him with the seeds for new ideas and works. He brings art and photography together to produce some visually stunning works. He takes images inspired by natural and man-made forms and transforms them through blending and interpreting colour and texture and, as the process evolves, so does his visual awareness of emerging qualities that continues to iterate through further reflection and making. His creative process involves exploring, selecting and combining towards his own unique interpretation of the visual image shaped by a love of fluidity, movement, and pattern seeking from the world about. His fascination with reflection, as shown in Figure 5.1 created with the iPad apps, is pivotal in his 'painting with light' an immediacy that promotes a fluid and improvisatory way of art making.[74] He has written about the artworks he has created since being diagnosed with prostate cancer in January 2018 in the illustrated book 'Improvising with Light'.[75]

In the interview that follows, he talks about the vital place of creative practice in his life and how digital technology provides him with a fluid and natural way of making visual art from photographic images.

Q: How would you characterise the way you work in your art practice?

A: It's a way of life so practicalities come into it, accessibility, and getting to the right place at the right time. At the point of being in front of something (say) water reflections it's just a fleeting moment that creates beautifully abstract patterns, if you have the right natural elements working together, wind speed and the direction of the light etc. I see a pattern emerging which is moving fast and constantly changing. I'm already going through the processes in my mind, how and what I might do with this image. It's taken me many years to have that sort of pre-visualisation technique on multiple images.

What interests me is viewing the world in reflection, which fundamentally changes the way I see and understand the environment that I am exploring. I have over the years created many artworks exploring the movement of water, these images draw their inspiration from the extraordinary properties of water. More than two thirds of the earth's surface is covered with liquid water. Pure water has no colour, taste or smell. A pinhead-size drop contains about one billion molecules, and these strongly attract each other especially at the surface, where their mutual attraction forms a strong skin known as surface tension. Under the right conditions this creates the illusion that the water has changed viscosity, allowing complex abstract patterns and colours to form for a fleeting moment on the surface. These reflections are constantly changing which is both mesmeric and metaphysical, the changing light and wind speed on any given day only adds to the dynamic.

I visit my locations many times as it is essential for me to form an intimate knowledge and connection to the landscape. I never arrive at a location by accident only by design. I can only create these images when the elements conspire to give just the right conditions, wind speed and direction and quality of the light which is constantly changing throughout the year. Put simply I have to get myself to the right place at the right time, whilst endeavouring to understand the local weather patterns, it is the same for all my locations.

Recently I was diagnosed with Prostate Cancer, inevitably I had many scans including MRI Scans of my spine were undertaken, it had never occurred to me that searching for patterns of cancer my own body would ever take place. Artists have long been aware of the therapeutic benefits of the creative process I believe it is fundamental to my future wellbeing. It was very important to me to connect this personal abstract image to the landscape, it was created using an Image of a tree in winter in the Botanical Gardens and an MRI scan of my spine. It is skeletal outline of tree combined with a piece of my own skeleton. Creatively

I found this a powerful statement which has had a very Positive effect on the way I view My ongoing illness.

Q: Take me through the process of taking a photo and using an iPad to change it.

A: Although my work starts with a photograph I think like a painter. My compositions are minimalist and use the visual language of shape, form, texture and colour. They are created using a very fluid intuitive technique of image capture, improvising with the light on any given day, then making composites by blending two or more images. Maintaining the integrity of the high-resolution sketches throughout is paramount as they will be used at a later stage to create the large exhibition artworks. In essence, this means retaining the file size of the original photographic sketch throughout the entire process.

This is where the improvisation kicks in. Now I have a new set of well-balanced composed photographic sketches to add to my archive. I call them sketches because none of the images at this stage would stand alone as an individual piece of work, they will only make sense when combined with other images. This is where I start to fundamentally change the sketches, intuitively bringing images together from my archive (around 1000 images) to try to create a finished piece of artwork, modifying shape, form, texture and colour. I usually start by changing the texture, and to this end I used a couple of my apps to create a series of textures to choose from. I will then add textures to both foreground and background images. Then I need to decide on the key foreground image, this is the one that will have the right compositional content, then blending a number of background images on to the foreground image (composites), also introducing some colour changes. I don't make a written or mental note of any of this work, I am just improvising with the material in my own archive.

The last stage of this work is finishing, in other words what am I going to do with this work. At some stage I will make a book but first I will be thinking about an exhibition and what form that might take. I have retained the file size of the original photograph throughout, which means I could make artworks over a metre wide. I have had a great deal of experience in transferring images onto a wide range of substrates such as textiles, metal, hand-made papers, ceramic, leather, silk and glass. If I take a conventional route of making a paper print and framing that would be fine, but by transferring onto glass the artwork could be both back lit and also lit from the top and sides. They can also be used inside or outside, which means that it would be in itself interactive, changing with the light, instead of just being passive. Therefore, they continue improvising even after the artwork is finished. I must also be aware that every time I use a different substrate, I will need to modify my artwork to suit a different process, lithographic printing, digital printing and textile printing etc.

Q: What effect has using the various iPad apps had on your creative process?

A: The most important aspect about working with the iPad is that it allows you to develop your image ideas in a less complex digital environment. Working with software like Photoshop, Painter, Lightroom and others became increasingly complex slow and cumbersome. Every time you have to stop to think through the next series of technical moves within the software this is detrimental to your creativity, by breaking the fluidity of the moment. It's now about continuing the improvisation letting your unconscious mind take over to intuitively concentrate on your own creativity. There are six apps all of which have been designed to do different things. I don't necessarily use them for the original intended use.

All the technical aspects I already know (tacit knowledge) it's now about continuing the improvisation letting your unconscious mind take over to intuitively concentrate on your own creativity. I call this process 'Improvising with Light'.

One of the extraordinary things you can do with the Pad is that I will sit down maybe after breakfast and I've just got this new body of work in there that always excites me because I don't know what I am going to do with it. I will sit while having a coffee with the iPad and start playing. There are things now I know instinctively that I can do that I know will be really interesting. And you don't have to stop doing everything else and go into a totally separate room and get your overalls on and start throwing the paint around. That is, I think, a great boon. And there's a digital pencil in my bag so I can draw with that and even that is now digital so I can program it to do certain things. It is just amazing to me.

When drawing using the iPad, there is an immediacy because the hand and the eye work closely together, whereas before, with the old systems you used to have to type in lots of things and use lots of buttons. Now there is a sense of unity between hand and eye and your brain. The appeal of the iPad is that there's no barrier between the close connection between the eye and the hand. . . . Most of the seven apps I now use have been around for some time, which means they have been developed and upgraded for a number of years. I chose each app to fulfil a specific role and to integrate with the other apps I use, there is real complexity here experimentation is the key. Working with the iPad has completely changed the way I think about creating art, it's about fluidity and the direct connection between my brain and fingers. It's extraordinary to think that this is just the beginning and where this technology could go in the future.

[76]Sue Hawksley: Dance Artist

> Technological mediation can open up amazing possibilities to augment and extend how this basic material is experienced.

Sue Hawksley is a dance artist and practitioner researcher currently based in Adelaide.[77] She trained at the Royal Ballet School in London and has performed with Rambert Dance Company, Mantis, Scottish Ballet and others. She has worked with choreographers Merce Cunningham, Trisha Brown, Siobhan Davies, Richard Alston, Ashley Page and Michael Clark, among others. She is artistic director of *articulate animal* – a platform for her critical and creative inquiry into embodiment, movement and environment, often within the context of interdisciplinary and collaborative practices. Sue holds a practice-led PhD from the University of Edinburgh.[78] She combines her dance practice with research investigations into the nature of felt experience and what it reveals about embodied knowledge. Sue's research employs choreographic and somatic practices that are mediated through performance and technology.[79] As a trained dancer and choreographer, she views her movement capability as a research tool that, in combination with the mediation of digital technology, affords new insights into the process. The amplification to her practice that this brings allows her to better understand the embodied experience of dance, both as a choreographer and a performer. Underlying her thinking is the idea that the body can inform creative cognition and that her choreographic practice can be used as a mode of enquiry to explore and reveal different kinds of embodiment. She believes that the movement awareness practices she has identified through her research have the potential not only to contribute to embodied understanding, but also to enrich everyday life through heightened reflective capability.

There is considerable impact on dancers working in complex interactive performance environments. To address the problem of heavy demand on their cognitive and embodied capacities, she developed what she calls an 'attention gym' to prepare performers for working in technologically mediated environments. In this way, her work in embodied practice and research involves creating solutions to some of the impacts that occur, not just identifying questions and problems. In this way, an iterative cycle of moving-reflecting-moving again (differently) generates insights that prompt further research and importantly, strategies and support for amplifying the dancer's experience of the interactive performance environment. In a certain sense, this process is akin to action research methodology which involves introducing a new way of doing something into a situation, observing and reflecting on the result of that intervention, from which new practices are devised to address the changed situation.

Crosstalk is an interactive collaborative performance work.[80] The participants can be either expert or not: in an art gallery, people on short visits can interact through the system with each other and the visual and sound elements. The performance begins with two dancers speaking descriptions of each other, and then setting up a score for operating as part of the system. Using voice-recognition software their words are written and projected onto a screen, and existing as virtual 3-D text-objects in the interactive virtual space. When the performers collide with the virtual text-objects this causes them to move.[81] As the texts collide with one another, new texts and sounds are created by an interpretative and generative grammar engine that shapes the interaction between all participating elements.

Sue's work is discussed in chapter 5 in relation to digital technology for mediated creative practice. An interview follows in which she talks about her dance practice and research in embodied cognition. Her written responses to my questions were preceded by a conversation at her studio in Cherryville in the Adelaide Hills.

Q: *How would you describe the new forms of knowledge identified in your PhD research?*

S: I think novel methods. My approach was heuristic, iterative and itinerative.[82] The aim was to 'follow the materials' as Ingold puts it, with the primary materials being movement, dance and the body, and a concern to apprehend notions of embodied cognition and knowledge through embodied creative practice – doing to understand. The particular methodologies for addressing each new question that arose in the course of the research evolved out of the creative practice, and it is unlikely I could have designed them at the start of the project. I was particularly concerned to give validity to embodied thinking and knowing, which tend to be classed more as 'experience' according to traditional academic definitions of Knowledge.

Q: *Can you give an example of a novel contribution?*

S: These questions about gesture were exciting and unexpected, revealed to me through my engagement with the creative task of talking-while-dancing. Much current research argues that the activity of gesturing and gesticulation plays a role in our thinking while speaking. This seemed to be reinforced in my work when the hands were taken up with following dance phrases and therefore not available to gesticulate, it became harder to think, or vice versa, hands getting drawn into gesture couldn't follow the dance logic. At the time, I knew little of the field of gesture research and subsequent reading in this area indicates that mine was a very lateral approach, which could potentially be used to positively trouble some of the classic methods, although there are clear difficulties for designing a quantitative methodology! Importantly I see these kinds of questions as affirming the value of creative inquiry.

Q: *Can you say more about what the technology mediation comprises from the practitioner-performer perspective, as distinct from how a system developer would characterise it?*

S: I would say (and this is a major generalisation!) that a systems developer tends to make a system as a tool for people to use, something separate or external from them that mediates how they feel or experience themselves or the world, for example, by them using or inhabiting it. As a practitioner, I am really interested in how the assemblage of people plus technology (low or hi-tech) alters how we sense, feel and act. Mediation affording agency rather than imposing objectification. As a performer, I am interested in how mediation allows an audience to gain a different perspective and insight on their or the performer's experience. Dance in its most basic form, is a very straightforward medium – bodies in movement in gravity. Technological mediation can open up amazing possibilities to augment and extend how this basic material is experienced. I can give two examples, one where I feel I characterised 'the system' as extrinsic to me, and one where I feel I had agency throughout the making and performing of the work – I was intrinsic to the system.

In an early collaboration with visual artist Simon Biggs, *I am, I was, a dying swan* (2001) I approached him with a choreographic idea for a version of Pavlova's famous solo, for which I wanted a visual environment to create a decay effect. He set up a system with three video projectors and three video cameras in a linear series, using digital delay to create temporal and visual degradation. Each camera was filming the projection of the previous one. I had very little experience at that time of working with technological mediation, so I approached it as a system separate from myself. I immersed myself in the system throughout the choreographic process and allowed the resultant dance work to be shaped by the tight constraints. For example, to be visible on a particular screen requires precise placing and timing of my actions, which creates huge tension in the resultant dance work. If I had developed my choreographic ideas out with the system, I doubt I would have chosen such tension levels.

Q: *Does the mediation allow the performer sufficient creative agency?*

S: The constraints in a work such as *Crosstalk* are very tight: the camera angles determine the size (small!) and shape of the interactive area, and the positions of the performers relative to each other so they do not occlude on another. The speech-to-text software requires clear articulation of words, etc. It can be frustrating and feel like a loss of freedom. But I would argue that accepting the constraints affords different possibilities that can only occur because of the mediation, so it's a case of weighing up whether it's a price worth paying. I know a lot of dancers who feel oppressed by technology, but often it's because it is new and unfamiliar. They are usually so used to dealing with other constraints, such as stage dimensions, the tempo of the music, the demands of a choreographer's movement style, awkward set and costumes etc., that these become invisible to them. I personally like to set constraints in all my work, such as delimiting and then systematically reducing the performance space or defining specific improvisation tasks but leaving lots of choice about how they are employed. Within these boundaries, I'm interested in how people solve the problems created by them, in witnessing their creative agency at play.

[83]Sarah Fdili Alaoui: Artist-Dance Maker

> In my research on embodied interaction, technology is considered as an extension of the body and the integration of the technology as a support or a partner for moving is what I study and write about.

Sarah Fdili Alaoui grew up in Morocco where she trained as a dancer in ballet and later in contemporary dance through which she discovered improvisation. Unusually she was also a gifted student in mathematics, a combination of movement and number that was to have a profound influence on her subsequent direction in education and life. As she studied for her master's degree in applied mathematics she engaged in yoga and somatic practices but it was not until she did her PhD[84] that these parallel paths came together. Discovering the intersection of dance with mathematics and computing through movement analysis was a revelatory moment when her creative and analytical talents found a natural home. This was the start of an extraordinary trajectory in research and practice that centres on movement qualities and embodied interaction. A key challenge for her resides in how to articulate and share the knowledge that emerges from 'felt movement'. Achieving an understanding of the relationship between the sensory body and the cognitive mind is explored through creating opportunities for observing movement both of the self and of others.[85] She is currently assistant professor at LRI-Université Paris-Sud and the INRIA *Exsitu* research team, teaches at a Dance conservatory in Paris and a dance collective on productions: Skin',[86]'Radical Choreographic Object'[87] and 'Ergonomics'[88]

In her interview, Sarah reflects on how digital technology contributes to her understanding of her reflective embodied practices.

Q: Could you say something about the way a new project begins, takes hold and starts to develop into something concrete?

S: I start sketching ideas, things I have put on paper from my readings, what I have seen, felt or experienced. The reason why I call myself an artist because a lot of what I do is for the creative process. But on the way knowledge is emerging and that knowledge has an academic value and a creative value. I like to give both an importance.

Q: *Is digital technology an answer to your questions or is it a way of provoking questions?*

S: They are ways of provoking my questions and ways of provoking a certain response or an opportunity for an exploration. . . . And then I use the somatic practice, which is an additional set of tools for observation, to be attuned to one another, to train your kinaesthetic empathy, to listen to what's going on in the body and how you observe it, how you make sense of it, how you translate it. . . . There have been various tools I have developed. Most of them are whole patches filled with programs and mappings. I can't say it was completely mine because some of it you grab from your colleague who has developed it. It raises a question of what belongs to who, which is a very interesting question in Computer Science, but also in Dance, because I borrow some of the techniques from choreographers with whom I train and different somatic practices just as much as I borrow programs and algorithms I find that I combine together to do the whole work. I've worked a lot with sound and image as part of the output that makes the dramaturgy of the piece and with whole body interaction so a lot of the tools I used were for motion capture. I recently worked a lot with EMGs for muscle activity[89] and IMUs for acceleration[90] as I started to be more interested in the Laban Effort qualities[91] that can be accessed via the forcefulness and the sense of acceleration of the movement (among others). I would say I have a collection of tools and I open up that box and choose which tool goes with what. For example, my last piece, which I choreographed recently called 'Skin' is perhaps too complex because I have chosen to use three different types of tools or instruments or interactions, one of which is machine learning for movement recognition. We filmed the whole piece in a remote house in Marseille in the south of France. There is a discourse or an interaction between what the dancers are doing on stage and the film that is triggered through the interaction and via a machine-learning algorithm. I am using Myos[92] for muscle activity but also proximity sensors and heart beat sensors. The muscle activity is recognized by the machine learning module and that triggers the corresponding videos in real time on stage. There is another part where the heartbeat is interacting with the sound rhythm – the tempo of the music for each of the dancers increases or decreases as their activity increases/decreases.

Q: *What sort of questions are you asking when creating a piece with tools for interaction?*

S: It's called 'Skin' because it's about that home of the self and how the skin is the border of that home of the self and how what is given to see is always what is outside of that. So, what can we capture from the inside of the 'home' and what intimacy does it allow for? Sensuality for example. And how much of that do we allow ourselves to show? And the reason why we are filming this whole piece in a house in Marseille is a metaphor of that house. There are two female dancers, very beautiful dancers that are walking us through different scenes and the whole piece is filmed as a film with different scenes. There is a narrative around it where you discover different parts of their lives, of their beings as they are on stage and the technology mediates the discovery throughout the whole piece.

Q: *You seem to be putting into practice the philosophical notion that our minds extend into our bodies and vice versa, the body extends into the mind. Can you say more about how you see that?*

S: There are multiple ways I use phenomenology or embodiment. One way is the methodology in which you discover through the body – the body is part of the knowledge. I constantly refer to that knowledge as knowledge when I am writing even in my academic work. I no longer or very rarely do controlled experiments, controlling different parameters and trying to get a person to show you whether they are faster or more accurate etc. In all of the work I do there is constantly the questions of how does the body respond and how do we make sense of it from a cognitive and embodied way? ... If I add a technology, if I give you a tool, a hammer, are you thinking about the hammer while you are ham-mering that nail? No you are not because that hammer has become an extension of your hand. And that nail, you know exactly how to move that shoulder and that elbow and that hand to nail that nail into the wall with impressive skills that your body completely understands. Our paradigm is that these tools might be digital, these technologies might be beyond that physical hammer but they work with the same kind of principles. These are the principles I'm interested in.

In my research on embodied interaction, technology is considered as an extension of the body and the integration of the technology as a support or a partner for moving is what I study and write about. We have reflected on this with my co-authors in many papers.[93] The complexity with these systems is extremely interesting I find. You can maybe predict what one of the particles does and then you add another particle and the complexity increases even more and with more numbers it becomes a complex system even if you want to give it certain physical qualities, there's always a certain amount of unpredictability and uncertainty. I think a system that brings opportunities and unpredictability is more interesting for a dancer than a system that allows you only to control as if you would have a remote control. That's very limiting. The embodied cogni-tion part is that I am always curious about how we integrate things in our body and how they make sense and how they start to be choreographic opportunities. I am attempting to do that by learning different techniques: the 'explicitation' technique[94] is part of my attempt to reconcile that and to get to the richness of what is felt, what is experienced and make an account of that and to build an academic knowledge as well.

Q: *What place does reflection have in your work?*

S: Reflection is a big part of it. There are times when you reflect on the outcome of an iteration, and you have to throw everything out. You have to accept to not get attached to anything. And the work itself is what matters, so in the last piece

SKIN, a student spent six months developing a hardware for capturing touch and heartbeat, at the end I throw it away because it wasn't as reliable as I needed and used mobile phones instead. It took me three days to make that decision, but eventually I did. Reflection was what helped with that, keeping an eye on where you are going, re-thinking the whole and not attaching to the details and definitely not to the technique . . . a lot of the practitioners we were working with were dealing with the struggle of not being able to articulate and make sense of what they felt in order for it to be operationalised from a design perspective.

The work of Varela[95] has allowed it to shift a little bit. The fact that you are claiming you have something to learn from your body is a big claim. I believe in this 100 per cent and that's what I am doing. It's the reason why I go to the studio. And there are some great challenges in how much of this knowledge can we make available and how do we make it valid? How can we perceive it as a valid type of knowledge? And that's where the reflection becomes really important; beyond your own practice it becomes knowledge you can share. I think you need a simple connection to the body. The easiest way is to have an embodied practice.

Q: *Is the partnering with the technologies a vital part of your creative exploration?*

S: They are media, instruments, tools – they are partners that have their own decision-making process. It is very strong in one of the works I collaborated in called 'Double Skin Double Mind'[96] where I used physical simulation and particle systems to represent abstractly what these movement qualities are in the body. Such an interactive feedback informs the dancer on her movement qualities rather than directly reacting to the postures or shapes or trajectories of her body while having their own behaviour and revealing some unpredictability. This type of relationship is perceived by the dancers as a partnership rather than a control which is very valuable in dance learning and performance. I have also used this type of interactive systems in a large-scale installation called 'A Light Touch'.[97] The visuals are responsive and have self-agency. They as well create an environment that seems to be alive in its own way. It was extremely impressive how much they were perceived as expressing those particle systems even if they didn't represent a body, they didn't represent anything concrete you could actually refer to but their dynamic and their behaviour was perceived as something that is physical and human related to movement qualities in dance. And that system, because of the physics behind it is responsible but at the same time it has its own dynamic, its own qualities and is also perceived as its own thing. People say it's responsive but also alive. In that sense, we start to talk about partners because partners don't only mimic what you are doing or tell you something about what you are doing but give you an opportunity by making choices.

[98]George Poonkhin Khut: Artist-Producer

> An important feature of reflective practice for me, is having some research questions underpinning your creative practice . . . there are processes of reflection **in** the work you do but I ultimately, it's reflection on action that is really pivotal in terms of deciding the kind of work you want to bring into the world, what you want people to pay attention to. It has to be some form of purposeful action with some intent to bring into the world some way of understanding, relating and experiencing.

George Poonkhin Khut is an artist who makes bio-sensing interactive and participatory artworks.[99] He completed his studies in fine arts at the University of Tasmania, in 1994, where he studied painting, sculpture, ceramics, video and electronic music. His Doctorate of Creative Arts from the University of Western Sydney, Australia explored the development and evaluation of participant-centred biofeedback-based interactive artworks. He teaches interactive art and design at the University of New South Wales Faculty of Art & Design and pursues his research interests in parallel with projects in health environments,[100] for example, The *Heart Library* Project and the *BrightHearts* research project at The Children's Hospital at Westmead Kids Rehab.

Because research is integral to practice, George's process is articulated in terms of questions, goals and outcomes for which a clear method is defined. Always there are questions, from the wider issues about identity and the role of art in culture to the detail of the interaction design in terms of sound quality or visual clarity. He is searching for a deeper understanding into the way we experience and conceptualise our embodiment through art and technology, and ways these interactive artworks can enhance our appreciation of our embodiment and perspective on living. A very interesting outcome of George's experiments in embodied reflective practice is his insight into the advantages of facilitated or guided interactions over simpler forms of audience engagement with interactive art. He has written about this work in books and journals.[101]

In the interview that follows, George discussed his creative practice and the central role of embodied thinking and how he develops interactive systems to facilitate highly focused audience engagement.

Q: How would you characterise the way you work in practice?

G: It's usually a combination of factors: I am always keeping an eye out for emerging technologies, checking when they come within reach in terms of their affordability and accessibility and thinking about what they might enable in terms of an interactive experience; then there are the deeper longer running preoccupations around the kinds of interactions I am interested in exploring and the different modalities and ways to structure that experience. So, a combination of exploring the emerging conceptual, aesthetic and technological possibilities.

Since 2002 my practice has been almost exclusively on body-focussed interaction, but I've also been slowly working away on a new body of work, which of course involves new collaborators and partners.

Q: Are there any particular reasons why you choose to work collaboratively?

G: Most of the projects I work on involve a combination of electronics engineering, computer graphics programming, sound design, and exhibition design. I concentrate mostly on the exhibition design, sound design and sensor data feature extraction and information mapping aspects of each project. But for the other aspects such as programming for data visualisation, and the electronics engineering aspects – I really depend on these partnerships with other specialist – especially for projects like the *BrightHearts* mobile app.[102]

Q: When you are developing works, what could you say about the process?

G: I usually begin some vague, felt-sense of an experience I want to create – some key experiential elements like certain sounds or visual imagery, as well as an overall quality of interaction and experience and usually some specific mode of interaction – such as interacting while lying down or sitting at a table for example. Then it's really about putting on my producer's hat, raising the funds to pay the collaborators I will need to realise the project, and then bringing these people together. But there are always some key images, sounds or body-sensation/orientation that is there at the beginning – that relates to a quality of experience and interaction that I want to realise.

A big part of the working process is meetings with collaborators about the material and methods we are working on – and identifying and making choices as they emerge. There are always many conversations, and negotiations within the constraints of the time available to different people on the team, the code we are working with, the hardware etc. It's never a case of simply having a vision and getting people to build it for you. It's always a conversation between people, and a push and pull process working with the constraints and properties of materials, codes and processes we've chosen to work with.

Q: *When you did your training and you did your PhD, did you come across this idea of reflective practice through reading Donald Schön?*

G: Not directly via Schön, but his notions of reflection in, and on practice was very much an assumed part of my doctoral supervision. My post-graduate degree was a Doctorate of Creative Arts, with practice-based research at its heart. I think the term 'research-led creative practice' could be a more accurate description of the process and methodology. I did have a very clear research question right from the start and each iteration was looking at a different facet of this. I set out trying to be reasonably clear about my expectations and what my goals were for each work – and then you present the completed work, observe people interacting with it, sometimes talk with them, interview them afterwards and then evaluate and reassess. Maybe there's things about the work that I didn't imagine – when you realise 'Oh right. That's what the work is doing'. These kinds of observations and insights into how the work is experienced can shift your understanding of what that work does through that process of evaluation and reflection. . . . Once I have all the electronics in place, I build an instrument – a collection graphic interfaces that I use to program and experiment with ways that the participant will influence the sound and visual appearance of the work. This is the really rewarding stage in which you begin to try out various mappings and scalings – a process and experience I describe as 'reaching through' all the sensors and technology – into the sounds and visuals – and this is very much a reflection-*in-action* process. Is this too loud? Is that too soft? Do I need to bring that up more? Is that too muddy? How do I find more contrast? How do I blend it? It's a very sensuous, and strangely embodied process. Even though I'm still working with a mouse and keyboard – I'm also wearing the sensors – and testing out various breathing patterns, mental states and stress or relaxation reflexes, and trying out different ways in which these mappings extend and transform my experience of these connections between body and mind. . . . With the body focussed interactions I want to draw people's attention inwards, and to frame these very subtle changes in nervous system orientation that can be difficult to notice. To develop the form for these works I have to pay a lot of attention to these changes inside myself, and then reflect on how the dynamics of the sounds and visuals can reflect this felt experience.

Q: *If you think of the reflection as being through the body how does it feel when you are actually engaged in it?*

G: The aesthetic is audio-visual but it's connecting to sensations in our body, our breath and autonomic nervous systems – so it is fused in that way. Embodiment is a fundamental fact of our existence We create the illusion of disembodiment through what we choose to include in our experience. Ultimately there are just different ways of using our body and directing attention. In most of my work so far – I'm wanting to facilitate an exploration about ways that thinking, experience and attention can influence and supported by the rest of the body, and then also how certain practices that focus attention on body and mind – can provide us with unique and otherwise inaccessible perspectives on what it is to be alive in this world.

Q: *Some people feel that when they are in the process of making something where the hands are engaged, that any kind of conscious awareness is an interruption to that process, are you aware of anything like that?*

G: I definitely disappear into another 'space' when I'm mapping and tuning the sounds and visuals – suddenly before I know it – five hours have passed! The more self-conscious and analytical ways of thinking take place before and after this period of immersion and 'feeling-through' the technology, back into the body-mind.

Q: *Would you say that your creative life goes on at a similar kind of pace to how it always has or do you have troughs and high points in terms of activity?*

G: It is very project based. I mentioned earlier on in this interview the importance of creative technical collaborations with programmers and electronics engineers. The other really important partners are the venue partners. I might develop a project with a particular venue in mind to present or test the work. There needs to be an audience or community to engage with but that is how I see my work as being meaningful in the sense that it goes into a public domain.

Q: *What does the phrase 'reflective practice' mean to you?*

G: What *I* mean by reflective practice is having a research question underpinning your creative practice. And that this question is tied to questions around culture, around identity, around representation and some understanding of the work that art does and how you bring that to your own individual practice with each work you make. So, there is reflection **in** the work you do but I ultimately, it's reflection *on* action that is really the pivotal one in terms of deciding the kind of work you want to bring into the world, what you want people to pay attention to. It has to be some form of purposeful action with some intent to bring into the world some way of understanding, relating and experiencing – even for seemingly 'purposeless' work.

[103]Andrew Bluff: Digital Artist Researcher

> It's hard for me to separate my practice as an artist and the programming because I think programming has actually shaped my brain and the way it thinks about everything.

In Andrew Bluff's creative practice, research, art and design are distinct but complementary elements of his reflective practice in which computer programming plays a central role.[104] He created the mobile apps *DrumStudio* and *RoboDrummer* and received the App Art Award for *Mobile Phone Orchestra*. He has collaborated with people from diverse backgrounds for several years during which time he completed a practice-based PhD on 3D techniques for the augmentation of live performance.[105] His art involves designing interactive software for live performances that can transform the traditional practices in drama and dance in collaboration with Stalker Theatre.[106] He combines his creative work with ongoing research at the Animal Logic Academy.[107] Creating artistic digital forms has become a way of life that transcends the need for solo activity and ownership. Co-creation offers more sources of inspiration and access to unusual perspectives that only working with people from diverse disciplines can bring. His satisfaction lies in knowing the value of a contribution that is in one sense concealed, but in another, is very apparent. As an artist and a researcher, he distinguishes between reflection in design, art and research. Reflecting through research is integral to exploring new ground for creating art. In the art making, he reflects on feedback from participants who experience the work but when designing software, reflecting involves reframing problems during the programming process.

An interview with Andrew follows in which he expands upon the part played by digital technology in amplifying his collaborative practice with Stalker Theatre performers. The full version of the interview is available on online.[108]

Q: What does the concept of reflective practice mean to you?

A: Reflective practice to me describes a practice which exists through a cyclical process of action and reflection. Do something (action) and then assess (reflect) the resulting pros and cons of this action in order to refine or redirect the next course of action. My art involves designing bespoke interactive software that I can use in live performances, and my research is around how this technology can alter the traditional practice of live performance. In my own work, this cycle occurs in different but inter-related scopes depending on my current role of artist, designer or researcher. As a designer, I use reflective practice to evaluate and find the optimum solution to a given problem. As an artist, I use reflective practice to find new problems to explore. These new problems result from reflecting on previous artworks and the design process of creating technology. As a researcher, I use reflective practice to identify frameworks and phenomenon across the body of artistic work, both mine and others, and use this framework to then find unexplored areas with which to focus new artistic works or research.

As the scope of reflective practice expands, the scope and formality of reflection and analysis expands. My reflection on design is very internal and solo, reframing problems in my own head or on a piece of paper, while my artistic reflection will often incorporate the criticism and suggestions of others via informal chats. The research will involve conducting and recording interviews with fellow artists and performers and applying formalised research methods to generate frameworks and identify phenomena in the hybridised artistic practices. I am not suggesting that this tiered notion of reflection and analysis is in any way universal, but it seems to apply to my particular brand of software design, interactive art and practice based research. I guess I'm doing an 'instant in-action reflection' . . . I like to make each parameter of the module I've just made easy to manipulate in real-time. Just looking at the response you're getting from the program especially when you are pushing it to the edge of its limits. I guess you are reflecting on the artistic potential of the object you've just made, judging it instantly as you are doing it-in-action. I'll do that for a period of time and then I'll sit there and reflect on what I felt worked and what didn't work. I do a lot of walking around the room. I 'm staring off into the distance, walking around the space and that's my reflecting on the programming side of things more than anything.

After I've made something artistic and I've played with it, my reflection is more going and having a break- watching some terrible television or something. And then my mind will wander back onto it. I think there are different stages. There probably is that same day and you are thinking about it a lot so when you are making spaghetti or something, it will pop into your head and you're re-assessing it. But then roughly two weeks later you find that you're thinking about it again, maybe in a different way, maybe in line with seeing some other artwork, seeing someone do something else and it will make you see some connection between what you are doing and you change it.

Q: *Can you say something about how you write computer programs?*

A: You think of each element of the program as being like a block, like a flow diagram. I think of programming in those terms, where you can see the whole picture of what you want to program, as a diagram and then you zoom in on that one little portion you are making and make that fit into the rest of the diagram. And in doing that it makes you reassess the diagram as a whole. I think that's one of my skills as a programmer: being able to put a complicated system into my brain and see how each component relates to it. . . . I like to think in little modules and the benefit for me as an artist, is that I can then reuse things in a different context, in an unexpected manner. I do a lot of reusing and sharing of modules so I can try to promote obscure thinking . . . shoehorning a round design into a square problem space to see if that opens up new opportunities. I have been programming since I was about 4 or 5 years old but the way I think about life and look at things in the world is almost using a programming logical flow. It's hard for me to separate my practice as an artist and the programming because I think programming has actually shaped my brain and the way it thinks about everything.

Q: Do you wait until you have done all the thinking about the nature of the program before-hand you start coding? Or do you code a bit and then go back to the overview?

A: I definitely code bit and then go back. There's several different ways. Sometimes you might go and see how the dancers are reacting to the system, but other times I jump in front and see what I think as a human and this back into the programming so I do iterate.

Q: What sort of things change as a result of looking at the dancers' movements?

A: It alters the way you see your end goal- what you think is interesting. I like to think about the motion tracking system we use with Stalker theatre which basically detects any kind of movement in the space. When you first go in there instantly you think, I want to track that dancer's movements and have the motion corresponding to that and I don't want to track the rope-like slings they use to perform. And then you start to look at the way it's working and the way they're using the slings and you realise, the slings are as much a part of this work as the humans are and we really should be tracking that movement as well. It makes you think, I'm going to this effort of separating this out for some logi-cal reason that doesn't marry well with the art form. So, let's just rethink that, embrace that. . . . I create visuals and sounds that react to the performer or par-ticipant's movements. This adds a sense of discovery and play for the audience, I give them a virtual sandbox to play in and they can create their own fun and meaning out of that. But I always try things out for myself. I find research top-ics to look into by doing them first: for instance, I found out that the system I developed to optimise the 3D perspective on a cylindrical screen is called 'omnistereo rendering'[109] which already has research on it. I went into the Data Arena with its 360-degree cylindrical screen and projected using the normal rendering system and found the perspective was wrong. I came up with my own system and because I'd gone through all the effort to rectify it myself, I then had some context to help me find out if anyone else had the same problem. Creating a solution helps me understand the problem.

Q: If suddenly you couldn't program would there be an alternative?

A: That's a good question. When I started my sound and music design course after eighteen years of coding, I was thinking let's give music a go without computers, especially without coding. I still used digital audio tools which I consider to be a different process than using programming. The audio tools are more for composing music, putting pre-recorded sounds onto a time line, playing back, re-ordering them. Things that a traditional music composer would have done on pen and paper. I used to make one of these tools professionally as a software engineer and when I was making the tool I used to really love using it to make music even though I was a really bad musician. Basically, I got bored with having to sit at my desk coding making tools for other people to go and work creatively. My reaction to the sound and music course was to abandon coding to see what I could do as an artist – as a sound artist. After a year of this, I found the traditional tools to be quite limiting and started to combine my coding skills with my artistic vision and seem to have found my niche.

Q: What is the balance now between using digital tools and your creative coding?

A: I rely on a lot of digital tools. I do a little bit of 3D modelling, a little bit of Photoshop work, a little bit of illustration, music composition, music synthesizer. I consider them to be tools not the core. I consider the coding to be where my artistic strengths lie. If you were to tell me you've got one chance to make an innovative artwork and that's all you got, I would say my skill is in coding and I will use that. I think perhaps I've got a skill there that lets me explore things that haven't been explored much because there are not as many people with those skills artistically exploring random ideas. I feel there's a lot there to be explored that hasn't been done. There's such a history of pencil work, beautiful oil on canvas that is so hard to compete with. Whereas with this computational thing there is always some extra aspect to explore. You have the control to create whatever you want and that's what I love about it. So, if you are using one of these digital tools, you don't feel like you've got complete control to do what you want to do. They've got very hard restrictions that make it easier to do whatever the tool is designed to do whereas if you go into more low-level coding you can create whatever you want to create. You are restricted by hardware but it gives me freedom – I never picture exactly what I'm making while I'm making it so it gives me the freedom to not realize that while I'm creating it and then to see what comes out in the end.

Q: Are the tools partners in the creative process?

A: Perhaps you could say that the underlying coding language is a part of you because you need to assimilate your own way of thinking with the flow of the programming language itself in order to effectively create large and complex applications. But it's not a one-way street, you also shape the program you are making to adhere to your own unique way of thinking. Then the software application that comes out of this coding, does act like a creative partner in an artwork. There is artistry and design on two separate levels; there is artistry in creating an interesting entity and then there is artistry in partnering with it to create an actual artwork. When you are heavily involved in both stages, the trick is to spend at least as much time partnering as you do creating. This provides a richer knowledge of what might be interesting to add or change in the creation stage. I think an artist will always use or 'partner' with a software application in a slightly different way than the creator imagined, even when it's the same person doing both. I think it's important to be open and to embrace this.

[110]Benjamin Carey: Musician Artist Researcher

> The surprise elements are very important for me so any kind of generative system or way of working using randomisation or algorithms that are kind of opaque is fascinating because when you stand away from that and interact with it as a performer, it provokes different ideas.

Benjamin Carey is a saxophonist, composer and technologist with interests in contemporary classical, improvised, interactive and electro-acoustic music. After completing a Bachelor of Music at the Sydney Conservatorium of Music in 2005, Benjamin moved to France to study saxophone and contemporary music under Marie-Bernadette Charrier at the Conservatoire de Bordeaux. Back in Australia, he completed his PhD which focused upon the design and development of interactive musical systems for improvised performance with instrumental musicians at the University of Technology, Sydney.[111] He has performed and exhibited work in Australia, New Zealand, France, Austria, the United States and Switzerland and published a number of research papers.[112] As a PhD researcher, Benjamin's approach to his work underwent much change and evolved into a deeply reflective process that is now an embedded part of his creative practice. He is fascinated by computational creativity because of its capability to provoke people to act in ways they might not by themselves. There is a sense of excitement that comes through interacting with software you have created yourself, and when it responds in a way you have not anticipated, it feels 'alive' as if partnering with another being.

In his interview, Benjamin talks about the way research has influenced his reflective practice and the importance of musical coherence in his interaction with a self-created digital partner. The full version is available online.[113]

Q: What is the practice — your creative practice?

B: For the vast majority of time, the creative practice is creating software. The end result, what the public sees is a performance and it might be a performance with myself with a piece of software, or it might be another musician interacting with that software and I'd be present or it could someone who has download the software elsewhere.

I first used MaxMSP to process my saxophone playing using Effects. Then I got more into it and started to think of my work with Max as creating larger systems to improvise with. Most of the practice is based in the computer. . . . I wanted it to be as unpredictable as possible so would feed new improvisations each time.

Q: *How do you begin?*

B: There is generally a seed for an idea so for instance if I am working on a piece of music and I want to use a process or an effect or some way of creating a musical composition or an interaction between myself and the computer that I have not encountered, I'll have an idea and it quite often comes from previous practice. Then I'll get into the software and start mocking up something, having not written down exactly what the idea was. Then it's sketching and I'll get into the software and sketch a little idea and usually that idea has some kind of input and output and that could be a microphone and that could be the mouse or something like that feeding off that initial process. Quite often the seed of the idea gets me to sit down at the computer and work and then that process of sketching that idea usually forms this kind of feedback loop where I'm thinking 'OK the idea I had at the start has changed and is continuing to evolve and it is only afterwards I start thinking where am I going, is it any different to what I initially started out with? I can't usually put my finger on what it is I want to do until I sit down and do it. I design very much from the bottom up whatever it is, the building blocks, rather than having a broad overview of the software I want to design. That comes from my performer background. As a classical player, you need to get into small sections and you only put the large piece together at the end of the process.

Q: *Is there a typical way of selecting how you want to move forward?*

B: That's a really good question. It depends on the level at which I am working and how long I have been working on something but generally I will work and idea through until its eventual demise. Quite often I will get to a technical hurdle and I'll save that sketch and think about it later. Then I'll move into something else, get frustrated and go off and do other creative work. That process is generally stop start. If I am working on an idea, I'll really work it through until I realise that no that's going to take me another couple of days. I don't have the time now, I'll put it aside. So rather than sitting down and saying I'm going to achieve this in the next two hours and then add it to a larger system, it's very much in the initial stages, head down not really knowing what I'm doing and then taking a breath later on.

You have a fresh look at it. You also draw connections between what it is you've done and other pieces of work. I keep all of my sketches so even if

I don't do anything with them, a lot of these small patches become the seeds for other things. Quite often I'll look at something I knew what a dead end at one time but I'll be able to connect it to something else. In the process of actually making that sketch I don't see those connections because I am involved in the doing at that point. But definitely later on, I either see that it was a naïve idea and I couldn't take it anywhere else or I find that it connects to other ideas that I didn't realise.

Q: *In terms of the programming process do you have a motivation for challenging yourself or getting the unexpected?*

B: Creating the _derivations software for my PhD thesis, it was finding ways of taking something that I knew, my saxophone performance, and presenting it in a way that could provoke me to do something different. If the computer can take something and draw connections and I don't understand what it's doing under the hood even as the person who has written it, then that's really exciting. The surprise elements are very important for me so any kind of generative system or way of working using randomisation or algorithms that are kind of opaque is fascinating because when you stand away from that and interact with it as a performer, it provokes different ideas- the performance is separate to writing the software. If you are interacting with something that is unpredictable it feels alive and that's thrilling as a performer and also as an interaction on stage. Also, for me interacting with something that is surprising gives you a different conception of what you want to create next. I created these random type systems and I'd perform with them and get quite excited but the more I spent time with them, I realised that I wanted them to be maybe a little bit less random or have more unpredictability but a sense of coherence, all of those kinds of things I didn't realise when I was first starting and it was the unpredictability that fed that I think.

Q: *What's the difference between a good surprise and a not so good surprise?*

B: A really good question. A good surprise is when the software does something I didn't expect but is actually musical and is coherent in the context of my performance and everything that's come previously. It's quite difficult to judge because it's also in the context of improvisation so you don't want it to do the same every time.

Q: *You don't want any predictability?*

B: No exactly – but you also don't want it to go off on its own tangent and not be able to relate to things it's heard or to be able to provoke something that's in the style or context of what is going on now. If I'm testing it and a surprise happens, and then another surprise happens, and another and there's no consistency between the algorithm's output then it becomes random and it's difficult for me as the person who's assessing it from the outside to see if I can perform with that. So, I play the role of the listener who created the algorithm. I'll test it and I'm thinking if I were in the audience, would that make any sense? When I interact with it, I am listening and responding to it and if it makes a decision that doesn't make any sense at all from what I've just given it, then it's not working and I can't connect that surprise to any musical idea that I'd like to pursue. I have a general idea of what I want, but I allow that testing process to be the arbiter of whether or not something works, in order to find out what it is that I want. I have this broad idea but I can't tell exactly what it is until I test it. The testing process takes a very long time and it's very much embedded in the writing of the software. I find that after while it's only after I've stepped away from it and I've listening to recordings of that interaction a few times that I realise what it is that makes this thing tick and where to go next. It is very difficult to map it out from the outset.

There's been a number of performances when I've been playing with the software and it will generate something that doesn't conform to the interaction that we've been having. So it will bring something from its database that doesn't relate at all to what we've been having. It's frustrating but it's a performance so I need to try and rein it in in some way so I might start playing differently. I might try and provoke it to do different things. For instance, if I've been playing quite quietly, and interacting with the system in that way and the system has been quite quiet, and we seem to be in some kind of coherent dialogue and then it spits out something unexpected and seems out of context, there's one of two things I can do: I can try and play even quieter and move into a different area or I can start playing as if it has provoked me to play louder. So, I'll go off with it and after I might go back to the software and think why did it do that? What is it about the internal algorithm that's happening there? And then I'll drill down into the code and start thinking about mitigating those things.

Q: *Tell me more about how you saw reflection as an approach in your PhD research.*

B: I think it has definitely been embedded in my practice. The way I used it was on a number of different levels. After reading a bit about reflective practice later on I realised that 'reflection-in-action' was very much what I was doing. It is very much what practitioners do, when you are doing something you are assessing it and actually reflecting on whether it is going the right way. In terms of actually reflecting as part of my practice, I write a lot.

Writing ideas about what I had been doing, where it is I think I wanted to go and how I was going to get there. Or it might be,' there's something really interesting about this process of interacting with the software but I can put my finger on it' and then I would tease out that through writing. Some of those extended reflections became part of my thesis. I initially thought that this process of writing as reflective memos would be something that I would go back on and they would be very small, a couple of paragraphs 'on this day this is what I was thinking' but it wasn't very formal like that. When I would reflect it was usually because I needed a way to communicate to myself where it was my head was at. They were usually quite long extended reflections.

The way I've used the word reflection is that I use the practice or the problems of practice to jump off and starting thinking about broader issues, or to drill down into an issue that I've found out in my practice is a problem. Evaluation can be part of it I think. I might start off by evaluating my own work and then that will get me into a broader theoretical discussion about what it is to perform with a computer. For me that's broader than 'self-reflection' as I've termed it in my own work but the whole process is still part of 'reflective practice' ... and yes 'evaluation' is a part of it- assessing whether or not something's working is definitely a part of it. . . . But I see reflection as being broader. . . . I think that makes a massive difference to how you view a surprise, how you view an unexpected event. The unexpected event for the professional is a problem to be solved, whereas for the creative person, not everyone, some may focus on the craft skills rather than the originality side of things- most of those who are interested in creating something new- they see that unexpected event, as a challenge, an opportunity.

Notes

1 Digital + Technology denotes all types of electronic equipment and applications that process information in the form of binary code, strings of the characters: zero and 1. Behind everything digital are zeros and ones in constant movement. The technology provides the devices and techniques.
2 Alan Turing formalized the underlying theory that allowed the modern computer to be built. The concept of the 'universal machine' was proposed in his 1937 paper as a theoretical machine that could solve any problem able to be described by simple instructions encoded on a paper tape. One 'Turing Machine' could calculate square roots, another might solve Sudoku puzzles and so on. See Turing (1937).
3 Kay (1984, pp. 53–59).
4 New media art is an umbrella term for artwork produced using forms of digital technology including software and hardware. Categories include digital art, computer art, animation, Internet art, interactive art etc. see Tribe et al. (2006). Cook and Graham (2010); Grau (2010).
5 These concepts and practices are discussed in Stanney et al. (2009); Anderson (2003). Farr et al. (2012) etc.
6 See Turkle's studies of the impact of digital technology on conversation Turkle (2015).
7 Alan Turing posed the question 'Can machines think?' triggering a debate about its possible implications Turing (1950). Much comment focused on achieving thinking machines by the end of the 20th century. However, if we look again there is a different implication: it was he said, meaningless because: *the use of the words and general educated opinion will have altered so much that one will be able to speak of machines thinking without expecting to be contradicted.* Turing's point was not that machines would 'think' in the same way as a human being but rather we would speak as if they do. For a comprehensive guide to Turing's contribution to computer science see Copeland et al. (2017).
8 For history of early creative computing see e.g. Brown et al. (2008); Poltronieri et al. (2018, pp. 3–29).
9 Augmented cognition research has inspired many creative practitioners: Englebart (1962).
10 Adobe Photoshop: www.photoshop.com.
11 The *Tipp-Ex* brand is a trademark of BIC corporation. *Tippex* is used in the sense of a fluid for correcting text on paper.
12 Adeyanu (2012).

13 An example is Grammarly, a tool for identifying grammar, spelling errors correct punctuation sentence structure.
14 Painting with Light (1985): www.creativebloq.com/video-production/remembering-quantel-paintbox-712401.
15 iPhone 2007: https://en.wikipedia.org/wiki/IPhone; iPad 2010: https://en.wikipedia.org/wiki/IPad.
16 Gayford (2016).
17 Hockney's exhibition 'A Bigger Picture' opened at the Royal Academy on January 21 until April 9, 2012.
18 En plein air – in open air painting leaves the studio and goes outdoors. The practice is centuries old but was made into an art form by the French Impressionists. Their desire to paint light and its changing, ephemeral qualities, coupled with the creation of transportable paint tubes and the box easel allowed artists the freedom to paint anywhere.
19 David Hockney: A Bigger Picture a film by Bruno Woldheim: www.a-bigger-picture.com.
20 Gayford (2016, p. 196).
21 Variations of reflection in and on action were discussed previously in Chapter 3 Reflective Creative Practice.
22 COSTART project: see Candy et al. (2002b, revised in 2018).
23 Quantrill (2002, pp. 225–230).
24 Yasunao Tone is an original member of the Fluxus movement and an artist, writer, theorist, and composer. He received a National Endowment for the Arts Fellowship (1982), a New York Foundation for the Arts Fellowship (1986), a New York State Council on the Arts Grant (1996–1997), and the Golden Nica Prize (2002).
25 Edmonds et al. (2003).
26 http://lindacandy.com/CRPBOOK/marshall.
27 See Edmonds et al. (2006) for categories of interaction.
28 Edmonds (2018).
29 Bilda et al. (2008), Bilda (2011): A creative engagement model was derived from interactive art experience studies.
30 Shusterman (2012).
31 Loke et al. (2012). See also Khut and Loke (2014)
32 This includes interpretive and generative grammar engines creating novel textual elements that the interactors may take direction from, creating a feedback loop of agency. A physics engine is also implemented in the work, such that the physical interactions of all the synthetic elements with each other and the interactors have further consequence, controlling which textual elements collide with and interact with one another and what is visible to the interactors and the audience. This introduces into the system a level of agency with a degree of autonomous behaviour. See Biggs et al. 2014 for further details.
33 An agent acts for another and has discretion to make decisions and complete tasks on behalf of clients. human agents include members of parliament and travel booking agents.
34 Sue Hawksley: http://lindacandy.com/CRPBOOK/hawksley.
35 Double Skin Double Mind: http://saralaoui.com/2015/03/double-skin-double-mind/.
36 Sarah Fdili Alaoui: http://lindacandy.com/CRPBOOK/alaoui.
37 George P. Khut: www.georgekhut.com/biography/.
38 George P. Khut: http://lindacandy.com/CRPBOOK/khut.
39 Mind-body dualism: Descartes' thesis was that mind and body are distinct entities with separate functions.
40 The term 'embodied cognition' suggests that the mind is not only connected to the body but that the true location of thinking is in the body interacting with the brain. Cognition is mediated by sensory and motor systems and differs radically from the notion of the brain as the thinking engine of a responsive body as exemplified in mind-body dualism.
41 Embodied Interaction in HCI: Dourish (2001).
42 Shusterman (2012).
43 Merleau-Ponty (1945, p. 148).

44 As the validity of the idea of the mind as a computational machine began to be questioned, ideas about embodiment gained ground supported by Lakoff and Johnson (1999) in 'Metaphors We Live By'.

45 Shusterman (2012).

46 Mahon (2015).

47 In the early days of artificial intelligence research, the main efforts were directed towards building a brain that performs as well or better than the human brain. This still dominates many parts of the field which has undergone a resurgence as machine learning systems have begun to prove more effective.

48 Anil Seth: Ted2017 :https://www.ted.com/talks/anil_seth_how_your_brain_hallucinates_your_ conscious_reality/transcript?language=en#t-1008792

49 Farr et al. (2012) introduce theoretical approaches to embodiment and ways in which embodiment is described within different disciplines. The article discusses how they are of interest in the context of digital technology research.

50 Brown (2002) and www.paul-brown.com/WORDS/STEPPING.HTM.

51 Brown (2008, p. 277).

52 Brown et al. (2008).

53 Biswas (2018) www.studiointernational.com/index.php/paul-brown-process-chance-serendipity-art-that-makes-itself-review-national-academy-sciences-washington.

54 ICA exhibition *Cybernetic Serendipity*: http://cyberneticserendipity.net.

55 A-Life agents are included in Paul's algorithms to replace random numbers with more deterministic mechanisms like Cellular Automata. These are simple rule-based computational procedures that interact with each other and reproduce and propagate themselves over time. Cellular automata became popular after an article about them in Scientific American in 1970 (Gardner, 1970). Soon after reading it Paul adopted the technique and later refined it at the Slade School of Art in London where he was exploring techniques that moved beyond using intuitive selection processes.

56 Processing is a language and an open-source development environment for the visual arts, new media art, and visual design communities. It uses the Java language and has a graphical user interface.

57 Cohen (2016, pp. 63–66).

58 Geroimenko (2014, revised 2018).

59 Nintendo Wiimote www.nintendo.co.uk/Wii/Accessories/Accessories-Wii-Nintendo-UK-626430.html and Xbox Kinect: https://thetechconnection675.weebly.com: The Nintendo Wii game console pioneered the market for motion based gaming. Then came the Sony PlayStation Move which was fairly comparable to the Wii. Then came the Microsoft Xbox 360 Kinect, which introduced a new method.

60 Gwilt (2011)

61 On the definition of the significance of AR, see Azuma et al. 2001; 2008, 2011.

62 Augmented Reality brings elements of the virtual world into the real world, enhancing the things we see, hear, and feel. The continuum ranges from a completely real and natural environment to a completely virtual environment and was first introduced by Milgram (1994).

63 Licklider (1960).

64 Mary Shelley (1797–1851) wrote Frankenstein or The Modern Prometheus tells the story of Victor Frankenstein, a young scientist who creates a hideous but sentient creature in a scientific experiment.

65 Sarah Knapton, science editor, *Daily Telegraph*: www.telegraph.co.uk/science/2016/03/12/meet-nadine-the-worlds-most-human-like-robot/.

66 Six Life-Like Robots: https://futurism.com/the-most-life-life-robots-ever-created/.

67 Ernest Edmonds: Fields Exhibition: http://rixc.org/fields/en/exhibition/4/Ernest_Edmonds/.

68 Johnston et al. (2008, pp. 220–221).

69 Andrew Bluff: http://lindacandy.com/CRPBOOK/bluff.

70 The software is available online freely via derivations.net.

71 Benjamin Carey: http://lindacandy.com/CRPBOOK/carey.
72 Full interviews are online at: http://lindacandy.com/CRPBOOK/.
73 Photograph by Christine Marshall.
74 In Search of a Pattern: A. Marshall: http://tony.7thwave.io.
75 Marshall (2018)
76 Photograph by Maria Falconer.
77 www.articulateanimal.org/sueh.htm.
78 Hawksley (2012) see PhD list.
79 Biggs et al. (2016)
80 Biggs et al. (2014).
81 A dictionary of words is included in the software, based on a general English vocabulary combined with the words created by the collaborating artists.
82 'Iterative' and 'Itinerative' – A distinction between 'iterative' (exact replications) and 'itinerative' (similar but variable) movements in making can be found in Ingold 2010, p. 97.
83 Photograph: Uwe Homm.
84 Alaoui (2012) see PhD list.
85 Alaoui et al. (2015).
86 Skin: http://saralaoui.com/2016/02/res-p-i-r/.
87 Radical Choreographic Object: http://saralaoui.com/2017/02/radical-choreographic-object/.
88 Ergonomics: http://saralaoui.com/2017/02/ergonimics/.
89 EMG: Electromyography is an electro-diagnostic medicine technique for evaluating and recording the electrical activity produced by skeletal muscles, performed with an electro-myograph instrument.
90 IMU: Inertial Measurement Unit- an electronic device that measures a body's force and magnetic field surrounding the body, using accelerometers sometimes magnetometers.
91 Laban human movement consists of four parts: Direction, Weight, Speed, Flow each with two elements combined as Eight Efforts: www.theatrefolk.com/blog/the-eight-efforts-laban-movement/.
92 Myos: www.myo.com.
93 Alaoui et al. (2013); Françoise et al. (2017).
94 Vermersch, P. (2003) *L'entretien d'explicitation* (Quatrième édition enrichie d'un glossaire) Issyles-Moulineaux: ESF Éditeur.
95 Varela built on Merleau-Ponty's work to develop a model of cognition as 'embodied action', a process they call 'enactive' (Varela et al., 1991).
96 Double Skin Double Mind: http://saralaoui.com/2015/03/double-skin-double-mind/.
97 A Light Touch: http://saralaoui.com/2015/03/a-light-touch/.
98 Photograph: Max Doyle, courtesy of The Australian Way magazine.
99 George P. Khut: www.georgekhut.com/biography/.
100 https://research.unsw.edu.au/people/dr-george-khut/.
101 Khut and Loke (2014) Loke et al. (2012).
102 www.brightheartsapp.co.
103 Photograph: Danielle Bluff.
104 Andrew Bluff personal website: www.rollerchimp.com.
105 Bluff (2017).
106 Stalker: www.stalker.com.au/.
107 Animal Logic Academy at University of Technology Sydney https://animallogicacademy.uts.edu.au.
108 Andrew Bluff: http://lindacandy.com/CRPBOOK/bluff.
109 Simon et al. (2004).
110 Photo: Benjamin Carey.
111 Carey (2016).
112 Carey (2013, 2016).
113 http://lindacandy.com/CRPBOOK/carey.

6

REFLECTION THROUGH RESEARCH

Chapter 6 explores practitioner approaches to making, appraising and document-ing their creative work in the context of private and shared research practices, here distinguished as personal or formal research. Reflective practice is undergoing a renaissance driven by new forms of research carried out in conjunction with crea-tive practice. This 'practice-based' research is an emerging field that is expanding our understanding of the nature of knowledge in and from practice. For practition-ers, research projects that connect closely with creative practice provide a means of extending their personal work at the same time as enhancing their ability to share and debate it with others. Practice-based research is relatively new and includes dis-ciplines from art, design and technology to education and health care, accompanied by an eclectic range of approaches and methods within which reflective practice has an important role. How research practices generate 'practice-based evidence' is discussed drawing on recent examples of practitioner research.

Donald Schön believed that reflection-in-action made the practitioner into a researcher who was then able to construct new theory from unique cases. He advo-cated giving 'attention to the system of knowing-in-practice and to reflection-in-action itself'.[1] Reflecting-in-action was, he said, the path to becoming a researcher:

> When someone reflects-in-action, he becomes a researcher in the practice context. He is not dependent on the categories of established theory and technique but construct a new theory of the unique case.[2]

Many practitioners in the creative arts today have embraced research through prac-tice and in doing so, have strengthened their reflective practices. An increasing number of university graduate courses that embrace practice-based research offer recognition by way of PhD qualifications. From these developments, new forms of knowledge are emerging that give access to 'knowing-in-practice', an expertise that is usually implicit and hence difficult to express. The practitioner's reflective voice has been strengthened by newly acquired research processes and we are beginning to understand much more about the nuts and bolts of thinking and making in creative practice. In this way, the outcomes from practice-based creative research can influence the ideas and actions of other practitioners as well as a wider community of interest. This is underpinned by practitioner documentation of the process of making artefacts, their creative intentions and goals and the results of experimentation with new forms and materials available in published articles.

Reflection through research can provide a rich source of new understanding about the nature of creative practice for the practitioners themselves. Naturally there are trade-offs, and the extra effort required to continue creative practice and, at the same time, carry out research, can be a difficult experience, especially in the early stages. The benefits come as unexpected discoveries and desirable surprises that can stimulate new ways of thinking. When research in practice and practice in research are bound together, this nurtures the ground for exploration and experimentation both on an individual basis as well as in collaborative work.

But what exactly do we mean by 'research' in a general sense and how does it differ from research in the context of creative practice?

Research as private versus and shared practices

In this section, we examine what is meant by the term 'research' in a general sense before homing in on practitioner research and how this kind of research facilitates and enhances reflection in practice. Research takes many forms and has different purposes and underpins many national and international educational qualifications. Research is a practice that requires training and experience for it to be done well.

Research practice involves a process as well as an outcome. The process consists of activities like asking questions, proposing theories, formulating problems and selecting methods for gathering and analysing information. The outcomes of the research process include data, information, results and findings, generated through a rigorous process of collection, analysis and interpretation. As discussed later, research is normally expected to contribute to the existing 'canon' of knowledge, that is, a body of tested facts and reliable information that is approved and agreed by experts in the field.

Research practice also suggests something about how we think and act more generally. When applied to individual people, the notion of a research mind-set or research ethos suggests an enquiring attitude of mind and an ability to look more deeply into matters rather than accepting things at face value. If doing research is your profession, you need training in methods and techniques for gathering and analysing data and you may choose to specialise in survey or statistical forms that produce results. In universities, graduate studies are training grounds for research and have a significant impact on the capabilities and expertise of the individual.

A comprehensive account of the nature of research processes and products is impossible to capture in a brief discussion, but in the context of creative practice, two kinds are distinguished here. The first is research that is purely for *private* purposes, and the second is that which is intended to be *shared* with others. Naturally, the two categories sometimes serve dual purposes and often overlap. However, in the examples that follow, there is a distinction which, for simplicity, I will refer to as 'personal' research and 'formal' research.

Most creative practitioners do personal research for exploring new ideas and gathering information about materials or tools and where to source expertise. The way it is done and what they do with the outcomes varies considerably. This kind of research is carried out mainly to progress the making of new works and is usually not intended to have relevance to the work of other practitioners, although what comes out is often something that will be of interest to others. Those who make the results of their personal research available to others do so for mixed reasons. Some prefer to explain the background to their work to interested parties whereas others use what they have learnt to teach others how to benefit from it. Its use, value and dissemination are for the individual practitioner alone to decide.

Research of a formal kind extends beyond the needs of the individual and operates under various conditions and expectations. Different traditions exist across disciplines and there is usually an accepted methodology that everyone is aware of and adheres to. When someone within a discipline challenges an existing theory, or proposes a new way of thinking, or identifies a gap in the canon of knowledge specific to that discipline, the experts in the area assess the worth of the claims and in due course, they are either rejected or accepted. The outcomes of such research appear as journal articles, reports and books, as well as surveys, charts, graphs, statistics etc. Combinations of all these forms of information are open to scrutiny and must be self-explanatory, most of all to the relevant communities of interest and expertise. The way such knowledge is created depends upon the methodologies of the particular discipline, within which there are standard techniques known to fellow researchers. Formal research requires methods, data and findings that can be scrutinised by peers. For the research to be considered as significant it has to show that something new and different and credible has resulted; in the personal case, this is not obligatory. Formal research that lays claim to making a novel contribution to knowledge must be open to scrutiny and evaluation, unlike the outcomes of personal research.

Seeking new information through research is a substantial part of a creative practitioner's everyday practice. It may always remain personal research that serves the objectives of a particular project. Alternatively, the research could be undertaken through a formal process of systematic exploration that involves sharing what emerges with a wider community of practice and making contributions to new knowledge in the field. In order to achieve advances in knowledge, the research process has to be defined and carried out in a manner that is commonly agreed. Differentiating between personal and formal research is especially important when it comes to describing the new developments in research that are intertwined with practice.

Research in creative practice has particular characteristics that do not necessarily conform to traditional norms. Practitioner research, with its focus on personal practice, involves reflecting on and documenting one's own creative process and interpreting any questions and insights arising from it. Reflection through research in creative practice is a strategy for interrogating existing practice and through that process, generating new knowledge. Practice based practitioner research of this kind is of necessity speculative and has its own protocols and new norms. The practitioner as researcher develops and adopts new frames of reference, designs and creates new forms and produces outcomes that are transformative and frequently challenging. For many practitioners, this has meant a shift away from conventional pathways in a search for opportunities outside the art and humanities fields. As Roy Ascott puts it:

> [A]rt research shares with science and technology its spirit of speculation, innovation and intellectual challenge. This is especially so where that research is practice-based.[3]

New avenues of practice-based research afford opportunities for practitioners to explore their knowing-in-practice in ways that were previously considered to be inaccessible because of the tacit nature of personal expertise.[4] This is an expanding area and there are a growing number of books and articles on practice-based research that give different views about it. I will try to sum up its main features drawing on my own texts which in turn, are informed by existing contributions to the field.[5]

Practice-based research

Practice based research consists of original investigations undertaken in order to gain new knowledge partly by means of practice and through the outcomes of that practice. The research and the practice of practice-based research operate as interdependent and complementary processes. The research component of practice-based research is, in most respects, similar to other kinds of research, a key element of which is the sharing of the outcomes of the research process. However, the results of practice-based research are intended to inform the practice itself and, in most cases, the creation of artefacts of some kind. This orientation is distinct from other forms of research such as 'blue skies' or basic research where the aim is to increase general knowledge and utility is not a primary goal. It is closer in intention to 'applied research' that seeks to answer immediate real-world questions and to solve specific problems. Practice-based research aims to produce outcomes that are applicable to the individual practitioner and, when undertaken in a more formal way, extends to generating original concepts and insights that contribute to a body of new practice-related knowledge. In an academic context, practice-based research is carried out in a structured process that is defined by university regulations.[6]

The practice that is central to practice-based research in the creative arts is primarily directed towards making things like visual or sound artefacts, installations, exhibitions or performances. The research is carried out through the process of creative practice from which questions arise and issues are explored. New works that emerge from this process are at the centre of the activity and in formal research, the significance of what has been done must be made available to others. Claims to have generated new understandings through this creation must be able to be scrutinised and evaluated. This new knowledge includes the artefacts which are central to the research process and are essential to a full understanding of what has been achieved. The sharing of the artefacts is often a critical element in the documenting of such research.

There are several interpretations of practice-based research and those differences are reflected in small but significant terminological variants, for example 'practice as research', 'research as practice'. The case for how creative practice can lead to research insights through practice-led research is counter-balanced with how research can impact positively on creative practice through research-led practice. This variant distinguishes between practice related research that leads to new understandings about practice and the kind where the main outcome is a work- an artefact. The artefact as a contribution to knowledge has been hotly debated with a strong argument against this without a linguistic articulation of context and significance. Scrivener contends that artworks offer perspectives or ways of seeing because they are made in order to create 'apprehensions'.[7]

Other types of practice-based research do not always differentiated research from practice giving the impression they are one and the same thing. This influences the manner in which the research is conducted and documented. The differences are partly explained by specific intentions and goals of the disciplines concerned but additionally, there can be a tension between highly individualised working practices and the requirements of research outcomes to be shared in a way that is accessible beyond the individual concerned. These variations in how practice-based research is conceived and carried out can diminish the value of practice-based research and even the significance of the contributions of practice-based PhDs to knowledge. Nevertheless, creative practitioners are everywhere taking up the challenge that PhD research involves.

Embarking on the PhD research track is not for all creative practitioners but increasingly it is a choice for many. There are different drivers: in many countries, it is fast becoming a basic requirement of teaching posts within higher education including in schools of art and design but there are often other factors such as seeking an environment conducive to satisfying personal goals and the attraction of funding, expert support and resources.[8] The emergence of practice-based research in universities has come about partly as a result of changes in educational expectations and culture and, in particular, the restructuring of regulatory frameworks which, for example, in the UK has driven changes in the way the creative arts are assessed through research performance.

Practitioners who pursue research through post-graduate academic programmes, are obliged to make what they produce available for external evaluation by examination which validate the outcomes of the PhD and future researchers learn from and build on what has been achieved. Where university rules permit, artefacts may form part of the PhD submission and they are accompanied by a written thesis that describes the significance and context of the claims.[9] Because the artefact plays a central role in the research, they have to be made available at the time and for future reference. The PhD submission must include the means to observe, hear and experience the artefact in whatever form it takes. However, being able to appraise a creative work is problematic if, as is usually the case, this is highly dependent on having direct experience of it. Audio and video recordings and printed material are poor substitutes for the actual experience of the works and can only achieve a limited idea. It is all the more important to have contextual material and empirical evidence to support the viewer's understanding of the work. The outcomes of doctoral level practice-based research constitute claims for originality and novelty and ideally, these claims are underpinned by a clear methodological position that includes methods and techniques for revealing and substantiating those claims. In this way, the role of making and evaluating artefacts contributes to a broadening of the definition of research, not a narrowing of the definition of practice. These issues are expanded in two articles published in the Leonardo Journal.[10]

Several practitioners interviewed for this book and others I have worked with have undertaken PhD research. The discussion that follows draws upon the ways and means they used to generate new understandings about practice. Completed PhD theses are listed after the main references.

Methodologies for practitioner research

Practice-based research is an emerging discipline and has yet to agree a unified methodological framework. This is because practitioner researchers are venturing into relatively unchartered territory and forging new ground. It is often necessary to explore and articulate the foundational concepts and ideas that have informed their approach as well as the rationale for choice of methods and techniques. This is not to say that other research disciplines do not set out the approaches and methods they use, but it is often within an existing framework that the community of research is familiar with and does not have to be spelt out from first principles. In science disciplines, there are tried and tested methods that can be applied to produce reliable results that can be replicated to test the validity of the findings.[11] Recognised forms of scientific research method are shared across research disciplines and can be scrutinised along with the results of experiments and studies. However, the foundations and justification for the overall scientific methodology itself is not normally required of the published texts. Once in the public domain, the validity of claims may be challenged on the grounds of the misapplication of data analysis methods and other issues such as whether this confirms the findings of earlier research. When researchers find their results challenged, they are expected to justify whether or not they have acquired and applied them correctly.

Practice-based research does not operate in the same circumstances as established disciplines and there is no comparable research methodology. This is complicated by the fact that there is a powerful interdisciplinary aspect to this kind of work. In many cases, practitioners combine the different approaches and customise existing methods in response to the demands of the situation. In the creative digital arts, practitioners are exposed to alternative perspectives as they brush up against different disciplines in the course of collaborative work. This leads to a more flexible attitude to using the rich store of existing methodologies in other fields. Such research is often *transdisciplinary* in the sense that it not only sits on the boundaries of more than one discipline but often forges new ground. For example, digital practice in interactive embodied creative work is transforming the performances of physical theatre, choreography and dance.[12]

Because of the eclectic nature of practice-based research, the methodologies being developed by practitioner researchers are drawing on, for example, design science, educational and health action research, anthropology and ethnography, all of which have provided a rich source of inspiration and practical ways forward. Methodologies that represent 'counterviews' to standard scientific experimental method[13] have proven to be a rich source for researchers investigating digital technology that interacts with humans. Action research ethnographic and qualitative approaches as well as techniques from Human-Computer Interaction (HCI) have proven to be very valuable and practical for studying audiences and interactive installation work.[14] Investigating audience experience in interactive art requires a research process that draws upon actual events or what we might call 'in vivo' situations, as distinct from 'in vitro' or laboratory based scenarios. Audio and video data is gathered in such a manner as to provide as accurate a picture of events as can be obtained. The data analysis that follows must also be carried out in a manner that affords genuine insight into the nature of the rich picture that has been obtained. All this is critical to how soundly based the findings are, as researchers into complex human processes, are all too aware. The findings may not pass the scientific test that experimental method affords but the requirement for systematic and principled research processes must be met if the findings are to prove useful and credible to the wider community of practice.

Identifying well-tested methods for eliciting audience views about their experience of interactive art is only the first step, however. Learning how to adapt and customise to suit the particular context is a necessary second step. In audience studies conducted in Beta_Space,[15] asking people what they were doing and thinking, using simple 'think aloud' techniques[16] even immediately after the interactive experience, did not always provide sufficiently rich information. This was partly because of the difficult nature of capturing the complexity of everything that was going on but mainly because of the (understandable) inability of the participants to recall everything in sufficient detail to satisfy the need for a rich, detailed picture of events. To address this problem, 'video-cued recall' was introduced into interactive art audience research. This involved re-playing video recordings of participant interactions and asking them to recall what they were thinking at the time: this proved to be a very much more effective method for acquiring such information.[17]

The question inevitably arises, why would a practitioner choose to embark upon a lengthy process of gathering data, devising analysis frameworks, implementing coding schemes and analysing many examples across different cases? This involves learning new skills and being sure to be rigorous about how the data is collected and analysed and how the results are interpreted at all times. It bears a resemblance to scientific research with all the attendant expectations of being reliable and repeatable that is a little too close for comfort for some. An alternative approach is for an artist to observe audience interaction with an artwork casually and to respond instinctively. If the evaluation is part of a formative process, the effect could be to alter particular aspects of the developing artwork in response to the way the audience responds.

Whilst practitioner researchers are able to draw upon existing methods from other disciplines and adapt them, this is only a first step towards developing a methodology for practice-based research in the creative arts. If practitioners decide they need evidence about audience interaction beyond what they can observe casually, this introduces a new imperative into their practice: you could say a new 'norm' of systematic evaluation. The experience of practitioner researchers in the interactive digital arts indicates that, for the most part, developing a methodology involves adapting and reformulating existing approaches in such a way as to address the creative art context. In a certain sense, this requires the creation of new 'norms' out of old, existing ones. I will focus on two broad categories of practice-based method: documented reflection in practice and practice-based evidence.

Documented reflection in practice-based research

Practitioner researchers are developing research methodologies that draw on theories of reflective practice. In locating research enquiry within practice and asserting the value of practitioner knowledge and its distinctive contributions, Schön's ideas give support to the notion that practitioners themselves are capable of bringing tacit understandings to solving problems in hand. Making artefacts whilst adopting a consciously reflective mode of research, leads to the emergence of questions and issues almost 'naturally' from the practice and it is often a relatively small step to articulate the context and methods associated with practice.

Documenting reflections in practice is a pathway of choice followed by many practitioner researchers. One of the most appealing aspects is that it enables them to record and respond to intuitive instincts about how to progress their practice as they engage with new challenges generated by research. The documentation can then be returned to later for further reflection. How to document reflective practice and use it effectively is a skill that has to be learnt and practical advice is useful.[18] The introduction of structured documentation using diaries, weblogs and other recording methods is an invaluable innovation that makes the process more transparent and, at the same time, sharable in those cases where collaboration is involved: see Chapter 7 to follow.

Documenting reflection in practice-based research has been a key pillar in the research of practitioners writing about their experiences.[19] Practitioners who have made Schön's theory an explicit part of their research methodology are discussed briefly in the following paragraphs.[20]

Lizzie Muller drew on Schön's concept of reflective practice in her research as a practising curator. Faced with the question as to how curatorial practice might produce new knowledge, she turned to his ideas about knowledge developed through action. She observes that he was not proposing a formal research methodology but aiming to throw light on the way professional practitioners generated knowledge in their daily work. For a series of practice-based experiments she used empirical methods adapted from human computer interaction design to the curatorial process from which she gained new knowledge about audience experience:

> This approach created a framework for understanding and describing the new knowledge produced through my practice-based curatorial experiments. The focus of my experimentation was audience experience. In particular, I adapted empirical and applied methods for working with 'user' experience from the field of human-centred interaction design to the process of curating. Reflective practice allowed me to integrate the outcomes of these experiments into an overarching cycle of reflection, theoretical development and practical innovation. The result was a set of new discoveries about the intellectual and strategic value of understanding and working with audience experience in curatorial practice.[21]

The gap in knowledge she wished to bridge was a lack of information about audience experience of artworks and how this might inform curatorial practice. Schön's concepts of repertoire and appreciative system inspired greater understanding of curatorial practice as a body of knowledge:

> [H]ow practitioners judge a 'satisfying outcome', and the concepts of 'repertoire' and 'appreciative system' that are for me, the most useful insights offered by Schön's in terms of how curatorial practice-based research can contribute to knowledge.[22]

Applying the concepts of reflection-in-and-on-action provided the means to describe how that practice can be expanded through research, something that continued to inform her career and ongoing research projects after the PhD was completed. The structural framework she developed is based on insights derived from conscious reflective practice within curatorial practice and has relevance for other practitioners in the same area.[23] It is new knowledge *about* practice derived from reflection *in* practice.

Dave Burraston also found Schön's ideas pivotal in guiding him towards an effective way of moving his thinking forward because, in adopting conscious reflective practice, his enquiry could remain open to the discovery of new phenomena, rather than be constrained too heavily by the initial questions and problems he had identified. His PhD research in the areas of generative music and Cellular Automata was a practice-based study that discovered new ways of making music and, in parallel, enabled a new approach to a complex systems science problem.

> Experimental music experiments have the capability to both produce music and inspire further development of complex systems research. The connection between creativity and complexity has positive implications for future work in both science and music.[24]

His contribution to knowledge in the area of Cellula Automata was considered to be a new contribution to the theory of the complexity field.[25]

Sue Hawksley's research provides an example of how a reflective practice approach, what she refers to as 'dancing to understand', offers fascinating insights into the richness of embodied practice. Her PhD included five dance-based performance works out of which the underlying concepts of embodied experience and knowledge are revealed and appraised.[26] Sue's methodology is based on a body (somatic) process of repeated and changing movements that provide the vehicle for elucidating questions about the thinking and action that takes place. Her research through practice prompted reflections that led to insights which, in turn, created new practices. For example, questions about the role of gesture in thinking emerged from a performance work (danced process #1: talking-while-dancing): when her hands were following dance phrases[27] at the same time as she was speaking, her inability to gesticulate made it harder to think. Conversely, hands that gestured during speech could not follow the dance phrases. This led her to look further into research knowledge about gesture and where her approach to enquiry did not conform to the conventions of the field.

> These questions about gesture were exciting and unexpected, revealed to me through my engagement with the creative task of talking-while-dancing. Much current research argues that the activity of gesturing and gesticulation plays a role in our thinking while speaking. This seemed to be reinforced in my work when the hands were taken up with following dance phrases and therefore not available to gesticulate, it became harder to think, or vice versa, hands getting drawn into gesture couldn't follow the dance logic. At the time I knew little of the field of gesture research and subsequent reading in this area indicates that it is a very lateral approach, which could potentially be used to positively trouble some of the classic methods, although there are clear difficulties for designing a quantitative methodology! Importantly I see these kinds of questions as affirming the value of creative inquiry.

Through creating and evaluating works in practice-based research, she was able to challenge her existing dance thinking and contribute to choreographic theory. The research gave rise to a significant change in her pre-existing assumptions about the role of language. Reflecting on the outcomes of the research process, she can see how much the embodied experience is far from a tacit and inarticulate one, but rather 'reveals itself fully as a linguistic entity'.[28] Her insight that language is integral to all lived experience has influenced her subsequent creative work. We can think about what is happening here as a process whereby practice based knowledge is created through thinking through movement, a powerful form of reflection-in-action-in-the-moment. Her work has been published in a number of articles that explore the interplay between action, reflection and the role of research.[29]

Sue's creative practice and works were discussed previously in relation to the mediating role of digital technology in Chapter 5 and her interview can be located on page 209: see also.[30]

Evidence in practice-based research

We seek 'evidence' when we wish to have more substantial grounds for believing something rather than simply relying on our personal gut feeling, someone's opinion or an anecdote that tells a story about a particular situation. There are, of course, many degrees of evidence and assessing what is generally true and reliably so is not straightforward. Finding evidence to support an action might be relatively simple if someone has already had a similar problem and has done some investigations to find the necessary information. If that is not the case, we may need to do our own research. A lack of evidence usually means that the situation at issue is a very new one or an unprecedented scenario such as is often the case in legal trials.

In the serious business of criminal and civil cases, the nature of evidence is at the heart of both jury and judge led trials. For some-one to be convicted, the prosecution legal team must produce evidence that proves a case 'beyond reasonable doubt'. To do that, evidence of many kinds from forensic data to witness statements has to be presented to the court, all of which must be substantiated by corroboration. The complexity of some cases can be daunting for those, like jurors and trial judges, who have to sift through it. However, sometimes we don't always appreciate what is needed from the police, coroners and forensic scientists who gather the basic information, as well as the prosecution and defence services whose job it is to create a narrative that explains what actually happened and who was responsible- and then convince the jurors and judge that the evidence is sound. A single piece of evidence can undermine a carefully constructed case either in defence or prosecution.

The stringency of the evidence required of different domains from law and medicine to the physical sciences does not have a single gold standard by which to measure all. Instead, evidence produced to support a case, therapy or theory has to meet the tests set by the rules and criteria that govern the field. The process of weighing the evidence depends greatly on the expertise of specialists with access to a large canon of knowledge. The true test of evidence is how well will it stand up to time and persistent scrutiny by knowledgeable peers and stakeholders.

In creative practice, evidence is an unfamiliar notion for the most part when it comes to appraising or assessing what has been done. Practitioners are usually much more comfortable with the role of story, intuition, emotion, choice, preference and other personal elements. Where the processes are highly individual, sometimes idiosyncratic, and the outcomes are entirely novel, chances are there will have been be no research and no evidence to drawn on. The very uniqueness of the creative context underlines this and in any case, why would a practitioner wish for or need 'evidence' and for what reason or purpose? And if they did, what exactly would that 'evidence' consist of?

Many creative practitioners are naturally cautious about so called 'evidence based' research because it is perceived as being overly 'scientific' with potential to exert a negative influence on creative work; moreover, it usually takes the form of quantitative measures- a numbers game. Even if we say 'systematic' rather than 'scientific', the connotations still suggest a highly rational process that is an anathema to some artists. It is not unreasonable to doubt the value of systematic research purely on the basis of its effect on the creative process. Being a creator, a maker of artworks, does not sit easily with the business of scientific and quantitative research. Not only does it require time and effort to learn the skills, but involves a radically different way of thinking and that in itself could have a distorting effect. Balancing the amount of effort needed on all fronts is a difficult one to achieve. That said, there are sometimes good reasons to adopt more structured and systematic approaches as practitioner researchers doing PhDs in particular contexts have discovered.

If evidence-based practice does not appeal because it smacks too closely of science, is there any place for evidence in practitioner research? Perhaps we need first to recover the word evidence from its scientific enclosure by taking a look at some evidence-based practice, or as I would rather refer to it, *practice-based evidence*. This is a term used in clinical medicine where a distinction with evidence-based practice is made.[31]

How should we differentiate practice-based evidence from evidence-based practice?

Practice-based evidence is acquired by gathering data by means of practice over time. Instead of asking a question and then searching for evidence on the basis of which action is decided, the process is turned around. The practitioner sets a target or goal, decides on a set of actions, carries them out and then appraises the result of those actions. If this sounds familiar when it comes to creative reflective practice, that's because in a very simplified way, that is the general pattern. There is an important dimension to reflective creative practice when the practitioner researcher chooses to take an empirical route to new understandings. By adding a principled enquiry stream to creative reflective practice, based on gathering and analysing observations of interactive works live with participating audiences, the process becomes one of 'creating-reflecting-creating-investigating-creating'. This process takes practitioner researchers into perspectives beyond those derived from individual self-reflection. Many practitioner researchers have taken that empirical path in addition, and sometimes in parallel with, the reflective one. This path relies on obtaining evidence from audience experience studies in the case of interactive art.

When we studied a number of practice-based researchers doing creative arts PhDs, there was a general pattern with individual variants depending on the individual. The practitioner typically follows a 'trajectory' or route, influenced by individual goals and intentions. Activities are undertaken during the creative process that may include things like coming up with a new framework for appraising the work, carrying out studies to check its functions or gathering comments to understand how audience participants feel. Creating artworks, exhibitions, installations, musical compositions and creative software systems, provide the basis for conducting research. In practice-based research, the place of theory is likely to consist of different ways of examining, critiquing and applying areas of knowledge that are considered relevant to the individual's practice. It may consist of a working assumption that the artwork will elicit certain emotions or qualities of experience in an audience; this will remain a personal theory until it is subject to a more rigorous form of study that involves investigation as to whether or not the assumption has any truth beyond an individual viewpoint. Evaluation includes reflecting on the process and any working assumptions that have been relevant to the making of the work. It may involve observation, recording and analysing as part of a semi-formal approach to generating understandings that go further than informal reflections on personal practice.

From a study of practitioner researchers, we derived several trajectory models of practice and research all of which were variants on a combination of practice, theory and evaluation. The trajectories work in a number of different ways. Where the primary driver is theory, a framework is developed that draws on theoretical knowledge and is used to shape the evaluation process and the creation of works A second type of trajectory is one where the practice drives the development of theory. In this case, research questions and design criteria are derived through the creation of works and this leads to the development of a theoretical framework which is used in the evaluation of the results of practice. In both cases, the process is cyclical, and there is often a tighter iterative sub-process in which the framework and practice develop together. The model represents how research and practice interrelate in the process of developing practitioner frameworks. The trajectories represent different kinds of relationships between theory, practice and evaluation as exemplified in the cases described. In each case, the interplay between practice, theory and evaluation involved many iterations and much interaction between the elements as the creative process drove a continuous process of change.[32]

The following examples illustrate the kinds of processes that practitioner researchers engage in when adopting a practice-based evidence approach.

Mike Leggett, a practising filmmaker, came to research with an expectation that he would acquire confirmation of his initial working hypothesis that when people interacted with his *Mnemovie* system, they would reveal their personal knowledge about the organisation of a moving image collection; from that he expected to be able to compare the types of knowledge in use. He produced graphical representations of the data from questionnaires and recorded observations. This revealed different patterns in the sample group and a 'persona' based view was identified, based upon the individual's interaction style. This evidence supported his belief that creative rather than functional approaches to interacting with movies was possible and could be encouraged by making the design of each system specific to each video collection. The results of carrying out systematic studies were not only valuable in confirming his initial assumptions but perhaps more importantly, they identified new patterns of user types that influenced his future designing. Being able to confirm a belief is helpful but when an unanticipated insight emerges as well, then the value for creative practice can be far reaching.[33]

Brigid Costello, as an artist looking to make interactive works that encouraged audiences to play carried out systematic evaluation studies of participant interaction in order to explore whether or not she had achieved her aim. She used observational techniques to study several of her own artworks, gathering data using video-cued recall and interviews and analysing the data using qualitative analysis methods and software analysis software in combination with mind-mapping software. The figures that resulted from the surveys were used to pinpoint trends and preliminary findings. These were then tested and refined during the analysis of the interview data. However, that process led to doubts about the value of systematic studies. Her reflections on the influence that systematic studies might have on her creative practice centred on the potential for confusing her artistic aims and diverting her focus and effort away from her creative practice. She found that the results of the audience studies yielded divergent opinions, which needed to be carefully considered; however, in the end, she found the process rewarding and creatively inspiring. Most important, she was able to understand her audience more clearly and design ways of interaction that were more effective on her own terms.[34]

Jennifer Seevinck, is an artist who conducted studies to derive understandings about interactive experience in parallel with creating her own art. Underlying this was a stream of enquiry about how an audience's response may be influenced by interaction with works of art designed to stimulate emergent responses in audiences. With each make-evaluate-make cycle, the artist moved towards her goal of creating artworks that stimulate particular responses in the audience. It was an approach not unlike that of a scientist: she was testing a working hypothesis embodied in the works she had made and then having gained insight into whether the design was appropriate, she used her insights from the studies to advance both art and theory. She later developed the work from her PhD into a significant book in the area of emergence.[35]

Self-reflective and evidence-based paths can be seen as different but complementary options for the practitioner researcher. Enhancing one's personal creative practice through reflection-in-action focuses inwardly, whereas conducting systematic studies turns the lens outwards towards the value of what other people can reveal.[36] In both situations, reflection is an essential element of generating practice-based knowledge.

Practice-based research and knowledge

Practitioner knowledge is embedded in understandings about the process of making and the creative works themselves: the artefacts, the compositions, the performances, the exhibitions and installations. In practice-based research, these works are given context through practitioner reflections on practice and gathering data or evidence that informs and shapes subsequent processes and outcomes.

How can practice-based research produce new knowledge?

Research in its different manifestations is usually expected to contribute to new knowledge that challenges existing theories and assumptions. Researchers everywhere seek to verify hypotheses or prove that existing theories are wrong. However, research in creative practice has particular characteristics that do not necessarily conform to traditional norms about the nature of knowledge and how it is generated. For one thing, the practice that is so central to practice-based research is primarily directed towards *making things*, whether they are visual or sound objects or installations, exhibitions or performances.

The contribution of creative practice is generally recognised to centre on the creation of novel works. Nevertheless, whilst the creative works are at the centre of the research, there are other outcomes that can be shared, scrutinised and evaluated. That practising artists might contribute to knowledge in other ways is a less familiar notion. The very idea that creating artistic works might play a part in generating new knowledge in a similar sense to conducting scientific experiments is contentious. That research from creative practice can contribute to knowledge in a more general sense flies in the face of widely held beliefs in the unique properties of art. Masterworks are valued for the contribution they make to culture in general and to aesthetic and emotional experiences. Knowledge is seen as verbal or numerical in expression and something that can be generalised to other processes or events that are outside those that gave rise to it. It is also considered to be transferable – and for that, verbal expression is paramount.[37]

Research within practice is concerned with the nature of artefacts and the processes used in their development. The role of the artefact in research is a contentious aspect of the practice-based research debate especially where the artefact is seen as a significant part of the research methodology and is implicated in the kind of knowledge that is generated. Practitioner research may use artefacts as the object of study or as experimental apparatus. The creation of an artefact can be central to the research process and may well represent the core of the new knowledge generated by the research. However, whether that knowledge is communicated directly through the artefact is questionable. If we accept that the artefact can, in some sense, represent new knowledge, the problem of sharing that knowledge implies a need for a parallel means of communication, in effect, a linguistic one that can help to frame the way that we view the artefact and grasp the knowledge.

What is important to understand about the creation of works within practice-based research is that the practitioner is typically investigating new artistic forms and that they are likely to make their claim to novelty explicit, often in textual form. This goes well beyond creating new content for old forms. This second kind of outcome, running in parallel with the works, is a vital part of any claims of new knowledge from practice-based research.

Conclusions

In this chapter, we discussed how practitioner research is generating knowledge from practice that has hitherto been hard to acquire. Practice-based research programmes that connect closely with creative practice are providing a means of extending creative work at the same time as enhancing the practitioner's ability to share and debate it with others. Reflection through practice-based research enables practitioners to generate fresh insights into their personal processes and the creative works that emerge. New methods are being deployed to generate practice-based evidence that can have wider relevance to creative practice. Contributions to knowledge from formal research that is fully documented and publicly available are adding to a wider understanding of practitioner expertise and how it is developed through experience.

Notes

1 Schön (1991, pp. 275–283).
2 Schön (1991, p. 68).
3 Ascott, R. (2011) in Candy and Edmonds (2011) Preface: Interacting: Art, Research and the Creative Practitioner.
4 'tacit knowledge' (Polanyi, 1983): internalised knowing that the person is unaware of and which is difficult to describe and therefore not articulated in words.
5 Selected practice-based research books: Biggs and Karlsson 2011; Barrett and Bolt 2007; Elkins 2014; Macleod and Holdridge 2006; Nelson 2013; Smith and Dean 2009; Sullivan 2010; Vaughan 2017.
6 Candy and Edmonds (2010): this chapter considers the way organisational frameworks are important and essential vehicles for giving the artefact a legitimate role in practice-based research. These developments have required changes to existing organisational rules and are relatively recent in the history of knowledge production.
7 Scrivener (2002).
8 In 2008–2009, a study of creative practitioners undergoing PhD research in three Australian universities was carried out. A majority already had well-established careers, often combined with a successful creative practice. In taking the important step of embarking on a lengthy, rigorous and impecunious formal research degree, they were inevitably influenced by more than one reason, including personal circumstances at the time. The decision to embark on a PhD was far from lightly undertaken and there were a number of barriers to be overcome: a lack of reliable funding, relocation from other countries, difficulties in finding the right environment for their needs, and inevitably, employment and time pressures. The main factors that influenced the decision to undertake a practice-based PhD were motivational and choice of environment. There was a clear differentiation between reasons given arising from intrinsic motives and those arising from extrinsic motives. All went on to complete successful theses and advance their creative practice: see Candy 2009; Candy and Edmonds 2018b.
9 Candy and Edmonds on how the university rules are important and essential vehicles for giving the artefact a legitimate role in practice-based research.
10 These issues are discussed in two Leonardo journal articles: Candy and Edmonds 2018a, 2018b.

11 The scientific method is a process for experimentation that is used to explore observations and answer questions. When direct experimentation is not possible, scientists modify the scientific method. The goal is to discover cause and effect relationships by asking questions, gathering and examining the evidence, and seeing if all the available information can be combined in to a logical answer. Scientific method involves backing up and repeating called an iterative process. The experimental method is usually taken to be the most scientific of all methods, the 'method of choice'. The main problem with all the non-experimental methods is lack of control over the situation. The experimental method is a means of trying to overcome this problem.

12 Bluff et al. (2018); Hawksley (2012).

13 Argyris et al. (1985).

14 The information gathering and analysis methods used by practitioner researchers from ethnographic research and HCI research (Crabtree, 2003) as well as strategies and methods for qualitative research such as grounded theory (Glaser and Strauss, 1999).

15 Beta_Space: Exhibiting and evaluating space at the Powerhouse Museum Sydney: www.betaspace.net.au/content/view/12/36/.

16 Lewis and Rieman (1994).

17 Costello et al. (2005).

18 Candy (2006); Edmonds (2018).

19 The book 'Interacting: Art, Research and the Creative Practitioner' includes articles by practitioners giving an account of their PhD methodologies and outcomes (Candy and Edmonds 2011).

20 See Candy (2011) for more details about these practitioners.

21 Muller (2011, p. 94).

22 Muller (2011, pp. 102–103).

23 Muller (2008) PhD.

24 Burraston (2011, p. 118).

25 Burraston (2006) PhD.

26 Hawksley (2012) PhD.

27 A choreographer designs a series of actions which linked by transitional movements to create a dance phrase, the basic unit of choreographed movement.

28 Lepecki (2006, p. 7).

29 Hawksley (2011) (2013) (2016).

30 Sue Hawksley: http://lindacandy.com/CRPBOOK/hawksley.

31 McIntosh (2010).

32 Edmonds and Candy (2010).

33 Leggett (2009); Leggett (2011).

34 Costello (2011).

35 Seevinck (2011); Seevinck (2017).

36 Candy and Edmonds (2011).

37 Smith and Dean (2009).

7

LEARNING FROM THE REFLECTIVE PRACTITIONER

Being a reflective practitioner means cultivating the many ways we can learn through experience. This can be expressed in simple terms as thinking about what you are doing or what happened as a result of your actions and then deciding what to do differently next time. Being reflective through everyday practice is essential to learning how to be effective when faced with new situations and unexpected events. Reflective practice has benefits in increasing self-awareness, a key element of emotional intelligence and, at the same time, in developing a better understanding of others. Chapter 7 considers what we can learn from reflective practitioners in professional and creative contexts, in collaboration with others, in digitally amplified practice and through research.

Can reflective practice be learnt?

Many people think so. The growth of advice and guidance in, for example, the medical, nursing and legal professions is testimony to the success of the claim that being reflective in practice is key to improving professional expertise. Reflection in and on practice has been made 'official', even mandatory, as new codes of practice and guidance on how to reflect as part of continuous professional development have been introduced. But is this a true measure of whether reflective practice can be learnt and does imposing it through appraisal systems really work? Those are difficult questions to answer and currently there are few studies that prove the value of this approach to embedding reflection in practice. In any case, practitioners were reflective well before it became a by-word for professional competence. Nevertheless, if take-up is anything to go by, reflective practice has been very successful as a concept. This is evident too in its dissemination in a wide range of practices, many of them in the creative sphere.

Can *creative* reflective practice be learnt?

This is even more difficult to answer in the same terms as there are few direct comparisons. In many ways, being reflective is a pathway to being creative and this is not confined to those areas traditionally thought to be more creative. Some people would argue that it is the personal qualities and cognitive attributes that lend themselves most to creativity and these are primarily genetically determined. On the other hand, others believe that if we can learn how to change our behaviour and acquire new skills, we can all become that much more creative. Both views have merit and especially if weighed up together. I happen to believe that whilst there is no doubt that genetically determined characteristics provide us with the basic ingredients for creative capability, our exposure to the social and educational environment plays a highly significant role as well. The relative contributions of nature and nurture will depend upon many factors and the debate, always contentious, as to which is more decisive, continues to engage researchers and educators without resolution.[1]

Human beings are thinkers and makers by nature and given the opportunity will seek to create and to learn from experience. Practitioners have enormously variable approaches when it comes to working creatively. As the practitioners who have inspired and informed the ideas presented throughout this book have shown, there are many ways to be creative. The individual and shared situations of practice shape the reflections that take place. Creative practice is a learning process and reflection is a mechanism for learning through practice. We can learn from creative and reflective practices that are revealed by listening to and observing experienced practitioners.

In the next section the focus, will be on lessons from the way practitioners create and the kind of reflective thinking that serves practice well in professional development, in creative practice, in collaboration with others, in digitally amplified practice and in research.

Lessons from reflective practitioners

Our understanding of the nature of practitioner knowledge has been undergoing a transformation since Donald Schön first challenged the dominance of the Technical Rationality model.[2] In the professions, to be accredited as a licenced practitioner, your knowledge has to be continually updated. This is why there are regulatory requirements and codes of practice that govern the standards of every profession. Many professional associations have adopted schemes that encourage practitioners to document their self-reflections during their professional lifetime, a practice seen increasingly as fundamental to upgrading professional expertise. In fields such as health care, medicine, nursing, social work and law, reflective practice has become an essential ingredient of professional development and the renewal of licences.

The aim of professional development schemes and courses is to encourage best practice in the individual practitioner, and as a consequence, improve the delivery of the service to clients. The danger arises when such schemes rely on mechanistic recording with little mind to whether it is really effective. This is particularly the case, where the implementation is new and insufficient attention has been paid to providing the practitioners with suitable ways of learning how to be reflective. Where the approach is focused on experiential learning through reflective practice and a learning culture is fostered in the organisation, practitioners are better able to develop the methods that lead to best practice.[3]

★★★

What do we learn from professional practitioners about being reflective in practice?

There are certain qualities of mind and ways of working that incline towards being reflective when faced with unexpected and puzzling problems: these situations of practice are frequently found in medicine, social work and other professions that aim to meet the needs of people often in difficult and complex circumstances. Some of the qualities and practices to be found in reflective professional practice are drawn from examples presented previously in Chapter 2. These attributes represent a sample of the thinking and actions of practitioners and may be found beyond the fields discussed. It is always important to remember that contextual factors influence the patterns of action and opportunities for reflection.

The ability to question one's deeply held assumptions, even prejudices, is a key quality of mind. Developing an open mind requires a questioning attitude, but also learning to observe closely, listen carefully and connect to people as patients, clients, customers, visitors. This is a case by case focus rather than applying generalised principles to a particular context. From understanding the individual situations, actions taken and reflected on build a repository of knowledge that can be modified and used again. In parallel with the individual case by case approach, there is also benefit to be gained from being aware of other perspectives outside the immediate situations of practice. Knowledge can be enriched by relating present actions to past cases in such a way as to broaden one's understanding of why something is done in the way it is done nowadays. A practitioner learns from mistaken remedies of the past, and in doing so, is better prepared to question the solutions of the moment, as we saw in the case of Suzanne O'Sullivan, the neurologist whose writings provide insight into the conundrum of being presented with patients with chronic illnesses for which there is no apparent physical explanation (see 'The medical practitioner' section from Chapter 2).

Making space for considered reflection amidst stressful and demanding situations is a tall order. Reflecting in the moment requires an extraordinary degree of calm and measured response, something which is expected by the public and desired by the professional, for example, in social work. In order to achieve any degree of considered reflection on action and at a distance, this cannot be left to chance opportunities during busy schedules. It is essential that time and resources are allocated by the organisation and managerial staff ensure it happens. Turning staff appraisal requirements into opportunities for reflective practice is a start but this must take place within a supportive framework for increasing professional knowledge. For practitioners to feel able to question their own approaches and actions there needs to be full confidence and trust in the environment they inhabit. This cannot always be assumed and building trust is a vital part of enhancing professional capability.

Being up to date in terms of professional knowledge is expected by the public but taking action − 'interventions' as in the case of social work, needs to be focused on immediate situations of need. This requires effort to coordinate and connect with other service practitioners, with full cognisance of the relevant law and being mindful of what the practice is committed to. Even in the face of huge difficulties, the reflective social worker is working to make a difference, a commitment to professional practice that brought them there in the first place (see 'The social work practitioner' section from Chapter 2).

Being a reflective practitioner implies a broader view of professional practice, one that embraces skills beyond domain specific knowledge. Knowing the law, for the solicitor, is a fundamental requirement of basic training, but this alone cannot serve the needs of every situation. If the client is in finance or energy, for example, there are general business and communication skills that can enhance the practitioner's ability to propose appropriate actions. Reflective practice is not a one-time set of actions based on the last case but a continuous process of self-directed learning from experience of many cases and situations. Learning through reflection on experience leads to higher levels of professional competence. The capacity to reflect on one's actions, evaluate the outcomes, learn from the situation and apply the new knowledge is integrated into the best practice of experienced practitioners. Making reflective practice a normal part of a lawyer's remit is the aim of the profession's regulatory framework, with the added benefit of addressing accountability and professional standards (see 'The legal practitioner' section from Chapter 2).

Reflective practice is not confined to individuals but also takes place in relation to group action. A single practitioner will try to work according to standards for him or herself but this is inevitably in the context of the field of practice, its rules, conventions and processes and what is more, what is expected by clients and society at large. Being professional means aiming high and responding to challenges as they arise and at the same time articulating a clear vision of the overall design of the enterprise in hand, as in the case of the architect. This is where creative thinking combined with a cohesive overarching idea is highly effective because these attributes are needed to draw discrete elements together whether it is coming up with a singular building design for an exceptional setting or solving a complex engineering problem. In these situations of practice, being able to create and communicate the big picture to others in the team and, at the same time, understand the detail that needs to be tested and evaluated by practitioners from different contributing disciplines, plays a vital, integrative role requiring a high level of reflection of all kinds. By embedding reflection in every thought and action, the reflective practitioner learns to live with uncertainty and face unexpected events and problems as a normal part of practice (see 'The architectural practitioner' section from Chapter 2.

The qualities of mind and working methods found amongst reflective professional practitioners may be found in many areas. These are not, however, independent of the particular conditions of a given situation such as whether the practice is public facing, collaborative or answerable to the practitioner alone. In particular where there is a requirement for reflection as part of competency assessment, this introduces a strong element of managed forms of reflection that does not necessarily accord with normal practice and may introduce new ways of working in order to accommodate externally imposed requirements.

What do we learn from creative practitioners about being reflective in practice?

In creative practice, managed forms of learning how to be reflective are not usual, and indeed, is not part of the cultural norms of creative practice. And yet, as the creative practitioners in this book can testify, reflection is ever present whether through individual preference or as a result of other factors such as doing formal research. The process of creating, whether in drawing, painting, constructing, designing, moving or any of the many options open to us, can be an enjoyable, if demanding, experience which in a certain sense 'teaches' the makers about themselves and their relationship to others. There is always some form of learning in the sense of being consciously aware of arriving at new insights, new directions or simply doing it better next time. Creating, reflecting and learning from experience is at the heart of such practice.

Does working creatively facilitate or encourage more reflection in practice? Or does reflective practice promote creative thinking? There is a reciprocal exchange of course but overall, I am inclined to the view that living and working creatively leads to more reflection overall because of the close interchange between making and evaluating. By taking the practitioner perspective, it was possible to identify reflection in creative practice. What we learn about creative practice does not necessarily conform to those views of creativity as an indefinable process. There are, of course, complex and interwoven aspects that do not lend themselves to categorisation and stubbornly remain impervious to reductive analysis. But that does not apply to everything. Far from being mysterious, certain aspects of creative work are well understood and can reveal different types of reflection as discussed in Chapter 3 and summarised in the following examples.

Reflection-for-Action is a systematic working practice that involves contemplating previous actions, thoughts and achievements and reassessing existing works and outcomes. To move forward, the practitioner often considers relevant information and prior strategies in order to identify any constraints that might impact the progress of a work. This awareness enabled Brigid Costello to reduce the many options open to her which were in danger of delaying or preventing actions at the beginning of a new project.

Reflection in the making moment by contrast, is responsive, requiring action in the immediate situation. Expressions like 'thinking on one's feet', 'thinking with the hands' and 'thinking through the body' capture some of the experiences of reflection in the moment which practitioners know well. In this situation, a practitioner needs alert senses: the looking, listening, feeling that is indicative of heightened awareness of mind and body and requires degree of conscious awareness that goes beyond intuitive actions and is critical to dynamic flow states. A good example is musical improvisation which demands responsiveness to the actions of others or self-set starting points, and as Roger Mills describes becomes a moment when time is suspended as he locks into the challenge of responding to the actions of others. This is a state where conscious and unconscious actions seem to work in parallel, as in the case of Esther Rolinson's drawing process.

Reflection at a distance can be achieved through detaching from the process in hand in order to disrupt over familiarity with work in progress. By moving location or materials or tools, the practitioner can change focus and sometimes arrive at new insights or alter direction of travel. The same effect can also be achieved by participative practices that involve exposing one's process and outcomes to others and responding to what you learn from their feedback. These are readily learned techniques that can be applied to any situation of practice. Julie Freeman builds experiences into her works that are intended to facilitate audience immersion and close engagement in a way that increases her own understanding.

Reflection on surprise requires a flexible attitude to the unexpected. Positive responses to surprises imply a willingness to embrace challenges. Even where a surprise outcome is not welcome – is 'undesirable' to use Schön's term, it can prompt valuable questions. Some practitioners provoke surprise as they look for ways to identify and disrupt tacit assumptions and in doing so, learn something new. In these ways, being open to surprise can bring rewards and engineering surprise as personal working method can provoke questions.

People are often urged to learn to 'think outside the box' assuming this is the route to generating more creative ideas. But how do we achieve that? One way that seems to be important is learning to take a lateral perspective.[4] But how does this work in practice as distinct from learning general purpose techniques? One way of stimulating more reflection is to deliberately adopt a tangential perspective in relation to one's own familiar ground, area of expertise or everyday practice. This kind of approach can be seen in scientists, curators and artists alike: in this book, Roger Kneebone (scientist), Ken Arnold (curator) and Sue Hawksley (artist) all demonstrate a propensity for taking the lateral view as they explore the different practices of their respective domains. In common with many creative practitioners, they feel more comfortable adopting perspectives that go beyond their own familiar ground rather than resting in the same cultural and disciplinary zones. By taking an unusual perspective, the basis for challenging existing assumptions and opening up new avenues of exploration is established in everyday practice. This is the kind of reflective ethos that may ultimately lead to larger challenges to the existing canon of knowledge.

In creative practice, it is often the learning from mentors and models that can be a very effective way to gain insight into your practice. For example, Csikszentmihalyi's state of flow[5] can be developed via other means such as studying and writing Zen calligraphy[6] in which making brush strokes onto special paper is an 'unconscious' meditative practice of focused intensity. This kind of practice is acquired through many years of study following the teachings of master practitioners. Gestural abstraction or action painting[7] such as those of American abstract expressionist, Jackson Pollock's dropping, spraying, splashing paint onto canvas laid out on the floor, appears at face value to be random splashes of colour on canvas but closer examination reveals they emerged from deep foundations in the process of painting as a performance.[8]

What do we learn from collaborative practitioners about being reflective in practice?

Collaboration is entering a renewed era across most fields of creative work. But many people are not prepared because they lack experience and have not learnt how to collaborate successfully. Making connections with other people can be a powerful stimulus to reflections in creative work. How to make those connections in productive and enriching ways is not always straightforward. Engaging in a dialogue with someone from different backgrounds, skills and experiences requires a sensitivity to divergent ways of thinking and communicating. To be able to build trust, practitioners need to be open and honest about their objectives and what they expect from collaborators. Sometimes, when world views are far apart, having someone else to mediate or facilitate the relationship, at least at the beginning, is necessary. In certain situations, loosely defined collaborations bring unexpected benefits and unexpected levels of surprise. In more structured situations, it is helpful to give all participants an opportunity to make a creative contribution and to recognise the potential of each person. Things are unlikely to run smoothly all the time and where difficulties arise, this does not have to be a negative thing as some degree of tension can be a stimulus to creative reflection. Leadership is usually necessary and if it can be both inspirational and responsive to the team, the chances of more sustainable collaboration are increased. know what role you want to play and what you expect of others.

Collaborative working enables greater reflection because the shared activity invites communication. Engaging in dialogue means that ideas have to be articulated in spoken and written form which contributes to shared understanding. Whilst talking and listening are important for co-reflection, the contribution and influence of each party to the shared enterprise becomes more evident as works take shape and come to fruition. Making works provides tangible outcomes that generate more mechanisms for shared reflection.

Learning how to empathise with practitioners of a different discipline can promote sustainable collaboration. Being exposed to different perspectives can stimulate reflection.

A few tips to think about:

• Inspire others and be inspired by others.
• Find out the expectations and constraints of the other parties.

- Value informal encounters as much as formal meetings.
- Take things on trust at times while you get to know everyone.
- Know what role you want to play and what you expect of others.
- Ask yourself if the risks outweigh the benefits.
- Recognise and celebrate the value of difference.
- Be sure you have a clear picture of what you expect but don't be too precious about owning every idea or piece of work if you can see you are gaining from it.
- Be upfront about what you can contribute and how you will do that.
- Build on longer term strength and reliability in your discoveries and relationships.
- Look for unexpected and surprising outcomes that can stimulate your creative thinking.
- Adopt an attitude of generosity especially with people you know will value it.
- Build networks of people with the kinds of qualities and know how you find stimulating.
- Identify someone you really want to talk to or form a working relationship for real benefit.

What do we learn from digital practitioners about being reflective in practice?

Many practitioners are exploring the possibilities that digital technology has for their creative practice and making new works that would otherwise not be possible. What begins as using a new tool to make an artefact eventually develops into something more compelling, as the full potential of computational processes becomes clearer. Moreover, the initial focus on making digitally enabled artefacts often gives way to a transformation in the practitioner's processes as their ambitions for what they can achieve increase. This varies according to how well versed they are in the technology itself. In the case of digital natives for whom writing computer code is a second language and software is a natural medium, there is a seamless movement between many varieties of digital offerings available. The more deeply ingrained the technology is in the materials and the making processes, the greater control the practitioner needs over its design and functions.

There are many lessons from the way that creative practitioners amplify their reflective practice with digital technology, some of them unsurprising, others less apparent. Reflection in practice is influenced in different ways depending on the type of technology and the practitioner's relationship with it. This can stimulate new insights into the process and its outcomes and, in turn, provoke more reflections. For digital immigrants used to traditional media, the process naturally requires adaptation in the way works are made, but beyond that stage, changes can be expected to extend beyond learning how to use ready-made digital tools. This is where there is a spectrum of difference between those who are content with digital as a means to enhance production of works and those for whom it is integral to the way they think, make and reflect on their actions and outcomes. This is likely to be a transitional situation as new generations of digital natives occupy the world of creative practice.

We can maximise the potential of digital technology to amplify creative work, by observing what successful practitioners do.

When choosing digital tools, keep your options open. Iteration is essential for exploratory ways of working and if, for example, a software application requires investment in significant amount of dedicated learning, this can restrict choices for future work. This might not matter at the time but it is important to keep that in mind and not be afraid to change direction.

Do the research to find what you need to satisfy your creative goals and if you want to have more control over how digital tools and media might suit your work. As we saw in the case of Anthony Marshall previously (page 205), the iPad apps he identified through research enabled him to keep his options open and work with all the functions he needed. His art making was enhanced by tools designed for ease of use which gave him room for reflection more generally because he did not have to struggle with 'clumsy' interaction methods.

Digital technology as a mediator implies a relationship between two or more parties who interact with one another and new forms are being created in creative embodied interaction. Mediation technology contributes to the creative reflective process as we saw in Sue Hawksley's interactive dance performances, in George Khut's body sense detection interactive works and Sarah Fdili Alaoui's mediated dance performances that break new ground both technically and artistically. Their embodied interactive art performances and reflective research practices are increasing our understanding about the role of the body in thinking (see Chapter 5).

Digital technologies as mediators can change the way practitioners think and make artworks in transformative ways. A different relationship between practitioner and technology is to see it as a medium for thinking and defining the artwork. The algorithm is the very material of the work itself as in the case of Paul Brown a pioneer in computational systems as a medium for the visual arts for over fifty years (page 195). This example and that of many other practitioners suggests that if you wish to enhance your control over the medium, learning to code is an essential skill. That does not suit everyone but it is advisable to at least become sufficiently well versed in the programming environment that the creative technologist is using in order to make key decisions together.

Augmented, mixed and virtual reality technologies have their own implications for the relationship between practitioner and technology. Research has explored the relationship between physical and virtual objects and raised questions about how this changes the way that we think about the interplay between these different states and the impact on the way participants see, hear, and feel, ranging from a completely real and natural environment to a completely virtual environment. It is an area that requires more research into the way these forms of technology impact on the creative process and the capacity for reflection.

In contemporary creative digital practice, the notion of partnerships between practitioner and technology is emerging. It is a relationship that is dependent on a more responsive relationship, for example in scenarios where digitally created works react to the human performer as if they are improvising together. For these creative exchanges to be possible the software has usually been programmed by the practitioners, as in the case of Benjamin Carey whose digital instrument gives him more scope for creative exploration because it is programmed to produce responses that are not easily predictable but are compatible with his expectations (page 203 and 226).

What do we learn from practitioners who do research?

Developing a research ethos through practice is a persistent state of mind not just a matter of learning skills and techniques although that is part of it. Practitioner research as described in Chapter 6 is, in many ways, an answer to Donald Schön's call for investigating and valuing the 'knowing in practice' that comes from reflecting in action when faced with unforeseen problems that demand new solutions. As we have seen previously, the very nature of creative practice involves setting challenges for oneself and treating surprises as opportunities for new insights and works. This often leads the practitioner down the road towards research, a process that involves reflection in every sense of the word. It also means that creative works are not the only outcomes.

Most practitioners do personal research to obtain information about materials or tools and where to source expertise. Some opt to share what they have learnt but that is a personal choice. What has been learnt may be embedded in the making of new works but that knowledge is not necessarily explicit unlike the outcomes of formal practice-based research that is assessed by independent experts in the field and is made publicly available. Many creative practitioners are doing PhDs and discovering what they can learn from those who have gone down that road before them. Reflection through research is a strategy for interrogating existing practice and through that process, generating new knowledge. It involves documenting the creative process and interpreting any questions and insights arising from it as a result of which new insights, appreciative and works emerge. Research of this kind will lead to change and that can be challenging and even transformative. Through studies of practitioner research, we are beginning to understand much more about how research and practice interrelate and the variations that occur. The interplay between practice, theory and research involves many cycles of change during which new questions arise through the actions taken.[9] Above all, research should be seen as a route towards strengthening one's practice which requires a systematic approach and a willingness to learn from the comments of others.

Developing a research through practice mind set is not a given and there are lessons to be learnt from the practitioners who have completed their studies and shared their new knowledge in theses, books and articles.[10] For practitioners considering a research path, the advice is to study those examples first before committing to what will be a demanding few years.

Documenting reflective practice

Reflective writing is seen as an increasingly important aspect of professional development in general. Developing reflective habits includes making time for documenting reflections on the day's events and actions, a process of setting down the salient issues and questioning whether the actions taken were optimal for the given case. The reflective writing habit is something that professionals in many spheres do, whether they call it a work around log, a red, blue or black note book or a field diary. It may never be consulted again after writing but it serves a purpose in embedding certain habits of mind. Alternatively, it may become a resource for future consultation. No matter the use, keeping such records is a feature of many practitioners' normal routine.

There are many ways to document, from handwritten notes, the writer's 'commonplace book' to video diaries, blog posts and podcasts, more often in use as digital natives overtake digital immigrants and those who have not yet ventured in that direction. Keeping records about working practice is a normal practice for many, if not most creative practitioners. For some it is the artwork itself that embodies years of creative effort and there is no additional value in producing verbal descriptions once they are made. However, writing down ideas or merely factual sources of information such as names of contacts, web links and phone numbers alongside sketches and diagrams, is a regular part of the daily work for many. These kinds of records operate not only as aids to thinking at the time but may also be turned to in later years as a source of reminders and stimulation. They may have no practical function at all but are a necessary part of the business of working through a current idea or exploring a new method without any intention of referring back to it later.

Monitoring and Recording Advice:

- Keep a written record either in the form of an online diary or blog, or a handwritten notebook.
- Keep a notebook with you to record any observations during the process of making a work.
- When collecting audio or video records, factor in time to transcribe or make notes on key events.
- Keep a chart to be able to see at a glance what has been recorded and what you plan to record.
- Designate time for reflection after your work session to record your reactions and emerging thoughts.
- Do not be tempted to only review and reflect on an ad hoc basis. Build it in to your timetable.

Good questions to ask yourself as you reflect are:

- What was proposed, discussed, decided and carried through?
- What stumbling blocks arose and how they were addressed?

- Were the ideas proposed workable, interesting, challenging?
- Did the group collaboration work well and if not why not?
- What were the reasons for success or otherwise?
- Did the solutions work well, if not why not?
- What were the viewpoints between collaborators and what did you learn from differences?
- What did you learn from any mistakes or things that failed?

Guidance for learning reflective practice

The student of reflective practice has plenty of advice to draw on from print literature and online web resources. Some texts are coupled with theoretical background which gives credit to foundational work, from Dewey to Schön and onwards in time. Much of the advice springs from the push brought about by regulatory codes of practice in professional spheres, either entirely new or as revised versions of past practices. I will not attempt to cover the ground fully, but instead offer some starting points and places to go for advice. The general guidance is useful for students and researchers coming to the practice and its theory for the first time. The domain specific advice is valuable for established practitioners undertaking new regimes for self-assessment as part of a programme of continuous professional development.

Multi-disciplinary reflective practice guidance

There are many sources of discussion about the relationship between professional knowledge and reflective practice. The work by Michael Eraut is particularly pertinent to the development of professional knowledge through practice. His paper on how professionals learn in their workplace covers a range of topics that relevant to our understanding of the learning process and several models that are helpful for devising ways and means to encourage observation, reflection and self-evaluation skills.[11] Barbara Bassot's guide to reflective practice presents an interdisciplinary perspective coupled with a practical approach to the subject.[12] By understanding what reflective practice means outside a specific field, the reader is invited to recognise the value of working at the boundaries of disciplines. It means examining theories and models of reflective practice that have a broader application to different professional situations. At the same time, Bassot advocates learning from cases and examples that have been tested in specific domains and can then be applied elsewhere. She presents a view of critical reflective practice as a process which does not capture the deeper dimensions of reflection over time which include questioning one's assumptions, engaging with one's feelings and developing greater self-awareness. This characterisation applies to the creative reflective practices explored previously in this book and in other collections of texts on practice-based research more generally.[13] Equally, the four styles of learning – activist, reflector, theorist and pragmatist[14] – that can influence reflecting in practice are to be found in the different roles and practices of creative practitioners working individually or in groups.

For the research student, Bassot's guide offers useful practical support to assist the learning necessary to become a reflective practitioner. Some professional practitioners could also benefit from the interdisciplinary outlook that is so helpful in breaking out of longstanding assumptions and constraints. For experienced creative practitioners, however, it is less helpful insofar as their practice already embraces an ethos of thinking, making and reflecting in iterative cycles, processes which are in integral to the very nature of creative practice. Those relatively new to creative practice might benefit more from writings by experienced practitioners particularly those who have undertaken research leading to post graduate degrees.[15] Bassot has followed this guide with an even more practically oriented book, this time concentrating on how to reflect in writing and what that can bring to the development of reflection in action skills.[16]

A different book based in education and the arts, aims to reveal the ways in which learning through reflection can enhance practice across a range of arts disciplines. Burnard and Hennessy's collection of essays is directed towards artists and educators.[17] For example, Cheung and Kung focus on how digital technologies can act as facilitators, catalysts, enhancers and role reversers in learning to think reflectively.[18] Overall, the book lacks a sufficiently coherent perspective on reflective practice across the many varieties of arts practice and education.

For those with a more theoretical interest, this can be found in Fook et al.'s 'Researching Critical Reflection' which addresses some of the fundamental questions arising from a closer examination of reflection in practice and its implications for research.[19]

Domain-specific guidance

For reflective practice in the professions, there are many online resources which deliver advice and templates for learning how to reflect. The domain specific guidance provided by professional associations is a good starting point. Some examples follow here:

For lawyers, professional bodies with legal remits, provide similar guidance: for example, the Solicitors Regulatory Authority (SRA) sets targets and methods for self-monitoring with toolkits tailored to assist practitioners to reflect on the quality of their practice and identify and address learning needs to ensure competency for practice.[20] There are also other sources that provide resources for initial training: for example, Casey's model of stages of reflective practice model is designed for legal education and represents reflective practice's relationship to cognitive and moral development.[21]

Reflection is a core feature of medical practice as well as an ethical duty and guidance is provided by the UK's General Medical Council.[22] It suggests ten key points for a reflective practitioner,[23] amongst them, reflection is personal and there is no one way to reflect; having time to reflect on both positive and negative experiences, and being supported to reflect, is important for individual wellbeing and development; Group reflection often leads to ideas or actions that can improve patient care. The reflective practitioner guide for doctors and medical students supports medical students, doctors in training and doctors engaging in revalidation on how to reflect as part of their practice.[24] It has been developed jointly by the Academy of Medical Royal Colleges, the UK Conference of Postgraduate Medical Deans (COPMeD), the General Medical Council (GMC), and the Medical Schools Council. A Guide to Reflective Practice for Primary Carers is directed at the Nursing and Midwifery Professions.[25] It was produced in response to a revised Nursing and Midwifery Council (NMC) Code of Professional standards.[26]

Conclusions

How will we know if we are learning to be a reflective practitioner? A quick way is to recognise some key features of a creative mind set as summarised in the following paragraph.

Being able to embrace the dynamism that doubt and scepticism engender often enables new ways of thinking. Have playful inclinations, coupled with a propensity to be bold, underlies creative thinking and action in many cases. New ideas arise in response to the materials for making but often the idea itself provokes a change of direction or decision to go with a novel technique. Whether working with artefacts or people, being open to new perspectives can be a powerful stimulus to creative thinking. Creative practitioners often move across field boundaries during their careers. They may be driven by restless curiosity or simply a refusal to rest easy in comfortable spaces. Being willing to seize the opportunity that turns up unexpectedly and follow the excitement of an unfamiliar path can be risky, but with courage and determination can lead one into fertile pastures. Above all, creative practitioners reflect and reflect again before, during and after everything they do.

Notes

1 Ridley (2004).
2 The TRM is discussed in Chapter 2 and thereafter.
3 Cole (2000, pp. 23–38).
4 Lateral thinking is a term coined by Edward de Bono (De Bono, 1967)
5 Csikszentmihalyi (1991).
6 Sato (2013).
7 The term 'action painting' was coined by Harold Rosenberg in his article The American Action Painters published in ARTnews in December 1952. Rosenberg was referring to artists such as Arshile Gorky, Franz Kline, Willem de Kooning, and Jackson Pollock. A related form of art making is Automatism which involves bodily movements that are not consciously controlled like breathing or sleepwalking.
8 The Painting Techniques of Jackson Pollock: www.khanacademy.org/humanities/art-1010/abstract-exp-nyschool/abstract-expressionism/v/moma-painting-technique-pollock: Created by The Museum of Modern Art.
9 Edmonds and Candy (2010).
10 See the books by practitioners in Chapter 6 and the list of completed PhDs at the end of the reference list.

11 Eraut (1994). Additionally see models, learning trajectories and other examples in http:// surreyprofessionaltraining.pbworks.com/f/How+Professionals+Learn+through+Work. pdf. Accessed September 3, 2019.

12 Bassot (2016a).

13 For example, Candy and Edmonds 2011c).

14 Honey and Mumford (2000) based the four distinctions on the work of Kolb (1984).

15 Candy and Edmonds (2011); Candy and Ferguson (2014); Candy et al. (2018).

16 Bassot (2016b).

17 Burnard and Hennessy (2009).

18 Cheung and Kung (2009, pp. 107–122).

19 Fook et al. (2016).

20 SRA Toolkit www.sra.org.uk/solicitors/cpd/tool-kit/continuing-competence-toolkit. page: what you need to do to remain competent.

21 Casey (2014, p. 321) for the stages of reflective practice model legal education. 'The goals of reflective practice are to provide the professional with a self-improvement algorithm, and to increase the capacity of the professional to exercise judgment in the professional context. In a basic sense, reflective practice forces the professional to increase awareness of the factors that affect judgment. . . . The goal of the Stages of Reflection model is to build a professional context for the student and to integrate reflective practice as a professional value'.

22 www.gmc-uk.org/news/news-archive/new-guidance-to-help-you-with-reflection.

23 www.gmc-uk.org/education/standards-guidance-and-curricula/guidance/reflective-practice/the-reflective-practitioner–guidance-for-doctors-and-medical-students/ten-key-points-on-being-a-reflective-practitioner.

24 www.gmc-uk.org/-/media/education/downloads/guidance/the-reflective-practioner-guidance.pdf.

25 www.pcrs-uk.org/sites/pcrs-uk.org/files/Guide%20to%20Reflective%20Practice_FINAL.pdf.

26 www.nmc-uk.org/code.

AFTERWORD

What have we added to our understanding of reflective practice by listening to the creative practitioner?

By making practitioner voices the primary sources of inspiration and guidance, it has been possible to describe key elements of reflective practice across a wide range of creative fields. This has been augmented by first-person narratives as well as research studies and historical accounts. Even more than previously, I am aware of how exploratory and experimental reflective creative practice is. It can also be a very challenging process for practitioners even though they often intend it to be that way. It seems too that the element of surprise is inherent to creative practice and responding to unexpected events can offer opportunities for pleasing creative outcomes. In collaborative practice, shared experience invites dialogue and stimulates reflection of different kinds, as does digital practice, where new technologies are central to exploratory, curiosity driven work. Those who delve more deeply discover different kinds of relationships as they learn to create new digital forms. Above all, it is clear that being a researcher at heart and in spirit is inherent to reflective creative practice. Embedding a research ethos in practice offers new ways for self-reflection as practitioners seek greater understanding about what it is to be human through the making and sharing of their creative works.

Creative practice is shared enrichment. Sharing stimulates awareness and this leads to reflection that prompts learning through experience – a new state of knowledge. Creative sharing offers something new to the individual but not only that. Creative people bring novel and potentially transformative experiences to a larger population. When the practitioner offers a service to others as professionals do, this is a sharing of knowledge from basic training and the experience of practice over time. It is knowledge applied for the benefit of others. When a creative practitioner offers something new, this is sharing an opportunity for both self-reflection and shared reflection. It is an exploration of the self that can transform the person's capacity for new insights through learned awareness.

REFERENCES

Adeyanu, I. (2012) Generating Weather Forecast Texts with Case Based Reasoning. *International Journal of Computer Applications*, Vol. 45 (10), pp. 35–40. Doi:10.5120/6819-9176

Alaoui, S.F., Bevilacqua, F., Bermudez, B. and Jacquemin, C. (2013) Dance Interaction with Physical Model Visualization Based on Movement Qualities. *International Journal of Arts and Technology (IJART)*, Vol. 6 (4), 357–387.

Alaoui, S.F., Schiphorst, T., Cuyckendal, S., Carlson, K., Studd, K. and Bradley, K. (2015) Strategies for Embodied Design: The Value and Challenges of Observing Movement. In *Proceedings of the 2015 ACM SIGCHI Conference on Creativity and Cognition*, pp. 121–130.

Allen, P. (2001) *Art, Not Chance: Nine Artists' Diaries*. Calouste Gulbenkian Foundation: London.

Anderson, M.L. (2003) Embodied Cognition: A Field Guide. *Artificial Intelligence*, Vol. 149, pp. 91–130.

Andreasen, N.C. (2006) *The Creative Brain: The Science of Genius*. Plume, Penguin Group: New York.

Argyris, C., Putnam, R. and McLain Smith, D. (1985) *Action Science: Concepts, Methods, and Skills for Research and Intervention*. Jossey-Bass Publishers Inc: San Francisco and London, pp. 82–83.

Argyris, C. and Schön, D.A. (1974) *Theory in Practice: Increasing Professional Effectiveness*. Jossey-Bass: San Francisco.

Arnold, K. (2017) A Very Public Affair: Art Meets Science. *Interdisciplinary Science Reviews*, part 1 of special edition on Art & Science, eds. Ball, P. and Ede, B., Vol. 42 (4), pp. 331–344, published by Taylor Francis: UK.

Ascott, R. (2011) *Preface to Interacting: Art, Research and the Creative Practitioner*. Editon by Candy, L. and Edmonds, E.A. Libri Publishing Ltd: Farringdon, UK.

Azuma, R., Baillot, Y., Behringer, R., Feiner, S., Julier, S. and MacIntyre, B. (2001) Recent Advances in Augmented Reality. *IEEE Computer Graphics and Applications*, Vol. 21 (6) (November–December), pp. 34–47.

Balloch, S., Mclean, J. and Fisher, M. (1999) *Social Service: Working Under Pressure*. Policy Press: Bristol.

Barrett, E. and Bolt, B. (eds.) (2007) *Practice as Research: Approaches to Creative Arts Enquiry*. I.B. Tauris: London.

Barrett, L. and Connell, M. (2006) Jevons and the Logic 'Piano': www.rutherfordjournal. org/article010103.html

Bassot, B. (2016a) *The Reflective Practice Guide: An interdisciplinary Approach to Critical Reflection*. Routledge: Abingdon, UK.

Bassot, B. (2016b) *The Reflective Journal*. Palgrave Macmillan: London, 2nd Edition.

Becker, H.S. (1982) *Art Worlds*. University of California Press: Berkeley.

Bengtsson, J. (1995) What Is Reflection? On Reflection in the Teaching Profession and Teacher Education. *Teachers and Teaching*, Vol. 1 (1), pp. 23–32.

Benkler, Y. (2006) *The Wealth of Networks: How Social Production Transforms Markets and Freedom*. Yale University Press: New Haven and London.

Biggs, M. and Karlsson, H. (eds.) (2011) *The Routledge Companion to Research in the Arts*. Routledge: London and New York.

Biggs, S., Hawksley, S. and Paine, G. (2014) Crosstalk: Making People in Interactive Spaces. In *MOCO '14 Proceedings of the 2014 International Workshop on Movement and Computing*. ACM Press: New York.

Biggs, S., Hawksley, S. and Paine, G. (2016) Bodytext: Somatic Data as Agency in Interactive Dance. In Fernandez, C. (ed.) *Multimodality and Performance*. Cambridge Scholars Publishing: Newcastle, pp. 179–186.

Bilda, Z. (2011) Designing for Creative Engagement. In Candy, L. and Edmonds, E.A. (eds.) *Interacting: Art, Research and the Creative Practitioner*. Libri Publishing Ltd: Farringdon, UK, pp. 163–181.

Bilda, Z., Edmonds, E.A. and Candy, L. (2008) Designing for Creative Engagement. *Design Studies*, Vol. 29 (6), pp. 525–540.

Biswas, A. (2018) Paul Brown: Process, Chance and Serendipity: Art That Makes Itself: www.studiointernational.com/index.php/paul-brown-process-chance-serendipity-art-that-makes-itself-review-national-academy-sciences-washington

Bloom, P. (2018) *Against Empathy*. Vintage, Penguin Random House: London UK.

Bluff, A., Johnston, A. and Clarkson, D. (2018) Interaction, Narrative and Animation in Live Theatre. *IEEE Computer Graphics and Applications*, Vol. 38 (2), pp. 8–14.

Boden, M.A. (1990) *The Creative Mind: Myths and Mechanisms*. Weidenfeld and Nicolson: London.

Brown, P. (2002) Stepping Stones in the Mist. In Bentley, P.J. and Corne, D. (eds.) *Creative Evolutionary Systems*. Morgan Kaufmann Publishers Inc and Academic Press: San Francisco, CA, pp. 1–75, 387–408: www.paul-brown.com/WORDS/STEPPING.HTM

Brown, P. (2008) From Systems Art to Artificial Life: Early Generative Art at the Slade School of Fine Art. In Gere, C., Brown, P., Lambert, N. and Mason, C. (eds.) *White Heat and Cold Logic: British Computer Arts 1960–1980 An Historical and Critical Analysis*. MIT Press: Cambridge MA and London, pp. 275–289.

Brown, P., Gere, C., Lambert, N. and Mason, C. (eds.) (2008) *White Heat and Cold Logic: British Computer Arts 1960–1980 An Historical and Critical Analysis*. MIT Press: Cambridge, MA and London.

Burnard, P. and Hennessy, S. (eds.) (2009) *Reflective Practices in Arts Education*. Springer: Dordrecht, NL.

Burraston, D. (2011) Creativity, Complexity and Reflective Practice. In Candy, L. and Edmonds, E.A. (eds.) *Interacting: Art, Research and the Creative Practitioner*. Libri Publishing Ltd: Farringdon, UK, pp. 107–118.

Cage, J. (1961) *Silence: Lectures and Writings*. Wesleyan University Press and MIT Press: Middletown, CT, 2nd Edition (February 1967), Indeterminacy, pp. 260–273.

Candy, L. (2006) Practice Based Research: A Guide. *Creativity and Cognition Studios Report V1.0* (November): www.creativityandcognition.com/wp-content/uploads/2011/04/PBR-Guide-1.1-2006.pdf

Candy, L. (2009) Practice-Based Research and the PhD: A Study. Doi:10.13140/RG.2.2.36552.98567

Candy, L. (2011) Research and Creative Practice. In Candy, L. and Edmonds, E.A. (eds.) *Interacting: Art, Research and the Creative Practitioner.* Libri Publishing Ltd: Farringdon, UK, pp. 33–59.

Candy, L. (2012) Evaluating Creativity. In Carroll, J.M. (ed.) *Creativity and Rationale: Enhancing Human Experience by Design.* Springer: New York, pp. 57–84.

Candy, L. (2018) Making Light Sculptures in Suspended Space: A Creative Collaboration. In Candy, L., Edmonds, E.A. and Poltronieri, F.A. (eds.) *Explorations in Art and Technology.* Springer Cultural Computing Series. Springer-Verlag: London, 2nd Edition, pp. 309–318.

Candy, L. and Edmonds, E.A. (1996) Creative Design of the Lotus Bicycle: Implications for Knowledge Support Systems Research. *Design Studies,* Vol. 17 (1), pp. 71–90.

Candy, L. and Edmonds, E.A. (2002a) Modeling Co-Creativity in Art and Technology. In Hewett, T.T. and Kavanagh, T. (eds.) *Proceedings of the Fourth International Conference on Creativity and Cognition.* ACM Press: New York, pp. 134–141.

Candy, L. and Edmonds, E.A. (eds.) (2002b) *Explorations in Art and Technology.* Springer Cultural Computing Series, Springer-Verlag: London, 2nd Edition, 2018.

Candy, L. and Edmonds, E.A. (eds.) (2011c) *Interacting: Art, Research and the Creative Practitioner.* Libri Publishing Ltd: Farringdon, UK.

Candy, L. and Edmonds, E.A. (2018a) Practice-Based Research in the Creative Arts: Foundations and Futures from the Front Line. *Leonardo,* MIT Press Cambridge MA, Vol. 51 (1) (February), pp. 63–69.

Candy, L. and Edmonds, E.A. (2018b) Practice-Based Research in Practice: Regulations and Recommendations. *Leonardo,* Vol. 51 (1) (February), Supplementary Article.

Candy, L., Edmonds, E.A. and Poltronieri, F.A. (2018) Collaboration. In *Explorations in Art and Technology.* Springer-Verlag Cultural Computing Series, 2nd Edition, Springer-Verlag: London. pp. 289–307.

Candy, L. and Ferguson, S. (eds.) (2014) *Interactive Experience in the Digital Age: Evaluating New Art Practice.* Springer Series on Cultural Computing. Springer-Verlag: London.

Carey, B. (2013) _derivations: Improvisation for Tenor Saxophone and Interactive Performance System. In *Proceedings of the 2013 ACM Conference of Creativity and Cognition,* Sydney, Australia.

Carey, B. (2016) Artefact Scripts and the Performer-Developer. *Leonardo,* Vol. 49 (1).

Casey, T. (2014) Reflective Practice in Legal Education: The Stages of Reflection. *Clinical Law Review,* Vol. 20 (March 15), pp. 317–354.

Cheung, J. and Kung, E. (2009) Reflective Use of Digital Technologies in the Arts. In Burnard, P. and Hennessy, S. (eds.) *Reflective Practices in Arts Education.* Springer: Dordrecht, NL, pp. 107–122.

Clark, S. (2018) Collaborative Practice in Systems Art. In Candy, L., Edmonds, E.A. and Poltronieri, F.A. (eds.) *Explorations in Art and Technology.* Springer-Verlag Cultural Computing Series, 2nd Edition, Springer-Verlag: London Ltd. pp. 327–332.

Clurman, H. (1975) *The Fervent Years: The Group Theater and the Thirties.* Harcourt Brace Jovanovich: New York.

Cohen, P. (2016) Harold Cohen and AARON. *AI Magazine,* Vol. 37 (4), pp. 63–66.

Cole, M. (2000) Learning Through Reflective Practice: A Professional Approach to Effective Continuing Professional Development Among Healthcare Professionals. *Research in Post-Compulsory Education,* Vol. 5 (1), pp. 23–38.

Connell, M. (2016) Materialising Innovation. In Lyons, J. (ed.) *Out of Hand.* Published by the Museum of Applied Arts and Sciences: Sydney.

Connell, M. and Turnbull, D. (2011) Prototyping Places: The Museum. In Candy, L. and Edmonds, E.A. (eds.) *Interacting: Art, Research and the Creative Practitioner.* Libri Publishing Ltd: Farringdon, UK, pp. 79–93.

Cook, S. and Graham, B. (2010) *Rethinking Curating: Art After New Media*. MIT Press: Cambridge, MA.

Copeland, J., Bowen, J., Sprevak, M., Wilson, R. et al. (2017) *The Turing Guide*. Oxford University Press: Oxford.

COSTART: http://research.it.uts.edu.au/creative/COSTART/overview.html, Accessed May 28, 2017.

Costello, B. (2009) Play and the Experience of Interactive Art. PhD thesis, Creativity and Cognition Studios, University of Technology, Sydney, Australia: https://opus.lib.uts.edu.au/handle/2100/984

Costello, B. (2011) Many Voices, One Project. In Candy, L. and Edmonds, E.A. (eds.) *Interacting: Art, Research and the Creative Practitioner*. Libri Publishing Ltd: Farringdon, UK pp. 182–194.

Costello, B.M. (2018) *Rhythm, Play and Interaction Design*. Springer Cultural Computing Series. Springer-Verlag: London.

Costello, B.M., Muller, L., Amitani, S. and Edmonds, E.A. (2005) Understanding the Experience of Interactive Art: Lamascope in Beta_Space. In Pisan, Y. (ed.) *Proceedings Interactive Entertainment*. Creative and Cognition Studios Press: Sydney, pp. 49–56.

Crabtree, A. (2003) *Designing Collaborative Systems: A Practical Guide to Ethnography*. Springer: Heidelberg.

Cree, V.E. and Davis, A. (2007) *Social Work: Voices from the Inside*. Routledge: London and New York.

Csikszentmihalyi, M. (1991) *Flow: The Psychology of Optimal Experience*. Harper Perennial, Harper Collins Publishers: New York.

Csikszentmihalyi, M. (1996) *Creativity: Flow and the Psychology of Discovery and Invention*. Harper Collins Publishers: New York.

Csikszentmihalyi, M. (1999) Implications of a Systems Perspective for the Study of Creativity. In Sternberg, R.J. (ed.) *Handbook of Creativity*. Cambridge University Press, UK, 1st Edition, p. 333.

Danchev, A. (ed.) (2011) *100 Artists' Manifestos: From the Futurists to the Stuckists*. Penguin Modern Classics, Penguin Books Ltd: London.

De Bono, E. (1967) *The Uses of Lateral Thinking*. Cape: London.

Deacon, M. (2016) *Michael Gove's Guide to Britain's Greatest Enemy . . . the Experts*: https://www.telegraph.co.uk/news/2016/06/10/michael-goves-guide-to-britains-greatest-enemy-the-experts/

Descartes, R. (originally published in 1637) *Discourse on the Method of Rightly Conducting One's Reason and of Seeking Truth in the Sciences*. Hackett Publishing Company, Inc, 1998.

Devere, R. (2017) Music and Dementia: An Overview. *Practical Neurology* (June), pp. 31–35.

De Wachter, E.M. (2017) *Co-Art: Artists on Creative Collaboration*. Phaidon Press Ltd: London.

Dewey, J. (1910) *How We Think*. D.C. Heath & Co.: Boston, New York and Chicago.

Dewey, J. (1934) *Art as Experience*. Penguin Books: London.

Dourish, P. (2001) *Where the Action Is*. MIT Press: Cambridge, MA.

Drake, J.E. and Winner, E. (2013) Who Will Become A Super Artist? *The Psychologist*, Vol. 26, pp. 730–733.

Dreyfus, H.I. and Dreyfus, S.L. (1988) *Mind over Machine Mind over Machine: The Power of Human Intuition and Expertise in the Era of the Computer*. Free Press: New York.

Dupré, J. (2001) *Human Nature and the Limits of Science*. Oxford University Press: Oxford.

Edmonds, E.A. (2018) *The Art of Interaction: What HCI Can Learn from Interactive Art*. Morgan & Claypool: San Rafael CA.

Edmonds, E.A. and Candy, L. (2010) Relating Theory, Practice and Evaluation in Practitioner Research. *Leonardo Journal*, MIT Press. Vol. 43 (5), pp. 470–476.

Edmonds, E.A., Candy, L., Fell, M., Knott, R. and Weakley, A. (2003) Macaroni Synthesis: A Creative Multi-Media Collaboration. In *IV '03: Proceedings of the Seventh International Conference on Information Visualization*. IEEE Computer Society.

Edmonds, E.A., Muller, L. and Connell, M. (2006) On Creative Engagement. *Visual Communication*, Vol. 5 (3), pp. 307–322.

Elkins, J. (ed.) (2014) *Artists with PhDs: On the New Doctoral Degree in Studio Art*. New Academia Publishing: Washington, DC, 2nd Edition.

Engelbart, D.C. (1962) *Augmenting Human Intellect: A Conceptual Framework SRI Summary Report AFOSR-3223 Prepared for: Director of Information Sciences*. Air Force Office of Scientific Research: Washington, DC, Contract AF 49(638)-1024 SRI Project No. 3578: http://dougengelbart.org/content/view/138

Eraut, M. How Professionals Learn Through Work: http://surreyprofessionaltraining. pbworks.com/f/How+Professionals+Learn+through+Work.pdf, Accessed July 6, 2019.

Eraut, M. (1994) *Developing Professional Knowledge and Competence*. Routledge: Abingdon, Oxon.

Eraut, M. (2007) Learning from Other People in the Workplace. *Oxford Review of Education*, Vol. 33 (4), pp. 403–422.

Ericsson, K.A. and Simon, H.A. (1993) *Protocol Analysis: Verbal Reports as Data*. MIT Press: Cambridge, MA.

Farr, W., Price, S. and Jewitt, C. (2012) *An Introduction to Embodiment and Digital Technology Research: Interdisciplinary Themes and Perspectives*. MODE Node, Institute of Education: London: http://eprints.ncrm.ac.uk/2257/4/NCRM_workingpaper_0212.pdf, Accessed February 8, 2019.

Finke, R.A., Smith, S.M. and Ward, T.B. (1992) *Creative Cognition*. MIT Press Cambridge, MA and London, UK.

Fish, D. (1998) *Appreciating Practice in the Caring Professions: Refocusing Professional Development and Practitioner Research*. Butterworth-Heinemann: Oxford.

Fook, J., Collington, V., Ross, F., Ruch, G. and West, L. (eds.) (2016) *Researching Critical Reflection: Multidisciplinary Perspectives*. Routledge: Abingdon, UK.

Franco, F. (2017) *Generative Systems Art: The Work of Ernest Edmonds*. 1st Edition. Routledge: London and New York.

Françoise, J., Candau, Y., Alaoui, S.F. and Schiphorst, T. (2017) Designing for Kinesthetic Awareness: Revealing User Experiences Through Second-Person Inquiry. In *Proceedings of ACM Conference on Human Factors in Computing Systems (CHI)*, Denver, pp. 4009–4020.

Freeman, J., Wiggins, G., Starks, G. and Sandler, M. (2017) A Concise Taxonomy for Describing Data as an Art Material. In *Open Access Concise Version*. MIT Press, Posted online February 16.

Frost, V. (2014) *Design Your Life*. Penguin Lantern: Australia.

Gardner, M. (1970) Mathematical Games: The Fantastic Combinations of John Conway's New Solitaire Game "Life". *Scientific American*, Vol. 223, pp. 120–123.

Gayford, M. (2016) *A Bigger Message: Conversations with David Hockney*. Thames and Hudson Ltd: London.

Geroimenko, V. (ed.) (2014 revised 2018) *Augmented Reality Art: From an Emerging Technology to a Novel Creative Medium*. Springer Series on Cultural Computing. Springer-Verlag: London.

Glaser, B.G. and Strauss, A.L. (1999) *Discovery of Grounded Theory: Strategies for Qualitative Research*. Routledge: New York.

Glinkowski, P. and Bamford, A. (2009) *Insight and Exchange: An Evaluation of the Wellcome Trust's Sciart Programme*. London: https://wellcome.ac.uk/sites/default/files/wtx057228_0. pdf, Accessed October 14, 2017.

Gombrich, E.H. (1950) *The Story of Art.* Republished by Book Club Associates: London, 1972.

Goodman, N. (1978) *Ways of Worldmaking.* Hackett Publishing: Company Inc. Indianapolis, IN.

Grau, O. (ed.) (2010) *MediaArtHistories.* MIT Press: Cambridge, MA.

Green, B. (ed.) (2009) *Understanding and Researching Professional Practice.* Published by: Sense Publishers: Rotterdam, The Netherlands. www.sensepublishers.com

Gwilt, I. (2008) Mixed Reality Art. Unpublished doctoral thesis, University of New South Wales, Australia.

Gwilt, I. (2011) Augmenting the White Cube. In Candy, L. and Edmonds, E.A. (eds.) *Interacting: Art, Research and the Creative Practitioner.* Libri Publishing, Farindon, UK. Ch. 5.3 pp. 257–267.

Harris, C. (1999) (ed.) *Art and Innovation: The Xerox PARC Artist-in-Residence Program.* MIT Press: Cambridge, MA.

Hawksley, S. (2011) Choreographic and Somatic Strategies for Navigating Bodyscapes and Tensegrity Schemata. *Journal of Dance & Somatic Practices,* Vol. 3 (1–2), pp. 101–110.

Hawksley, S. (2012) *Traces of Places.* The Peripatetic Studio Weblog, University of Bedfordshire Repository

Hawksley, S. (2013) Dancing on the Head of a Sin. *Leonardo Electronic Almanac,* Vol. 19 (4), pp. 84–97, Special Issue: Without Sin: Taboo and Freedom within Digital Media.

Hawksley, S. (2016) Coping with the (interactive) Environment: The Performative Potential of Interactivity. *Journal of Dance and Somatic Practices – Special Issue, Embodiment, Interactivity and Digital Performance,* Vol. 8 (1), pp. 43–56.

Holtzman, H. and James, M.S. (1986) *The New Art – the New Life: The Collected Writings of Piet Mondrian.* G.K. Hall: Boston.

Honey, P. and Mumford, A. (2000) *The Learning Styles Helper's Guide.* Peter Honey Publications Ltd: Maidenhead.

Ingold, T. (2010) The Textility of Making. *Cambridge Journal of Economics,* Vol. 34, pp. 91–102.

Ingold, T. (2013) *Making.* Routledge: Abingdon, Oxon and New York.

Ixer, G. (1999) There's No Such Thing as Reflection. *The British Journal of Social Work,* Vol. 29 (4), pp. 513–527.

John-Steiner, V. (2000) *Creative Collaboration.* Oxford University Press: Oxford, New York.

Johnston, A., Candy, L. and Edmonds, E.A. (2008) Designing and Evaluating Virtual Musical Instruments: Facilitating Conversational User Interaction, in Interaction Design and Creative Practice. *Design Studies,* Vol. 29 (6), pp. 556–571. Elsevier.

Johnston, A.J. (2014) Keeping Research in Tune with Practice. In Candy, L. and Ferguson, S. (eds.) *Interactive Experience in the Digital Age.* Springer Cultural Computing Series, Springer-Verlag: London, pp. 49–62.

Johnston, A.J. (2015) Conceptualising Interaction in Live Performance: Reflections on 'Encoded'. In *Proceedings of the International Workshop on Movement and Computing (MOCO2015),* Vancouver, Canada, pp. 60–67.

Johnston, A.J. and Bluff, A. (2018) Collaborative Creation in Interactive Theatre. In Candy, E. and Poltronieri, F. (eds.) *Explorations in Art and Technology.* Springer Cultural Computing Series, 2nd Edition, Springer-Verlag: London, pp. 341–351.

Kay, A. (1984) Computer Software. *Scientific American,* Vol. 251 (3), pp. 53–59.

Khut, G.P. and Loke, L. (2014) Intimate Aesthetics and Facilitated Interaction. In Candy, L. and Ferguson, S. (ed.) *Interactive Experience in the Digital Age.* Springer: New York, pp. 91–108.

Killion, J. and Todnem, G. (1991) A Process for Personal Theory Building. *Educational Leadership,* Vol. 48 (7), pp. 14–16.

Kim, H.S. (2002) Research: Cultural vs Innate Factors: We Talk, Therefore We Think? A Cultural Analysis of the Effect of Talking on Thinking, Stanford University. *Journal of Personality and Social Psychology,* Vol. 83 (4), pp. 828–842.

Kinsella, E.A. (2007) Technical Rationality in Schön's Reflective Practice: Dichotomous or Non-Dualistic Epistemological Position. *Nursing Philosophy*, Vol. 8 (2), pp. 102–113. Blackwell Publishing Ltd.

Kinsella, E.A. (2009) Constructivist Underpinnings in Donald Schön's Theory of Reflective Practice: Echoes of Nelson Goodman. *Reflective Practice*, Vol. 7 (3) (August 2006), pp. 277–286. Routledge-Taylor & Francis.

Kneebone, R.L. (2016) Performing Surgery: Commonalities with Performers Outside Medicine. In *Frontiers in Psychology*, Vol. 7 (August 1), Article 1233, pp. 3–4: www.fron tiersin.org

Kolb, D.A. (1984) *Experiential Learning: Experience as the Source of Learning and Development*. Prentice Hall: Englewood Cliffs, NJ.

Kuh, K. (1962) *The Artist's Voice: Talks with Seventeen Artists*. Harper & Row and Da Capo Press, 1st Edition, 2000.

Lakoff, G. and Johnson, M. (1999) *Philosophy in the Flesh: The Embodied Mind and Its Challenge to Western Thought*. Basic Books: New York.

Lawson, B. (1994) *Design in Mind*. Butterworth Architecture: Oxford.

Ledgard, A. (2006) Fair Exchange: Shared Professional Development and Reflective Action. In Burnard, P. and Hennessy, S. (eds.) *Reflective Practice in Arts Education*. Springer: Dordrecht, NL, pp. 169–182.

Leggett (2011) Memory, Schema and Interactive Video. In Candy, L. and Edmonds, E.A. (eds.) *Interacting: Art, Research and the Creative Practitioner*. Libri Publishing Ltd: Farringdon, UK, pp. 282–284.

Lepecki, A. (2006) *Exhausting Dance: Performance and the Politics of Movement*. Routledge: London.

Lewis, C. and Rieman, J. (1994) *Task-Centered User Interface Design: A Practical Introduction*: https://hcibib.org/tcuid/, Accessed March 1, 2019.

Licklider, J.C.R. (1960) Man-Computer Symbiosis. *IRE Transactions on Human Factors in Electronics*, Vol. HFE-1 (March), pp. 4–11. MIT Computer Science and Artificial Intelligence Laboratory.

Loke, L., Khut, G.P. and Kocaballi, A.B. (2012) Bodily Experience and Imagination: Designing Ritual Interactions for Participatory Live-Art Contexts. In *Proceedings of the Designing Interactive Systems Conference, DIS '12*, pp. 779–788.

Lufityanto, G., Donkin, C. and Pearson, J. (2016) Measuring Intuition: Nonconscious Emotional Information Boosts Decision Accuracy and Confidence: https://journals.sagepub. com/doi/abs/10.1177/0956797616629403

Macleod, K. and Holdridge, L. (2006) *Thinking Through Art: Reflections on Art as Research*. Routledge, New York.

Mahon, B.Z. (2015) What Is Embodied About Cognition? *Language, Cognition and Neuroscience*, Vol. 30 (4), pp. 420–429.

Marinetti, F.T. (1909) http://bactra.org/T4PM/futurist-manifesto.html.

Marsh, H. (2014) *Do No Harm: Stories of Life, Death and Brain Surgery*. Orion Publishing Co: Weidenfeld and Nicolson.

Marshall, A. (2018) *Improvising with Light*. Bob Books' book of the month September.

McIntosh, P. (2010) *Action Research and Reflective Practice*. Routledge: Abingdon, Oxon and New York.

Merleau-Ponty, M. (1945) *Phenomenology: Language and Society*. Heinemann: Portsmouth, New Hampshire, 1974 Edition.

Merleau-Ponty, M. (1952) Indirect Language and the Voices of Silence. In Johnson, G. (1993) (ed.), Smith, M. (trans.) *The Merleau-Ponty Aesthetics Reader: Philosophy and Painting*. North Western University Press: Evanston, IL, pp. 76–120 (Original work published 1952).

Milgram, P., Takemura, H., Utsumi, A. and Kishino, F. (1994) Augmented Reality: A Class of Displays on the Reality-Virtuality Continuum. In *Proceedings of Telemanipulator and Telepresence Technologies* (Issue 2351–34).

Miller, G. (1956) The Magical Number Seven, Plus or Minus Two. *Psychology Review*, Vol. 63, pp. 81–97.

Mills, R. (2014) The Metaphorical Basis of Perception in Intercultural Networked Improvisation. In Abrahams, A. and Jamieson, H.V. (eds.) *Cyposium: The Book*. Link Editions: Brescia, Italy, pp. 103–116.

Mills, R. (2019) *Tele-Improvisation: Intercultural Interaction in the Online Global Music Jam Session*. Springer Cultural Computing Series, Springer-Verlag: London.

Mills, R. and Beilharz, K.A. (2014) The Networked Unveiled: Evaluating Tele-Musical Interaction. In Candy, L. and Ferguson, S. (eds.) *Interactive Experience in the Digital Age: Evaluating New Art Practice*. Springer-Verlag: London, pp. 109–122.

Molderings, H. (2010) *Duchamp and the Aesthetics of Chance*. Columbia University Press: New York.

Montero, B.G. (2016) *Thought and Action: Expertise and the Conscious Mind*. Oxford University Press: Oxford.

Muhly, N. (2018) How I Write Music. *London Review of Books*, Vol. 40 (20) (October 25), pp. 38–39.

Muller, L. (2011) Learning from Experience: A Reflective Curatorial Practice. In Candy, L. and Edmonds, E.A. (eds.) *Interacting: Art, Research and the Creative Practitioner*. Libri Publishing Ltd: Farringdon, UK, pp. 94–106.

Nakamura, J. and Csikszentmihalyi, M. (2001) *The Oxford Handbook of Positive Psychology*. Edited by Lopez, S.J. and Snyder, C.R. Oxford University Press: New York, pp. 85–105.

Nelson, R. (2013) *Practice as Research in the Arts: Principles, Protocols, Pedagogies, Resistances*. Palgrave Macmillan: UK.

Noë, A. (2015) *Strange Tools: Art and Human Nature*. Hill and Wang, Farrar, Straus and Giroux: New York.

Norbert, L. (1994) Futurism. In Stangos, N. (ed.) *Concepts of Modern Art: From Fauvism to Postmodernism*. Thames & Hudson: London, 3rd Edition, p. 97.

O'Sullivan, S. (2016) *It's All in Your Head: Stories from the Frontline of Psychosomatic Illness*. Vintage, Penguin Random House.

Polanyi, M. (1983) *The Tacit Dimension*. Peter Smith: Gloucester, MA.

Poltronieri, F.A., Edmonds, E.A. and Candy, L. (2018) Part 1: History. In *Explorations in Art and Technology*. Springer Cultural Computing Series, 2nd Edition, Springer-Verlag: London, pp. 3–29.

Quantrill, M. (2002) Integrating Computers as Explorers in Art Practice. In *Explorations in Art and Technology*. Springer-Verlag: London, pp. 225–230.

Reichardt, J. (ed.) (1968) *Cybernetic Serendipity: The Computer and the Arts*. Studio International: London.

Reichardt, J. (1971) *The Computer in Art*. Studio Vista: London.

Ridley, M. (2004) *Nature via Nurture: Genes, Experience and What Makes Us Human*. Fourth Estate, Harper Collins Publishers: London.

Rolinson, E. (2018) Drawing Spaces. In *Explorations in Art and Technology*. Springer-Verlag Cultural Computing Series, 2nd Edition, pp. 319–326.

Rowe, A. (2015) Immersion in Mixed Reality Spaces. A doctoral thesis submitted to The Oslo School of Architecture and Design. Arkitektur- og designhøgskolen i Oslo: Norway.

Rowe, A. (2018) Creativity, Technology and Collaboration: Towards Hoped-for and Unexpected Serendipities. In Candy, L., Edmonds, E.A. and Poltronieri, F.A. (eds.) *Explorations in Art and Technology*. Springer Cultural Computing Series, 2nd Edition, pp. 333–340.

Rusbridger, A. (2018) *Breaking News: The Remaking of Journalism and Why It Matters Now.* Cannongate Books Ltd: Edinburgh.

Ryle, G. (1949) *The Concept of Mind.* Penguin Books: Hutchinson, 1963.

Sato, S. (2013) *Shodo: The Quiet Art of Japanese Zen Calligraphy.* Tuttle Publishing Company, an Imprint of Periplus Editions (HK) Ltd.

Schön, D.A. (1987a) *Educating the Reflective Practitioner: Towards a New Design for Teaching in the Professions.* Jossey-Bass: San Francisco.

Schön, D.A. (1987b) Changing Patterns of Inquiry in Work and Living. *Journal Royal Society of the Arts,* Vol. 135 (5367) (February), pp. 225–237.

Schön, D.A. (1991) *The Reflective Practitioner: How Professionals Think in Action.* Ashgate Publishing Ltd: Aldershot. First published by Basic Books in 1983.

Schön, D.A. and Wiggins, G. (1992) Kinds of Seeing and Their Functions in Designing. *Design Studies,* Vol. 13 (2) (April), pp. 135–156. Butterworth-Heinemann Ltd.

Schulkind, J. (1985) Moments of Being: Virginia Woolf. In *A Sketch of the Past.* Harcourt, Inc: San Diego.

Scrivener, S. (2002) The Art Object Does Not Embody a Form of Knowledge. Working Papers in Art and Design 2: www.herts.ac.uk/__data/assets/pdf_file/0008/12311/WPI AAD_vol2_scrivener.pdf

Scrivener, S. (2013) Towards a Practice of Novel Epistemic Artefacts. In *Experimental Systems: Future Knowledge in Artistic Research.* Orpheus Institute. Leuven University Press: Leuven, pp. 135–150.

Seevinck, J. (2017) *Emergence in Interactive Art.* Springer Cultural Computing Series, Springer Verlag: London.

Shusterman, R. (2012) *Thinking Through the Body: Essays in Somaesthetics.* Cambridge University Press: London.

Simms, B.R. (1986) *Music of the Twentieth Century: Style and Structure.* Schirmer Books: New York; Collier Macmillan Publishers: London.

Simon, A., Smith, R.C. and Pawlicki, R.R. (2004) Omnistereo for Panoramic Virtual Environment Display Systems. In *Virtual Reality 2004. Proceedings IEEE,* pp. 67–279.

Simon, H. (1969) *The Sciences of the Artificial.* MIT Press: Cambridge, MA.

Smith, A. (2006) Cognitive Empathy and Emotional Empathy in Human Behaviour and Evolution. *The Psychological Record,* Vol. 56, pp. 3–21.

Smith, H. and Dean, R.T. (2009) *Practice-Led Research, Research-Led Practice in the Creative Arts.* Edinburgh University Press Ltd.

Snow, C.P. (2001) [1959] *The Two Cultures.* Cambridge University Press: London.

Stanney, K.M., Schmorrow, D.D., Johnston, M., Fuchs, S., Jones, D., Hale, K.S., Ahmad, A. and Young, P. (2009) Augmented Cognition: An Overview. *Reviews of Human Factors and Ergonomics,* Vol. 5 (1), pp. 195–224.

Sternberg, R.J. (ed.) (1999) *The Handbook of Creativity.* Cambridge University Press: Cambridge, UK and New York.

Stocker, G. and Hirsch, A.J. (2017) The Practice of Art and Science: http://archive.aec.at/media/archive/2017/228790/File_06390_AEC_RES_2017.pdf, Accessed November 16, 2017.

Stonbely, S. (2017) Comparing Models of Collaborative Journalism: Center for Cooperative Media. Monclair State University (September): https://collaborativejournalism.org/models/, Accessed October 14, 2017.

Sullivan, G. (2010) *Art Practice as Research: Inquiry in the Visual Arts,* Sage: Thousand Oaks, CA, 2nd Edition.

Sweller, J. (1988) Cognitive Load During Problem Solving: Effects on Learning. *Cognitive Science,* Vol. 12 (2), pp. 257–285.

Sylvester, D. (1975) *Interviews with Francis Bacon*. Thames and Hudson, Illustrated Edition.

Tribe, M., Jana, R. and Grosenick, U. (2006) *New Media Art*. Taschen: Cologne.

Turing, A.M. (1937) On Computable Numbers, with an Application to the Entscheidungs-problem. *Proceedings of the London Mathematical Society*, Vol. 2–42 (1), pp. 230–265.

Turing, A.M. (1950) Computing Machinery and Intelligence. *Mind*, Vol. 49, pp. 433–460.

Turkle, S. (2015) *Reclaiming Conversation: The Power of Talk in the Digital Age*. Penguin Press: New York.

Turney, J. (2003) *Science, Not Art: Ten Scientists' Diaries*. Calouste Gulbenkian Foundation: London.

Varela, F.J., Thompson, E. and Rosch, E. (1991) *The Embodied Mind: Cognitive Science and Human Experience*. MIT Press: Cambridge, MA.

Vaughan, L. (2017) *Practice-Based Design Research*. Bloomsbury Academic: London and New York.

Vermersch, P. (2003) *L'entretien d'explicitation. (Quatrième édition enrichie d'un glossaire)* Issyles-Moulineaux. ESF Éditeur: France.

Vygotsky, L.S. (1978) *Mind in Society: The Development of Higher Psychological Processes*. Edited by Cole, M., John-Steiner, V., Scribner, S. and Souberman, E. Harvard University Press: Cambridge, MA and London.

Wallas, G. (1926) *The Art of Thought*. First published by Solis Press Kent England in 2014.

Webster, S. (2005) Art and Science Collaborations in the United Kingdom. *Nature Reviews Immunology* | AOP, published online November 18, 2005. Doi:10.1038/nri1730

Webster, S. (2008) Encounters: Contemporary Art-Science Collaborations in the UK. PhD thesis submitted to the Open University, February 1.

Wilson, M. (2002) Six Views of Embodied Cognition. *Psychonomic Bulletin and Review*, Vol. 9 (4), pp. 625–636.

Wilson, S. (1999) Reflections on Pair. In Harris, C. (ed.) *Art and Innovation: The Xerox PARC Artist-in-Residence Program*. MIT Press: Cambridge, MA.

Wilson, S. (2002) *Information Arts*. Leonardo Book Series, MIT Press: Cambridge, MA.

Wilson, S. (2010) *Art + Science Now: How Scientific Research and Technological Innovation Are Becoming Key to 21st-Century Aesthetics*. Thames and Hudson: London.

Practice-based Research PhD Theses

Alaoui, S.F. (2012) Dance Gesture Analysis and Physical Models Based Visual Feedback: Contribution of Movement Qualities to Interaction. PhD thesis, University Paris-Sud, France.

Bluff, A.J. (2017) Interactive Art, Immersive Technology and Live Performance. PhD thesis, University of Technology Sydney: http://hdl.handle.net/10453/120340

Burraston, D. (2006) Generative Music and Cellular Automata. PhD thesis, Creativity and Cognition Studios, University of Technology, Sydney, Australia.

Carey, B. (2016) _derivations and the Performer-Developer: Co-Evolving Digital Arte-facts and Human-Machine Performance Practices. PhD thesis, University of Technology, Sydney.

Costello, B. (2009) Play and the Experience of Interactive Art. PhD thesis, Creativity and Cognition Studios, University of Technology, Sydney, Australia: https://opus.lib.uts.edu.au/handle/2100/984

Freeman, J. (2018) Defining Data as an Art Material. PhD thesis, Queen Mary University of London.

Gwilt, I. (2008) Mixed Reality Art. Unpublished doctoral thesis, University of New South Wales, Australia.

Hawksley, S. (2012) Dancing to an Understanding of Embodiment. PhD thesis, Edinburgh College of Art, The University of Edinburgh.

Johnston, A. (2009) Interfaces for Musical Expression Based on Simulated Physical Models. PhD thesis, Creativity and Cognition Studios, University of Technology, Sydney, Australia.

Leggett, M. (2009) Mnemovie: Visual Mnemonics for Creative Interactive Video. PhD thesis, Creativity and Cognition Studios, University of Technology, Sydney, Australia.

Mills, R. (2014) *Tele-Improvisation: A Multimodal Analysis of Intercultural Improvisation in Networked Music Performance* (University of Technology, Sydney PhD thesis).

Muller, E. (2008) The Experience of Interactive Art: A Curatorial Study. PhD thesis, Creativity and Cognition Studios, University of Technology, Sydney, Australia.

Rowe, A. (2015) Immersion in Mixed Reality Spaces. A Doctoral thesis submitted to The Oslo School of Architecture and Design, Norway, Publisher: Arkitektur- og designhøgskolen i Oslo.

Seevinck, J. (2011) Emergence in Interactive Art. PhD thesis, Creativity and Cognition Studios, University of Technology, Sydney, Australia.

INDEX